KU-184-835

*edited by*

*Larry L. Barker*
*Robert J. Kibler*
Florida State University

# SPEECH COMMUNICATION BEHAVIOR

## Perspectives and Principles

*Prentice-Hall, Inc.*
*Englewood Cliffs, N.J.*

LIBRARY NOTTINGHAM UNIVERSITY

© 1971 by Prentice-Hall, Inc., Englewood Cliffs, New Jersey

All rights reserved. No part of this book may be reproduced in any form or by any means without permission in writing from the publisher.

Library of Congress Catalog Card Number: 74–143586

Printed in the United States of America

C 13–827345–6
P 13–827337–5

Current Printing (last digit):
10 9 8 7 6 5 4 3 2 1

PRENTICE-HALL INTERNATIONAL, INC., London
PRENTICE-HALL OF AUSTRALIA, PTY. LTD., Sydney
PRENTICE-HALL OF CANADA, LTD., Toronto
PRENTICE-HALL OF INDIA PRIVATE LIMITED, New Delhi
PRENTICE-HALL OF JAPAN, INC., Tokyo

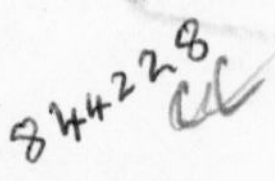

*To our wives*
*Jeanne and Sharon*

# PREFACE

This book is designed to be used as either a primary or supplementary textbook for introductory, undergraduate speech-communication courses. It might be used as a primary text for courses in which emphasis is placed on content and theory, in which students might also be required to apply the principles and research findings of the field in an examination of real communication events, through individual or group projects. This book also might serve as a supplement to texts designed for performance-oriented courses in speech, such as James McCroskey's *An Introduction to Rhetorical Communication* or Gordon Wiseman and Larry Barker's *Speech: Interpersonal Communication.* In addition, the book may be useful as reference material in a variety of communication courses.

There are nine major chapters in the text. The first chapter provides a conceptual overview of selected aspects of communication. Chapters 2 through 8 are on the following aspects of communication: *Theories and Models of Communication Processes; Acquisition and Performance of Communication Behaviors; Human Information Processing and Diffusion; Persuasion and Attitude Change; Psychophysiological Approaches to Studying Communication; Interpersonal Communication within Transracial Contexts;* and *Measuring Communication Effects.* The key principles discussed in the text are identified in the Epilogue.

Obviously, no effort has been made to develop an encyclopedic overview of all aspects of communication behavior or to provide comprehensive answers to man's communication problems—even *if* we had them. We have tried to provide a *status report* by reviewing where we are in examining selected perspectives concerning human communication processes.

We selected the body of knowledge reflected in these topics for two major reasons. First, we believe it to be representative of the theoretical background and the basic content which is requisite to an understanding of how the process of human communication evolves and functions. Second, it is representative of the new perspectives, those which in recent years have become important to people who want to be informed observers and participants in our complex Twentieth-Century world. In general, the vantage point is that of the behavioral scientist, but we have attempted to adapt the ideas and the style of the book to the needs of lower-division college undergraduates.

Each chapter is composed of a lead article and several related readings. Each chapter can be read independently of others. At the same time, there is a logical progression of ideas which permeates the sequence of chapters. We have attempted to organize the book in such a way as to avoid some of the criticisms leveled against other collections of readings. Particularly, we are hopeful that the original, introductory article in each chapter will provide a summary of the literature and a frame of reference for the readings to follow, integrating them into a cohesive examination of one or more aspects of the communication process. One section of each introductory article is on the principles derived from the theory and the research reported, along with their possible applications to real communication events. Thus, students should find practical employment for the ideas discussed, but they also will need to make an additional effort to transfer these ideas to their daily communication behavior. (Obviously, because of the nature of their subject matter, some authors have been more successful than others in their treatment of the "principles and implications" section.) Established scholars in the respective areas of communication have prepared the lead article for the various chapters and have selected readings which both complement and extend the ideas examined in their own article.

An effort has been made to make the book useful and flexible from an instructional point of view. Ideas and concepts in the various chapters have been cross-referenced. Students are systematically referred to the readings when ideas are developed only briefly. Each reading is prefaced by an introduction stating the importance of the selection, and several questions for discussion appear at the end of each chapter.

Probably the most unique aid to the teacher appearing in the text, particularly in a book of readings, are the sets of instructional objectives in each chapter. Some teachers, and perhaps some students, will feel we have been too prescriptive by providing instructional objectives for both the lead articles and the readings. Our bias toward the use of objectives in instruction is well-documented.* We believe that instructional objectives are a critical ingredient in the instructional process and that both teachers and students benefit when they are used. However, just because the instructional objectives are stated does not mean that all teachers *must* use them, or that teachers may not use the book with quite different objectives in mind. The instructional objectives can be used flexibly. Some teachers may agree with our objectives and use them as stated; others may use only part

*R. J. Kibler, L. L. Barker, and D. T. Miles, *Behavioral Objectives and Instruction* (Boston: Allyn & Bacon, Inc., 1970).

of the objectives stated and perhaps create a few of their own; still others may decide not to make use of any of the objectives. Necessarily, this is a matter of choice for each individual instructor. The objectives are there for those who wish to use all or any part of them. And regardless of whether teachers do or do not elect to employ the stated objectives, students can increase the efficiency of their learning by using them. The objectives serve as a preview of the material and help students to focus their attention on the important ideas and concepts included in the chapters.

The authors wish to express their appreciation to several persons who contributed to this book. First, we are indebted to the authors of the original lead articles for their painstaking efforts to make the book valuable to students and relevant to their world. We are also indebted to the copyright holders of the readings and, in many cases, to the authors, for permitting the selections to be reprinted. We thank our wives for typing various parts of the manuscript and for their patience during the construction of the book. We acknowledge the special contributions of Donald J. Cegala and Kathy J. Wahlers during the final stages of assembling the manuscript. Valerie Kibler helped us to retain our rationality by managing our children during key stages of the manuscript's production. Finally, our appreciation to Arthur Rittenberg of Prentice-Hall, who encouraged us to undertake the book.

*Larry L. Barker*
*Robert J. Kibler*

# CONTENTS

# SPEECH COMMUNICATION BEHAVIOR

*chapter* **1**

# A CONCEPTUAL OVERVIEW OF COMMUNICATION DIMENSIONS

*Objectives for Chapter*

After reading this chapter you should be able to:

1. State in writing at least nine aspects or characteristics of communication discussed in the chapter.
2. Define in writing at least seven of these characteristics.
3. Describe in writing the current status of the development of a comprehensive theory of communication.
4. List and describe in writing at least five techniques which have been employed by the authors of chapters to make your learning more efficient and/or less painful.

*Larry L. Barker and Robert J. Kibler*

# A CONCEPTUAL OVERVIEW OF COMMUNICATION DIMENSIONS

Most texts on communication begin by emphasizing the importance of communication in contemporary society. We feel that such an emphasis at this point in time is similar to telling the owner of a horse that has just won the Kentucky Derby that he has a "pretty fast" horse. The obvious should not be belabored. In fact, it is more of a concern to us that people tend to view communication as a panacea for all social ills. How many times have you heard the expression: "It must have been a communication breakdown?" True, many problems in society may be traced to failures in communication, incorrect interpretation of messages and, in some instances, overcommunication. However, there is a considerably larger body of problems which are not a result of communication failures. There are ideological and theological conflicts that are real—and not the result of misunderstanding.

This book, therefore, does not purport to help correct all of society's problems. It is intended to help you recognize some of the techniques and, as well, some of the limitations of communication. The book is a statement of contemporary thinking and a report of current knowledge about the problems and processes of communication. It can be extremely useful and practical if viewed in the proper perspective, but it will not guarantee immediate personal and financial success to those who follow the precepts included.

One of the problems inherent in the study of communication, is that we actually know very little about it *for certain*. Most of the principles in this text are based on empirical research, sound theory, or both: To date, however, most research in the communication sciences has been of limited generalizability and may not extend to the majority of communication settings. Another problem in examining communication in a text is the different views that scholars hold concerning communication. Scholars have classified the aspects of communication in a multitude of different ways.

## *Selected Aspects of Communication*

The way any particular aspect of communication is viewed in this or any other book is a function of the interests, perceptions, and philosophical position of the particular researcher and author. Because interests, perceptions, and philosophical backgrounds differ, the specific views expressed may differ substantially.

A few of the many aspects of communication are discussed below. Each represents a specific way in which researchers and textbook writers have chosen to examine communication in the past. Note that some aspects are "dimensions": They are, in essence, bipolar (i.e., they represent variables at each end of the same continuum). Others do not necessarily range along a single continuum: They involve a variety of "topical" classifications.

VERBAL AND NONVERBAL COMMUNICATION. Perhaps the most common system for classifying communication into component parts is the examination of words separately from nonwords (which may also communicate). *Verbal communication* refers to those language symbols which, it is assumed, have meanings agreed on by all parties involved in communication. (Whether or not this theoretorical assumption is valid is a different concern, and one which will be discussed several times later in this text). Some of the variables of verbal communication which are often studied include language structure (e.g., grammar, linguistic analysis, syntax), message organization, word choice, use of examples and illustrations, and use of emotion and logic. Nonwords which may communicate include, e.g., objects, actions, gestures, shape, color, space, and time. These nonwords are grouped together into a class of communication called *nonverbal.*

The distinction between nonverbal behavior and nonverbal communication is rather tenuous, but important. Nonverbal behavior generally refers to vocal and physical human behavior—which may "communicate" messages to other human beings in the communication setting when they are symbolic. Nonverbal (symbolic) behavior often complements verbal messages or replaces them entirely. Nonverbal communication includes not only symbolic nonverbal behavior but the entire range of objects, events, and temporal and spatial variables which have communicative impact. When national guardsmen or policemen carry weapons on a college campus, there are certain nonverbal messages communicated to college students.

INTRAPERSONAL, INTERPERSONAL, GROUP, MASS, CULTURAL COMMUNICATION. *Intrapersonal communication* is the basic level from which all other forms of human communication are derived. It is that communication which occurs *within* the individual. It involves the evaluating of and reacting to internal and external stimuli. These evaluative and reactive processes help human beings to cope with and understand ideas, events, objects, and experiences. Thinking is one form of intrapersonal communication.

*Interpersonal communication* is the exchange of messages between two or more persons. On the formal–informal continuum (see below) both intrapersonal and interpersonal communication are ranked as informal. Interpersonal communication involves all forms of two-person and small-group interaction in social, business, and conversational settings. It includes also the dialog, which, according to some experts, is the third (and most recent) revolution in the field of communication.

*Group communication* must be differentiated from small-group communication. *Small-group communication* is classified, in this system, as a form of interpersonal communication (for practical purposes, small groups range in size from 3 to 15 members). However, it is assumed that small-group communication is not from one person to the rest of the group or from the group to one person, but a unique type of communication which typically involves a variety of interaction within and among members of the group. Group communication, on the other hand, includes "one-to-many" communication (e.g., public speaking) as well as the more infrequent "many-to-one" communication (e.g., a group of Black Panthers ostracizing a storekeeper for buying merchandise from a white salesman). Group communication may fall on either side of the formal-informal continuum, but is generally considered more formal than interpersonal communication.

*Mass communication* involves the transmission of a message via a mass medium of communication. Even though large public lectures are attended by "masses" of people, they are not considered to be mass communication. Radio, television, motion pictures, newspapers, books, and magazines are primary examples of the media through which mass communication occurs. Although mass communication tends to be classified as more formal than informal, it is generally conceded that mass communication messages which *appear* to be informal or at least "interpersonal" to the listeners are most effective.

*Cultural communication* is the most abstract form of communication and yet one of the most pervasive. It involves the symbolic interaction of cultures (i.e., communicating) with other cultures as well as the effects of culture on the individual. Culture conditions such things as the food you eat, the kind of shelter you choose, the clothes you wear, the language you use, and so on. It combines verbal and nonverbal elements of communication and might even be classified on the formal–informal continuum. For example, "rapping" may be perceived as a more informal kind of communication than a sermon, by those living in a black colony. However, the complex behavior required for effective communication is learned in both instances, and the rules for what is effective are implicit in the norms specified by the subculture.

ORAL AND WRITTEN COMMUNICATION. This distinction between types of communication is probably the easiest to discern. *Oral communication*, as the name suggests, refers to messages (primarily verbal, but with some nonverbal messages included) which are transmitted via sound waves from a human being to other communicatees. Oral communication may occur in interpersonal settings, in public speaking settings, or via the mass media. The defining characteristic is that it involves the production and transmission systems of the human voice and is directed to the *auditory* reception system of one or more human beings.

*Written communication* is that form of communication by which messages are recorded on paper (or some other semipermanent recording medium) for transmission to other human beings. The written message is first channeled through the central nervous system, which controls the fine muscles that coordinate to produce typed or written messages, and is directed to the *visual* reception system of one or more human beings. Written communication is primarily verbal, and little or no nonverbal (in the previously defined sense) communication accompanies it. The conditions that determine whether oral or written communication will be the more effective, and whether they should be used independently or in combination sometimes differ appreciably. Presenting to a college president a list of grievances and a written petition which has been signed by 70 per cent of the student body, may be a more effective way of moving him to act to redress those grievances than public speeches by student leaders, conferences on the individual issues, or oral reports from student groups.

FORMAL–INFORMAL COMMUNICATION. Most human communication may be characterized as having an air of formality or informality. Most interpersonal and small-group communication tends to be informal, while public speaking and mass communication are usually characterized by a more formalized mode of communication.

Communication is usually identified as informal when the speaker sounds "like himself". In informal communication, more errors in grammar and word choice, and more pauses are expected, because this is the way most people talk. Formal communication usually assumes elements of artistic form, and the manner of presentation is frequently emphasized more than the content.

INTENTIONAL AND UNINTENTIONAL COMMUNICATION. Most communication is purposeful. That is, a message is transmitted from one person to another to achieve a specific goal (e.g., to inform or persuade).

However, some communication may take place without the originator of the message being aware it has occurred. This is especially true of nonverbal behavior and other forms of nonverbal communication. A disheveled appearance may arouse negative attitudes toward the speaker in some members of his audience—without his even being aware that he is transmitting any message. A beautiful girl may arouse very positive attitudes about her personality in a young man without uttering a word. Thus, when examining the effects of communication, it is useful not only to examine those that were intended by the originating communicator, but also those which were transmitted or received unintentionally.

MAN, MACHINE, AND ANIMAL. Early communication theorists examined electronic communication systems as possible models of human communication systems. Gradually, scholars have come to realize that although there may be some similarities between electronic circuits and human communication, the differences are greater than the similarities. At least three broad classes of communication have been analyzed: man, machine, and animal—as well as symbolic interaction between these classes.

*Human (man) communication*, the primary focus of this text, refers to symbolic interaction of human psychological and physiological processes, primarily in social settings. *Machine communication* includes a variety of communication subtypes. For example, you may examine man-to-machine, machine-to-man, or even machine-to-machine communication. This particular area of study, which has been labeled "cybernetics," focuses primarily on the use of computers in communication—either to help man process information or to compose new information and transmit it to men or other machines.

The study of *animal communication* is characterized by research on the patterns of interaction in bee and ant colonies, porpoise communication, monkey and ape communication, and the abilities of some birds to communicate. Although there are interrelations among these three classes of communication, caution must be exercised in applying principles derived from one class to the other.

CONTENT, MEDIUM, AND DELIVERY.* These three variables of communication are frequently identified by speech teachers when analyzing the effectiveness of a speaker or a series of spoken messages. *Content* refers to the conceptualization of ideas, their organization, the evidence

*The historical origins of this view of communication date back to Ancient Greece and Rome. Early scholars developed several "canons" of rhetoric which are reflected somewhat in this "content, medium, and delivery" categorization. Four of the early canons were invention, disposition, elocution, and style.

adduced, the examples cited, and so forth, in a given message. *Medium* refers to the channel used to impart the message. McLuhan* has emphasized the impact of the medium on the reception and interpretation of a message. Examples of media are air waves, light waves, (these are transformed via electronic transmitters and receivers, and result in radio and television broadcasts, films, recordings, and so on.) Media may be both verbal and nonverbal.

*Delivery* refers to the way a message is presented. In public-speaking settings, "delivery" means the speaker's vocal variety, inflection, pitch, volume, gesture, movement, facial expression, and so on. In mass communication, it may refer to the colors used in a television commercial, the volume at which a commercial is broadcast, the "hard-sell" of an announcer, and so on. Delivery is often interrelated with media—especially in mass communications.

*Informative–persuasive communication.* Early rhetorical scholars defined all communication as persuasion. Theoretorically, it can be argued that when new information is presented to an organism, this changes the nature of the organism (even though the change may be microscopic) and, therefore, that the presence of information is persuasive. This argument appears to be somewhat vulnerable, however. It is more reasonable to accept the notion that relatively little communication is purely informative (in terms of its impact on the receiver), although there are several general communication settings (e.g., classroom) where the intent of the communicator is primarily to impart information to the receiver. There also are a substantial number of situations in which the expressed purpose of the speaker is to change the attitudes or behavior of the audience. The differentiation of communication events on the basis of their intended effect on the audience has been a useful one in helping scholars to classify and examine the entire range of communication behavior.

SENDER AND RECEIVER. Most communication scholars have elected to focus their primary attention on the sender (speaker) when examining the communication process. This is partially because the speaker is the more modifiable of the participants in the communication process. He is more likely to change his behavior as he learns effective techniques, because he has some degree of motivation to achieve his purpose in communication. Few scholars have elected to focus significant attention on the receiver (listener) in the communication process. A few have contended that listeners must improve their reception and decoding skills before communication can be maximally effective.

It is obvious that both senders and receivers are critical components

*For example see Marshall McLuhan, *Understanding Media: The Extensions of Man.* New York: McGraw-Hill, 1964.

in the communication process. Communication cannot take place effectively without both parties becoming active participants. Focusing on one participant in the communication process to the exclusion of the other is often convenient and even necessary, but such isolation can result in distorted views of the nature of the communication process.

LOGICAL–EMOTIONAL. Some communication scholars have viewed the nature of the arguments in a message as a defining characteristic. Several scholars contend that logical arguments should be used almost exclusively in communication; others have tended to favor less use of logical argument and a more substantial use of emotional appeal. In most instances, the type of argument used depends on the speaker, the audience, and the occasion.

Generally, a balance of the two—but with a favoring of logical argument—is most effective. It should be realized, however, that few, if any, arguments can be classified as purely logical. (The same holds true of emotional arguments.) Theoretically, logical and emotional arguments tend to lie on different ends of the same continuum. In fact, although an argument may tend to lie more toward one end of the continuum than the other, it rarely lies in an extreme position. If you were asked to classify the arguments used by an SDS speaker at a student rally, you might find the arguments more on the emotional than on the logical side of the continuum, but you still might find that certain logical arguments were used.

PUBLIC SPEAKING AND COMMUNICATION. This distinction of communication processes is emphasized by an ongoing controversy among scholars in the field of verbal communication. Traditionally, speech teachers have been primarily concerned with public speaking. In the past decade, however, their emphasis has gradually shifted to interpersonal and small-group communication, while they have maintained some degree of interest in public speaking. Although the distinction between public speaking and communication is more academic than practical, it is one that speech students should be aware of because it suggests a direction in which the field of speech communication appears to be moving. It is an emerging point of view, and is expressed throughout this book.

ASPECTS OF COMMUNICATION DISCUSSED IN THIS BOOK. While both verbal and nonverbal communication are discussed in the rest of the book, most of the chapters focus more on *verbal communication* than on nonverbal. In Chapters 3 and 7 nonverbal behavior is considered to a limited degree, but all chapters include information on verbal communication.

As the title of the book implies, *oral communication*, rather than written, is emphasized in all chapters. And even though Chapters 4, 5, and 7 deal somewhat with formal communication, the primary emphasis throughout the book is on *informal communication.* Similarly, *interpersonal communication* is given more attention than public speaking. Only Chapters 2 and 8 and, to a lesser extent, Chapters 3, 5, and 7, focus on the distinction between intentional and unintentional communication. Almost no attention is devoted to a man, machine, and animal classification, or to their interactions, as a way of examining communication processes. Related matters are considered only indirectly in Chapters 2, 4, and 6.

Content, medium, and delivery are considered at some point in almost every chapter. The variables, or factors, associated with content and medium appear to receive slightly greater emphasis in Chapters 2, 4, 5, and 8; in Chapters 3, 6, and 7, the variables identified with delivery or the way people communicate are stressed slightly. While aspects of both informative and persuasive communication are considered in Chapters 2, 3, 6, 7, and 8, the material in Chapter 4 is primarily on informative communication settings, and, in Chapter 5, on persuasive communication. Most chapters in this book are reasonably balanced with respect to the sender and receiver in various communication processes. To some extent, in Chapter 8, major attention is given to the receiver, or to respondent communication. Few of our authors discuss the distinction between logical and emotional arguments: only in Chapter 5 has this matter been considered, and in a limited fashion.

The aspects of communication we have discussed in this introduction are not all-inclusive—and, as we noted earlier, many are not even mutually exclusive. However, they should give you some idea of the great variety of ways in which those who study communication have classified the process. If this whole business of classifying and examining various aspects of communication seems confusing, join the crowd. There is currently a great deal of indecision among communication experts as to which aspects, along with their related variables, are the most significant to study.

STATUS OF COMMUNICATION THEORY. We cannot end this section without making a few observations concerning the primitive state of theories of communication. (As you will see, it is reflected in the following chapters.) Even though considerable effort has been directed toward its formulation, no comprehensive and satisfactory theory of communication has emerged. For that matter, a considerable number of communication experts feel that we have probably not developed any *adequate* theory of communication—at any level. An adequate theory would: (1) lead to accurate predictions; (2) be marked by successful predictions or antecedent probability, or be based on empirical evidence; (3) would link constructs in the theory to observable evidence; (4) would possess heuristic value; (5) would be parsimonious; and so on. In Chapter 2 this point is discussed in greater detail, but you should continue to think about the relatively crude level of theory construction in communication as you read the remaining chapters in this book. As you read the chapters which follow, you will observe that the systematic study of communication has evolved from theories about human behavior which contribute to an understanding of communication, rather than from the development and testing of specific or comprehensive theories of communication.

## *Organization of the Text*

The text is organized into eight major chapters. The first is an introductory chapter and the Epilogue serves as a summary. Chapters 2 through 8 contain the major content of the text. Each chapter is composed of a lead article and several related readings, and each is, in a sense, independent of the others: You can read and understand almost any chapter without having read the preceding chapters. Since there is a logical progression of ideas, however, it is probable that maximum understanding will be gained if the chapters are read sequentially. Below is a brief preview of the content of Chapters 2 through 8.

CHAPTER 2. The lead article in the second chapter is an examination of the nature and uses of models and theories, particularly with respect to the communication process. It provides a variety of examples of communication models and theories, and discusses the close interrelationships between theories and models. The readings in Chapter 2 are discussions of the general nature of theory construction, the uses of models and analogies, some aspects of information theory, a relatively thought-provoking transactional model of communication, and the flow of information in communication.

CHAPTER 3. The lead article in Chapter 3 is about the acquisition and performance of verbal and nonverbal communication behavior by human beings. The emphasis is on the interrelationship of communication behavior and human developmental and learning processes. The readings relate to the assessment of the language and cognitive learning of black children, some elements of psycholinguistics, the stages in the acquisition of standard English, and a sociolinguistic approach to socialization.

CHAPTER 4. The lead article of this chapter is an exploration of such issues as how people acquire information, effective means of diffusing information, and the relationship between information theory and communication theory. The readings are discussions of selectivity in exposure to mass communications, a modified revision of the two-step flow-of-communication hypothesis, and the effect on communication of similarities and differences in attributes, beliefs, values, and education.

CHAPTER 5. The lead article of the fifth chapter is concerned with attitudinal changes and persuasion in communication. Several theories of attitudinal and behavioral change, as well as the broader question of how attitudinal change and persuasion are related to the entire scope of man's communication behavior, are explored. In the readings, the doctrine of suggestion, some practical applications of principles of attitudinal and behavioral change, the use of the principles of persuasion in President Nixon's 1968 campaign, and a functional approach to the study of attitudes are discussed.

CHAPTER 6. The lead article in Chapter 6 provides the student with information he should have about psychophysiological variables and communication behavior. The nature of man's psychophysiological behavior is identified, and a few theories which have been used to explain psychophysiological behavior are presented. The readings in this chapter include a discussion of the general nature of psychophysiology and of a very practical and useful application of psychophysiology, lie detection.

CHAPTER 7. The lead article in Chapter 7 directs attention to the relevant topic of transracial and interracial communication. Normalization of communication, overlapping language codes between races, nonverbal communication in a transracial context, and interracial sensitivity are discussed. The reading included is a provocative analysis of "rapping" in a black ghetto.

CHAPTER 8. The focus of the lead article in Chapter 8 is on the measurement of communication effects. The classes of measurement relevant to communication behavior are identified and discussed, some problems of measurement are introduced, and some practical ways of measuring the effectiveness of communication are suggested. In the readings are emphasized some critical problems in the indirect observation of communication behavior, some methods of measuring effect on the audience, and some basic problems in using direct observation for recording and measuring communication behavior.

## *Organization Within Each Chapter*

Organizationally, each chapter is divided into two major sections. The first section, Overview and Perspective, is an original article written especially for this book by a communication scholar who has a special interest in the particular topic. Each of these original lead articles is composed of two parts: The first is a summary of the theory and research related to one or more aspects of the communication process, designed to provide a frame of reference for a particular approach to the study of communication and for the readings to follow; in the second part, principles derived from the theory and research reported in the first part of it are specified, and their implications are discussed. While various authors necessarily have treated the "principles and implications" part in different ways, all have made an effort to make the theory and research, discussed in the first part of the article, meaningful for you. However, you too are expected to put forth an effort to make the ideas and principles in the first section *relevant*: You must try to transfer or translate the idea expressed into your daily communication behavior, if you are to obtain the maximum benefit from this book.

Now, some of you are going to be stimulated by ideas expressed in the lead articles and will want to examine them in greater depth. With this in mind, we created the second section, a set of related readings. The readings which follow the lead article are designed to let you explore in greater depth some of the ideas presented in the introductory article. In effect, we have created two books into one. The first book is a collection of the original introductory articles, which provides you with an overview of various aspects of the communication process and with the related principles and their implications, with which you can improve your communication behavior; the second is a book of related readings which expands the ideas expressed in the introductory articles. (Knowing how undergraduates dislike spending time in libraries roaming through the stacks to find journal articles, sitting in reserve rooms, and waiting for journals to be returned so they can read their assignments, we thought you might appreciate having all these materials under one cover.)

We also have thought about you in establishing the structure for the chapters. First, we have tried to make your learning more efficient by setting forth objectives—so that you know what information you are expected to acquire as a result of reading. Objectives have been provided for both the introductory articles and each of the readings. Second, because you may be curious about who wrote the introductory articles, we have provided a brief statement about each author, containing information about his background and his work in communication. Third, our authors have made an effort to cross-reference the ideas they discuss with related ideas examined in other chapters. Fourth, you are referred to the readings periodically throughout the introductory articles, so you will understand which readings are related to ideas discussed in the lead articles. Fifth, when specifying principles and their implications, the authors have attempted to keep college students in mind, providing examples and illuminating implications that are relevant to you and the problems to which you are sensitive. Obviously, this is easier to do with some topics than with some others. Sixth, each reading is preceded by an introduction designed to orient you to the major thrust and concerns in the selection to follow. Seventh, because we want you to think about each chapter as a whole—the introductory article and the selected readings—Questions for Discussion appear at the end of each chapter. Even if your teacher does not require that these be discussed in class, we think you will find them useful for review and in making your personal assessment of whether the ideas presented will be useful to you in thinking about the communication process.

## QUESTIONS FOR DISCUSSION

1. What conditions or reasons occur to you which might have influenced teachers of communication to shift emphasis away from public speaking and toward interpersonal communication?
2. Why haven't we determined all the conditions necessary to produce consistently effective communication?
3. Given the present state of our knowledge of communication, can you learn enough to ever really *know* how to be an effective communicator? What reasons can you give for your answer?
4. What are some of the problems which result when we look at *only two* or *three* of the various aspects of communication? When we look at *all* the various aspects of communication?
5. Assume that when you finish this book you will have acquired information about how communication takes place, about some conditions which might increase effective communication, and so on. What specific steps will you have to take to make this information useful to you to: (a) improve your own communication behavior; and (b) become a critical observer of others' communication behavior?

# chapter 2

# THEORIES AND MODELS OF COMMUNICATION PROCESSES

## SECTION ONE: OVERVIEW AND PERSPECTIVE

*Objectives for Section One*

After reading the first section of the article, "What Do We Mean—Communication?" you should be able to:

1. List a few personal theories of communication which you have developed from your own experience.
2. Describe communication courses you have taken and compare them with the behavioral approach to communication.
3. Distinguish between the field of communication as a scholarly discipline, a behavioral science, and a profession.
4. List at least 10 academic disciplines related to communication and relate each one to the communication event typically studied.
5. Distinguish between communication and communications.
6. Describe communication as a process.
7. List the characteristics of communication at four levels: intrapersonal, interpersonal, group or mass, and cultural.
8. Distinguish between internal and external communication.
9. Name and define five different nonverbal languages.
10. Distinguish between the content and relationship aspects of communication.
11. Give your own definition of communication.
12. Summarize the communication variables presented in Berlo's SMCR diagram.

After reading the second section of this article, "Models of Communication Processes," you should be able to:

13. Distinguish between the research and instruction functions of a model.
14. Define and give examples of models according to their structure: iconic, verbal and graphic, and mathematical.
15. Describe the process of intrapersonal communication.
16. Describe the process of interpersonal communication.
17. Describe the process of mass communication.

After reading the third and final section of this article, "Theories of Communication Processes," you should be able to:

18. Cite an example of the practical use of a communication theory.
19. Summarize the typical steps in the scientific method.

*Ronald L. Smith*

# THEORIES AND MODELS OF COMMUNICATION PROCESSES

When you leave classes and return home, chances are good that a younger brother, sister, or friend will ask you what has been happening on your campus. Your reply will affect his perception of what it is like to attend college. If your friend has not been around many college students, you will help shape his ideas about the role of a college student. As the two of you interact, he may begin to share *your* perception of being a college student. The more you talk, the easier it is to understand each other. You have established common reference points for your conversation.

Suppose your conversation turns to communication—perhaps communciation problems with parents. Now you have shifted to a subject in which your friend, and all people, have considerable experience. Communication seems as easy as thinking and breathing; but precisely because it is such a universal human experience, it is normal for you and your friend to *assume* that you understand the process by which it occurs. This assump-

Ronald L. Smith *is professor of communication and chairman, Department of Communication and Organizational Behavior, General Motors Institute. He received his degree as Bachelor of Mechanical Engineering from General Motors Institute in 1960, and his M.S. (in industrial relations in 1962) and Ph.D. (in organizational communication, in 1967) from Purdue University. He is president of the International Communication Association (1971–72) and a director of the Council of Communication Societies.*

*Dr. Smith's interest in communication models began with a 1962 paper,* "General Models of Communication," *which received wide attention. At GMI, he teaches courses in interpersonal and organizational communication for undergraduate engineering and industrial administration majors. His research interests include interpersonal sensitivity and performance appraisal.*

tion may cause a breakdown in communication as soon as the two of you discuss communication problems. You may discover that you have different ideas about what communication is and is not; or, worse yet, different interpretations may exist, and you may casually discuss communication without ever discovering that fact.

Even as you study communication in a more formal, theoretical way, it is all around you. You already know thousands of facts about communication. There is probably no course subject with which you have had more experience. This familiarity may be a disadvantage, for all of us have jumped to conclusions about communication which are not supported by systematic, scientific investigation. For example, we accept the maxim, "Seeing is believing," although experiments have shown that our eyes often play tricks on us. Moreover, past experience or group pressure may interfere with accurate visual perception. We really cannot believe all that we see; breakdowns can occur in visual communication.

Experience has led each of us to formulate personal theories about the effects of communication. If these theories accurately predicted or described the outcomes of communication in a variety of situations, there would be more consistency among our personal theories and they would have helped us to become more effective communicators. Even though we have observed and participated in communication since birth, the frequency of breakdowns in personal communication suggests that experience alone does not provide adequate data for predicting how one ingredient in a situation will affect another ingredient.

In a specific situation, you may show considerable skill in predicting communication behavior. You may know how dad, a roommate, or an instructor will react to a certain message—and how you will react to their reaction. You may even make some plausible generalizations about communication from such a specific situation and similar events in your experience. But many of your intuitive generalizations may not be supported by careful investigations of communication. Some unlearning may have to take place during your initial contact with a science of speech-communication behavior.

We hope you will also discover some new aspects of communication. For many years, you have probably been taught an approach to communication which emphasized the form of the message: where to insert commas and periods, how to improve voice and diction. In this book you will encounter a behavioral approach to the study of human communication, one which emphasizes personal interaction—the relationships between senders, receivers, and messages.

In this chapter we consider what is meant by communication, and how theories and models from the behavioral sciences can increase our understanding and effectiveness in speech communication. We will focus on the general role of models and theories in scientific explanation, since theory building is the most important objective of the behavioral sciences. The ideas in this chapter come generally from the area of thought labeled "philosophy of science." Examples from communication theory and research will be introduced to strengthen your understanding of the general processes of communication.

## *What Do We Mean—Communication?*

The suggestion that we already may be having a problem as we try to communicate about communication seems ludicrous, but that may be the case! Let us examine several different ideas which could pop into your mind when a friend says: "I'm having a problem with *communication.*"

### COMMUNICATION AS A FIELD OF STUDY

Your friend may mean he received a poor grade on the last examination in his communication course. In this sense, communication can be defined as a field of study which focuses on message-related behavior. Like other areas of study, communication has professionals engaged in teaching, research, and practice. As a *scholarly discipline*, communication represents an emerging field in many academic institutions, which emphasizes the explanation of communication behavior and its teaching through classroom-laboratory experience in group problem solving, speaking, interviewing, and role playing. As a *behavioral science*, communication is a focus of theory building and research in which investigators collect, quantify, analyze, and interpret data in an attempt to discover how some ingredients, or variables, of communication affect others. As a *profession*, communication involves the practical application of knowledge, skills, and techniques in improving communication in two-person relationships, families and work groups, organizations, nations, and in the total family of man. Counselors, teachers, speech writers, and journalists, as well as radio, TV, and film professionals are all communication practitioners.

Some academicians now claim that communication has developed as a distinct discipline; however, organizations such as the International Communication Association attract professionals from a wide variety of academic disciplines. This book presents a selected inventory of communication theories and principles from many different fields. Some of these disciplines and a few of their major communication interests are:

<table>
<tr><th></th><th>Academic Discipline</th><th>Communication Event Typically Studied</th></tr>
<tr><td rowspan="4">frequently labeled behavioral sciences</td><td>Psychology and Social Psychology</td><td>Language behavior (as in Chapter 3) and Interpersonal communication between individuals (as in Chapter 5)</td></tr>
<tr><td>Physiology</td><td>Intrapersonal communication, within individuals (as in Chapter 6)</td></tr>
<tr><td>Sociology</td><td>Group and mass communication</td></tr>
<tr><td>Anthropology</td><td>Culture and communication</td></tr>
<tr><td></td><td>Speech</td><td>Rhetoric, public address, speech pathology</td></tr>
<tr><td></td><td>Journalism, Radio, TV, and Film making</td><td>Mass communication</td></tr>
<tr><td></td><td>Linguistics</td><td>Languages</td></tr>
<tr><td></td><td>English</td><td>Writing</td></tr>
<tr><td></td><td>Education</td><td>Learning and communication (as in Chapter 3)</td></tr>
<tr><td></td><td>Business</td><td>Organizational communication; information systems</td></tr>
<tr><td></td><td>Library Science</td><td>Information storage and retrieval (as in Chapter 4)</td></tr>
<tr><td></td><td>Engineering</td><td>Telecommunication</td></tr>
</table>

Here a strong cautionary note is necessary. The above list illustrates the multidisciplinary nature of communication studies; but it is not complete in either the left or right column. All chapters in this book have a multidisciplinary flavor; hence, references in the preceding list merely indicate chapters which describe some research from the identified discipline.

Even if we know that the word "communication" evokes the idea of a field of study, we still cannot be certain whether the other person is thinking about psychology, journalism, speech, or some other area in which he has taken a course or read a book.

## COMMUNICATION AS A MESSAGE

When your friend says he is having a problem with communication, he may be thinking about a particular communication, a single message such as an editorial for the college newspaper. Or he may be having difficulty with a series of messages, with communications. The difficulty may be behavioral in nature—a problem, for example, of selecting the language or symbols to use or of anticipating the receiver's interpretation. The problem may lie in the mechanical transmission of the physical signal—a problem in acoustics or equipment failure.

You may have noticed that this book uses the word "communication" rather than "communications." Consider the following comparison with other areas of study:

| | |
|---|---|
| Medicine | medicine*s* (individual pharmaceuticals) |
| Law | law*s* (individual statutes) |
| History | historie*s* (individual accounts) |
| Communication | communication*s* (individual messages) |

In this sense, "communication" is used to identify a process, while "communications" refers to single events in the process.

## COMMUNICATION AS A PROCESS

This book is about verbal behavior in the process of communication. Throughout the book, the term "communication" will connote a *process.*

When your friend says, "I'm having a problem with communication," he may be including more than difficulties with a college course or a specific message or group of messages. He may be saying, "I have trouble understanding [or being understood] by my girl." Or "I don't relate well to my fraternity brothers." When your friend says that, he implies something more than a single, static communication event. He is saying that he is concerned about a dynamic, ongoing, complex communication relationship with another person or group of people. He is talking about an ongoing process of interacting with another rather than a single event.

Behavioral communication theory must reflect the point of view that communication is a process. We cannot identify beginnings or ends of communication. We can only make observations at points in time, almost like using a camera to record communication events as frames within the process. Your communication relationship with another person an hour or a moment from now will be affected by what happened an hour or a moment ago.

Single ingredients or variables of communication are difficult to isolate because they are so interwoven with other variables. For example, when managers in an industrial plant decide to communicate product information (one variable), it does not seem to matter which medium (another variable) they use—oral presentation or written memoranda—for these media appear to be equally effective (a third variable) when employees are highly motivated (a fourth variable) to receive the message (Smith, 1961).

Many variables interact within the process of communication and within a variety of communication settings. As you read this book, you should begin to have a greater understanding of the relationships among those variables.

Considered as a process, communication can be defined and classified in many ways: as internal or external, verbal or nonverbal, as expressing content or relationship, as being intentional or unintentional, and so on. As these aspects are discussed, we will introduce a few definitions of communication that have been offered by influential scholars. These will help us to understand some important questions about what can be included or excluded when we talk about communication.

INTERNAL AND EXTERNAL COMMUNICATION. When we study communication, we are really analyzing different levels of communication *systems*. The molecule, the cell, the organ, the individual, the group, and the society are all different levels of living systems. These living systems are made of matter and energy organized by information.

Consider the following general definition: "Communication means that information is passed from one place to another" (G. A. Miller, 1951, p. 6). Such a definition implies that the process of communication can take place internally (within a system) or externally (between systems). Then, too, a single message can be called either internal or external communication, depending on the systems which are being analyzed. As you read this page, different classes of communication are occurring. Information is being passed between your eyes and brain. For you as an individual (a single system), this can be analyzed as internal communication; in an analysis of cells and organs, it is external communication between lower-level systems.

When we discuss communication, it is important to identify the level of system we have in mind. Ruesch and Bateson have prepared a table which describes communication at four levels, which they call intrapersonal, interpersonal, group, and cultural. This analysis is reproduced in Table 1. Sometimes Ruesch and Bateson's concept of group communication is called "mass communication."

VERBAL AND NONVERBAL COMMUNICATION. One frequently cited definition concludes that communication "involves not only written and oral speech, but also music, the pictorial arts, the theatre, the ballet, and in fact all human behavior" (Shannon and Weaver, 1949, p. 95). That opens up the whole area of communication without words, or nonverbal communication.

*Verbal communication* is usually defined as message behavior in which words are used as symbols to represent objects and ideas. *Nonverbal communication* includes all other forms of message behavior, such as: (1) sign language; (2) action language; (3) object language; (4) space; and (5) time. Sign language is used when a gesture, such as a "V" made with two fingers, is used to communicate an idea like peace. A nod of the head may mean "yes." Action language is the language of the body, such as facial expression and posture, which communicate unintended or at least unconscious messages. Object language is the display of tangible items, such as hair styles, cars, clothes, and jewelry, which communicate roles and status. The use of time, especially punctuality or tardiness, com-

Table 1. The Specification of Networks at the Four Levels of Communication

| *Levels* | *Origin of Message* | *Sender* | *Channels* | *Receiver* | *Destination of Message* |
|---|---|---|---|---|---|
| I. Intrapersonal "within one" | Sensory end organ or Communication center. | | Neural, humoral pathways and contiguous pathways. | Communication center or the effector organs. | |
| II. Interpersonal "one to one" | Communication center of person sending message. | Effector organ of sending person. | Sound, light, heat, odor, vibrations traveling across space on the one hand, chemical or mechanical contact with material or person on the other hand. | Sensory end organs of receiving person. | Communication center of person receiving message. |
| III. A. Group "One to many" (centrifugal messages) | Communication center of group: head man or committee. | Person specializing in being a mouthpiece or executive for the communication center. | Multiplication of message through press, radio, loudspeaker system, movies, circulars, etc. | Persons engaged in receiving and interpreting incoming messages for the group—readers, listeners, theater spectators, critics. | Many persons who are members of a group. Identity of persons is unspecified by name: they are known by role. Group is specified. |
| B. Group "Many to one" | Many persons who are members of a | Spokesman who expresses the voice of | Mail, word of mouth, or other | Professional specialists who engage | Communication center of group— |

| (centripetal messages) | group. Identity of persons is unspecified by name; they are known by role. Group is specified. | the people, the family, or other small groups at the periphery. | instrumental actions of people. | in receiving messages: news analysts, intelligence service, government agencies. Condensation and abstraction of incoming messages. | executive, committee, or head man. |
|---|---|---|---|---|---|
| IV. A. Cultural<br>"Space binding" messages of "many to many" | Many groups unspecified by name, known by role, which express moral, aesthetic, or religious views—e.g., the clergy, children. | Groups specializing in the formulation of standards of living: legislators. | Script, written and unwritten regulations and laws. Customs transmitted by personal contact often implicit in action. Persons become channel. | Groups engaging in the reception and interpretation of cultural messages such as judges, lawyers, scientists, ministers. | Many groups composed of living people, unspecified by name, known by role. |
| B. Cultural "Time binding" messages of "many to many" | Many unspecified groups the members of which are older than the receivers or already dead. | The voice of the past, frequently a mythological or historical figure. | Script, material culture such as objects, architectural structures, etc., and personal contact from generation to generation often implicit in action. | Group specializing in the reception and interpretation of the messages of the past—archaeologists, historians, clergy. | Many unspecified groups the members of which are younger than the originators of the message. |

Reprinted from *Communication, The Social Matrix of Psychiatry* by Jurgen Ruesch, M.D. and Gregory Bateson. By permission of W.W. Norton & Company, Inc. Copyright 1951 by W.W. Norton & Company, Inc.

municates, as does space—how close or far away we choose to be when we talk to another person. Finally, silence communicates. If you have a friend, and you do not call or write for a long period of time, you are probably communicating either that you do not care about the relationship or that you are so sure of its stability that you do not feel it necessary to send periodic messages. It seems to be true that "one cannot NOT communicate" (Watzlawick, Beavin, and Jackson, 1967, p. 51). Nonverbal messages are critical, and often actions *do* speak louder than words.

CONTENT AND RELATIONSHIP COMMUNICATION. Every message transaction has a content and a relationship aspect. A message not only conveys bits of information; at the same time it defines how the information is to be taken—the nature of interpersonal transactions between the communicants. The relationship aspect of communication answers questions such as:

How do I see myself?
How do I see you?
How do I see you seeing me?

Thus, when mother receives two messages—one from daughter: "Gee, that's the third dent you've put in the car in five weeks," and one from husband: "Well, I see you've done it again"—these verbal messages contain approximately the same information. The content of both is that a physical change in the car has been perceived. But the two messages obviously define very different relationships between the sender and receiver.

INTENTIONAL AND UNINTENTIONAL COMMUNICATION. We all send many unintended messages. Often these unintended messages are nonverbal. *Time* magazine recently carried a photograph of President Nixon reading a document, with both corners of his mouth turned down. Was he angry? We might infer so. But *Time* reported that those "who have worked with him say that his turned-down-mouth expression is really one of concentration on the matter before him. When he is really displeased, they say, his most characteristic expression is a tight smile, accompanied by excessive politeness" (1970, p. 9). (See photograph, p. 29.)

Some communication research focuses on intentional communication: One pioneer in persuasion studies defined communication as "the process by which an individual (the communicator) transmits stimuli (usually verbal symbols) to modify the behavior of other individuals (communicatees)" (Hovland, 1948, p. 391). Another researcher is even more explicit about his focus on the intentional when he defines communication as "those behavioral situations in which a source transmits a message to a receiver(s) *with conscious intent to affect the latter's behaviors*" (G. R.

Miller, 1966, p. 92). Miller acknowledges the presence of unintentional messages, but he thinks we can learn more by concentrating our studies on intentional message behavior.

Another writer, on the other hand, includes unintentional messages by focusing his definition on the receiver's interpretation rather than the sender's intent: "In its broadest perspective, communication occurs whenever an individual assigns significance or meaning to an internal or external stimulus" (Thayer, 1961, p. 43).

In addition to unintended messages, we frequently encounter unintended receivers who misinterpret messages intended for others. A few years ago, the Poole, England, General Hospital staff newsletter reported the following conversation:

> "It was God who took out my tonsils," the boy told his mother after his operation.
> "When I was taken into the big white room, there were two lady angels dressed in white. Then two men angels came in. Then God came in."
> "How did you know it was God?" asked the mother.
> "Well, one of the men angels looked down my throat and said—'God, look at that child's tonsils.' "
> "Then God took a look and said, 'I'll take them out at once.' "

The doctor's verbal exchange obviously wasn't intended for the young patient. Adding to the confusion was the boy's misinterpretation of certain nonverbal signs such as the white coats.

You should by now be able to recognize some communication variables which operate in a variety of situations: the level of system at which communication is taking place, the nature of signs and symbols (verbal and nonverbal) used to express messages, the information content and the relationship which it defines, the intent or purpose of the sender, and the assignment of meaning (interpretation) by the receiver.

Many lists of communication variables have been compiled. One of the earliest and most influential was Berlo's SMCR diagram, which appears in Figure 1. This might be called a "pre-model diagram," since it sets forth major variables without performing the function of a model: suggesting specific relationships between the variables.

## *Models of Communication Processes*

In our everyday language, we use the word "model" in many different ways. You may be a "model" student—an ideal student worthy of imitation. A "model" may be the doll a little girl cuddles and the photogenic "doll" whose picture appears on the *Playboy* centerfold. Scientists have

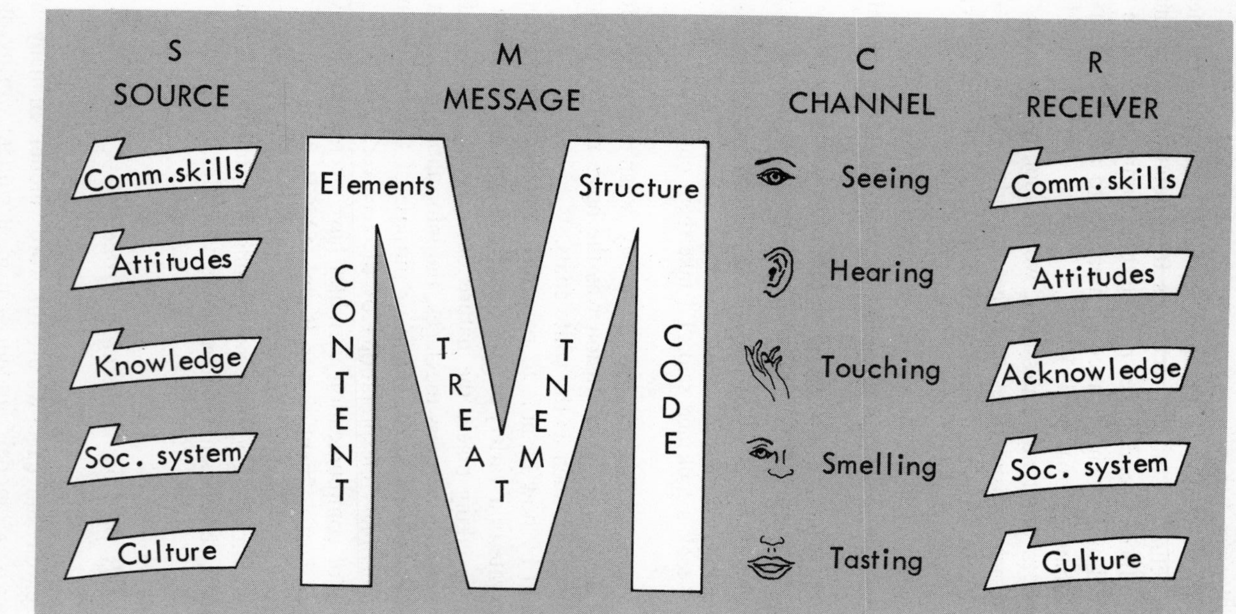


**Figure 1.** The Ingredients of Communication. [From David K. Berlo, *The Process of Communication: An Introduction to Theory and Practice* (New York: Holt, Rinehart & Winston, Inc., 1960), p. 72. Reprinted by permission of the publisher.]

not adopted a uniform definition of the term. Even so, "model" and "theory" should not be used synonymously because the two have different characteristics.

In order to understand the discussion of models and theories which follow, you will need to know the definitions of some terms, such as *law, hypothesis, theory, construct,* and *concept.* These are defined early in the first reading which follows this article, "The General Nature of Theory Construction," and you should read the first section, "Some Basic Definitions." As you read the definitions, bear in mind that we are using the terms "ingredient" and "concept" synonymously.

## FUNCTIONAL CLASSES OF MODELS

Scholars use two different definitions of "model," which can best be understood by examining the two different functions which a model can serve.

THE RESEARCH FUNCTION. One function of models is to help the researcher make the relationship between constructs clear and to organize them. To consider this the primary function of the model is to view it as a step in theory construction (Margenau, 1950; Hempel, 1952; and Torgerson, 1958).

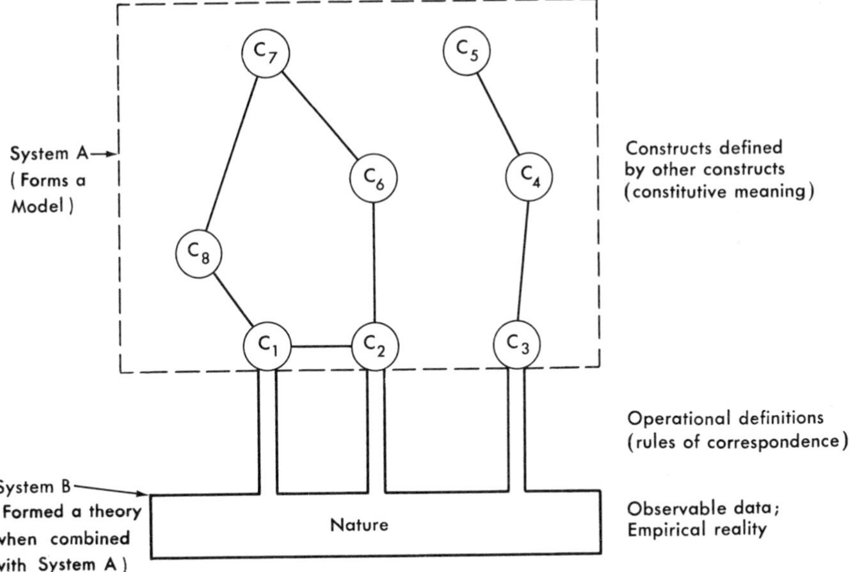


**Figure 2.** A Typical Theory in the Behavioral Sciences [Adapted from W. S. Torgerson, *Theory and Methods of Scaling* (New York: John Wiley & Sons, Inc., 1958), p. 5. Reprinted by permission of the publisher and author.]

The diagram in Figure 2 shows the research function of a model. The model is pictured as System *A*, a network in which the constructs are represented by knots (circles), and the definitions are represented by the threads (single lines) connecting the knots. Constructs are defined by other constructs, which is called "constitutive meaning." The model floats above the plane of observation (System *B*: Nature) and is anchored to it by "rules of correspondence," or interpretation. These rules of correspondence, or operational definitions, might be viewed as strings which are not part of the model but which link certain parts of the model with specific points on the plane of observation. When such interpretive connections are made (combining Systems A and B), the network can function as a scientific theory.

THE INSTRUCTIONAL FUNCTION. Models are also used to explain and clarify theories. A teacher may use a communication model, for example, to help a student understand the sequence of events in the process or to identify areas in which personal communication can be improved. To consider instruction as the main function of the model is to view it as a separate representation of the communication process, an analog brought in from some other field.

The dangers of analogical models are pointed out in the second reading which follows this article, "The Use of Models and Analogies." The authors of this reading argue that mathematical models hold the greatest promise for fulfilling the research function, and that analogies should be largely limited to the instructional function.

## STRUCTURAL CLASSES OF MODELS

At least three types of structures of models are widely used. In ascending levels of abstraction they are iconic models, verbal and graphic models, and mathematical models.

ICONIC MODELS. Some analogical models, such as the model airplane, look like the subject they represent. Often these are called "physical" models, but a more precise term is "iconic" (Churchman, Ackoff, and Arnoff, 1957, p. 159). The term is taken from the Latin word *iconicus*, which means "representing a figure" or "copied." Photographs, paintings, and sculptures are iconic models of persons, objects, or scenes. A globe is an iconic model of the earth. In general, the properties of an iconic model are proportional to those of the subject, but they are usually scaled to meet the dimensions desired in the model. The earth model is scaled down, but the molecular model is magnified many thousand times to give it a useful size.

Iconic models are particularly well-suited for representing either static subjects or dynamic subjects at a specific moment of time. The photograph of President Nixon* is the one referred to earlier; it clarifies the "turned-

Used by permission of United Press International Photo.

down mouth" which was described earlier in this chapter.

The fact that iconic models contain many of the same properties, in the same proportions, as the subject, does not mean that all the properties of the original are represented. A plastic model of a head may contain lifesize replicas of the human articulatory mechanism (tongue, lips, teeth, jaw, and palates), but these parts do not have to be of the proper relative weight or color, or contain arteries, capillaries, and veins, to be a useful physiological model.

VERBAL AND GRAPHIC MODELS. At one time or another, every theory is stated in words, or in a verbal model. Verbal models have played

*The original caption that appeared with the photograph is as follows: "4/9/70 Washington: Pres. Nixon said 4/9 he wants his next Supreme Court nominee to be from outside the South because he feels the Senate will not accept a conservative Southerner. He said he has told Attorney General John N. Mitchell (left) to recommend someone from outside the South for his third nominee for a vacant seat on the court."

an important role in science, especially in the preliminary exploration of a topic and in the presentation of results.

A graphic representation of a verbal model often clarifies or emphasizes relationships among variables defined in the verbal model. The graphic representation of the verbal model differs from the iconic model: It does *not* look like the subject which is represents.

It is not always convenient to reproduce all the properties of a subject, even scaled, yet it may be desirable to describe these properties with a model more precise than the verbal model. The geological structure of the earth cannot be conveniently reproduced on a map, for example, but various types of geological formations can be represented by different colors. Thus one property (color) is substituted for another (geological structure) according to some convention of transformation which is usually explained in a legend on the map. Graphs are models in which distance represents such properties as time, number, age, and weight.

Most communication models have been verbal descriptions of networks of constructs or graphic representations of these networks. These models have served to define and classify constructs in the communication process and to suggest relations among constructs.

MATHEMATICAL MODELS. Most scientists consider their ultimate objective to be the expression of theories in sets of mathematical or logical equations. Mathematical models are a step toward this goal and allow substantial ease in manipulating the subject of inquiry. Computers perform hundreds of quantitative manipulations in a few seconds when formal mathematical structures can be programed. Few attempts have been made to mathematize communication theories. Two exceptions are the statistical concepts of information processing and the application of graph theory to the analysis of communication networks.

## A SAMPLE OF COMMUNICATION MODELS

A 1962 survey (Smith) located 15 different communication models; since then many others have appeared in communication literature. Although attempts have been made to classify these models (DeVito, 1968), there are no universally accepted categories. The models which appear in this chapter were selected to help clarify variables operating in the communication process at different levels of systems, but many of these models have had a preliminary research function as well as an instructional function.

AN INFORMATION-PROCESSING MODEL. In 1949, Shannon and Weaver published *The Mathematical Theory of Communication*. This model has been a singularly influential analog, using principles of telecommunication to explain human communication.

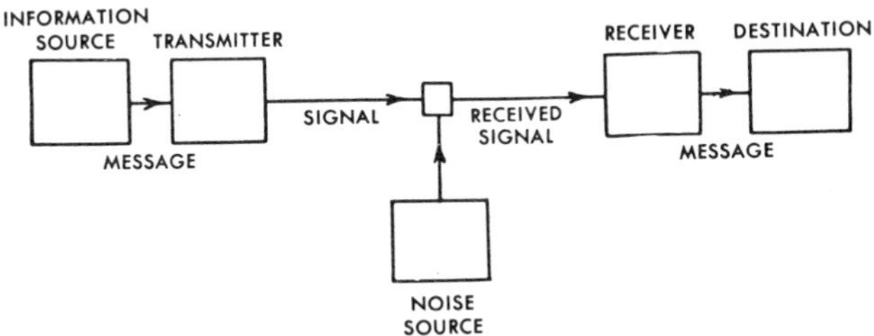


**Figure 3.** An Information-Processing Model. [From Claude E. Shannon and Warren Weaver, *The Mathematical Theory of Communication* (Urbana, Ill.: The University of Illinois Press, 1949), p. 5. Reprinted by permission of the publisher.]

In the Shannon-Weaver model (Figure 3), the information source selects a desired message out of a set of possible messages: Thus, the model is based upon the statistical concept of probability. The transmitter changes this message into a physical signal which is sent over the communication channel from the transmitter to the receiver. In speech communication, the information source is the brain and the transmitter is the voice mechanism producing the varying sound pressure (the signal) which is transmitted through the air (the channel). Noise sometimes interferes with reception. The receiver is an inverse transmitter, changing the transmitted signal back into a message and sending this message on to the destination. This model is elaborated further in the third reading following this article, "The Information Theory."

AN INTRAPERSONAL COMMUNICATION MODEL. Barker and Wiseman (1966) have constructed a model of intrapersonal communication. Their graphical analog appears in Figure 4.

Internal and external stimuli are received by the body's sensory organs. Internal receptors such as nerve endings relate information in the form of feelings or sensations which reflect the psychophysical state of the individual. External receptors located near the surface of the body react to physical and chemical stimuli and relate the individual to his environment. Stimuli are screened for relative strength in a "discrimination" process, the weaker stimuli being filtered out. Stimuli are "regrouped" according to their urgency; and while discrimination and regrouping are taking place, meaning is attached to stimuli in the symbol-decoding process. These processes occur almost simultaneously, interacting with the individual's life orientation or field of experience.

Ideation (thinking, planning, organizing) occurs; incubation allows the ideas to jell; and the individual prepares to transmit the idea by encoding it into words, gestures, or movements. Internal feedback occurs through bone conduction, muscular contractions, or neurocircuitry of the central nervous system.

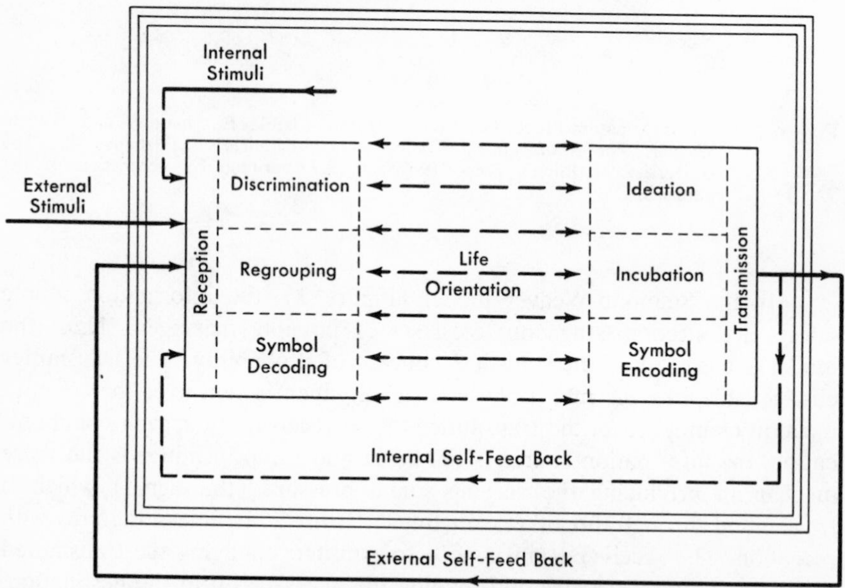


**Figure 4.** An Intrapersonal Communication Model. [From L. L. Barker and G. Wiseman, "A Model of Intrapersonal Communication," *Journal of Communication,* XVI (1966), 174. Reprinted by permission of the International Communication Association and the authors.]

An Interpersonal Communication Model. Early models pictured communication as a circular response, the communicators alternately exchanging roles as sender and receiver (Monroe and Ehninger, 1967, pp. 16–19). Dance pointed out that a circle implies that communication returns to the same point at which it started, which is impossible because the process occurs in time. Dance proposed a helical representation, giving "geometrical testimony to the concept that communication while moving forward is at the same moment coming back upon itself and being affected by its past behavior" (1967, p. 296).

Tubbs (1970) has further refined and elaborated the helical model of interpersonal communication. His pictorial diagram appears in Figure 5. In his scheme, the primary originator starts out with inputs such as his social and cultural system and the nature of the physical space he is occupying. His physiological and psychological system constitute a filter through

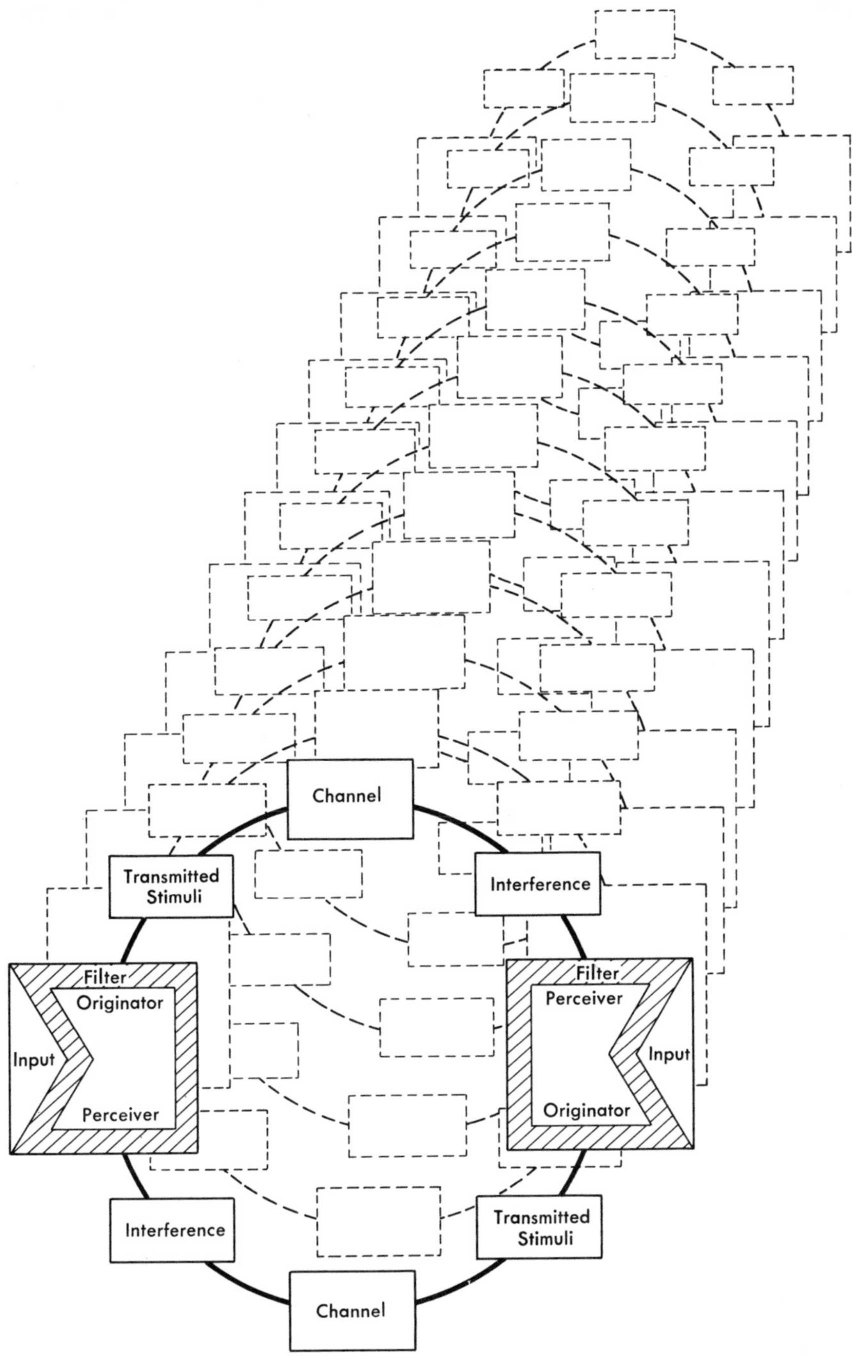


**Figure 5.** An Interpersonal Communication Model. [From S. L. Tubbs, *An Introduction to Interpersonal Communication* (in preparation, 1970), p. 12. Reprinted by permission of the author.]

which stimuli—internal and external, verbal and nonverbal, and intentional and unintentional—are transmitted. Channels such as sound waves and light waves are used to transmit physical signals through technical barriers such as noise, semantic barriers such as different meanings, and psychological barriers such as fear. A portion of these signals pass through the perceiver's filter; his response is feedback, which gives him the role of originator. As this process continues, the helix grows larger in circumference, symbolizing increasing interpersonal awareness, trust, and competency in communicating.

A GROUP OR MASS COMMUNICATION MODEL. Mass communication, compared to interpersonal communication, involves a smaller variety of sensory stimuli and less immediate feedback. Westley and MacLean (1957) have built a model of mass communication, using as their foundation Newcomb's (1953) simple model of interpersonal communication: Person *A* transmits something about object *X* to person *B*. Westley and MacLean add a new element *C*, which has as its purpose to:

1. Select the abstractions of object *X* appropriate to *B*'s need satisfactions or problem solutions;
2. Transform them into some form of symbol containing meanings shared with *B*; and
3. Transmit such symbols by means of some channel or medium to *B*.

*B* might be a housewife who does not have time to visit with each neighbor and observe the details of her environment. The neighborhood gossip performs function *C* by observing, selecting, encoding, and transmitting a limited portion of all possible messages, which fulfills the need of *B* for information.

The addition of role *C* provides *B* with a more extended environment. It generalizes the simple model by enlarging the number of levels of communication which can be explained. *B* now does not have to be a person; *B* can be a primary group or a total social system.

A graphical representation of the model appears in Figure 6. Part 1 represents intrapersonal communication; Part 2, interpersonal communication. *C* is introduced in Part 3, and Part 4 is the fully developed mass-communication model.

The principal elements of the mass communication model are these:

*A* (Advocacy role). Usually called "the communicator," *A* is a person or social system engaged in selecting and transmitting messages purposively.

*B* (Behavioral system role). Usually called "the receiver," "the public," and such, *B* is a person or social system requiring and using communications about the condition of its environment for the satisfaction of its needs and the solution of its problems.

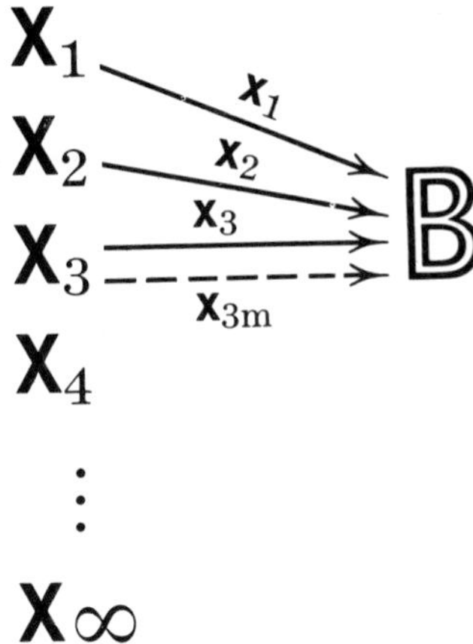


1. Objects of orientation $(X_1 \ldots X_x)$ in the sensory field of the receiver (b) are transmitted directly to him in abstracted form $(X_1 \ldots X_3)$ after a process of selection from among all Xs, such selection being based at least in part on the needs and problems of B. Some or all are transmitted in more than one sense ($X_{3m}$, for example).

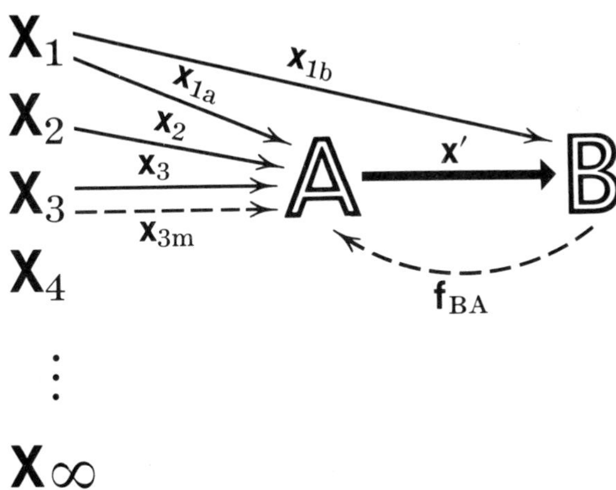


2. The same Xs are selected and abstracted by communicator (A) and transmitted as a message (X') to B, who may or may not have part or all of the Xs in his own sensory field ($X_{1b}$). Either purposively or non-purposively B transmits feedback ($f_{BA}$) to A.)

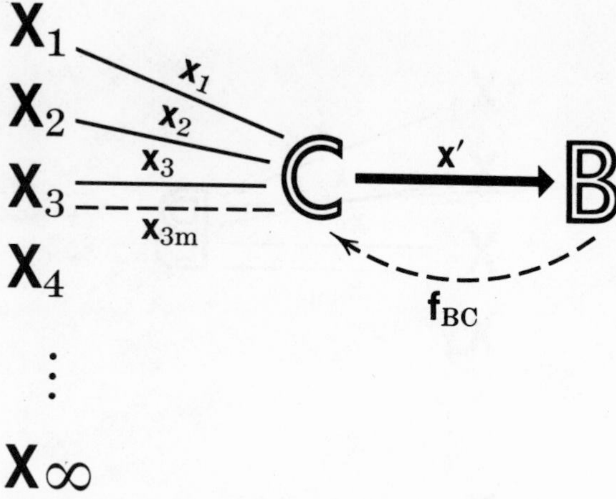


3. What Xs B receives may be owing to selected abstractions transmitted by a non-purposive encoder (C), acting for B and thus extending B's environment. C's selections are necessarily based in part on feedback ($f_{BC}$) from B.

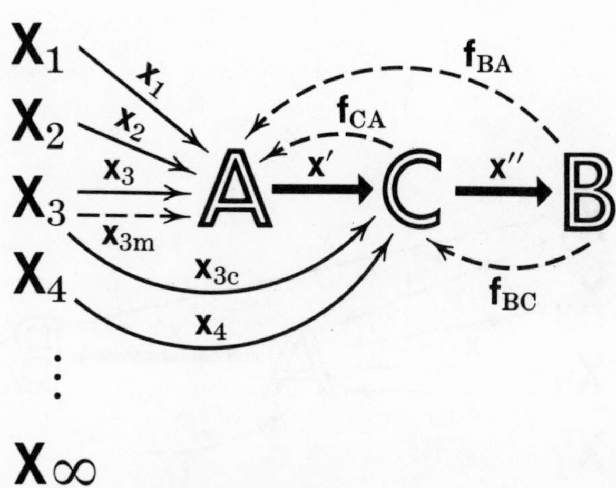


4. The messages C transmits to B (X″) represent his selections from both messages to him from A's (X′) and C's selections and abstractions from Xs in his own sensory field ($X_{3c}$, $X_4$), which may or may not be Xs in A's field. Feedback not only moves from B to A (fBA) and from B to C ($f_{BC}$) but also from C to A ($f_{CA}$). Clearly, in the mass communication situation, a large number of Cs receive from a very large number of As and transmit to a vastly larger number of Bs, who simultaneously receive from other Cs.

**Figure 6.** A Mass Communication Model. [From Bruce H. Westley and Malcolm S. MacLean, Jr., "A Conceptual Model for Communications Research," *Journalism Quarterly,* XXXIV (1957), 8–9. Reprinted by permission of the publisher and the authors.]

*C* (Channel role). Often confounded with *A*'s, *C*'s serve as the agents of *B*'s in selecting and transmitting fortuitously the information *B*'s require, especially when the information is beyond the immedate reach of *B*.
*X*. The totality of objects and events "out there." *X′* is these objects and events as abstracted into transmissible form: "messages" about *X*'s and *A-X* relationships (such as "opinions").
*Channels*. The means by which *X*'s are moved, by way of *A*'s or *C*'s, to *B*'s. Channels include "gates," manned by *C*'s who in various ways alter messages.
*Encoding*. The process by which *A*'s and *C*'s transform *X*'s into *X*″s. Decoding is the process by which *B*'s interiorize messages.
*Feedback*. The means by which *A*'s and *C*'s obtain information about the effects of messages on *B*'s.

The fourth reading which follows this article is "A Transactional Model of Communication." Barnlund's model is another good illustration of a single model developed for analysis of different levels of systems: Intrapersonal, interpersonal, and mass communication.

A SUMMARY MODEL OF COMMUNICATION SYSTEMS. Figure 7 shows Thayer's diagram (1968) which takes into account the levels of analysis and their relationship with information systems. The first level of analysis

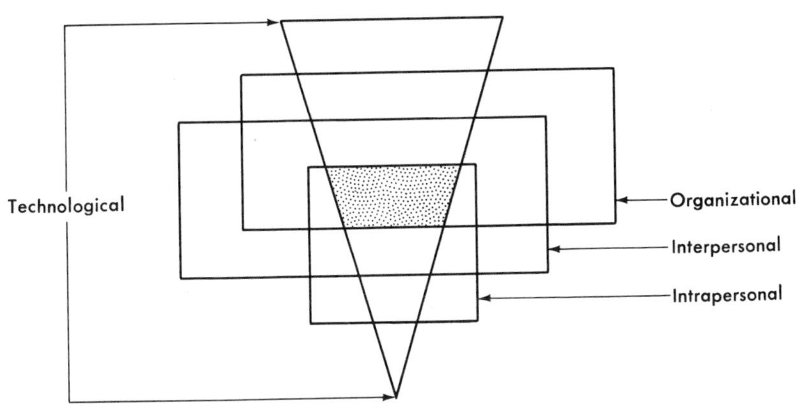


**Figure 7.** Levels of Communication Analysis. [From L. Thayer, *Communication and Communication Systems* (Homewood, Ill.: Richard D. Irwin, Inc., 1968), p. 32. Reprinted by permission of the publisher and author.]

is intrapersonal input and the processing of information. The next level, the interpersonal level, focuses on two-person (or *n*-persons) systems of communication. A third level of organizational analysis is concerned with networks of data systems that link individuals to each other and to the environment: A fourth level of technological analysis takes into account the "hardware" for mechanically generating, storing, processing, translating, distributing, or displaying data—and the multitude of symbolic systems available. Thayer does not even claim that his diagram is a model. He presents it as only an outline of a comprehensive communication theory, but it is a start toward the systems concept which Katz and Kahn discuss in the fifth reading following this article, "Communication: The Flow of Information."

## *Theories of Communication Processes*

Behavioral sciences are much more recent contributors to man's knowledge than physical sciences such as chemistry, physics, and astronomy. So it is natural for many people to limit their association of science and the scientific method to physical inquiries. In this section, we will examine science and theory and the scientific method as they apply to behavioral studies.

### SCIENCE AND THEORY

Kerlinger (1964) describes three popular stereotypes which sometimes impede the broad understanding of science. One such notion is that the scientist uses complicated equipment in a laboratory merely to generate facts. Now, communication events can be described in terms of facts, observations, or data. You can be observed as you read this book. The observation can be permanently recorded with a movie camera or video-tape recorder. Someone can measure the frequency and duration of nonverbal cues such as turned-up or turned-down corners of the mouth, blinking, or half-closed eyes. Each bit of raw data is an observation, a fact about an event.

But as Skinner put it: "Science is more than the mere description of events as they occur. It is an attempt to discover order, to show that certain events stand in lawful relations to other events" (1953, p. 6). Does the introduction of a picture or a concrete example in a book like this regularly elicit the same response from different readers? If so, how does that observable response relate to learning, attitudes, and other desired responses? Scientific theory is constructed to produce just such explanations and predictions. Science is more than an accumulated body of knowledge; it is the act of discovering new ways to explain and predict the unknown.

A second stereotype pictures the scientist as a brilliant—probably eccentric—theoretician in an ivory tower, whose thinking and whose theory are largely impractical. Theorizing (making symbolic constructions) is different from practice (acting out events). But theorizing may be a very practical activity. Kaplan (1964) pointed out that lower animals learn *by* experience but not *from* it, while humans may make symbolic constructions—the "leaping ability" which characterizes the scientist.

In 30 years, we have seen models of public-opinion measurement develop into sophisticated theories which produce fairly precise predictions of voting patterns, buying habits, and other elements of consumer behavior. Any politician, marketing manager, or advertising consultant will testify to the practicality of these theories.

Kerlinger's third stereotype suggests that science is sometimes equated with engineering and technology. Building expressways, automobiles to drive on the expressways, and stereo-tape decks to play while driving the automobiles—these are products of man's inventiveness which make life smooth and efficient and more pleasurable. This view of science suggests that its goal is the materialistic betterment of mankind. It is not. The objective of science is theory which expands our base of knowledge about natural events such as communication.

## THE SCIENTIFIC METHOD

How is a theory constructed? What is the scientific method? Kerlinger's (1964) adaptation of Dewey's famous pattern of reflective thinking is the pattern followed in most communication research. Table 2 focuses on the single experiment, but many experiments must be conducted before a theory takes form.

TABLE 2. THE SCIENTIFIC METHOD

| *Dewey's Pattern of Reflective Thinking* | *Kerlinger's Scientific Approach* | *Characterized by:* |
|---|---|---|
| 1. Felt need | Problem–Obstacle–Idea | Unrest, curiosity |
| 2. Definition of problem | Hypothesis construction | Turning back to experience, observations |
| 3. Problem analysis | Reasoning–Deduction | Deducing consequences of the hypothesis |
| 4. Establishing criteria<br>5. Testing solution | {Observation–Test–Experiment} | Observation of events; data |
| 6. Accept or reject solution | Accept or reject hypothesis | A return to the original problem; modification |

Both Dewey and Kerlinger state that the steps do not always occur in this order, nor is one step neatly completed before the next begins. Cattell also emphasizes the diversity of the scientific method. An hypothesis need not be fully developed before the thinking about research begins. This thinking phase may be triggered simply by an intriguing observation of some regular behavior. There may be no stated hypothesis in the initial thinking phase, but eventually an hypothesis is needed for the formal stages of research.

Cattell's depiction of the continuing spiral of theory construction is illustrated in Figure 8. With the unending spiral, Cattell shows how theory functions both as a tool and as a goal. The goal of theory is to put laws into a system. But while reaching for this goal, construction of a theory leads to the discovery of new laws (deductions), and thus new theories. Scientists call this the heuristic or self-discovery function of theory.

At this point, you should return to the first reading, "The General Nature of Theory Construction," and read the second section entitled "Basic Element of Theory Construction: An Overview."

Then go to the sixth and final reading following this article. Here Gergen (1969) offers five "Criteria for Theory Construction" and illustrates them with research about the event posed at the very beginning of this chapter: what happens when you leave classes and go home.

## PRINCIPLES*

Although a substantial portion of this chapter has focused on specific theoretical aspects of the communication process, several generalized principles may be derived. These include:

1. Experience alone does not make one a good communicator.
2. The term "communication" means different things to different people.
3. Communication is a process rather than an event.
4. The study of communication involves the analysis of different levels of communication systems—i.e., intrapersonal interpersonal, group, and cultural.
5. Since all human behavior is communicative we might say that one cannot *not* communicate.
6. Every message transaction has content and is affected by relationship.
7. There are basically two types of messages: intentional and unintentional.
8. A model and a theory are closely related, but they are not synonymous.

*The author is indebted to Donald J. Cegala for preparing these principles for the chapter.

9. The basic requirement of a model is that it specifies relationships among variables.
10. The scientist uses models to make his hypotheses more concrete and to select ways of organizing and analyzing his data.
11. Models can be used to clarify and explain theories.
12. Models tend to oversimplify the communication process.

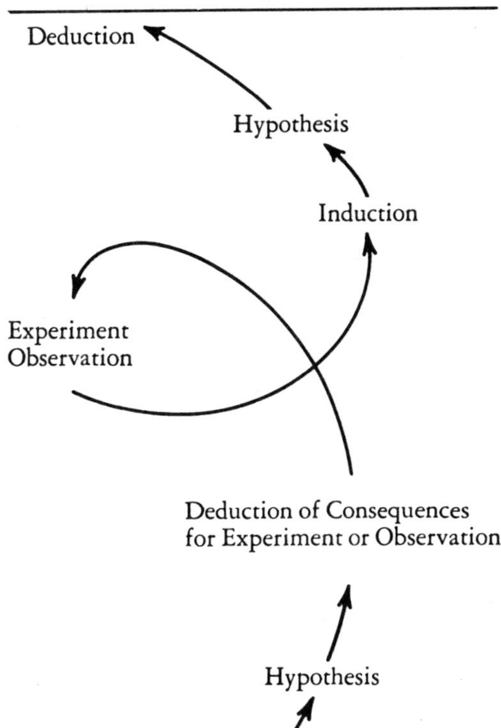


**Figure 8.** The Inductive - Hypothetico - Deductive Spiral. [Raymond B. Cattell, "Psychological Theory and Scientific Method," in Raymond B. Cattell, (Ed.), *Handbook of Multivariate Experimental Psychology* © 1966 by Rand McNally and Company, Chicago, Diagram 1–1, p. 16. Reprinted by permission of the publisher and author.]

13. Generally, mass-communication models involve less varied sensory stimuli and less immediate feedback than interpersonal communication models.
14. Scientific theory is constructed to explain and predict phenomena.
15. The basic objective of science is theory.
16. The goal of theory is to put laws into a system.

Comprehensive theories of human communication processes have not yet been developed. There are, however, many narrow theories about specific types of communication events such as language acquisition, information processing, attitudinal change, physiological responses, and assignment of meaning. Chapters 3 through 9 provide a compendium of many of these theories—our present state in man's spiral of knowledge about human communication.

## *REFERENCES*

Barker, L. L., and Wiseman, G. A model of intrapersonal communication. *Journal of Communication*, 1966, 16, 172–179.

Berlo, D. K. *The process of communication.* New York: Holt, Rinehart & Winston, Inc., 1960.

Cattell, R. B. (Ed.). *Handbook of multivariate experimental psychology.* Skokie, Ill.: Rand McNally & Co., 1966.

Churchman, C. W., Ackoff, R. L., and Arnoff, E. L. *Introduction to operations research.* New York: John Wiley & Sons, Inc., 1957.

Dance, F. E. X. (Ed.). *Human communication theory: original essays.* New York: Holt, Rinehart & Winston, Inc., 1967.

DeVito, J. A. Communication models—a conceptual scheme. Unpublished manuscript, 1968.

Dewey, J. *How we think.* Boston: D. C. Heath and Company, 1933.

Hempel, C. G. *Fundamentals of concept formation in empirical science.* Chicago: University of Chicago Press, 1952.

Hovland, C. Social communication. *Proceedings of the American Philosophical Society*, 1948, 92, 371–75.

Kaplan, A. *The conduct of inquiry.* San Francisco: Chandler, 1964.

Kerlinger, F. N. *Foundations of behavioral research.* New York: Holt, Rinehart, & Winston, Inc., 1964.

Margenau, H. *Nature of physical reality.* New York: McGraw-Hill Book Company, 1950.

Miller, G. A. *Language and communication.* New York: McGraw-Hill Book Company, 1951.

Miller, G. R. On defining communication: another stab. *Journal of Communication,* 1966, 16, 88–98.

Monroe, A. H., and Ehninger, D. *Principles and types of speech.* (6th ed.) Glenview, Ill.: Scott, Foresman & Company, 1967.

Newcomb, T. M. An approach to the study of communicative acts. *Psychological Review,* 1953, 60, 393–404.

Shannon, C. E., and Weaver, W. *The mathematical theory of communication.* Urbana, Ill.: University of Illinois Press, 1949.

Skinner, B. F. *Science and human behavior.* New York: The Macmillan Company, 1953.

Smith, R. L. An experimental comparison of oral and written media for communicating information in industry. Unpublished masters thesis, Purdue University, 1961.

________, General models of communication. Paper presented at the annual conference of the National Society for the Study of Communication, Purdue University, 1962.

Thayer, L. *Administrative communication.* Homewood, Ill.: Richard D. Irwin, Inc., 1961.

________, *Communication and communication systems.* Homewood, Ill.: Richard D. Irwin, Inc., 1968.

*Time.* The seventh crisis of Richard Nixon. April 20, 1970, 8–15.

Torgerson, W. S. *Theory and methods of scaling.* New York: John Wiley & Sons, Inc., 1958.

Tubbs, S. L. Interpersonal communication. Unpublished manuscript, 1970.

Watzlawick, P., Beavin, J. H., and Jackson, D. D. *Pragmatics of human communication.* New York: W. W. Norton & Company, Inc., 1967.

Westley, B. H., and MacLean, M. S., Jr. A conceptual model for communications research. *Journalism Quarterly*, 1957, 34, 31–38.

# SECTION TWO: READINGS

## *Introduction and Objectives for Reading One: "The General Nature of Theory Construction"*

In the first reading, psychologist Melvin Marx examines the general role of theory building in science. Important terms are defined, and the major elements of theory construction are examined as they relate to both everyday experiences and science.

When you have completed the first section, "Some Basic Definitions," you should be able to:

1. Define law, hypothesis, theory, construct, and concept.
2. Give an example of a communication law, hypothesis, theory, construct, and concept.

When you have completed the second section, "Basic Elements of Theory Construction: An Overview," you should be able to:

1. Explain why scientific advances are related to the control of variables.
2. List the two criteria for operational specificity and explain these qualities in terms of Figure 2, "A Typical Theory in the Behavioral Sciences," presented in the lead article.

Melvin H. Marx

# THE GENERAL NATURE OF THEORY CONSTRUCTION

## *Some Basic Definitions*

LAW. A scientific law is most often defined as a statement of regular, predictable relationship among empirical variables. Sometimes, especially in older usages, the term law means a strongly established theoretical or abstract principle. However, it is increasingly being used to refer to the basic regularities observed in natural phenomena and thus typically to represent the descriptive and the empirical, rather than the abstracted and the inferred, properties of data. (The term data refers to the recorded results of observations, often but not necessarily in quantitative form; the term variable refers to a factor or condition involved in the investigation—to a class of objects or events, or to a class of properties of objects or events.)

HYPOTHESIS. Loosely defined, an hypothesis is any conjecture or surmise that states a relationship among variables. This term is a veritable workhorse in the scientific vocabulary and is defined "loosely" almost by necessity, so many and varied are the ways in which it is used. However, the hard core of usage involves the notion of a provisional explanatory proposition which makes certain definite predictions concerning empirical data.

Scientific hypotheses vary along a number of dimensions, certain of the more important of which may be here specified. First, hypotheses vary in regard to the directness with which they may be tested. The experimen-

Reprinted with permission of The Macmillan Company from *Theories in Contemporary Psychology* by Melvin H. Marx. Copyright © by The Macmillan Company, 1963.

tal hypothesis, for example, is directly tested by means of observations, whereas certain abstract hypotheses, from which experimental hypotheses may be derived, can be tested only indirectly by determining the cumulative effect of many observations. A second, and closely related, dimension is that of specificity. In general, of course, the more specific the hypothesis, the more amenable it is to direct test; but this is not a perfect relationship, since some abstract hypotheses can be stated with a high degree of theoretical specificity, and conversely, some experimental hypotheses may be unfortunately vague and ambiguous. A most significant subclass of this dimension is the degree of logical tightness that the investigator is able to build between his experimental (data-oriented) and his abstract (theory-oriented) hypotheses.

A third important dimension, the importance of which is not often adequately recognized, is the public-private continuum. Here the range is from the vaguest of hunches, which one scarcely recognizes himself, much less formulates or announces, to the most highly formalized and publicized of logical propositions. The decision as to when to publicize a hypothetical proposition is a difficult one, one on which scientists with different temperaments or work habits quite clearly differ. Indeed, this difference of opinion seems to be the basis for much of the controversy between the typical positivist, who prefers to keep his hunches to himself while letting them direct his research, and the formal theorist, who prefers to state them openly and publicly, once they have acquired sufficient promise to satisfy him.

The term "postulate" is sometimes used as a kind of synonym for hypothesis, especially in a more or less logically formalized, systematic procedure (e.g., cf. Hull, 1943). Here the postulate is a proposition that is indirectly tested by means of its implications, or theorems.

THEORY. It is especially important to keep separate the various different meanings of "theory," since a large part of the confusion surrounding this topic is attributable to a failure to do so. Thus, critical or derogatory statements intended to apply to one kind of theory are often indiscriminately attributed to a different kind, or to "theory" in general. Conversely, a commendatory statement about one kind of theory may similarly be indiscriminately and inaccurately applied. The following sections indicate four of the major ways in which the term has been used within science.

1. Most generally, theory is used to refer in a very broad sense to any aspect of the formal, or conceptual, processes of science as contrasted with the strictly empirical, or observational, aspects. This usage, while not necessarily harmful in and of itself, is of limited value and does help to confuse the other, more specific usages. (A comparable usage is to refer loosely to any innovation as an "experiment.") Frequently, moreover,

theory as thus popularly used has a distinctly negative connotation, in the sense that the practicability of the proposition is challenged (cf. "theory," def. 2, English and English, 1958). Nevertheless, in spite of these limitations, this usage is so well established as to require recognition. In the present chapter, therefore, the term, when not qualified, will be used in this general sense, but with particular reference to the conceptual and inferential processes which attempt to organize and order empirical data.

2. Theory is used to refer to any generalized explanatory principle. Ordinarily, this kind of theory consists of a statement of functional relationship among variables. If the variables are expressed in empirical terms, then the term law is more likely to be applied to such a principle. If, on the other hand, the variables tend to be more abstract and less directly empirical, the term theory is more often used.

Theories of this sort are obviously very closely related to *hypotheses.* For this reason the latter term will be used in the present paper to refer generally to provisional explanatory propositions. It should be noted, however, that the theory is often distinguished from hypothesis mainly on the basis of a somewhat greater amount of confirmation or scientific acceptability. In this usage, hypothesis refers to the least confirmed proposition, theory to a more confirmed one, and law to the one which has the greatest degree of confirmation, having usually survived the test of time as well as direct empirical investigation. This distinction (cf. "theory," def. 1, English and English, 1958) is increasingly being replaced by the usages described elsewhere in this paper.

3. Theory is used to refer to a group of logically organized (deductively related) laws. This usage is coming to be a preferred one (cf. Bergmann, 1957). It is clearly more pertinent to the better developed sciences, such as physics, from which it originated. Also, it has an obvious affinity to the concept of *system,* in the sense in which that term broadly refers within psychology to a cluster of theoretical propositions and methodological biases (e.g., behaviorism, psychoanalysis), and even more to the less ambitious *minature system.* The decline in popularity of the classic systems within recent years may help to account for the increased utilization of this sense of the term, since it can serve as a kind of substitute concept for "system."

4. In its most restricted sense, theory refers merely to summary statements which give order, in an essentially descriptive manner, to the cluster of laws which have been empircally developed in some subject matter. Here the emphasis is upon a radical empiricism or positivism, with an absolute minimum of inference and postulation, and dependence upon generalization within an inductive procedure. Obviously, this use of "theory" has only a slight affinity to the other ones.

Construct. A construct is a special kind of concept. These rather closely related terms are frequently used as synonyms. However, the distinction here made would seem to be a useful one, following the typical sense in which they are more precisely used within scientific work.

A concept is a class name which refers to certain abstracted properties of the class. It is a generalized term, because it is intended to apply to all cases showing the referent properties. It is a symbol, because it stands for or represents something else.

As class names, concepts are used in a wide variety of situations. Three major types are here differentiated.

1. Concepts refer to *things* (objects, organisms) and *properties* of things. Man, child, dog, rodent, table, school—along with large, small, black, white, round, and elementary—are thus all concepts, since they apply as class names (in the main, as nouns and adjectives) to a number of individual examples of each class. As Pratt (1939) has clearly pointed out, all concepts contain both *more than* and *less than* the observations from which they are derived. Thus, the concept "dog"—"dog in general," that is—is at the same time more meaningful than the observation of any particular dog, since it summarizes in a single word or other symbol the essence of an infinite number of observations, and less meaningful, since it invariably loses in concreteness and individuality.

2. Concepts refer to *events* (things in action) and properties of events. This usage is more complex than the first, since the nature of the action (play, fight, eat, sing, roll, burn; quickly, awkwardly, gaily, etc.) needs to be abstracted. Direct description of behavior utilizes this kind of concept (grammatically, verbs and adverbs).

3. Concepts refer to *relationships among things and/or events, and their various properties*. Here, in this most complex case, the term *construct* is generally used. The "building" or "making" implication of the term is evident in that more inference is required in the process of abstracting the properties identified by the construct. Justice, school spirit, statesmanship, loyalty, and friendship are everyday examples of this kind of complex concept, or construct; gene, atom, habit, personality, and anxiety are scientific examples. Since so much meaning needs to be inferred, and the construct often is so broad as to include a great variety of different relationships, difficulties of communication are compounded, relative to the simple concepts of type (1) and (2). Much of the controversy concerning the role of theory in science, and particularly within psychology, stems more or less directly from this fact. Precise description of referent behaviors are frequently lacking; as a result, psychological constructs, which generally refer to the inferred properties of the organism, tend to be imprecisely and ambiguously used.

Although the kinds of concepts outlined above represent salient cases, it should not be assumed that the particular hierarchical organization suggested is anything more than one way of ordering the tremendous linguistic complexity involved in conceptualizations. As an initial step into this jungle of words and other symbols, the proposed distinction between simpler concepts and constructs should be helpful.

## *Basic Elements of Theory Construction: An Overview*

Three basic elements of theory construction are shown in Figure 1. *Observation* is recognized as fundamental to all science. *Constructs* are seen as the major substantive units of which theories are composed. *Hypotheses* are considered to be the major conceptual tools by which theories are constructed.

The major purpose of Figure 1 is to provide a kind of overview of the way in which these three salient elements of theory construction vary with regard to their major dimensions. Each of the three continua from practical affairs to science will be considered briefly; more detailed attention is accorded certain aspects of these problems in later sections. The present treatment is in no sense exhaustive but is intended to highlight certain of the more critical problems of theory construction.

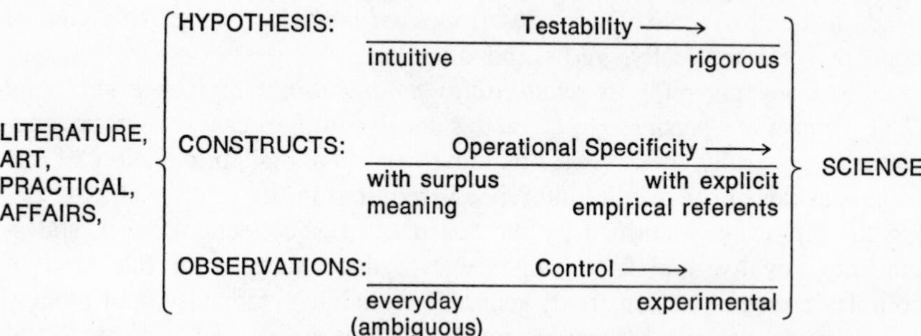


**Figure 1.** The three basic elements of scientific theory construction.

Observations: Control. Control of variables is held to be the essential characteristic of science, differentiating it from non-scientific procedures (see Marx and Hillix, 1963, Ch. 1, for a further discussion of this point; see also Boring, 1954, and Valentine and Wickens, 1949). It may be granted that everyday-life observations often constitute the groundwork for the origin of scientific problems and for preliminary conceptual and theoretical formulations. However, notwithstanding the ability and ingenuity of some especially keen observers and reporters in literature, art, and related fields of endeavor, a certain degree of control of variables must be developed if science is to advance. Control in this sense refers to a reduction in the ambiguity with which variations in the data (dependent-variable measures) may be assigned to the major conditions whose influence is under investigation (independent variables). Elimination of extraneous conditions (controlled variables) is achieved in the main by experimental or statistical techniques.

It follows from the foregoing considerations that scientific progress is marked by a progressive shift from left to right in the diagram in Figure 1 for all three phases of theory construction. In each case there is a reduction in ambiguity of relations between the various components and an increasingly clear and often formal differentiation of their respective functions. The fact that scientific progress results in increasingly less natural and less lifelike concepts and theories obviously increases the difficulties of popularization and translation into practical action, but this is hardly avoidable (cf. Pratt, 1939, for an especially good discussion of this point). It is instructive to note, in this respect, how even Kurt Lewin, who may be considered to have been perhaps the most responsive of recent leading theorists to important human problems, translated such problems into the highly "artificial" terms and concepts of topological and vector psychology. Even in the case of popular vs. technically coined terminology, only an apparent advantage may accrue by using already familiar terms in new scientific and unnatural settings. As Thouless (1949) has observed, the use of popular, familiar terms may actually be disadvantageous in spite of its superficial appeal, because it is likely to result in a false and misleading sense of popular understanding, based upon the old but now inadequate meanings. This then simply increases the difficulties of popularization and re-translation.

CONSTRUCTS: OPERATIONAL SPECIFICITY. Operational specificity—the clearly stated relationship of the construct to its empirical basis in operations producing the data—is the most important characteristic of construct formation. Animistic concepts (e.g., "mind," "libido") and others having what Reichenbach (1938) has called "surplus meaning" may be tolerated in the early, pre-scientific development of a field, but their replacement by constructs more closely tied to the empirical operations must occur for effective scientific theory construction.

Although the physicist Bridgman (1927) is generally credited with the first emphasis on the importance of the operational principle in science, the need for clarity in definitions had long before been recognized, at least in practice, especially in the physical sciences. What was new in Bridgman's emphasis was the recognition that when different operations are involved, different concepts are generated, irrespective of any verbal similarities which may exist. Within psychology, both aspects of operationism are important: 1) the clarity of meaning in communication—the specification of empirical referents for concepts—and 2) the multiplicity of concepts, or meanings, which come from a corresponding multiplicity of operations, or empirical referents. Examples of this latter problem are discussed below, where the application of operationism to psychological constructs is considered in greater detail.

HYPOTHESIS: TESTABILITY. Testability is the absolutely essential characteristic of any scientifically useful hypothesis. A conjecture which cannot be tested in some way is of no immediate use to science, attractive as it may be for forensic and similar purposes. Moreover, the hypothesis must be so constructed as to be clearly *disconfirmable*—that is, it must be precise enough so that not all possible outcomes can be incorporated within its framework (a defect commonly ascribed to certain theoretical positions, such as the psychoanalytic).

The "intuitive-rigorous" continuum for testability of hypotheses refers to the extent to which adequate empirical (observational) tests can be performed. Adequacy here consists primarily of satisfactory logical relationships between hypothesis and data and reasonable control of variables in the observations. Since the latter point takes us back to the control dimension already discussed, the situation is obviously circular. But this is no accident. This is exactly the way in which science operates, with a continuous interplay of observation and hypothesis (or induction, if one prefers) medicated by constructs.

At this point it seems appropriate to emphasize a distinction between the so-called contexts of *discovery* and *confirmation*. The latter function, that of rigorously controlled tests of propositions, is the hallmark of science and has therefore been emphasized in this section; we have confidence in scientific propositions precisely because of their confirmation. *But*, we are also concerned with the significance or importance of scientific propositions, and in this regard confirmability has no direct relevance. That is, the significance of a proposition—its potential theoretical or implied importance—is independent of the empirical support it may subsequently receive. Problems of significance therefore belong to the context of discovery, and here science is similar to all other creative endeavors (which tend toward the left side of Figure 1). The only generally practical guideline that can be laid down for the encouragement of creativity is that the worker be thoroughly immersed in his work. The place for daring and imagination, the time for striking out boldly in new and previously uncharted directions—this is obviously the context of discovery, just as the place for caution and restraint and for the careful evaluation of hypothesis and data is in the context of confirmation.

We need to recognize most explicitly that *both* discovery *and* confirmation are necessary to effective scientific work. The most ingenious theories are limited scientific value until empirical tests are produced; the best confirmed proposition is of little value unless it deals with meaningful variables. Unfortunately, much controversy, even within science, has arisen from a failure to accept this dual necessity. This dichotomy enables us to understand and see in better perspective the overemphasis on either the discovery aspect (as is sometimes claimed to occur in psychoanalysis, for example) or the confirmation aspect (as is sometimes claimed to occur in scientific empiricism, for example). Finally, much useless argumentation seems to occur on strictly semantic issues, such as the question as to whether a particular person (say, Freud) is or is not a scientist; obviously, one's own definition of "scientist" determines the answer here. But however one defines a scientist, the necessity remains to recognize that both of these functions, whether or not they occur within a single individual, are essential to fruitful and productive science.

## *References*

Bergmann, G. *Philosophy of science.* Madison, Wis.: Univ. of Wisconsin Press, 1957.

Boring, E. G. The nature and history of experimental control. *Amer. J. Psychol.,* 1954, 67, 573–589.

Bridgman, P. W. *The logic of modern physics.* New York: Macmillan, 1927.

English, H. B., and English, Ava C. *A comprehensive dictionary of psychological and psychoanalytic terms.* New York: Longmans, Green, 1958.

Hull, C. L. *Principles of behavior.* New York: Appleton-Century, 1943.

Marx, M. H., and Hillix, W. A. *Systems and theories in psychology.* New York: McGraw-Hill, 1963.

Pratt, C. C. *The logic of modern psychology.* New York: Macmillan, 1939.

Reichenbach, H. *Experience and prediction.* Chicago: Univ. of Chicago Press, 1938.

Valentine, W. L., and Wickens, D. D. *Experimental foundations of general psychology* (3rd ed.). New York: Rinehart, 1949.

## *Introduction and Objectives for Reading Two: "The Use of Models and Analogies"*

In the second reading, there are many examples of analogical models which have been borrowed from one field of science to clarify a phenomenon in another field. The authors point out the pitfalls of analogies and argue that the models which serve a research function should be mathematical.

When you have completed this reading, you should be able to:

1. Describe at least two analogical models from the physical sciences.
2. Relate the "partial character" and "just-like" qualities of analogs to their potential deficiencies.
3. Explain why mathematical models have less "surplus meaning" than analogs.

George Mandler and William Kessen

## *THE USE OF MODELS AND ANALOGIES*

In their attempts to understand novel or unusual phenomena, men are often forced to draw on explanations which are appropriate to well-understood phenomena. They use what they are confident about in order to comprehend what is still unclear. This sort of theorizing by extension of the old to the new may be called *explanation by analogy,* and its common occurrence in science at large and in psychology suggests the importance of its function in the work of explanation.

Analogical treatments can be seen at a simple level in the pedagogy of elementary science. In order to get across the notion of "valence," chemistry students are told to imagine that each atom has a specified number of hands or hooks which determines the proper combination with other atoms; electricity is often discussed in analogy to hydraulic systems; the mathematical laws of electron activity are set in a comprehensible model about the planetary orbit of particles; and so on. If the student goes beyond the fundamentals expressed in such analogical fashion, he is usually weaned away from this primitive kind of presentation, and slowly taught the system of general principles which is appropriate to the subject matter under study.

As we have noted earlier, the road from the vernacular to the scientific language is of gradual slope, and the use of analogies is an important guide and crutch. Piaget's theory of adaptation is an elegant expression of the fact that we can assimilate or use only what can be fitted somehow into

From George Mandler and William Kessen, *The Language of Psychology* (New York: John Wiley & Sons, Inc., 1959), pp. 269–274. Copyright 1959 by John Wiley & Sons, Inc. Reprinted by permission of the publisher.

an earlier "theory" of natural phenomena. The choice of analogy is of course dependent on the prototheories which a human being brings with him—e.g., the analogy in explanation of electrical phenomena given a five-year-old will usually be quite different from that given a college freshman—but there is doubtlessly systematic variation in what will be a popular form of analogy at any particular time in the history of science. From the Newtonian reconstruction in the seventeenth century until well into the twentieth, analogies based on the movement of particles—billiard balls, planetary systems, molecules of gas—have dominated the field. More recently, analogies based on quantum theory and on "field" effects have begun, as they grow more familar, to take a place among the popular models of explanation. Fruitful scientific theories seem to show a regular progression from incomprehensibility and rejection through acceptance and test to an uncritical extension beyond their original range of intent. This "extension" usually takes place through the technique of analogical reasoning.

The use of models and analogies in science is by no means confined to the classroom; there is ample biographical evidence that they frequently appear in the creative work of scientific theorists. Newton, for all his reluctance to invent hypotheses, was led to a wave theory of color by an extension of his observations on sound. He anticipated that color would depend on vibration "much after the manner, that in the sense of hearing, nature makes use of aereal vibrations of several bignesses to generate sounds of divers tones; for the analogy of nature is to be observed" (Birch, 1757, p. 262). The fact that he was on the right track has added another gem to the Newtonian crown, but the "analogy of nature" is not always so kind; Titchener's mental chemistry was not too unlike Newton's generalization from sound to color.

The place of models in scientific explanation can perhaps best be typified in Maxwell's handling of electromagnetic induction. In an early presentation and commentary on Faraday's results, he developed an ingenious model with cylinders and spherical balls, turning and rolling against one another in a way which permitted him to account for the empirical results. In a later exposition, the mechanical model gave way to a hydrodynamical one, in which he drew his analogy from notions of lines of flow in an incompressible fluid. Side by side with the hydraulic model were the mathematical equations containing his theoretical principles, from which so much of modern physics derives. The nonmathematical analogies served two purposes; they provided Maxwell with instructive leads to a formal theory, and they made possible the presentation of his results in forms comprehensible to his colleagues. But, as Einstein has noted, he took none of his mechanical constructions very seriously; "it was clear that the equations themselves were all that was essential" (Thomson et al., 1931, p. 70).

Maxwell himself had a remarkably clear view of what analogies were good for and his comments are relevant to scientific explanation today.

> If we adopt a physical [i.e., analogical] hypothesis, we see the phenomena only through a medium, and are liable to that blindness to facts and rashness in assumption which a partial explanation encourages. We must therefore discover some method of investigation which allows the mind at every step to lay hold of a clear physical conception, without being committed to any theory founded on the physical science from which the conception is borrowed. (Quoted in Thomson et al., 1931, p. 99.)

It is the partial character of analogical treatments that makes them of ambiguous value in the work of scientific explanation. For the very reason that a model is drawn from a different area of discourse, it is likely that its extended application will at some point break down. The "valence-as-hooks" analogy cannot meaningfully be broadened to include all that is known about hooks; the water-in-tubes model for electricity provides no way of dealing with phenomena of magnetic induction; the planetary model for electrons is limited in its handling of modern discoveries of subatomic phenomena. To take examples from psychology, the theory of Oedipal conflict does not include the prediction that a son will be driven to blind himself or a mother to hang, regardless of the Sophoclean solution. Nor does the generalization about ontogeny recapitulating phylogeny entail the growth of feathers in children during the birdlike stage of their development. Analogies or models often go too far and land in absurdity or they do not go far enough to account for the phenomena under examination. These devices can be seen as special cases of plausible explanation, and they have both the advantages and disadvantages of other plausible systems. Analogies may serve to facilitate communication of novel ideas, and they almost certainly are important aids to the creative scientist, but like their vernacular cousins, the prototheories, they often fall short of producing a consistent set of general principles which lead to the prediction of confirmable outcomes. Frank has noted, for the special study of physics, a change in the scientific climate which may be applicable to other disciplines as well.

> The rise of twentieth-century physics, of relativity and the quantum theory, was closely connected with a new view of the basic principles. It was no longer taken for granted that the principles from which the facts had to be derived should contain a specific analogy, either to an organism or to a mechanism. Nothing was required except that the observed phenomena could be derived from the principles in a consistent way and as simply as possible. The words and symbols that occurred in the principles, and the way these were connected, could be invented according to their fitness as bases for deriving the phenomena discovered by the experimental physicist. (Frank, 1949, p. 252f.)

From the point of view of the psychology of thought, this is undoubtedly overoptimistic. Human beings, scientists as well as laymen, will continue to find their way toward new conceptualizations by means of old ones, and the analogy will continue to serve didactic and heuristic ends. Nonetheless, Frank correctly emphasizes the absence of a priori restrictions on the language of explanation. Science is indissolubly tied to its groundings in reliable observation, but the superstructure of theory has surprisingly few limitations on its language beyond the bounded ingenuity of creative men.

Analogical reasoning in psychology can often produce a group of problems which closely resemble the ones raised in the discussion of reductionism. If the human organism is assumed to behave "just like" a hydraulic or a thermodynamic or a chemical or a neurophysiological system, the use of the appropriate analogy may provide the explainer with a feeling of having a "more basic" theory. Surely, if he turns to highly developed scientific systems, he will find well-confirmed principles and a rich source of interlocking theoretical relationships. This wealth is not easily claimed, however; until his system is so revised and edited that it permits accurate prediction of behavior, it remains analogical, with whatever virtues and encumbrances this mode of explanation brings with it.

There is another somewhat more elusive relationship between analogical explanation and the reductionist controversy. Much of MacCorquodale and Meehl's argument for a dichotomy of theoretical words depends on the notion of "actual existence," and this criterion for hypothetical constructs parallels the older demand in the physics of wave phenomena for what Maxwell called a "physical hypothesis." Both positions imply strongly that good explanations are those which draw on well-established, or at least well-accepted, theories for their basic constructs. The argument from "actual existence" is one of the thorniest problems in the philosophy of science, but the experience of physicists, who some time ago gave up such a prototheoretical commitment, should be a warning to psychologists not to be cheered too much if their theories are "existential." The analogy from other sciences would seem to support with heavy underlining that "the equations themselves are all that is essential."

Thanks to an unhappy development in psychological argot, a group of theories of behavior which are almost antithetical to analogical treatments have also been called "models." These explanatory systems—the so-called mathematical models—are of interest in the present context precisely because they have so few of the disabilities attached to analogical reasoning. The stochastic theories (see Bush and Mosteller, 1955) have as their central theoretical terms certain mathematical operators which, unlike almost all other psychological explanations, do not have any obvious relationship to the language of the vernacular or to the language of other empirical disciplines. The initial statements of the explanation are chosen only with regard to their mathematical consistency and their usefulness in producing meaningful descriptions of observed phenomena in the field of learning. The result of this strategy is twofold. In the first place, there results a calculus of explanation and a set of rules for its manipulation which, on grounds of explicitness and clarity, is unrivaled in present-day psychology. Moreover, such a system can be manipulated quite independently of any specific empirical interpretation, and the work of theoretical revision and addition can be carried on without contamination from "physical" or archaic analogies. Mathematical "models" are free from any taint of surplus meaning in the sense either of prototheoretical associations or of the reductionist contention.

The nature of this achievement can be illustrated by comparing the stochastic theories with earlier attempts to set up mathematical treatments of behavior. Hull, for example, carefully chose association-free symbols (e.g., $_{S}H_{R}$, $D$, $r$) in his theoretical principles, but his textual discussion of the theory and its use by other researchers quickly demonstrated the infiltration of associations to "habit," "drive," and so on. Similarly, Lewin's attempt to build a topological explanation of behavior was soon overlaid with extratheoretical associations to terms like "force" and "valence." To the present date, the mathematical theories of behavior have remained relatively clear of this kind of increase in "meaning." It is, of course, matter for the future testing and refinement of the theories to determine their utility in the explanation of behavior, but they have the apparent advantage of being disconnected in their public statement from the "analogies of organism and mechanism" which have characterized psychological theory in the past.

If we except the mathematical "models," the function of analogies and models in psychology can be seen as largely that of plausible explanation. They often promote communication, particularly between teacher and student, and they frequently serve as guides to creative researchers in the construction of formal theories and in the design of research, but the value of analogical reasoning in the explicit statement of deductive theories is not so clearly demonstrable. The gain in vernacular comprehensibility that comes from the exposition of an apt analogy may be more than offset by the illusion of having achieved a genuinely deductive explanation.

## *References*

Birch, T. (1757) *The History of the Royal Society of London,* Vol. III. London: A. Millar.

Bush, R. R., and Mosteller, F. (1955) *Stochastic Models for Learning.* New York: Wiley.

Frank, P. (1949) *Modern Science and Its Philosophy*. Cambridge: Harvard University Press.

Thomson, J. J., et al. (1931) *James Clerk Maxwell*. Cambridge: Cambridge University Press.

## *Introduction and Objectives for Reading Three: "The Information Theory"*

The third reading presents the analog from the physical sciences, which has had the most profound influence on human communication theory. Norbert Wiener, Claude Shannon, and Warren Weaver developed a scientific theory of information for telecommunication and digital computer transactions which has clarified the process of human communication.

When you have completed this reading, you should be able to:

1. Define information, bit, redundancy, channel capacity, and entropy.
2. Explain why the Shannon-Weaver model is called a "statistical approach which enlists probability theory (uncertainty)."
3. Construct an empirically testable hypothesis about human channel capacity.
4. Reproduce the Shannon-Weaver graphical model.

Francis Bello

# *THE INFORMATION THEORY*

Great scientific theories, like great symphonies and great novels, are among man's proudest—and rarest—creations. What sets the scientific theory apart from and, in a sense, above the other creations is that it may profoundly and rapidly alter man's view of his world.

In this century man's views, not to say his life, have already been deeply altered by such scientific insights as relativity theory and quantum theory. Within the last five years a new theory has appeared that seems to bear some of the same hallmarks of greatness. The new theory, still almost

Francis Bello, "The Information Theory," *Fortune*, Dec., 1953, 136–140ff. Reprinted in part by permission of the publisher and author.

unknown to the general public, goes under either of two names: communication theory or information theory. Whether or not it will ultimately rank with the enduring great is a question now being resolved in a score of major laboratories here and abroad.

The central teachings of the theory are directed at electrical engineers. It gives them, for the first time, a comprehensive understanding of their trade. It tells them how to measure the commodity they are called upon to transmit—the commodity called "information"—and how to measure the efficiency of their machinery for transmitting it. Thus the theory applies directly to telegraph, telephone, radio, television, and radar systems; to electronic computers and to automatic controls for factories as well as for weapons.

It may be no exaggeration to say that man's progress in peace, and security in war, depend more on fruitful applications of information theory than on physical demonstrations, either in bombs or in power plants, that Einstein's famous equation works. As might be expected, military applications are coming first. For example: The recently disclosed "Distant Early Warning Line" of automatic radar stations, stretching from Alaska to Greenland, almost certainly incorporates more of the lessons of information theory than any other communication system yet devised. The warning line was designed by the two organizations that should know more about the theory than anyone else: Massachusetts Institute of Technology (working through its Lincoln Laboratory) and Bell Telephone Laboratories.

The theory has an unusual joint origin. To M.I.T.'s eminent mathematician, Norbert Wiener, goes the major credit for discovering the new continent and grasping its dimensions; to Claude Shannon of Bell Laboratories goes the credit for mapping the new territory in detail and charting some breath-taking peaks. Wiener's basic contribution was to recognize that communication of information is a problem in statistics, a view he first stated clearly in a secret World War II document that dealt with the problem of shooting down airplanes. He followed this in 1948 with his now famous book *Cybernetics, or Control and Communication in the Animal and the Machine*. The same year Shannon published his great work, *The Mathematical Theory of Communication,* aimed specifically at the electrical engineer.

The fascination of the theory, as *Cybernetics* indicates, is that it insists on thrusting beyond the confines of electrical engineering. In particular it is Wiener's belief, shared by many others, that one of the lessons of cybernetics is "that any organism is held together by the possession of means for the acquisition, use, retention, and transmission of information." Naturally, therefore, attempts are being made to use information theory in a dozen fields from psychiatry to sociology. In a few fields, notably psychology, neurophysiology, and linguistics, the theory has already been applied with considerable success.

## *What Information Means*

What the theory does for the first time is provide a precise unit of measure for the "amount of information" in various broad classes of messages. The class may be represented by a voice on the telephone, a picture on a television screen, the language of Shakespeare, or the music of Beethoven. When the engineer has used the theory to measure the information content, or information density, of such messages, he can tell how large his transmission channel must be to carry each.

Information, as used in the theory, is very carefully defined and information theorists have trouble forcing people to stick with the definition. To Wiener and Shannon, information is contained, to great or less degree, in any message a communication engineer is asked to transmit. He is not interested in semantics or meaning; he must assume that even gibberish may have meaning if someone is willing to pay to have it transmitted. "You have to realize," says one student of the theory, "that this is a little like Alice in Wonderland. The word 'information' means exactly what we say it means."

Shannon once had to tell a group of prominent scientists who had become badly confused by his use of the word: "I think perhaps the word 'information' is causing more trouble . . . than it is worth, except that it is difficult to find another word that is anywhere near right. It should be kept solidly in mind that [information] is only a measure of the difficulty in transmitting the sequences [i.e., messages] produced by some information source."

If Samuel Morse had been listening he would have felt perfectly at home with the concept of transmission difficulty. And he would have been quick to appreciate that the way to measure difficulty is by statistical techniques. In setting up his dot-dash code, Morse made one of the first applications of statistics to a communication problem. On the basis of type counts made in a printing shop, Morse assigned a short code to the most frequent letters and longer codes to the less frequent. Thus he would transmit E, the most frequent, by simply sending a dot, but for V, one of the least frequent, he had to send dot-dot-dot-dash.

Thus Morse would expect to have more difficulty, i.e., expend more dots and dashes, transmitting 100 letters of gibberish, which might use V as frequently as E, than sensible English in which letters appeared with their familiar frequency. However, Morse might have been as astonished as anyone else to hear Shannon equate difficulty and information, because by this equation gibberish, to the extent that it is good *random* gibberish, will always contain more "information" than an equally long sequence of letters from, say, *Hamlet* or the *Britannica.* Lest the reader, at this point, balk and say that Shannon and Wiener have no right to call gibberish "information," he must let them continue.

Most people will agree that any message communicates information only to the extent that it contains "news." If a message source generates an endless succession of A's, the engineer need not transmit it at all. He would simply build a device for creating the message at the receiving end. The lesson in this for the engineer is that *whatever* part of a message he can predict, he need not transmit. In this light all existing communication systems—telephone, radio, television—are vastly overdesigned, hence vastly inefficient.

Wiener and Shannon show, with their statistical approach, that all ordinary messages—speech, music, pictures—are highly predictable. They are not composed of random sequences of sounds, notes, or light and dark areas. They contain familiar patterns. When the engineer has familiarized himself with all the possible patterns in his messages, he can start omitting redundancies and start transmitting only what is essential—that is, only the unpredictable.

### *The Value of the Theory*

It is doubtful if many communication engineers, before Wiener and Shannon, grasped the essence of their job in quite this light, obvious as it may seem now. The theory, of course, does more than express a philosophy of communication, it provides universal measures. Before the theory, engineers knew that when "something"—it couldn't yet be called information—in a message changed rapidly, they had to provide bigger transmission "pipes," i.e., channels, to carry it. Thus music produced vibrations in air that had an upper frequency of about 15,000 cycles per second. To transmit these vibrations with "high fidelity" they knew they had to use a channel with a "bandwidth" of 15,000 cycles. Actually, in AM radio they settled for 5,000 cycles, and lower fidelity. Telephone engineers used a bandwidth of about 3,500 cycles for speech. Then came television, in which "something" changed very rapidly indeed. The engineer found that to paint a picture on a screen with a beam of electrons he had to be prepared to vary the intensity of every dot on every one of the 525 scanning lines thirty times a second. To do this required a bandwidth of some four million cycles, or nearly 1,000 times that required for ordinary radio. Shannon recalls that one of the questions motivating his early work was: could television be compressed into a smaller bandwidth, or couldn't it?

While information theory now shows that it can, no one has progressed much beyond paper plans, for the job is extremely tricky and takes a lot of hardware. . . .

It is precisely here that the value and power of a good theory become difficult to describe. A theory builds no machinery. But inevitably, when good theories are enunciated, they make machinery easier to build. "Before we had the theory a lot of us were deeply troubled," says Jerome Wiesner, director of M.I.T.'s Research Laboratory of Electronics. "We had been dealing with a commodity that we could never see or really define. We were in the situation petroleum engineers would be in if they didn't have a measuring unit like the gallon. We had intuitive feelings about these matters, but we didn't have a clear understanding."

### *One "Bit" of Information*

To provide a measure for information, which makes it possible to measure the "something" in different sorts of messages, information theory builds from the simplest of all bases. It considers two symbols, say A and B, and the way they may be combined into messages. We have already seen that an endless string of A's presents nothing that needs transmitting. Information begins with uncertainty—with the first B. As more B's are mixed in with the A's the engineer has to send out more signals. In the extreme case when there are as many B's as A's and they appear at random, i.e., unpredictably, the flow of signals—hence the flow of information —reaches a maximum. The simplest possible code for A and B is 0 and 1. If the engineer sends the 1 over a channel as one electric impulse, and the 0 as "no impulse," he has achieved all the economy possible.

Thus the engineer is working hardest, in the simplest case, when transmitting two symbols of equal probability. This suggested to Wiener and Shannon that *the unit of information be defined as that which makes a decision between two equally probable events.* This unit was baptized the "bit" because the symbols 0 and 1 are technically known as "binary digits," which someone had previously abbreviated to "bits." Thus to transmit a random string of A's and B's the engineer has to transmit one full bit of information, either 0 or 1, every time the message source utters one letter or the other.

By stringing together code groups composed of bits—just as Morse used dots and dashes—it is possible to code the entire alphabet of twenty-six letters, or "alphabets" of any desired length. A code group two bits long provides four combinations, 00, 01, 10, 11, hence can be used to encode a four-letter "alphabet," say, A, B, C, D. A three-bit code can be arranged in eight possible combinations: 000, 001, 010, 011, 100, 101,

110, 111, hence will specify an eight-letter alphabet. Note that as the code lengthens by *one* bit, the number of combinations *doubles*. Thus an eight-bit code provides 256 combinations starting with 00000000 and ending with 11111111.

Information theory tells the engineer that his codes are efficient only when each 0 and 1, i.e., each bit, is working just as hard as it can. When this is achieved, says the theory, the engineer can count up the number of bits he has used, and this will tell him the *net* amount of information in the original message.

Since the engineer, obviously, cannot be expected to sit down and test every possible way of encoding a message into 0's and 1's, the theory provides him with an equation that gives, in bits, the amount of information per symbol in any message—be it speech, music, or pictures.[1] All the engineer has to put into the equation is the relative frequency with which each symbol appears in the message. This is not hard to do for a single message, but the answer obtained in this way is not very useful. What should go into the equation are frequencies with which *groups of symbols* are used in a large sample of messages.

This concept is easiest to follow if we consider written English. Morse dealt only with frequencies for each letter. However, he might have counted the frequencies of letter *pairs,* of which there are 676 possibilities from AA to ZZ. These he could have ranked in decreasing order of frequency, assigning a longer code to each as he went down the list. (Had he done this, of course, telegraphers would have given up in despair.) If letter pairs were coded into binary digits, with no regard to frequencies, the average code length would be about 9.4 bits. Such a code could be devised by drawing up a "code mobile" similar to that shown for the twenty-six-letter alphabet on page 00. If the mobile were extended to support 676 symbols (i.e., 676 letter pairs), the number of bits needed to specify each would usually be nine, though some symbols would require ten.

If, however, the 676 symbols were hung, according to frequency, on what page 00 describes as an asymmetrical "mobile," some commonplace letter pairs (for example, TH and IE) would be assigned codes only two or three bits long, while the least frequent pairs would carry codes sixteen or seventeen bits long. If ordinary English were translated into such a code, a count would show that, on the average, only 7.1 instead of 9.4 bits

[1]In written messages the symbols are the letters of the alphabet; in spoken messages the symbols are the various phonetic sounds, of which there are about forty; in pictures the symbols are the number of distinguishable tones from white to black of which each "dot" of the picture is composed. In played music, the number of possible symbols may be obtained by "quantizing" the complex sound wave of the music into a succession of numerical values.

had been used to encode each pair of letters. This works out to 3.56 bits per letter as against the 4.7 bits required when the code is assigned without *any* reference to frequencies.

The question that fascinated Shannon was how *little* information does ordinary English really contain. If he could determine this he would know how tightly English might theoretically be encoded. With existing frequency tables he could go only one step beyond two-letter frequencies to three-letter frequencies (calculated as an aid to cryptographers). These, in Shannon's equation, reduced the code requirement to 3.3 bits per letter.

It is easy to see why no one ever carried the frequency tables beyond three-letter groups: there are 17,576 possible ways to arrange twenty-six letters into groups of three, and nearly half a million combinations of four-letter groups, from AAAA to ZZZZ. Shannon, however, was determined to press further, so he reasoned that any average speaker of English ought to have a tremendous "built-in" knowledge of English statistics. To tap this knowledge, Shannon resorted to ingenious guessing games.

## *The Guessing Game*

In one game he would pick a passage at random, from a book, and ask someone to guess the letters, one by one. He would tell the subject only if he were wrong, and the subject would continue until he finally guessed the right letter (or space). Shannon quickly discovered that the average person requires substantially fewer than 3.3 guesses to identify the correct letter in ordinary text. The relation between guesses and bits of information should become clearer in what follows.[2]

One of Shannon's favorite passages for this type of game was *"There is no reverse on a motorcycle a friend of mine found this out rather dramatically the other day."* In this passage there are 102 letters and spaces, including a final space after "day." Going through the passage letter by letter, one of Shannon's subjects guessed right on his first guess 79 times, and correctly identified all 102 letters and spaces with only 198 guesses, or less than two guesses per letter or space.

[2]Information theorists view the game Twenty Questions as an exercise in their theory. If the game were played perfectly, they say, each yes or no should provide the contestant with one bit of information. In this view, twenty bits would suffice to identify $2^{20}$, or one out of a million-plus, possible objects. This indicates why the twenty-first question would frequently be so helpful; with twenty-one questions it should be possible to identify one of $2^{21}$, or over two million objects.

## *In Joyce, A Compression?*

After mathematical analysis of many such experiments Shannon concluded that in ordinary literary English the long-range statistical effects reduce the information content to about *one bit per letter*. That is to say, if one sees the first 50 or 100 letters of a message, he can be reasonably certain, on the average, that the next following letter (which he hasn't seen) will be one of only two equally probable letters. To remove this much uncertainty requires, by definition, only one bit of information.

Naturally, the amount of uncertainty, hence amount of information, varies among different samples of English. In his basic paper on communication theory, Shannon writes: "Two [opposite] extremes of redundancy in English prose are represented by Basic English and by James Joyce's book *Finnegans Wake*. The Basic English vocabulary is limited to 850 words and the redundancy is very high. This is reflected in the expansion that occurs when a passage is translated into Basic English. Joyce on the other hand enlarges the vocabulary and is alleged to achieve a compression of semantic content."

Shannon's calculation that the average letter of English (in a long passage) contains only one bit of information has this surprising implication. It says that with proper encoding it should be possible to translate any page of ordinary English into a succession of binary digits, 0 and 1, so that there are no more digits than there were letters in the original text. In other words, twenty-four of the twenty-six letters of the alphabet are superfluous. So far as printed English is concerned, this is the goal that information theory establishes for the communication engineer.[3]

To help engineers visualize how English might be tightly encoded, Shannon asks them to imagine a communication system in which the transmitting device "guesses" upcoming letters in the way his subject guesses the letters in *"There is no reverse on a motorcycle."* The numbers under each of the following letters (and spaces) indicate the number of guesses the human subject required for the first words:

```
T H E R E   I S   N O
1 1 1 5 1 1 2 1 1 2 1 1

R E V E R S E
15 1 17 1 1 1 2
```

[3]However, the theory recognizes that redundancy often has value. It is English's high redundancy, for example, that makes typographical errors fairly easy to catch. By using a few extra binary digits, it is possible to design error-checking and error-correcting codes.

In theory, one could build a transmitter or encoding device that would approach this performance by providing it with a suitable set of operating instructions or program. It might, for example, be programed to guess T to start every message. After T it might always guess H, then E. After E, however, its programed sequence of guesses, in order, might be space, S, I, Y, and R. Presumably the human subject ran through some such sequence before guessing R. Like the human, the machine finds that its program of first and second choices works fine until it reaches the R and V in REVERSE.

With such a transmitter, the symbols that go over the channel are not the letters in the message but the numbers (in binary code) corresponding to the transmitter's guesses. (Naturally, strings of 1's would be coded into more economical form.) The receiver at the other end is an "identical twin" of the transmitter, hence it "knows," for example, that its own fifth guess after T-H-E would be R, and so on.

To reach the goal of two bits per letter—let alone the theoretical one bit—such a transmitter should not even start to guess until it had inspected at least the first ten letters of the message. Once it starts guessing it should make every guess on the basis of probabilities established by the preceding ten letters. This means that to program such a transmitter someone would have to establish these probabilities by tabulating all combinations of eleven letters in a fair sample of all the English ever written. Since there are nearly four million billion ways to arrange twenty-six letters in groups of eleven, the task is all but unthinkable. Even so it might be done electronically if anyone thought the project worth while.

. . . . . . . . . . . . . . . . . . .

## *The Encoding of Information*

To transmit information—words, music, pictures—the communication engineer must encode it. A central teaching of the Wiener-Shannon theory of communication is that encoding should take advantage of the statistical nature of messages.

One code system of great value uses only two symbols, O and 1, which are called binary digits, or "bits" for short. The diagrams at right show how ordinary letters can be coded into bits. If two letters, A and B, appear in a message at random (hence with equal probability), an efficient code (center right) will let A=0 and B=1 (or vice versa). Similarly, each letter in a four-letter "alphabet," A, B, C, D, will require a two-bit code, *provided*, again, that one letter is as probable as another.

Suppose, however, an information source has an A-B-C-D alphabet but uses some letters more frequently than others. Then, says the theory,

*Communication's basic network*

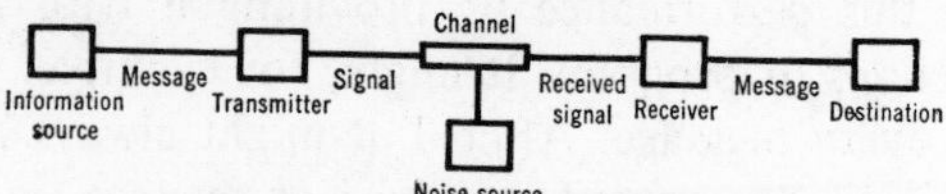


Communication theory deals with the generalized communication system shown above. The key to efficient communication is maximum compression (i.e., proper encoding) of the message at the transmitter.

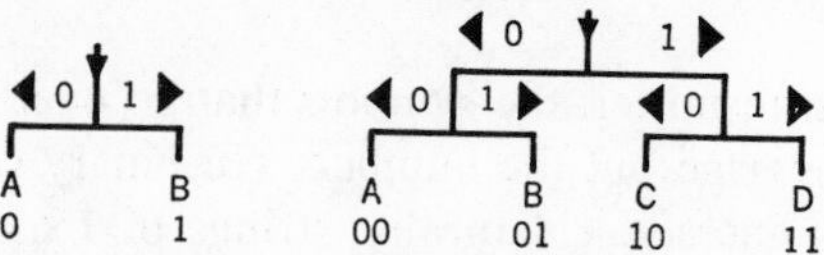


The symmetrical "code mobiles," above, indicate the basic method for establishing an efficient binary-digit (0 and 1) code for two or four letters, provided the letters appear in a message with equal frequency. The code is determined by the "0" and "1" signposts that are passed en route to each letter. The asymmetrical "mobile," below, yields an efficient code if the engineer is trying to transmit messages composed half of A's, one-quarter of B's, one-eighth C's and D's.

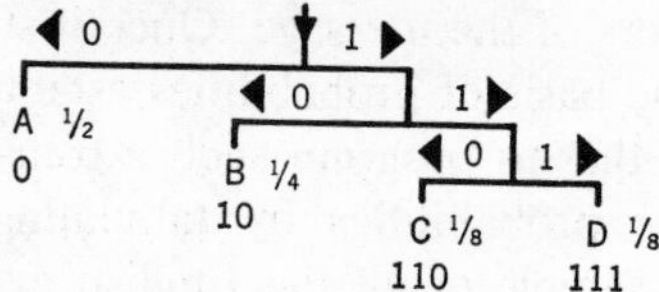


*The alphabet in 4.7 bits per letter*

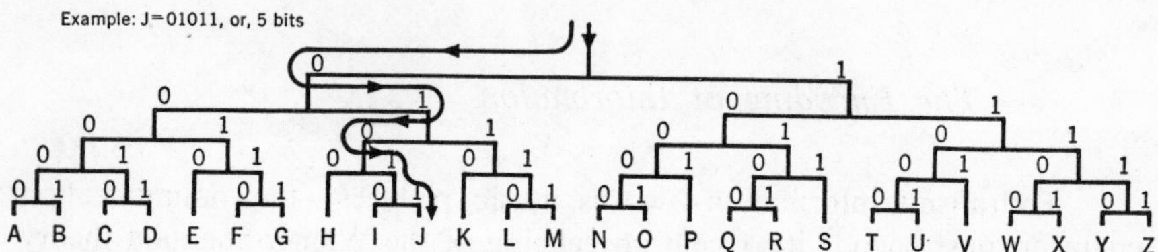


each letter does not carry a full two bits' worth of information, hence does not deserve a two-bit code. If a source creates messages that contain, on the average, half A's, one-quarter B's, and one-eighth C's and D's, it can be shown that an efficient code lets A=0, B=10 ("one-zero," not "ten"), C=110, and D=111. With this code a typical message BDAAABCA becomes: 10111000101100. So coded the total message contains only fourteen bits, or 1¾ bits per letter—not two bits.

The basic method for creating an efficient code is shown at lower right. The symbols are hung on an asymmetrical "mobile" so that the first decision point (marked 0 or 1) divides the symbols into two equally probable groups. (Here, A is as probable as B, C, and D combined.) The next decision point again divides the remaining symbols into two equally probable groups, and so on. The "mobile" is rigged correctly if random trips through it will generate messages that have the same letter frequencies as those composed by the information source itself.

Information theorists say that it is possible to make a similar, but gigantic, "code mobile" that would provide a coding of maximum efficiency for ordinary literary English. As the diagram below indicates, an ordinary (equal-probability) mobile for the alphabet calls for between four and five bits per letter (4.7, to be exact). Shannon's surprising conclusion is that sensible written English carries, on the average, only about one bit of information per letter.

## *Man As Communicator*

Some of the most interesting applications of information theory, outside of electrical engineering, are being made in experimental psychology. To the psychologist, man may be considered as a message source or as a channel, but not very readily as a transmitter or a receiver. If you try to measure his abilities purely as a transmitter or receiver, you find you are really using him as a channel. Thus there seems to be no good way to ascertain the rate at which the eye or ear may receive information except by measuring the amount that is remembered or otherwise played back.

In tests run at M.I.T., subjects were asked to point to numbered squares as fast as they could read numbers flashed in random sequence. The test was run with two numbers and two squares, four numbers and four squares, and so on up to 4,096 numbers and 4,096 squares. As might be expected, the subject can hit quite a few squares per second when he has only a few to choose from, but when he has 1,024 (each worth ten bits) he does well to average 1.5 per second. In terms of information theory, it turns out that the average person can handle about fifteen bits per second.

The highest human channel capacity that M.I.T. psychologists have measured is forty-five bits per second, determined by a variant of the experiment just described. The world's fastest typist, in typing 149 words per minute, is handling just about twenty-five bits per second, if each letter be given a value of two bits. (This seems fair since she probably cannot grasp the long-range clues that, according to Shannon, reduce the information to one bit per letter.) The world's shorthand record is 282 words per minute, which, on the same basis, works out to about forty-seven bits per second.

These figures provide an upper limit for the amount of information a person may handle in a lifetime. The upper limit: roughly 50 billion bits.[4] One can now appreciate the immense channel capacity used to transmit television. The information handled in the most diligently spent lifetime could, if suitably encoded, be transmitted over a television channel in about sixteen minutes. The information handled in an *average* lifetime could hardly keep a TV channel occupied more than ten seconds.

There are dangers, of course, in overworking any concept, no matter how helpful. Some psychologists who originally encouraged their colleagues to study information theory and to apply it in their experiments now feel that the theory is frequently misapplied by psychologists—and almost inevitably misapplied by sociologists.

### *Inside The Nerve*

As Norbert Wiener perceived with his characteristic great enthusiasm, the concepts of information theory apply directly to neurophysiology. Largely as a result of his inspiration, M.I.T. has become one of the leading centers for the study of the central nervous system. The work, which comes under the Research Laboratory of Electronics, not only has high significance in its own right, but since biological reflexes are the most economical known, it may suggest ways to improve man-made systems.

To learn more of fundamental nerve circuitry, the M.I.T. investigators insert dozens of ultra-tiny electrodes into the spinal cords of anesthetized animals to chart the detailed flow of nerve messages. In the old technique for recording nerve impulses, a relatively large electrode was clamped outside a bundle of nerve fibers. This methods, explains one M.I.T. scientist, was about as helpful as trying to analyze the communication network of the entire U.S. using only the signals picked up by ships stationed off the coast. The new electrode-insertion method requires complex electronic recording gear that is available only at a relatively few places like M.I.T., and the work goes slowly.

### *Information and Life*

So far no mention has been made of a word that appears in information theory with great frequency. The word is "entropy," and Shannon uses it as synonymous with "amount of information." When Shannon had derived his equation for calculating "amount of information," he found it was precisely the same equation that physicists use to calculate the quantity known as "entropy" in thermodynamics. What the physicists means by "en-

[4]Fifty bits per second, twelve hours a day for sixty years.

tropy" has stumped freshman physics students for well over seventy-five years, but it is really not too difficult a concept. In thermodynamics, entropy measures the degree of randomness, or disorder, in atomic and molecular systems. The more disorder, the higher the entropy. The famous second law of thermodynamics states that in an isolated system, entropy may stay constant or increase, but never decrease. For an analogy, consider a shoebox into which one puts a handful of white beads at one end and a handful of black beads at the other. If the box is never touched, the beads will stay in their respective ends, i.e., entropy (disorder) will stay constant. However, the moment the box is disturbed the beads will begin to mix, and disorder, i.e., entropy, will increase.

In Shannon's view, entropy (or amount of information) reaches a maximum when all the symbols in a message appear independently with equal probability, i.e., in random order.[5] Shannon does not suggest that there is any real identity between his entropy and thermodynamic entropy. Other scientists, however, have speculated that some deep, underlying identity *may* exist.

The identity seems tantalizingly real when one considers the nature of life. Life appears to refute the second law of thermodynamics, until one considers that life cannot continue in a closed system. In his book, *What Is Life?,* Erwin Schrödinger, the Austrian-born physicist, stated a view that has gained popularity when he observed that life feeds on high-grade energy or negative entropy, that is, on substances with highly ordered structures. But the question remains: How does a simple leaf utilize solar energy to erect the primary ordered structures (e.g., sugar, starch, proteins)? It does this, Wiener and others suspect, because photosynthesis employs catalysts that somehow have the power to suspend the second law of thermodynamics, locally and temporarily. Such sorting agents, first proposed by Clerk Maxwell, have been called "Maxwell Demons." For the demon (catalyst) to operate it has to obtain information about the particles it is sorting. If life is thus viewed as a manipulation of energy and information, Wiener and others consider it fitting that both carry "entropy" as a common measure.

## *Information and Meaning*

While some extremely gifted minds have tried to use information theory as the foundation for a new theory of meaning, they have not been too successful, or at least they have not convinced their colleagues of their

[5]Some information theorists, including Wiener, prefer to view information as equivalent to *negative* entropy—seemingly because information, to them, represents *order* not disorder. It is doubtful, however, if this reflects anything more than a bookkeeping difference.

success. Yet even many of the unconvinced continue to hope that a foundation exists. One of the most hopeful is Warren Weaver, president-elect of the American Association for the Advancement of Science. Soon after Shannon's work appeared, Weaver wrote: "The theory . . . has so penetratingly cleared the air that one is now perhaps for the first time ready for a real theory of meaning. . . . One has the vague feeling . . . that information and meaning may be subject to some joint restriction that compels the sacrifice of one if you insist on having much of the other."

Until Warren Weaver's hope is fulfilled, perhaps the hardest thing for the average person to keep steadily in mind is that information theory says nothing whatever about meaning. It is content to tell the engineer that a surprisingly large part of any English sentence (or of any other ordinary message) is predictable. But with all its quaint redundancies the English sentence is still, in Churchill's phrase, "a noble thing." The mind cannot conceive its all but infinite variety. In a billion years even television's capacious channel could not transmit more than a sub*sub*microscopic fraction of the ways Churchill might have written a single speech.

The power of the theory lies in its ability to cope with messages of any nature. It will, for example, help the neurologist analyze communication networks that transmit apparently meaningless strings of coded symbols. Indeed, neurologists have already discovered that the signals that transmit information from the eye to the brain appear to be wholly random. However, to the brain, which knows the code, the signals are not meaningless; their apparent randomness simply reflects a high degree—conceivably the optimum degree—of compression. It is this same compression that information theory invites the communication engineer to achieve.

It is hard to see how information theory can fail to rank with the enduring great. For it goes to the heart of what appears to be life's most essential feature—the ability to communicate information.

## *Introduction and Objectives for Reading Four: "A Transactional Model of Communication"*

The fourth reading presents a new communication model capable of extension to several levels of systems analysis. It is accompanied by a verbal description rich with examples of communication at many levels.

When you have completed this reading, you should be able to:

1. Explain in your own words the processes of intrapersonal and interpersonal communication.

2. Summarize the place of nonverbal communication in this model.
3. Compare the Barnlund model to the Tubbs, Newcomb, and Westley-MacLean models presented in the lead article of this chapter.

Dean C. Barnlund

# A TRANSACTIONAL MODEL OF COMMUNICATION

## A Pilot Model

A pilot study is an "experimental experiment" in which an investigator attempts a gross manipulation of his variables to determine the feasibility of his study, clarify his assumptions and refine his measuring instruments. The drawings that follow are "pilot models" in the same spirit, for they are preliminary experiments in diagramming self-to-environment, self-to-self and self-to-other communication.

## Intra-Personal Communication

It may help to explain the diagrams that follow if the abstract elements and relations in the models are given concrete illustration by using a hypothetical case. Let us assume a simple communicative setting. In Figure 1, a person ($P_1$), let us say a Mr. A, sits alone in the reception room of a clinic waiting to see his doctor. As a communication system Mr. A decodes (D), or assigns meaning to the various cues available in his perceptual field by transforming sensory discriminations into neuro-muscular sets (E) so that they are manifest to others in the form of verbal and nonverbal cues. Evidence is not available which will permit us to establish if encoding and decoding are separate functions of the organism, successive phases of a single on-going process, or the same operation viewed from opposite ends of the system, but it is reasonable to assume until we have solid proof that they are closely articulated and interdependent processes.

From Johnnye Akin, Alvin Goldberg, Gail Myers, and Joseph Stewart, eds., *Language Behavior: A Book of Readings* (The Hague, The Netherlands: Mouton & Co., 1970), pp. 53–61. Reproduced by permission of the publisher.

The spiral line connecting encoding and decoding processes is used to give diagrammatic representation to the continuous, unrepeatable and irreversible nature of communication that was postulated earlier.

The meanings presented in Mr. A at any given moment will be a result of his alertness to, and detection of, objects and circumstances in his

*Dean C. Barnlund*

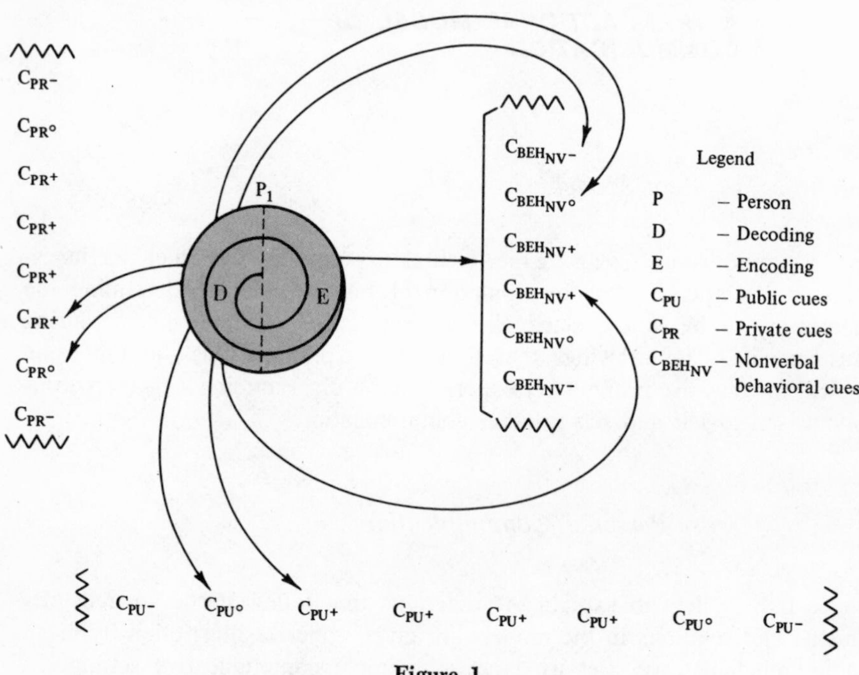


**Figure 1.**

environment. The lines terminating in arrows on Figure 1 can be used to indicate either the different stimuli that come into focus as Mr. A's attention shifts from moment to moment, or that a single "experience" may be a mosaic of many simultaneous perceptions. The direction of the arrows illustrates the postulate that meaning will be assigned to, rather than received from, the objects admitted to perception.

There are at least three sets of signs—or cues—to which Mr. A may attribute meaning in this setting.[1] Any of them may trigger interpretations or reactions of one kind or another. One set of cues derives from the environment itself. These cues are identified in Figure 1 as public cues

[1]The more generic term of cues has been adopted to avoid some of the difficulties that attend the sign-symbol distinction.

($C_{PU}$). To qualify as a public cue any object or sound or circumstance must fulfill two criteria. First, it must be a part of, or available to, the perceptual field of all potential communicants. Second, it must have been created prior to the event under analysis and must remain outside the control of the persons under observation. Two types of public cues can be distinguished. Natural cues, those supplied by the physical world without the intervention of man, include atmospheric conditions of temperature and humidity, the visual and tactual properties of minerals, the color and forms of vegetable life and climatic crises such as hurricanes and rainstorms. Artificial cues, those resulting from man's modification and manipulation of his environment, include the effects created by the processing and arranging of wood, steel and glass, the weaving and patterning of clothing, the control of climate through air or sound conditioning.

As Mr. A glances about the office he may be aware of the arrangement of furniture, a worn carpet, a framed reproduction of a Miro painting, a slightly antiseptic odor, an end table covered with magazines. To any of them he may attach significance, altering his attitude toward his doctor or himself. In some instances the cues may be authored and edited by a number of persons. The painting, for example, is a message from Joan Miro, its framing a message from the decorator, its choice and location a message from the doctor. All these cues are available potentially to anyone who enters the reception room. The perception of any specific cue, or the meaning assigned to it, however, will be similar for various people only to the extent that they possess the same sensory acuity, overlapping fields of perception, parallel background experiences, and similar needs or purposes.

A second set of cues consists of those elements or events that are essentially private in nature, that come from sources not automatically available to any other person who enters a communicative field. Private cues might include the sounds heard through a pair of earphones, the sights visible through opera glasses, or the vast array of cues that have their origin in the taste buds or viscera of the interpreter. In the case of Mr. A, the private cues ($C_{PR}$) might include the words and pictures he finds as he riffles through a magazine, the potpourri of objects he finds in his pocket, or a sudden twitch of pain he notices in his chest. Public and private cues may be verbal or nonverbal in form, but the critical quality they share is that they were brought into existence and remain beyond the control of the communicants.

Although no one else has yet entered the communicative field, Mr. A has to contend with one additional set of cues. These, however, are generated by, and are substantially under the control of, Mr. A himself. They consist of the observations he makes of himself as he turns the pages of his magazine, sees himself reflected in the mirror, or changes positions in his chair. The articulation and movement of his body are as much a part of his phenomenological field as any other cue provided by the environment.[2] Indeed if this were not true he would be incapable of coordinated acts. To turn a page requires the assessment of dozens of subtle muscular changes. These cues are identified in Figure 1 as behavioral, nonverbal cues ($C_{BEH_{NV}}$). They comprise the deliberate acts of Mr. A in straightening his tie or picking up a magazine as well as his unconscious mannerisms in holding a cigarette or slouching in his chair. They differ from public cues in that they are initiated or controlled by the communicant himself. When public or private cues are assigned meaning, Mr. A is free to interpret as he will, but his meanings are circumscribed to some extent by the environment around him. Where his own behavior is involved, he controls (consciously or unconsciously) *both* the cues that are supplied and their interpretations as well. Two sets of lines are required in Figure 1 to reflect the circularity of this communication process, one to indicate the encoding of meaning in the nonverbal behavior of Mr. A, the other to show interpretation of these acts by Mr. A.

The jagged lines ( ^^^^ ) at either end of the series of public, private and behavioral cues in Figure 1 simply illustrate that the number of cues to which meaning may be assigned is probably without limit. But, although unlimited in number, they can be ordered in terms of their attractiveness, or potency, for any viewer. Men do not occupy a neutral environment. The assumptive world of Mr. A, a product of his sensory-motor successes and failures in the past, combined with his current appetites and needs, will establish his set toward the environment so that all available cues do not have equal valence for him. Each will carry a value that depends upon its power to assist or defeat him in pursuit of adequate meanings. Tentative valences have been assigned to the public, private, and behavioral cues in Figure 1 through the addition of a plus, zero or minus sign (+, 0, −) following each of them.

The complexity of the process of abstracting can readily be illustrated through the diagram simply by specifying the precise objects which Mr. A includes or excludes from his perception. Research on dissonance and balance theory suggests the direction followed in the discrimination, or-

[2]While this sort of intra-personal communication is usually identified as feedback, the connotation of this term may be unfortunate when applied loosely to human communication for it suggests a sender-receiver dualism where there may be none, and implies that a person receives information about his performance from his environment. Actions, however, are incapable of sending meanings back to the source. The individual acts and as he acts observes *and* interprets his own behavior. As long as this is understood the term need not cause difficulty but this does not always seem to be the case in the literature on communication.

ganizing and interpreting of available cues.[3] Unless other factors intervene, individuals tend to draw toward the cues to which positive valences can be assigned, that is toward cues capable of reinforcing past or emerging interpretations, and away from cues to which negative valences are attached or those that contradict established opinions and behavior patterns.

> By a balanced state is meant a situation in which the relations among the entities fit together harmoniously; there is no stress towards change. A basic assumption is that sentiment relations and unit relations tend toward a balanced state. This means that sentiments are not entirely independent of the perceptions of unit connections between entities and that the latter, in turn, are not entirely independent of sentiments. Sentiments and unit relations are mutually interdependent. It also means that if a balanced state does not exist, then forces toward this state will arise. If a change is not possible, the state of imbalance will produce tension.[4]

Successive diagrams of a particular communicative event could be made to demonstrate in a cognitively dissonant setting how a person avoids negatively-loaded cues, maximizes or minimizes competing cues, or reassigns valences in order to produce consonance.

An illustration, even though oversimplified, will suggest the course of Mr. A's communication with himself. At the moment he is faintly aware of an antiseptic odor in the room, which reinforces his confidence in the doctor's ability to diagnose his illness ($C_{PU}+$). As he glances through a magazine ($C_{PR}0$) he is conscious of how comfortable his chair feels after a long day on his feet ($C_{PR}+$). Looking up, he glances at the Miro reproduction on the wall, but is unable to decipher it ($C_{PU}0$). He decides to call the nurse. As he rises he clumsily drops his magazine ($C_{BEH_{NV}}-$) and stoops to pick it up, crosses the room ($C_{BEH_{NV}}0$), and rings the call bell firmly and with dignity ($C_{BEH_{NV}}+$).

## *Interpersonal Communication*

The communication process is complicated still further in Figure 2 by the appearance of a second person ($P_2$), let us say Dr. B, who enters the reception room to look for his next patient. The perceptual field of Dr. B, as that of Mr. A, will include the public cues supplied by the environment ($C_{PU}$). These cues, however, will not be identical for both persons, nor will they carry the same valences, because of differences in their

[3]See Leon Festinger, *A Theory of Cognitive Dissonance* (Row Peterson, 1957) and Fritz Heider, *The Psychology of Interpersonal Relations* (Wiley, 1958).

[4]Heider, Ibid., p. 201.

backgrounds and immediate purposes. Dr. B may notice the time on the wall clock or the absence of other patients, and he may assign different valences to the disarray of magazines on the table or to the Miro print. In addition, Dr. B will be interpreting private cues ($C_{PR}$) that belong exclusively to his own phenomenological field, such as his own fatigue at the moment, and these may alter the interpretations he attaches to Mr. A's conduct. Finally, there are the behavioral cues ($C_{BEH_{NV}}$) that accompany his own movements to which he must be tuned in order to act with reasonable efficiency.

Even before any verbal exchange takes place, however, there will be a shift in communicative orientation of both individuals. As Mr. A and Dr. B become aware of the presence of the other (sometimes before), each will become more self-conscious, more acutely aware of his own acts, and more alert to the nonverbal cues of the other as an aid to defining their relationship. Each will bring his own actions under closer surveillance and greater control. The doctor, as he enters, may assume a professional air as a means of keeping the patient at the proper psychological distance; the patient, upon hearing the door open, may hastily straighten his tie to make a good impression. A heightened sensitivity and a shift from environmental to behavioral cues identifies the process of social facilitation. Men do not act or—communicate—in private as they do in the presence of others. While audiences represent a special case of social facilitation, and mobs an unusually powerful and dramatic one, the mere appearance of a second person in an elevator or office will change the character and content of self-to-self communication in both parties.[5]

At some point in their contact, and well before they have spoken, Mr. A and Dr. B will have become sufficiently aware of each other that it is possible to speak of behavioral cues as comprising a message (M). That is, each person will begin to regulate the cues he provides the other, each will recognize the possible meanings the other may attach to his actions, and each will begin to interpret his own acts as if he were the other. These two features, the deliberate choice and control of cues and the projection of interpretation, constitute what is criterial for identifying interpersonal messages.

Dr. B, crossing the room, may initiate the conversation. Extending his hand, he says, "Mr. A! So glad to see you. How are you?"[6] At this

[5]See Erving Goffman, *The Presentation of Self in Everyday Life* (Doubleday Anchor Books, 1959).

[6]We do not have, as yet, in spite of the efforts of linguists and students of nonverbal behavior, an adequate typology for identifying message cues. In the case of this simple remark, is the unit of meaning the phoneme, morpheme, word, or phrase? And, in the case of nonverbal cues, is it to be bodily position, gesture, or some smaller unit? Until we have better descriptive categories the careful analysis of communicative acts cannot proceed very far.

point, despite the seeming simplicity of the setting and prosaic content of the message, Mr. A must solve a riddle in meaning of considerable complexity. In a nonclinical environment where the public cues would be different, perhaps on a street corner ($C_{PU}$), Mr. A would regard this message

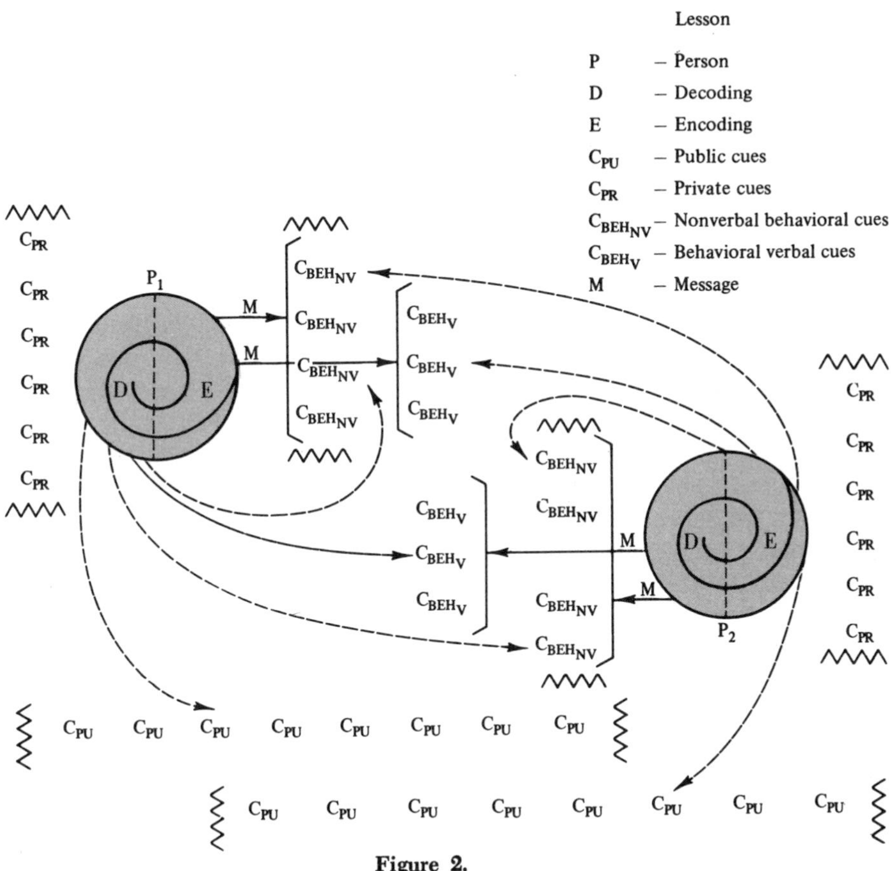


**Figure 2.**

($C_{BEH_V}$) as no more than a social gesture, and he would respond in kind. This on the other hand, is a clinic ($C_{PU}$). Is this remark, therefore, to be given the usual interpretation? Even here, the nonverbal cues ($C_{BEH_{NV}}$) of Dr. B, the friendly facial expression and extended hand, may reinforce its usual meaning in spite of the special setting. On the other hand, these words ($C_{BEH}$ ) may be interpreted only as showing the sympathetic interest of Dr. B in Mr. A. In this case, the message requires no answer at all but is a signal for Mr. A to come into the office. In spite of the clinical setting ($C_{PU}$) and the gracious gesture ($C_{BEH_{NV}}$), however, the last phrase ($C_{BEH_V}$), because of a momentary hesitation just before it ($C_{BEH_{NV}}$), might be an invitation for Mr. A to begin giving an account of his symptoms. In deciphering the meaning, Mr. A will have to assign and reassign valences so that a coherent interpretation emerges. (No valences are assigned in Figure 2 because their positive, negative or neutral value would depend upon the interpretive decisions of Mr. A and Dr. B.) All three contexts, the environmental, behavioral and verbal will have to be scanned, assigned meanings, and compared in order for Mr. A to determine a suitable response.

Meanwhile, Dr. B is involved in weaving some interpretations of his own out of the cues he detects and the valences he assigns to them. Mr. A smiles back and says, "Nice to see you again, too. I wish the circumstances were different." At this moment Dr. B turns his attention from the carpet which needs repairing ($C_{PU}$) to Mr. A. How should he interpret this message? Since they are in a clinic ($C_{PU}$) it is not surprising that Mr. A should speak of the "circumstances" of his visit. Yet, could this be a warning that the visit concerns a serious medical problem rather than a trivial one? Mr. A's relaxed posture ($C_{BEH_{NV}}$) does not reinforce the former meaning, but his flushed face does ($C_{BEH_{NV}}$). Or could this remark be no more than a semi-humorous reference to a past episode on the golf links ($C_{PR}$)? In any case, Dr. B, like Mr. A, must reduce the ambiguity in the situation by experimentally assigning meanings to public, private, nonverbal and verbal cues, relating them to the surrounding conditions of time and place, and determining the extent of congruence or incongruence in the meanings given them. Not until further verbal and nonverbal cues are supplied will Dr. B be confident that he has sized up the message properly.

This analysis suggests that meanings are assigned to verbal cues according to the same principles that govern the interpretations of all other cues. Indeed, this seems to be the case.[7] Meaning is cumulative (or ambiguity reductive) and grows as each new cue, of whatever type, is detected and assigned some sort of valence. Verbal cues are distinctive only in the sense that they constitute a special form of behavior, are finite in number, and are presented in a linear sequence.

One further clarification must be added concerning the transferability of cues. A public cue can be transformed into a private cue by manipulating it so that it is no longer available to all communicants. Mr. A may refold his coat so that a worn cuff cannot be seen by Dr. B, or the doctor may turn over his medical chart so that Mr. A cannot read his entry. Private cues may be converted into public ones. Mr. A may want Dr. B to see a cartoon in the *New Yorker* he has been reading or Dr. B may choose to show Mr. A the latest photograph of his daughter. Sometimes an action

[7]James M. Richards, "The Cue Additivity Principle in a Restricted Social Interaction Situation," *Journal of Experimental Psychology* (1952), p. 452.

on the part of a communicant involves manipulating or altering an environmental cue. Dr. B may unconsciously rearrange the magazines on the table while speaking to Mr. A and, in this case, environmental and behavioral cues merge.

The aim of communication is to reduce uncertainty. Each cue has potential value in carrying out this purpose. But it requires that the organism be open to all available cues and that it be willing to alter meanings until a coherent and adequate picture emerges. Conditionality becomes the criterion of functional communication which, according to Llewellyn Gross, "involves the attitude of thinking in terms of varying degrees and changing proportions; the habit of acting provisionally and instrumentally with a keen awareness of the qualifying influence of time, place, people, and circumstances upon aspirations and expectations; the emotional appreciation for varieties and nuances of feeling."[8]

What is regarded in various academic fields as an "error of judgment," or "a communication breakdown," or a "personality disturbance," appears to be a consequence of a sort of communicative negligence. The nature of this negligence is intimated in what a British psychiatrist has called "The Law of the Total Situation."[9] To the extent that a person is unable to respond to the total situation—because he denies critical cues from the environment, distorts verbal or nonverbal cues from the opposite person, fails to revise inappropriate assumptions regarding time and place—to that extent will it be difficult, or impossible, for him to construct meanings that will allow him to function in productive and satisfying ways.

The observance and disregard of the Law of the Total Situation can be documented again and again in human affairs, at the most intimate interpersonal levels, and at the most serious public levels. Since comunicative negligence is so omnipresent, it might be refreshing to consider an instance that illustrates a sensitive observance of the Law of the Total Situation.

Betty Smith, writing in *A Tree Grows in Brooklyn*, tells of a neighborhood custom. On the night before Christmas a child could win a tree if he stood without falling while it was thrown at him. When Francie was ten and Neeley nine, they went to the lot and asked the owner to throw his biggest tree at the two of them. The small children clasped each other to meet the force of the great tree. For just a moment the man agonized, wanting simply to give it to them, but knowing that if he did he would have to give away all his trees, and the next year no one would pay for a

[8]Llewellyn Gross, "The Construction and Partial Standardization of a Scale for Measuring Self-Insight," *Journal of Social Psychology* (November, 1948), p. 222.

[9]Henry Harris, *The Group Approach to Leadership Testing* (Routledge and Kegan Paul, 1949), p. 258.

tree. Realizing he must do it, he threw the tree as hard as he could. Though the children almost fell, they were able to withstand the impact and claimed the tree. As they started to pick it up Francie heard the man shout after them, "And now get the hell out of here, you lousy bastards." There was no doubt about what he said. But Francie was able to hear beyond the rough words. She knew that this tone of voice, on Christmas Eve, from one who had no other language really meant, "Merry Christmas, God bless you." The man could not have said that, and Francie recognized it. He used the only words he had and she was able to understand him, not from his words alone, but from the totality of time, place, personality, and circumstance.

The complexities of human communication present an unbelievably difficult challenge to the student of human affairs. To build a satisfactory theory about so complex an event through sole reliance upon the resources of ordinary language seems less and less promising. Any conceptual device which might give order to the many and volatile forces at work when people communicate deserves attention. The value of any theoretical innovation, such as a symbolic model, may be measured by its capacity to withstand critical attack, its value in prompting new hypotheses and data, or finally, by its contribution to the improvement of human communication. The pilot models described here may not fulfill any of these criteria completely, but they will have served a useful purpose if they prompt the search for better ways of representing the inner dynamics of the communication process.[10]

### *Introduction and Objectives for Reading Five: "Communication: The Flow of Information"*

The fifth reading discusses communication in organizations. The organization is viewed as an open system in continual interaction with its external environment.

When you have completed this reading, you should be able to:

1. Give reasons why "more and better communication" will necessarily not solve organizational problems.
2. Define coding and translation as they apply to organizational communication.

[10]Only slight modifications are needed to adapt these models for use in representing the dynamics of mass communication.

Daniel Katz and Robert L. Kahn

# *COMMUNICATION: THE FLOW OF INFORMATION*

The world we live in is basically a world of people. Most of our actions toward others and their actions toward us are communicative acts in whole or in part, whether or not they reach verbal expression. This is as true of behavior in organizations as in other contexts. We have said that human organizations are informational as well as energic systems, and that every organization must take in and utilize information. The intake and distribution of information are also energic processes, of course; acts of sending and receiving information demand energy for their accomplishment. Their energic demands, however, are negligible in comparison with their significance and implications as symbolic acts—as acts of communication and control.

When one walks from a factory to the adjoining head-house or office, the contrast is conspicuous. One goes from noise to quiet, from heavy electrical cables and steam pipes to slim telephone lines, from a machine-dominated to a people-dominated environment. One goes, in short, from a sector of the organization in which energic exchange is primary and information exchange secondary, to a sector where the priorities are reversed. The closer one gets to the organizational center of control and decision-making, the more pronounced is the emphasis on information exchange.

In this sense, communication—the exchange of information and the transmission of meaning—is the very essence of a social system or an organization. The input of physical energy is dependent upon information about it, and the input of human energy is made possible through communicative acts. Similarly the transformation of energy (the accomplishment of work) depends upon communication between people in each organizational subsystem and upon communication between subsystems. The product exported carries meaning as it meets needs and wants, and

From Daniel Katz and Robert L. Kahn, *The Social Psychology of Organizations.* (New York: John Wiley & Sons, Inc., 1966), pp. 223–29. Copyright 1966 by John Wiley & Sons, Inc. Reprinted by permission of the publisher.

its use is futher influenced by the advertising or public relations material about it. The amount of support which an organization receives from its social environment is also affected by the information which elite groups and wider publics have acquired about its goals, activities, and accomplishments.

Communication is thus a social process of the broadest relevance in the functioning of any group, organization, or society. It is possible to subsume under it such forms of social interaction as the exertion of influence, cooperation, social contagion or imitation, and leadership. We shall consider communication in this broad sense, with emphasis upon the structural aspects of the information process in organizations, but with attention also to the motivational basis for transmitting and receiving messages.

It is a common assumption that many of our problems, individual and social, are the result of inadequate and faulty communication. As Newcomb (1947) points out, autistic hostility decreases communication and in turn decreased communication enhances autistic hostility. If we can only increase the flow of information, we are told, we can solve these problems. This assumption is found in our doctrine of universal education. It is fundamental in most campaigns of public relations and public enlightenment. Our democratic institutions, with their concern for freedom of speech and assembly, their rejection of censorship, and their acceptance of the principle of equal time for the arguments of opposing political parties, have extended the notion of competition in the market place to a free market for ideas. Truth will prevail if there is ready access to all the relevant information.

The glorification of a full and free information flow is a healthy step forward in intraorganizational problems as well as in the relations of an organization to the larger social system. It is, however, a gross oversimplification. Communication may reveal problems as well as eliminate them. A conflict in values, for example, may go unnoticed until communication is attempted. Communication may also have the effect, intended or unintended, of obscuring and confusing existing problems. The vogue enjoyed by the word *image* in recent years reflects in part an unattractive preoccupation with communication as a means of changing the perception of things without the expense and inconvenience of changing the things themselves. The television commercials, with their incessant and spurious assertion of new products and properties are the worst of numberless examples. In short, the advocacy of communication needs to be qualified with respect to the kind of information relevant to the solution of given problems and with respect to the nature of the communication process between individuals, between groups, and between subsystems.

Communication needs to be seen not as a process occurring between any sender of messages and any potential recipient, but in relation to the social system in which it occurs and the particular function it performs in that system. General principles of communication as a social-psychological process are fine; they set the limits within which we must operate. But they need to be supplemented by an analysis of the social system, so that they can be applied correctly to given situations.

The discovery of the crucial role of communication led to an enthusiastic advocacy of increased information as the solution to many organizational problems. More and better communication (especially, more) was the slogan. Information to rank-and-file employees about company goals and policies was the doctrine; the means too often were stylized programs and house organs homogenized by the Flesch formula for basic English. Communication up the line to give top echelons a more accurate picture of the lower levels was a complementary emphasis.

### *Social Systems as Restricted Communication Networks*

Though there were and are good outcomes of this simplistic approach, there are also weak, negligible, and negative outcomes. The blanket emphasis upon more communication fails to take into account the functioning of an organization as a social system and the specific needs of the subsystems.

In the first place, as Thelen (1960) points out, an organized state of affairs, a social system, implies the restriction of communication among its members. If we take an unorganized group, say 60 people milling around at random in a large room, the number of potential channels of communication is $n(n\text{-}1)/2$ or 1770. If, however, they are organized into a network of twelve combinations of five such that each person on a five-man team has one clearly defined role and is interdependent with four other people, the number of channels within the work group is reduced to *ten* in a completely interdependent condition or to *four* in a serial dependent position.

Without going into such complexities as task-relevant communication, the major point is clear. To move from an unorganized state to an organzied state requires the introduction of constraints and restrictions to reduce diffuse and random communication to channels appropriate for the accomplishment of organizational objectives. It may require also the introduction of incentives to use those channels and use them appropriately, rather than leave them silent or use them for organizationally irrelevant purposes. Organizational development sometimes demands the creation of new communication channels. The very nature of a social system, however, implies a selectivity of channels and communicative acts—a mandate to avoid some and to utilize others.

In terms of information theory, unrestricted communication produces noise in the system. Without patterning, without pauses, without precision, there is sound but there is no music. Without structure, without spacing, without specifications, there is a Babel of tongues but there is no meaning.

The same basic problem of selectivity in communications can be considered in terms of Ashby's (1952) conceptual model. Thelen summarizes the Ashby contribution in these terms.[1]

> *Any living system* is an infinitely complex association of subsystems. The complex suprasystem has all the properties of a subsystem plus communication across the boundaries of subsystems. Ashby's brilliant treatment (1952) shows that stability of the suprasystem would take infinitely long to achieve *if* there were "full and rich communication" among the subsystems (because in effect all the variables of all the subsystems would have to be satisfied at once—a most unlikely event). If communication among subsystems is restricted or if they are temporarily isolated, then each subsystem achieves its own stability with minimum interference by the changing environment of other systems seeking *their* stability. With restricted communication, success can accumulate (from successive trials, for example), whereas in the single suprasystem, success is all-or-none. . . . Thus the way an overall system moves toward its equilibrium depends very much on the functional connectedness of its parts. Adaptation of the whole system makes use of two conditions: enough connectedness that operation of one subsystem can activate another so that the contributions of all can contribute to the whole; and enough separation of subsystems that some specialization of function is possible and such that "equilibrium" can be approached in the system as a whole. But no complex suprasystem would ever have equilibrium in all its subsystems at the same time. Each subsystem has the "power of veto" over equilibria in other subsystems, and under a variety of conditions one subsystem can dominate another.

Our loosely organized political system reflects the system requirements of restriction of full and free communication. Chaos in national decision-making is avoided by the device of the two-party system. Instead of representing in clear fashion in Congress all the factional groups and subsystems within the nation, we go through a quadrennial process of successive agreements within the major parties, culminating in the nomination of a presidential candidate by each of them. This is in effect a restriction and channeling of the communication process. Once candidates are selected, the factional groups within each party tend to unite behind one ticket, and the amount of communication to the candidates is restricted.

[1]Mimeographed paper, 1960.

The rank-and-file voter neither communicates up the line nor receives much in the way of communication down the line except for the projected image of the candidate and the general image of the party.

In fact, the average voter is woefully ignorant of the stand of his party on most political issues. On sixteen major issues of the 1956 presidential election, the proportion of people who had an opinion, knew what the government was doing, and saw some differences between the parties never exceeded 36 per cent and for some issues was as low as 18 per cent (Campbell, Converse, Miller, and Stokes, 1960). This is one price we pay for the organizational restrictions of a two-party system and the communication distance between the voters and political leaders. Nevertheless, the two-party system has the advantage of overall political stability and facilitation of national decision-making. If all interested groups and ideological factions had their own parties and their own representatives in Congress, we would have more complete communication between the people and their elected leaders but we would have terrific problems of attaining system stability. We would have many possibilities of veto by coalition of minority groups, of legislative stalemates, and of national indecision. Some European countries with multiple-party systems, with more communication, and perhaps better-informed electorates have had such problems.

## *The Coding Process*

Individuals, groups, and organizations share a general characteristic which must be recognized as a major determinant of communication: the coding process. Any system which is the recipient of information, whether it be an individual or an organization, has a characteristic coding process, a limited set of coding categories to which it assimilates the information received. The nature of the system imposes omission, selection, refinement, elaboration, distortion, and transformation upon the incoming communications. Just as the human eye selects and transforms light waves to which it is attuned to give perceptions of color and objects, so too does any system convert stimulation according to its own properties. It has been demonstrated that human beings bring with them into most situations sets of categories for judging the facts before them. Walter Lippmann (1922) called attention to the coding process years ago in the following famous passages. Even then he was merely putting into dramatic form what had been recognized by the ancient philosophers.

> For the most part we do not first see, and then define, we define first and then see. In the great blooming, buzzing confusion of the outer world, we pick out what our culture has already defined for us, and we

> tend to perceive that which we have picked out in the form stereotyped for us by our culture. (p. 31)
>
> What matters is the character of the stereotypes and the gullibility with which we employ them. And these in the end depend upon those inclusive patterns which constitute our philosophy of life. If in that philosophy we assume that the world is codified according to a code we possess, we are likely to make our reports of what is going on describe a world run by our code. (p. 90)
>
> Most of us would deal with affairs through a rather haphazard and shifting assortment of stereotypes, if a comparatively few men in each generation were not constantly engaged in arranging, standardizing, and improving them into logical systems, known as the Laws of Political Economy, the Principles of Politics, and the like. (pp. 104–105)

Organizations, too, have their own coding systems which determine the amount and type of information they receive from the external world and the transformation of it according to their own systemic properties. The most general limitation is that the position people occupy in organizational space will determine their perception and interpretation of incoming information and their search for additional information. In other words, the structure and functions of a given subsystem will be reflected in the frame of reference and way of thinking of the role incumbents of that sector of organizational space. The different functions and dynamics of the production structure, the maintenance system, and the adaptive system (described in Chapter 4) imply that each of these subsystems will respond to the same intelligence input in different ways and that each will seek out particular information to meet its needs.

All members of an organization are affected by the fact that they occupy a common organizational space in contrast to those who are not members. By passing the boundary and becoming a functioning member of the organization, the person takes on some of the coding system of the organization since he accepts some of its norms and values, absorbs some of its subculture, and develops shared expectations and values with other members. The boundary condition is thus responsible for the dilemma that the person within the system cannot perceive things and communicate about them in the same way that an outsider would. If a person is within a system, he sees its operations differently than if he were on the outside looking in. It is extremely difficult to occupy different positions in social space without a resulting differential perception. Where boundary conditions are fluid and organizational members are very loosely confined within the system (as with people sent abroad to live among foreign nationals for some governmental agency) there will be limited tours of duty, alternation between foreign and domestic service, and careful debriefing sessions to insure that life outside the physical boundaries of the country has not imparted too much of the point of view of the outsider.

## *The Problem of Translation across Subsystem Boundaries*

Within an organization there are problems of clear communication across subsystems. The messages emanating in one part of the organization need translation if they are to be fully effective in other parts. In an earlier chapter, reference was made to Parsons' (1960) specific application of this principle to the chain of command. Instead of a unitary chain from the top to the bottom of an organization, Parsons pointed out that there are significant breaks between the institutional and managerial levels and again between the managerial and technical levels. Communications, then, must be transmitted in general enough terms to permit modification within each of these levels. The same type of translation problem occurs between any pair of substructures having their own functions and their own coding schema. Without adequate translation across subsystem boundaries, communications can add to the noise in the system.

. . . . . . . . . . . . . . . . . . .

## *References*


Ashby, W. R. 1952. *Design for a brain.* New York: Wiley.

Campbell, A., P. E. Converse, W. E. Miller, and D. E. Stokes. 1960. *The American voter.* New York: Wiley.

Lippmann, W. 1922. *Public opinion.* New York: Harcourt, Brace.

Newcomb, T. M. 1947. Autistic hostility and social reality. *Human Relations,* 1, 69–86.

Parsons, T. 1960. *Structure and process in modern societies.* New York: Free Press.

Thelen, H. A. 1960(a). Exploration of a growth model for psychic, biological, and social systems. Mimeographed paper.

Thelen, H. A. 1960 (b). Personal communication to authors.


## *Introduction and Objectives for Reading Six: "Criteria for Theory Construction"*

In the sixth and final reading in Chapter 2 are presented and illustrated five major criteria for judging the quality of a theory of behavior. The reader should keep these criteria in mind as he continues through this book and examines theories about specific types of communication events.

When you have completed this reading, you should be able to:

1. Define predictive capability and relate it to the application of speech-communication theories to behavioral change, such as increasing interpersonal effectivesness.
2. Compare or contrast: linkage with observables (Reading No. 5), operational specificity (Reading No. 1), and rules of correspondence (lead article).
3. Define heuristic value and parsimony.

Kenneth J. Gergen

## *CRITERIA FOR THEORY CONSTRUCTION*

Let us begin with a concrete question. College students often find that they disagree sharply with those outside the college environment—particularly if the latter are over 30, and more often than not, if they happen to be parents. Research has also shown that values and attitudes within a group tend to become more homogeneous over time. Thus, a college student will tend to develop values that are common within the college population. These values are often different from those found in, let us say, the middle class, middle-aged population. However, we must proceed to the question: What happens to a person's values as he moves from one group to another? College students do not always remain at college. They may spend their vacation at home and reside there for the summer. In such situations their views may be alien to those around them. The specific question, then, is: What changes occur in a student's values as a result of his sojourn in an alien culture? Would you expect his values to change? If so, in what direction—toward the values in the home environment or away? And most important, for what reason would you expect the change to occur? What is your *theory?*

As it happens, there are data relevant to this issue. Philip Brickman, while a senior honors student at Harvard, explored the problem in the following way. Some weeks prior to Christmas vacation some 72 undergraduates filled out two questionnaires. Both of the questionnaires dealt

Kenneth J. Gergen, *The Psychology of Behavior Exchange*, 1969, Addison-Wesley, Reading, Mass.

with values. Standardized items explored the students' feelings about such issues as obeying authority, sensuality, equality, and the manipulation of other people. The second questionnaire asked about the students' perceptions of the norms both at Harvard and at home. The student thus indicated what he felt to be the norm at Harvard on each of the dimensions, as well as the norm in his home environment. When the students returned from spending some three weeks at home over Christmas, they were again asked to fill out a questionnaire—a repeat of the initial measure exploring their own values.

The data analysis was confined to those items in which the following configuration occurred in the *initial* testing period: the student's perception of the Harvard norm fell to one side of his own value, and the perceived home norm to the other. In the following example we see a 10-point scale for one of the items concerning social equality:

Poverty could be almost entirely done away with if we made certain basic changes in our social and economic system.

| | *Disagree* | | | | | | | | | *Agree* |
|---|---|---|---|---|---|---|---|---|---|---|
| Own View: | −5 | −4 | −3 | −2 | −1 | (+1) | +2 | +3 | +4 | +5 |
| Harvard Norm: | −5 | −4 | −3 | −2 | −1 | +1 | +2 | +3 | (+4) | +5 |
| Home Norm: | −5 | (−4) | −3 | −2 | −1 | +1 | +2 | +3 | +4 | +5 |

As you can see, the student perceives the Harvard environment as being extremely liberal (as most students did), while his own value is not quite so liberal (as most weren't) and the view he saw most prevalent at home was on the conservative end of the continuum (with generally high agreement). In effect, Brickman confined his analysis to cases of maximal conflict—where the students' values fell somewhere between the polarities represented by the two reference groups. In concrete terms, the focus of the study was on whether the students' value ratings would move toward the perceived home or perceived Harvard norm as a result of their having spent several weeks in the former environment. Perhaps by now you have formulated your own prediction about what Brickman was to find, and a supporting rationale for the prediction.

It is with the question of rationale that we can return to the original issue: What makes one theory or rationale better than another? What criteria can be used to compare theories? Using the study of student values as a point of departure, we list the following criteria as most important to consider:

1. Predictive Capability. The most elementary criterion that may be brought to bear is whether one's reasoning, or theory building, leads him to a correct prediction or not. For example, the Marxian theory of class struggle and the inevitable emergence of a classless society may ac-

count nicely for events in a number of cultures. In the main, however, it has failed to predict the course of history for most countries, and thus it does not in this respect constitute a "good" theory.

But what about student values? What did your reasoning lead you to predict? Brickman reasoned that if a person was a member of one reference group (e.g., college) and moved for a short period into an alien reference group (home), those in the latter group would react to him primarily as a member of the former. Thus, the family and friends of the student would generally behave toward him as if he held the views prevailing at college. In questioning or discussing the values held in the college community, he would be called upon to defend the college norm by virtue of his membership in that community. He would thus be forced to *play the role* of the typical student at his college, with the net effect that he would become even more committed to the values he felt to be normative at his college. He would think of reasons to support these values, search for criticisms of potential opponents, and, over time, convince himself. His values would not change toward those of his friends and family, but on the contrary, would move toward the perceived college norm.

Did this reasoning lead to an accurate prediction? As it turned out, student values did undergo a statistically significant shift in the direction of the perceived college norm. College students essentially became *more* collegiate as a result of spending time away from college. In terms of predictive capability, the theory proved to be a good one.

Now it is also quite likely that some readers have made the opposite prediction. After all, you know of situations in which a person has moved from one reference group to another and has simply shed the skin of his older existence. If this were not so, immigrants would never be assimilated into society and incoming freshmen at a college would never shed their homespun values for those they stumble upon in college (and later shed again). And it does make sense that the attempt of people to please others and to be liked by them usually brings them into closer agreement. This appears to be perfectly valid reasoning. Should we, because this reasoning did not predict in the present case, jettison this latter approach altogether?

No, what we can do is search for characteristics that distinguish between the case of the college student going home and that of the immigrant or incoming freshman. Such distinctions may ultimately be used to expand and enrich the theory. For example, one difference between the student going home and the immigrant is that the former is not seeking to establish membership in the alien culture, whereas the latter is. Another difference is that the freshman and the immigrant are spending a far greater period of time in the new culture. Perhaps under such conditions as these, the opposite of Brickman's results would be expected. In fact, Brickman's data showed that students who spent the greatest amount of time at home during the vacation were least likely to move toward the Harvard norm. By drawing these distinctions and examining relevant data, we have managed to expand the theory in important ways and to further the predictive capabilities of the theory.

2. LINKAGE WITH OBSERVABLES. Theories are by nature stated in abstract terms. To be sure, some theories are more abstract than others. To say that frustration leads to aggression is a broad, inclusive, and highly general theoretical statement. It is much more abstract than a theory about what your brother will do when he finds his bicycle is stolen. But regardless of level of abstraction or generality, theoretical terms may also differ in another very important way: the extent to which they can be linked to observable entities. We can point to many examples of aggression, and also agree on what the terms "reference group" and "norms" refer to in the Brickman study of students' values. On the other hand, if we had used concepts such as "will" or "soul," we might have had a very difficult time in specifying observable referents.

The degree of linkage between abstract terms and real-world entities is of cardinal significance when one wishes to test a theory, to assess its capacity to make correct predictions. If a theoretical prediction cannot be tied to a set of events or entities with what are termed *operational definitions*, the theory is virtually untestable. Its value in predicting can never be known. The hypothesis that God saves the souls of sinners when he feels generous is of no utility to science. We cannot point to events or phenomena around us that could either confirm or disconfirm such a hypothesis.

We shall not have to worry extensively about this problem of linkage in the present volume. However, there is a more subtle issue at stake that will become increasingly problematic as the book progresses. This is the issue of "psychologizing." A very important distinction can be made between theoretical terms that refer to processes, events, or structures *inside* the person, and terms that refer to overt behavior. Such terms as "feeling," "perception," "emotion," "cognition," and "thought" are of the former kind, while such terms as "body movement," "response increment," "attraction ratings," and "self-description" are of the latter. You may recall from earlier courses in psychology the notion of "hypothetical construct," a notion that has often been used to refer to processes or structures within the person to which we can have no direct access. If we accept the admonition that a theory is better insofar as its concepts refer to immediately observable events, then we must also conclude that hypothetical constructs are inferior as theoretical terms. This may be a bitter pill to swallow inasmuch as most of the terms we use in talking about why people do certain things, and most of the characteristics we feel to be crucial to us personally (our values, loves, aspirations), are considered hypothetical constructs.

This is not to say that such terms must never be used. But the conditions under which they may be used should be limited, and the purist might wish to rule them out altogether.

Two conditions favorable for the use of hypothetical constructs may be elucidated by returning to our original research example. One theoretical speculation was that when the student was engaged in defending a position, he would think of supporting arguments for the position and against the opposition, and this process would cause him to become more committed to the position he was defending. The terms "think of supporting arguments" and "beliefs" fall into the category of hypothetical constructs. In what senses are they defensible?

First, there are observable operations that are designed to assess these ineffables. That is, we assume that certain types of overt behavior are indicative or are measures of these so-called internal events. Beliefs or "values" can be measured with questionnaires, as we have seen above; similarly, we could have subjects talk about or write down their "thoughts" in support of these beliefs. The hypothetical terms thus have a *second-order* anchor in reality. Second, such terms are helpful in explaining the results. They are *useful* and point to additional areas of relevant investigation. However, it must still be concluded that if an especially useful theory could be developed that did not rely on such constructs, it would be a better candidate for our attention.

3. EXTENT OF DATA BASE. There is a small but active group of psychologists who feel that it is possible for people to send and receive information without making use of any of the normal senses, that is, by extrasensory means. However, the assumption is not shared by the majority of scientists in this country. They consider the theoretical assumption inferior, and seldom hesitate to criticize. Why should there be such a vehement reaction on the part of so many? What is it they find so objectionable?

The primary reason why people are loath to accept such a premise is that it violates the overwhelming evidence that science, as well as their daily lives, supplies to them. The term *antecedent probability* is often used in this context. In elementary form, it can be said that any theoretical prediction or hypothesis has a certain probability of being verified whenever it is tested. If a theory has had a history marked by successful predictions, the probability of its being correct in any new instance is quite high. In this case, it is said that the theory has a high antecedent probability. The degree to which there is a supportive data base contributes to the probability of its holding true in the present instance. Given the history of science to date, the ESP assumption has a very low antecedent probability. This is not to say that the theory is false, but simply that a considerable volume of data is required to establish a reasonable degree of antecedent probability.

Resistance exists because accepting the ESP assumption means abandoning or drastically revising other theories of very high antecedent probability.

To return to the study of student values, how extensive was the data base underlying Brickman's theory? As it turns out, there is abundant evidence supporting the notion that publicly defending a position increases one's belief in that position. The literature dealing with the effects of role playing on attitude change is rife with examples. However, the study also assumed that the "folks" back home generally treat college students as examples of the college environment and cause them to defend the liberality found in the college setting. Here there is little supporting evidence, and this link in the reasoning remains untested. Perhaps you can examine your own experience and derive some intuitive feeling for the antecedent probability of the assumption.

4. Heuristic Value. A theory may make accurate predictions, be linked to real-world events, and be based on abundant evidence, but at the same time essentially lead nowhere. The value of a theory in stimulating the field may be independent of these other considerations. The theorizing of Sigmund Freud is a good case in point. Psychoanalytic theory can hardly be said to have great predictive value (although it often proves handy after the fact); the concepts are difficult to pin down operationally; and the great controversy which it has created is a good indication of its low antecedent probability. And yet, almost all would agree that Freud's theory was one of the most significant contributions to Western thinking in the twentieth century. Why? Primarily because it has stimulated large numbers of investigators, both within the field of psychology and without, to develop new insights, generate discoveries, and restructure their research in more profitable ways. In effect, psychoanalytic theory is most important because of its heuristic value.

But what about the theorizing going into the study of student values? What heuristic value does it have? A moment's thought will reveal that the reasoning does lead in some interesting directions. For example, one might wish to investigate changes taking place in students' values as a result of going abroad. It is typically assumed that the *grand tour* broadens one's understanding, causes one to be more flexible, highlights the shortcomings in one's own narrow systems of belief. Does this always take place? Brickman's study suggests that there are circumstances under which a person returns home more committed to his narrowness than ever before.

5. Parsimony. It may be a commentary on human nature itself (although after reading enough psychology you may thoroughly disagree), but scientists generally hold that the briefer a theoretical statement the better. If two theories are equal in every other respect, the theory using the fewer theoretical terms is considered superior. Applying such a criterion might

appear simple enough, but as you will see, application in practice is fraught with difficulty. In the first place, reality may be sufficiently complex that parsimony in any satisfactory sense is an impossible goal. The world may just not be amenable to understanding through simple propositions. In fact, the demand for parsimony can sometimes blind the investigator to subtle nuances within his data. Theories have a way of directing and guiding our perception. They cause us to be selective. And then again, even if an investigator realized that there were subtle findings that his theory could not account for, would it be worthwhile to add an entirely new set of concepts if 95% of his evidence supported his theory?

On another level, most hypothetical constructs are considered superfluous baggage by many theorists. They consider concepts such as love, hate, and anxiety unnecessary for understanding behavior, and advocate their banishment from the field of psychology. Having separate concepts to deal with the subjective experience of love as well as the overt expression of love seems a needless multiplication of terms. If you agree with the criterion of parsimony, you are at loggerheads with theorists who use such concepts. It should be noted in this respect that the theory applied to the data on student values is not very parsimonious. Many assumptions have to be made, many terms employed. Perhaps the rationale which you developed accounted for the data more succinctly.

These five criteria, then, are most important in evaluating a theory. There are other more ambiguous or less important criteria. For example, one might want to add the criterion of richness of the deductions made from a theory. A given theory might be extremely good in predicting behavior in an artificial laboratory setting. Many psychologists confine themselves entirely to such endeavors. When all theoretical deductions are relevant to the same situation, they may well become progressively more trivial. It is a matter of personal bias, but for many, a theory that has ramifications for a broad number of issues, both in and out of the laboratory, would be considered superior to one of limited scope. On much the same biased grounds, one could argue that a theory is more valuable if it has relevance to pressing social problems. However, what one calls "rich" in the way of theory depends primarily on his particular values and world outlook. One man's triviality may be another's god.

While on the topic of debate, you have no doubt realized that various theories may be good for different reasons. This raises the question of which criteria are more important. If a theory were based on solid factual evidence, but heuristically impoverished, for example, would it be better than an unsupported theory that stimulated many others in the field? There are no simple ground rules to follow in such situations. Suffice it for now that as we proceed we shall have to compromise a number of times among competing criteria. We shall simply have to negotiate such settlements, each within its own context. Armed with these criteria of evaluation, we are now prepared for the onrushing legions of abstraction.

## *References*

Brickman, P., Attitudes out of context: Harvard students go home. Undergraduate Honors Thesis, Harvard University, 1964.

Brown, R., *Explanation in Social Science*. Chicago: Aldine, 1963.

Direnzo, G. J. (ed.), *Concepts, Theory and Explanation in the Behavioral Sciences*. New York: Random House, 1966.

Janis, I. L., and B. T. King, The influence of role playing on opinion change. *Journal of Abnormal and Social Psychology*, 49, 211–218, 1954.

Mandler, G., and W. Kessen, *The Language of Psychology*. New York: John Wiley and Sons, 1959.

Sarbin, T. R., Role theory, in *The Handbook of Social Psychology* (2nd edition, G. Lindzey and E. Aronson, eds.), Vol. I. Reading, Mass.: Addison-Wesley, 1968.

## *QUESTIONS FOR DISCUSSION*

1. If a friend asks you to discuss some communication problems, how can you make certain that the two of you define "communication" similarly?
2. Train yourself to be a more careful observer of communication events. Begin a notebook and record specific nonverbal transactions, semantic barriers, or other categories of interesting variables.
3. Select one model of interpersonal communication and identify the steps in the process where your interpersonal breakdowns seem to occur most frequently. How can you modify your behavior to increase your effectiveness?
4. Select a radio or TV program, newspaper article, or movie, and analyze it using the Westley-MacLean notation system. Identify *A, B, X, X′, C,* and so on.
5. Evaluate the information theory, using the criteria suggested by Gergen.

# chapter 3

# ACQUISITION AND PERFORMANCE OF COMMUNICATION BEHAVIORS

## SECTION ONE: OVERVIEW AND PERSPECTIVE

*Objectives for Section One*

After reading the first section of this unit (Some Views in Theory and Research), you should be able to:

1. Define and distinguish between stimulus-substitution and response-substitution theories of language acquisition.
2. Describe a mediational account of language and distinguish it from behaviorist accounts.
3. Define the major shortcomings of learning-theory accounts of phonemitization, syntactic knowledge, reference as distinct from meaning, and linguistic experience.
4. Describe the concept of linguistic knowledge and relate it to the acquisition of language.
5. Describe the genetic component in verbal development and the speculations about its role in the acquisition process.
6. Summarize the over-all picture of language development from the perspective of developmental psycholinguistics.
7. Distinguish between the psycholinguistic and sociolinguistic views of verbal development.
8. Define dialect as a sociolinguistic phenomenon and give examples.
9. Define modes of speech as a sociolinguistic phenomenon and give examples.

10. Summarize speculations on how nonverbal communication may enter into the developmental picture.
11. Summarize the main classes of types of speech and their constituent types, which are cited as examples of development levels.

After reading the second section of this unit (Principles and Practices), you should be able to:

12. Describe the role and implications of the genetic component in language acquisition.
13. Describe the role and the implications of the nature of linguistic knowledge in language acquisition.
14. Describe the implications of the principle that specific communication behavior is culturally bound.
15. Describe the implications of the theory that language must vary to meet the demands of communication situations.
16. Describe the implication that classes of communication situations may reflect developmental stages.

*Frederick Williams*

# ACQUISITION AND PERFORMANCE OF COMMUNICATION BEHAVIORS

## *Introduction*

The materials in this chapter have been selected and arranged for you upon the basis of a practical premise: *If you know something of the nature of the development of communication behavior in humans, you will be in a better position not only to improve your own communication skills, but to understand and adapt to differences in the communication habits and skills of others.*

If you were to do a term paper on communication development and begin to look up entries on this topic in bibliographies or your library card catalog, you would soon agree that nearly every discipline has its own use for the word "communication," and its study might encompass anything from *language learning* by human beings to the postal system in the Soviet Union. Although there is no one well-defined body of knowledge called "the development of communication behavior," we can work from what is known about verbal development and develop its implications for our topic.

Frederick Williams *is Director of the Center for Communication Research and Professor in the School of Communication, University of Texas at Austin. His doctorate was granted in an interdisciplinary communications program at the University of Southern California in 1962. Williams has conducted language research under various grants from the National Science Foundation, the Office of Economic Opportunity, and the Office of Education. He is the author of some 40 research papers in language and communication, and recently edited* Language and Poverty: Perspectives on a Theme *(Chicago: Markham Publishing Co., 1970), a volume commissioned by the Office of Economic Opportunity.*

Our fundamental assumption in preparing this chapter is that any type of human communication behavior, whether it be speaking or listening, reading or writing, or even facial expression or gestures, is a coalescence of genetic, psychological, and social factors. Your behavior in reading this page depends, among other things, upon your being human. Because of your genetic endowment you have a linguistic capability unknown in any other species. That you know and use the language on this page is a function of the social aspect of your existence. You have learned the verbal code used by the society which shares a knowledge of the English language.

This chapter has three main sections. The first is devoted to an overview of theory pertaining to the acquisition of language, including learning theory, developmental psycholinguistics, and developmental sociolinguistics. The second section attempts to draw together from these theories some of the constituent principles pertaining to what we call *the development of communication behavior* and to explore their implications for your own communication behavior. The final section contains readings which will provide you with some first-hand examples of current thinking about the acquisition of communication behavior and the behavior itself.

## *Some Views in Theory and Research*

Views on the acquisition of language are often in partial disagreement with one another. Most of them reflect different theoretical perspectives, and really none of them can completely serve our needs in studying the acquisition of communication behavior.

After a review of some different learning theories of the acquisition of language, we will emphasize a psycholinguistic explanation of verbal development, *developmental psycholinguistics.* This approach is an attempt to explain, mainly on genetic and psychological bases, how a child is able to learn to create and understand sentences. Next, we will examine a slightly broader area, now sometimes called *developmental sociolinguistics*, which moves from the genetic and psychological aspects to a sociological theory of language learning. The sociological perspective gives us a basis for considering human differences in the use of language not only in terms of linguistic details but also in terms of how and why members of a subculture or culture use language the way they do. Eventually, sociolinguistics enables us to associate some types of language uses with the communication demands of social structures. This view comes closest to that of communication theorists.

## LEARNING THEORY AND LANGUAGE ACQUISITION

Much of what existed in textbooks until the mid-1960's about the nature of language learning drew heavily upon learning-theory accounts of the acquisition process. This stress upon learning, rather than on genetic or social factors, reflected the long-time emphasis of psychologists on the nature of human learning. Given this emphasis, it was not unusual that much of what was said about language was said within the context of different kinds of explanations of learning.

BEHAVIORIST ACCOUNTS. One of the learning-theory explanations of language was based upon *classical conditioning*, or the *stimulus substitution* theory. Basically, it proceeded as follows: Infants learn to discriminate among stimuli in their environment. Some of these stimuli are the sounds of language which occur simultaneously with the presentation of some type of object or with some action that is important to the child. Some such associations probably occur during feeding or as a parent plays with the baby. These sounds would come to be associated with the actions or things themselves, by the child. Thus, for example, the sounds that precede feeding would come to indicate to the child that feeding was about to occur. This is what is meant by *stimulus substitution*: The sounds that accompany feeding come to stimulate the same type of response as the feeding itself. As you may already know, this is the type of conditioning that the Russian physiologist, Ivan Pavlov, wrote about when he explained how a dog would eventually salivate upon hearing a bell, if beforehand the bell and meat powder had been presented simultaneously to the dog a number of times.

Although classical conditioning gives us one way of explaining how a child may associate the sounds of language with actions or things, it is not so useful in explaining how the child himself becomes an active user of language. In terms of classical conditioning, we have to look at utterances as stimulus substitutions, and this tells us little of why or how a child *creates* an utterance. An alternative theory of conditioning, called *instrumental conditioning*, or *response substitution,* has sought to explain such verbal behavior.

According to the theory of response substitution, the acquisition of language typically comes about as follows: The child begins as a random babbler. Sometimes his babbling is meaningful to a more mature user of language, and this person responds in a favorable way to the child—that is, he *reinforces*, or rewards, the child's behavior. The child senses the reinforcement and eventually learns the association between the sounds *he* made and the kind of favorable response he might receive. It is not difficult, then, to imagine that a child would eventually learn a repertoire of sounds that would obtain favorable responses for him, and that eventually these sounds could become his instruments for affecting the behavior of others.

The elaborated version of this conditioning explanation was stated in more formal terms in B. F. Skinner's well-known book *Verbal Behavior* (1957). In his theorizing, Skinner considered verbal responses of the instrumental type to be a kind of behavior whose reinforcement depended upon the behavior of a listener. Skinner called these kinds of responses *operants*, and a major share of his book *Verbal Behavior* is devoted to the classification and explanation of different types of operants. He even coined some original terms to name these categories. One type is called a "mand," a kind of verbal behavior that stems from a state of need. If you were to ask a person for food or water, for example, your verbal behavior would belong largely to the mand category. Another example of an operant is the "tact," or the association between a referent and an utterance: for example, when a child says "ball" in association with an actual ball. Skinner has created a variety of categories of operants which will presumably account for the basic kinds of associations that underlie our learning of language. He considers everyday verbal behavior as a confluence, or complex combination, of different operants.

When we consider Skinner's work, it is important to bear a few points in mind. One is that Skinner's theorizing reflects the position of a staunch behaviorist. He chooses to build the essence of his theory only upon that which he can directly observe, manipulate, and eventually predict under experimental controls. Thus it is not unusual that, at the outset of his treatise on verbal behavior, Skinner emphasizes that he is trying to develop a theory that would not have to depend upon the usual speculations concerning the nature of meaning. To Skinner, "meaning" is an elusive mentalistic concept, something we cannot observe, hence something we cannot incorporate into our theorizing. A more practical way to look at Skinner's position is that his work on verbal behavior is an attempt to say as much as possible about verbal behavior and its acquisition without running into the problem of meaning. In short, Skinner has chosen *not* to incorporate within his theory a consideration of the kinds of processes which may go on within the human mind as it interprets an utterance and formulates a verbal response.

MEDIATIONAL ACCOUNTS. Other learning theorists, however, have attempted explanations of language acquisition and verbal behavior which do incorporate various assumptions about internal processes of the mind. Often we call these "mediational" accounts of learning, because they stress the intermediate behavior which occurs within the human organism both as a response to an outside stimulus and as an initiator of overt behavior. Such behavior internally links response and stimulus, or is said to "mediate" the linkage between the two. The theorist perhaps best known for an account of this type is Charles Osgood (1963).

Osgood speculates that there are three different levels of intermediate behavior in the organism. One is a kind of *reflexive*, or motor, linkage between an organism's response to a stimulus and its own self-stimulation. An example of this is the behavior that occurs if we put our hand on a hot stove. Heat (external stimulus) is sensed by the organism (mediational response) which initiates (mediational stimulus) the reflex action of jerking your hand away (external response). The behavior in this case is largely automatic; we might even say that it is almost "wired into" the organism. A second level of intermediate behavior, the *integrational* level, comprises well-learned associations. An example of this might be the way we immediately pay attention when someone calls our name. We did not have to learn to pull our hand away from a hot stove, but we did have to learn our name and the pertinence of somebody calling it out to us—even though we have learned it so well that we do not have to "think" about it in order to respond. Finally, Osgood theorizes that there is a *representational* level of intermediate behavior, which is the kind of internal behavior that we would call "meaning."

In simple terms, Osgood's description of the representational level goes as follows: Assuming that our responses to stimuli involve a total range of behavior, both internal and external, he speculates that some increment of the internal portion of this behavior comes to represent for us the totality of the original response. This explanation is somewhat akin to what we already discussed as instrumental conditioning, or response substitution. Here, in contrast, the response substitution is that some internal portion of the total response comes to substitute for ("represent") the original total response. Osgood goes on to say that such internal responses are themselves capable of stimulating the organism to make different types of overt responses. That is, if we experience an external stimulus, we make an internal response, and this internal response in turn leads to some overt behavior on our part. For example, someone may say "apple" (external stimulus) and this stimulus would initiate a representational response (meaning) within us, as a function of our internal response to apples themselves. This meaning or representation would then serve to stimulate our overt response, which might be to salivate slightly, to ask for an apple, and so on. If, for example, someone said, "What's your name?" Osgood's theory would pose the following sequence of events between your sensing this utterance and responding to it.

"What's your name?" (external, acoustic stimulus)

Auditory sensing (internal, reflexive response translated to neural signals or internal, reflex-level stimulation)

Decoding on integration level (neural signals decoded as language forms or integrational-level response, which in turn stimulates meaning)
Representational mediation (meaning of utterance as a mediational response stimulates initial encoding of answer)
Encoding on integrational level (neural signals translated into neural commands for articulation)
Articulatory activity (articulators respond on reflex level to neural commands, result is creation of an acoustic stimulus)
"John" (external, acoustic stimulus)

Obviously, there is considerable speculation involved in such description. Some theorists, in fact, would deny that any of the steps take place as Osgood says. However, the point is that Osgood, in a mediational account, has tried to deduce what might take place. This description gives researchers a basis for raising more detailed questions about the nature of verbal behavior.

## DEVELOPMENTAL PSYCHOLINGUISTICS

As we mentioned earlier, there is a relatively new view of language acquisition which dates from the early 1960's. This approach was associated, in its early stages, with the work of the psychologist George Miller (1962, 1965), among others. As you can read at first hand in the section reprinted in this unit, Miller raised a series of objections to learning theories, on the grounds that they are inadequate to explain what we can observe everyday in language behavior. Let us consider some of these objections.

One of the best ways to be introduced to current psycholinguistic theory is to see how it was developed as a reaction to the inadequacies of learning theory explanations of language acquisition behavior.

PHONEMITIZATION. A first main criticism of learning-theory explanations of the acquisition of language is that they do not account adequately for what we call "phonemitization." Any human language is made up of basic sound categories, or the phonemes of that language. If we count the consonant, vowel, and semi-vowel sounds, we have about 33 categories of sounds, or phonemes, in the English language. It is important to realize that each phoneme is not an individual sound but is a category of sounds. For example, the /r/ phoneme in English may be articulated in such different ways as in "grown," "tree," "around," or "argosy." In each of these words you can feel your tongue in a slightly different position for each articulation of /r/. The question then is: How does a child learn that these different articulations of/r/ are all members of the same phoneme? Somehow it seems that by the time a child is one year old he has usually abstracted from his language experiences some notions of the basic sets of sound categories that underlie the language of his environment.

The implication of phonemitization is that a child does not seem to learn language as an exact repetition or imitation of what he hears. He appears, instead, to induce from these heard experiences a knowledge of the basic sound categories that comprise the language of his community. After the child becomes a mature user of that language (say, at adolescence) he will have problems with phonemes if he is to learn another language, as in learning French after English. The use of English phonemes will have become so habitual that he will carry them over into the other language: In short, he will speak French with an American accent. In contrast, the lack of phonemitization can be seen in animals who appear to replicate human utterances. If, for example, a parrot who has learned a few words of Spanish is shifted to English words, he will not have an accent. This is because he is imitating what we typically call the "surface features" of the utterance. He does not seem to induce from his training a set of categories of sounds. The human child, as we have said, appears to internalize a knowledge of the phonemes which underlie his language.

To account for the learning of a phoneme is a major challenge to explanations which assume that the child acquires only what he directly experiences of a language. The only way that learning theories can account for phonemitization is to apply the concept of reinforcement to a child's differentiation of every acoustic detail of a language. That is, they must assume that the child is such a keen listener to details, and such a keen observer of the reinforcement which follows his making use of these details, that he learns to select and use the phonemes. But this stretches learning-theory explanations far beyond the point where scientists are capable of validating them experimentally. To put it another way, we simply lack the objective data to support these extensions of learning-theory explanations.

SYNTACTIC KNOWLEDGE. Another problem is the need for a suitable explanation of the human ability to learn and use the syntactic aspect of language. It is our syntactic capabilities which allow us to combine words, each of which has its individual meaning, into a language construct that has some new type of collective meaning. For example, consider the sentence:

Bill hit the ball.

The understanding of this sentence involves not only our knowing the meanings of the individual words "ball," "hit," "the," and "Bill," but it also requires that we know that these meanings have been combined to form a statement which depends upon relations among these individual meanings. Thus we know, for example, that Bill hit the ball rather than the ball hit Bill. It is syntactic knowledge that allows us to determine the alternative meanings of sentences such as,

| *They are flying planes.* (These are nonflying planes.) | and | *They are flying planes.* (We are fueling planes.) |
|---|---|---|

or allows us to detect the difference between the underlying syntactic structure of,

*The letters were sent by mail.*
as against
*The letters were sent by me.*

Even though the latter pair are sentences with similar words, the syntactic structures which relate those words point to a major difference in the role of the word "mail" in the first sentence and that of the word "me" in the second one. Thus, like phonemitization, it seems that humans learn the underlying syntactic rules of their language. Again, one is hard pressed to explain such learning in terms of a typical learning-theory model. How is it that a child learns the underlying syntactic regularities of his language? What are the cues in the details of what he hears in speech which eventually lead to the formulation of syntactic knowledge?

REFERENCE AND MEANING. Another consideration is the problem that learning theorists have in distinguishing between what we often call "reference" as contrasted with "meaning." For example, the name "Neil Armstrong," the phrase "the first man on the moon," or the phrase "the man who first stepped on the moon in July 1969," all *refer* to the same person or thing. However, slightly different meanings are associated with each of these ways of labeling the same referent. The challenge to learning theory is to explain how we have learned these subtle distinctions in meaning when, in fact, all the labels refer to the same referent. Most learning-theory explanations which incorporate some account of meaning typically treat it as a learned association between a referent and some utterance. The problem with this explanation is that it does not provide us with a basis for explaining the differences among the meanings in the present example.

We can add to this challenge the problem of accounting for the learning of the meaning of those many words in a language that have abstract or unobservable referents. How, for example, do you learn the meaning of "democracy," or of "atom"? You might say that you have learned their meaning because of their definitions in terms of the meaning of other words —as you might do when you look up a definition in a dictionary—, but this process would require an extremely complicated learning-theory explanation. That is, the learning of the meaning of any abstract word would have to be accounted for in terms of your knowledge of the meanings of associated words that are less abstract, and perhaps the knowledge of those words in terms of words that are still less abstract, and so on. If we were to account for reinforcement and conditioning at all stages of such learning, we would be faced with a fantastically complex explanation of a simple word such as "why."

LINGUISTIC EXPERIENCE. Although learning-theory accounts can and have been extended to phonemitization, syntax, or meaning, a further argument presents an even greater challenge to learning-theory explanations of the learning of language. Consider all the different utterances of which a five-year-old child is capable. George Miller, in an article reprinted in this chapter, tells us that it has been estimated that if we try to explain the child's linguistic knowledge in terms of his experiencing all these utterances, he would have had to live for something like 1,000 times the age of our earth. Needless to say, this is an unanswerable challenge to learning-theory accounts of the acquisition of language. A child seems to learn more language, and to learn it in a shorter time, than could be explained only by learning theory. George Miller's essay is a first-hand example of the kinds of objections made about learning-theory explanations of language.

LINGUISTIC KNOWLEDGE. The contemporary view in psycholinguistics is also associated with the writing of Noam Chomsky (1965) and Eric Lenneberg (1967). Let us see how the ideas of Miller, Chomsky, and Lenneberg have coalesced into a theoretical account of language behavior and its acquisition. As you can read for yourself in the article by Miller, he has stressed that a child must be biologically equipped to learn language. To put it another way, Miller is saying that the language of the human organism appears so rich at such an early age that it would seem nearly impossible that he had learned it all. Some aspects of language must be genetically endowed. As we have already said, Miller argues that much of what we call a person's knowledge of his language does not seem to be a knowledge of the surface or immediately perceptible aspects of what is heard, but seems to be a deeper knowledge of the sound (phonology), the word (morphology), and the organization (syntax) of language. The need, then, is to characterize or explain the underlying linguistic knowledge that appears to be what a child develops when he learns a language.

Questions about the nature of the knowledge that seems to underlie our language capabilities are also to be found in the theorizing of the linguist Chomsky (1965). Chomsky has proposed that the adequate description of language is not a concentration upon its observable features in our everyday speech, but a concentration upon the kinds of knowledge we would have to have in order to create and to understand sentences.

This knowledge, according to Chomsky, can be described in terms of what he has called "generative" rules, the collection of which is called a *generative grammar*. Chomsky's writings about the nature of a generative grammar have involved the attempt to state rules which would adequately generate the grammatical sentences of a language.

GENETIC COMPONENT. Like Miller, Chomsky believes that there is a substantial genetic component in language learning and verbal behavior. In fact, Chomsky argues that a major facet of this genetic component is the human capability for inducing linguistic (i.e., grammatical) knowledge from a finite set of linguistic experiences. It is this knowledge which enables the organism to create and understand an infinite variety of sentences.

The genetic component in the acquisition of language has been substantially elaborated in the works of Lenneberg (1967). He has drawn together evidence which argues that language is an uniquely human trait, part of our biological evolution. He goes on to argue that if a genetic component is recognized, it simplifies the challenges made to learning theory in explaining language development. The learning component of an acquisition theory would therefore not be required to account for so many of the detailed aspects of a child's knowledge of language. The genetic component, in effect, makes more precise the definition of what it is a child has to learn when he learns language. Among Lenneberg's most persuasive arguments favoring a biological basis for the development of speech is his plot of the relation between indexes of brain development and different stages of language acquisition, such as when a child begins to put words together to form phrases, when his sentences are more complex, and so on.

NEW VIEWS. Given the psycholinguistic approach, contemporary theorists such as David McNeill have attempted to formulate new questions about the process of language acquisition, or what is now called *developmental psycholinguistics*. In an influential essay on this topic, McNeill (1966) focuses upon the need for: (1) a detailed definition of the human genetic endowment in language acquisition; (2) a description of the processes whereby finite linguistic experiences allow a child to induce linguistic knowledge; and (3) an explanation of how, given this linguistic knowledge, a child comes to employ it actively in his own speaking and listening.

In approaching these questions, McNeill attemps to describe some of the stages of linguistic knowledge that an English-speaking child appears to go through. Such stages, for example, characterize the kind of syntactic knowledge a child seems to be using when he says "Daddy gone" and not "gone Daddy," or "my ball" rather than "ball my." Sometimes the errors that a child makes reveal to us that he is using some underlying knowledge of the rules of his language. He might say there are "two gooses in that picture," or "I goed." These examples are also evidence that mere frequency of exposure is not a critical variable in the acquisition process. It is doubtful that the child has ever heard "gooses" or "I goed"—in fact, he has probably only heard their alternatives.

The processes of language acquisition as viewed within developmental psycholinguistics can be summarized as follows: By virtue of being human, a child is genetically endowed with a predisposition to learn a language. Much of the timetable for his verbal development is based upon maturational stages of the human organism. As a child develops according to this genetically endowed timetable, he is ready for different stages of verbal development. At each of these stages it is thought that the environment serves to trigger what the child is ready to do with language. In the main, then, the process is seen as an interaction of genetic factors and environmental factors which results in the learning of a specific language (English, French, or so on). At each stage, the development is seen as the child's capability of inducing from his linguistic experiences the specific knowledge that enables him to create and understand sentences in his specific language.

There is an increasing body of evidence that this kind of developmental timetable described above prevails throughout the world—that is, whether a child is learning standard English in a middle-class white home, French in a lower-class home, Swahili in Africa, or a Negro dialect in inner-city Chicago, he will go through certain predetermined stages of language acquisition. The extent or quality of what he develops at each of these stages may vary, however. At a particular stage children learn the combining of words into phrases, but the diversity of the combinations and their use may vary from child to child. As one turns from this species-specific account of human-language learning and attempts to account for cultural, subcultural, or even individual differences, an environmental component becomes increasingly important. At this point, it is useful to formulate a systematic view of the role of the environment in language acquisition. This view has most recently been called "developmental sociolinguistics."

## DEVELOPMENTAL SOCIOLINGUISTICS

An emerging generalization of developmental sociolinguistics is that a child's language development at any given stage, although scheduled by his maturational timetable, can vary considerably according to the demands of his social environment. Although this may seem obvious in terms of the differences between children who speak English and those who speak Bantu, it is not always so obvious when the contrasts among the speakers of the same language are considered. These contrasts have often been discussed as *dialects*—i.e., language differences among speakers who can nevertheless understand one another. You already know about regional dialects, such as exist among Southerners and Westerners in the United States. What has not been so widely discussed in an objective manner are the language differences observed in people from different social strata, or even the differences that we are capable of exhibiting as we find ourselves communicating with different people in different speech situations. These aspects of sociolinguistics are especially pertinent to a consideration of the acquisition of communication behavior.

SOCIAL DIALECTS. Some of the most insightful research into social dialects in the United States is the work of William Labov (1966) in New York City. Labov has investigated a concept that he calls "socially conditioned variation," that dialectical differences may exist among different social classes, or even in different speech situations. In one phase of his New York City research, Labov selected speakers from a number of different social strata and studied variations in how they articulated such sounds as: /r/ as in "car," "fire," "Saturday"; the vowel in such words as "bad," "bag," "cash"; the vowel in such words as "caught," "dog," "all"; "th" in such words as "thing" or "then." Labov not only found a reliable correlation between a person's social class and his pronunciation of these different sounds but also found that, if he presented brief samples of these sounds to listeners from New York City, they could reliably predict the social class of the speaker. In the same series of studies, Labov described how the features of a person's dialect would also shift as he found himself in formal or informal speaking situations (e.g., you speaking to your class or conversing with a classmate, respectively).

Another variant that has recently been systematically studied is the speech of certain ethnic groups in the United States, particularly the Black population. Beginning in the mid-1960's, the linguist William Stewart (1965) made the point that American Negro dialect was being inaccurately portrayed as substandard English rather than simply another dialect of English that might better be called nonstandard. Stewart and others (Labov, 1970; Wolfram, 1969) have developed detailed descriptions of selected features of what most linguists now call *nonstandard Negro English.*

A study by Baratz (1969) illustrates the consequences of having a child perform as a speaker of and listener to one dialect of English when another dialect has been his primary one. Baratz had white children who spoke standard English and Black children who spoke Negro nonstandard English perform a sentence-repetition task. The sentences to be repeated by the children were in two versions, one in standard English and the other in Negro nonstandard English. The children's repetitions were most like the original sentences when they were repeating sentences in the version of their primary dialect—that is, Black and white children scored approximately the same when they were repeating sentences in their own dialect. When either group of children was repeating sentences in the other group's primary dialect, many of the "errors" they made could be predicted by references to the rules of their primary dialects.

Baratz's experiment illustrated that a child's verbal performance reflects the details of his underlying grammatical knowledge. What the white children repeated intact of the Negro nonstandard English sentences were those parts that could "survive" a standard English grammatical translation. All of this is not too far removed from our earlier comment about accents and how they reveal a person's primary language when he is learning a second one. Here, however, was illustrated a carryover on all levels—the phonological, lexical, and syntactic aspects—of language. In Baratz's paper in this chapter, she discusses some of the implications of a careful consideration of the Black child's dialect by our educators. Many of these implications can be readily extended to the language of the Mexican-American child, the Appalachian child, or the American-Indian child.

One generalization that can be derived from our discussion of dialects is that dialectal differences are reliably related to social variables. We mentioned earlier that dialects are often considered in terms of regions, but we have now seen that dialect may vary with the social status or ethnicity of the speaker. Even within these variations, one's dialect may vary additionally with the formality of a speech situation.

To be frank about it, the educational system and teachers of speech or English, in particular, have too often looked upon many of the dialects of English as deficient or less-developed versions of standard English. On the contrary, there are no good arguments to indicate that any dialect of English is inherently inferior, as language, to any other. Most dialects are highly efficient in the situations in which they are spoken. It is when one version of a language is used in a situation where speakers expect another that problems arise. That is to say, the language used during an employment interview will certainly differ from that used at a football game. Neither usage is any "better" than the other. "Appropriateness" is a more realistic criterion. The linguist Fries (1940) pointed out long ago that no one truly speaks precisely what we call "standard English." It is a version of English that is mainly what grammarians have chosen to set down as a *prescription* for formal usage and for writing, rather than an objective description of the language. When we naïvely assume that this prescription for standard English should be applied to all speakers in the United States in all of the communication situations in which they may find themselves, a problem naturally arises. As we shall see in the next section of this article, the way a person typically speaks in different situations is usually a very practical consequence of what he has learned about the relation between language and the demands of different situations. In his paper in this chapter, Labov discusses how standard English can be seen within this kind of developmental context.

MODES OF SPEECH. Beyond dialect, the consideration of developmental sociolinguistics leads us to relation of forms, or expression, in language, and the functions that these forms serve. That is, *how* (form) and *why* (function) we speak can be considered in relation to the demands that are made upon us. Some researchers have called this combination of form and function "mode of speech." A practical illustration of this is reported in the recent writings of the British sociologist Basil Bernstein (1970). In a variety of studies, Bernstein and his colleagues have found that the language of the middle and working classes in Great Britain differs in function and in the forms associated with the functions. These differences have led to differences in ability to meet the demands of certain communication situations. In describing the form-function, or mode-of-speech differences, Bernstein makes a distinction between what he calls *restricted* and *elaborated* language codes.

A restricted code, according to Bernstein, is used among friends of long standing, where specialized meanings are implicitly assumed and where discourse involves maintenance and control of social relationships. A restricted code would probably be observed, for example, in conversations between husband and wife, members of a fraternity or sorority, members of a military unit, football fans discussing last Saturday's game, or in cocktail-party chatter. To an outsider, the restricted code will seem to be fragmented and stereotyped in form, particularly in syntactic alternatives, but to its users it is presumably a rich and efficient means of expression. This latter point serves to illustrate a point. A restricted code does not connote a "poor" or "underdeveloped" version of language forms or functions. It is simply a version with a range of forms which fits certain interpersonal communications.

An elaborated language code, according to Bernstein, makes meaning explicit to its users. It is not dependent upon the assumption of implicit meanings being held by its users; it "spells out" the message explicitly. To an outsider, an elaborated code will appear to involve a rich array of language forms, particularly a marked variety of complex syntactic structures. An elaborated code would be typically found in scientific reports, in the language used to talk about abstract concepts, and in the language of instruction in the schools.

Incorporated in Bernstein's definitions of restricted and elaborated language codes are the kinds of context within which these codes are typically observed. The context for the restricted code would be everyday situations in which people know one another fairly well or know about one another on the basis of social-role identification (e.g., a shopkeeper and a customer). Additionally, what they know about one another can be based upon their joint experiences with the topic immediately under discussion. It is because of shared knowledge or experience that the actual speech which they exchange may be abbreviated or unelaborated. This is somewhat like the situation where one person says, "Do you remember the one about the traveling salesman?" and everybody breaks out laughing and the joke is never told because they knew it already. The elaborated-code situation, on the other hand, does not incorporate so many assumptions of shared knowledge. Thus, what is said must be explicit and must be elaborated, lest communication be incomplete. This is not the language of everyday conversation, but more like the language we use when we want to explain something in detail, the language of description or explanation. Broadly, then, the use of restricted or elaborated language codes is correlated with differences in social situations and in the kinds of communication demands imposed by the situations. In view of these distinctions, it is not unreasonable to consider that some of the differences which we observe in the verbal development of children are a function of differences in the kinds of speech or communication contexts typically encountered by the child. (Bernstein's own description of the restricted and elaborated codes constitutes one of the readings in this chapter.)

An example of differences in contexts of language development is reported in the research of Robert Hess and Virginia Shipman (1968). Briefly, they investigated what they called "maternal language behavior" as a key variable in the shaping of a child's language or communication styles. In some of their research, Hess and Shipman made the differentiation between a mother who tends to talk to her child mostly in terms of commands, or the imperative mode, as contrasted with a mother who, although she may give commands to her child, often explains the reason or the consequences of the commands. These two styles of maternal language almost directly fit within Bernstein's distinction between restricted and elaborated codes. The direct imperative style of language requires only a limited range of linguistic forms and focuses upon a single function; the elaborated code is the one used by the mother who explains her commands, since explanation requires a greater range of complex linguistic forms than command and serves an additional function as well. This mother may even invite a verbal response or counterexplanation from her child, and thus prompt a continued verbal exchange. Although some researchers have questioned the validity of Hess and Shipman's observations, the concept of maternal-language style illustrates for us the kinds of differences in developmental contexts children may experience in their acquisitional years.

NONVERBAL COMMUNICATION. Most of what we have discussed

thus far has been restricted to linguistic or verbal facets of development—that is, to vocalized expressions which have some arbitrary associations with referents or meanings and which are shared by the members of a given speech community. We now consider expressions which are not vocalized but have the form of facial expressions or gestures, and which may or may not have arbitrarily assigned references or meanings. Often such expressions are studied under the heading of "nonverbal communication." If we are to explore the boundaries of a developmental sociolinguistic theory, or the larger boundaries of communication development, nonverbal expression must somehow be incorporated.

Contemporary research (especially Ekman, 1964, and Williams and Tolch, 1965) yields strong evidence that many facial expressions have general meaning. Some theorists (e.g., Schlosberg, 1954) have speculated that these expressions have their basic forms and origins in affective (emotional) states of the organism. Thus, for example, we can differentiate between such basic expressive states as surprise and passivity or satisfaction and dissatisfaction. Whether we learn the relation between someone looking a certain way and knowing that he is angry or whether this is an association we know innately is a question for research. Nor has it been ascertained at what age the human can begin to know such associations, although we know that infants as young as a few months may respond differentially to an adult's smile or scowl.

Anyone who undertakes research with young children will inevitably encounter a child's preferences for gesturing over vocalizing answers to questions. Typically, a question to a three-year-old child of which of two toys (one familiar, the other strange) belongs to him will result in his pointing by way of answer. If vocalization occurs, it will typically complement the gesture (e.g., "That") rather than serve as an independent expression of the answer. One line of explanation is that the younger a child is, the more he will depend upon the physical context itself as a part of his communication; presumably, gesturing fits efficiently into this bias. Vocalization at this stage typically complements gesturing. However, when communication demands are sufficiently complex and context cannot be made a part of an answer, a child must rely upon language to communicate his response. Subsequently, gestures come to complement words rather than vice-versa, and eventually these gestures may develop into the conventional forms which one learns as the effective bodily and visual aspects of speaking in his society. As this last statement implies, as a child matures in a given society, his nonverbal forms of communication become increasingly culture-bound.

Although nonverbal communication receives nowhere the research attention it deserves, there are studies of methods for describing nonverbal symbols (Birdwhistell, 1952), nonverbal communication in psychiatric interviews (Sainsbury, 1955), and theories of nonverbal communication in cultures as a whole (Hall, 1959).

## TOWARD A THEORY OF THE DEVELOPMENT OF THE ABILITY TO COMMUNICATE

Where do we stand in our task of discussing the implications of the nature of learning to communicate? One thing we have assumed is that a basic capability for verbal development underlies its unfolding; we referred to this capability in terms of developmental psycholinguistics. Second, we have assumed that as the ability to speak develops in the organism, it develops to serve the communicative demands of a given social structure. This we have examined as developmental sociolinguistics.

Recently, the anthropologist Dell Hymes (in press) has proposed a concept which integrates psycholinguistic and sociolinguistic components of development into what he calls *communicative competence*. An individual's communicative competence refers to what he must be able to do communicatively in order to function as a member of a given speech community. Hymes has developed this concept as part of his theorizing about how modes of speech serve in the functioning of social structures. Along with Bernstein (1970), Hymes has also argued that as a child learns to meet the communicative demands of his community, he is internalizing his future role in that community. Eventually, when he exercises this role he will be perpetuating some of the characteristics of his community. This topic is treated in the selection from Hymes in this chapter.

What kinds of stages might characterize the verbal development of a child? Table 1 is an attempt to outline one answer to this question. Here, three classes of communication situations are proposed. In the first class are types of *context-centered* speech, where what is said is most relevant only within that particular situation. Three types of context-centered speech—*impulsive, contactive,* and *conversative*—are defined, and all are considered to be situations in which Bernstein's restricted conversational code might be employed. The next main class of situation—*sender-receiver* centered—is considered to be constrained most by the sender or receiver who is part of the topic of discourse. What is said refers concretely to the speaker's own experiences or consists of directions or commands he is giving the receiver. The third class of situation is *topic-centered.* Discourse focuses on some topic other than the sender or receiver's individual behavior or experiences and, in particular, on topics which can only be defined verbally, e.g., "democracy." This class of speech is akin to Bernstein's elaborated code.

Each of these main classes of speech is also considered (see Table 1) in relation to an accompanying set of function-form characteristics of language. Context-centered speech depends much upon context as a part of the message. Much can be expressed with few words, and sometimes nonverbal expressions or gestures may suffice. Sender-receiver centered speech usually requires that words at least be combined into minimal syntactic fragments. Topic-centered discourse may require the maximal use of lexical and syntactic alternatives and attention to such higher-level constructions as the organization of the over-all message.

The foregoing classes of speech situations, thought to be relatively general in most cultures, could represent the kinds of social situations within which the developing child finds the demand for communication imposed upon him. In fact, just as the classes represent increasing demands upon the use of language forms, they also to some degree represent the stages of communicative competency that are known to develop in a child, although some children become more facile than others. We could say that these are the types of situations within which a child would have to learn to meet communicative demands if he is to function within the norms of his speech community.

## *Principles and Practices*

At the outset of this unit we said that you, as a speaker and listener, could improve your own skills by having some idea about the nature of the development of the ability to communicate. In this section we will summarize some principles and try to point out their implications for you in speech-communication practice.

### SELECTED PRINCIPLES

1. *There is a major genetic component in the acquisition of language.* By virtue of biological endowment, humans are predisposed to learn language. Talking, like walking, develops within a maturational timetable. That we communicate the way we do is, at bottom, a genetic trait. The genetic component allows the human to induce, from a finite number of experiences, a knowledge of language that makes him capable of creating and understanding an infinite variety of messages.

A practical aspect of this principle is that if we are to use instructional schemes to facilitate the improvement of individual communication —the learning of new languages, speech "improvement," and so on—then we need to take into account where a person falls in the maturational timetable. We can make assumptions that stages of development will be biologically scheduled (in the absence of pathology), but that the details of what develops at each stage will be mainly a function of experience. Thus, the child of 12 to 48 months might be a far superior learner of the phonemes of a language than a child of 6 years, and the older child may be within the age range where the potential syntactic learning is at a peak.

Such considerations are equally important for the college student. A college student is well into linguistic maturity—perhaps up to 90 per

TABLE 1

| *Context-centered* | Function | Form | Examples |
|---|---|---|---|
| (impulsive) | Utterance bound to contextual factors. Receiver and topic are irrelevant. | Typically very minimal forms, even those which are vocal and nonverbal (e.g., a scream). Single words, no syntactic requirements. Many forms could be expressed nonvocally through facial and gestural expressions. | "Ouch," "wow," "oh," "ah," screaming, laughter, crying, swearing, etc. |
| (contactive) | Utterances reflect upon the sender's attempt to initiate, evaluate, or maintain linkage with a receiver or receivers. Topic is irrelevant. | Minimal word forms, even where meaning is insignificant. Minimal phrase constructs, stereotyped in structure, syntactic distinctions insignificant. Some forms could be expressed nonverbally (hand waving). | "Hello," "hey," "John?" "waiter!" "How do you do?" "you know," "do you hear me?" |
| (conversative) | Utterances reinforce and maintain linkage with receiver. Topic may be relevant, but is seen more in the context of the discourse than in the speech of an individual. | Minimal word forms and syntactic fragments allowable, but can range to relatively developed sequences. Typically complemented by nonverbal forms. | Cocktail party chatter, language exchanged between persons just introduced, elaborated greetings and farewells, simple yes-no answers, names, etc. |

TABLE 1 (continued)

| | | | |
|---|---|---|---|
| *Sender-receiver centered* | Topic is relevant as the object of discourse, but elaboration, if any, is through reference to concrete and particular experiences. Description reveals such experience from a sender-centered perspective, whereas direction prescribes an experience for the receiver's actions. | Minimal word forms and syntactic fragments are allowable for naming or commands, but syntactic elaboration is required to verbally symbolize the structure of the experience. Illustrative gesturing may serve as rudimentary forms or to compliment verbal elaborations. Elaboration depends upon expansion of predicate phrase structures. | Recounting some event which has been experienced; delineating in verbal terms a "picture" of something; telling a person how to play a game, step-by-step; giving instructions to a traveller; commanding some action. |
| *Topic-centered* | Topic is explicitly relevant as the object of discourse, and such discourse may be adapted to the perceptions of the receiver, including distinctions among either individual receivers or groups of receivers. Explicit topical elaboration reaches to levels which can only be obtained through verbal symbolism. Primarily a topical mode. | Demands are imposed for maximal lexical and syntactic alternatives. The structure of discourse is achieved through syntactic and compositional features which are organizing devices in themselves and are not dependent upon the reference to concrete experience. Nonverbal forms are minimally relevant at this level. | Interpretation, or explaining one's understanding of the meaning of some event which has been experienced, or of some concept or idea (e.g., what "freedom" means). Narration, of developing a topic in story form (e.g., retelling the story of a movie or TV show). Persuasion, or inducing direction in thinking or behavior by overt verbal appeal (e.g., a mother reasoning with her child). |

Adapted from Frederick Williams and Rita C. Naremore, "On the Functional Analysis of Social Class Differences in Modes of Speech," *Speech Monographs*, XXXVI (1969), 98. Reprinted by permission of authors and publisher.

cent of his linguistic knowledge has been acquired. He is already a poor learner of new language sounds (and thus very prone to speak them with an accent); his learning of new words may be restricted to specialized vocabulary obtained from dictionaries, books, or direct instruction; his syntactic learning may be on a high level—learning to write more complex sentences. As compared with the two-year-old, learning an entirely new language is for this person comparable to running the 100-yard dash at the age of 80. He will have to work at it (and may never quite succeed!). On the other hand, the college student may be starting to realize the vast contrasts in different types of communication situations and the necessity of adapting to their different demands. Effective participation in these different situations requires some modifications or elaborations of existing linguistic habits. Here, as in sharpening his writing or speaking skills, linguistic maturity is to his advantage.

2. *The acquired knowledge of a language is not in terms of utterances (or sentences) themselves but is a kind of underlying knowledge (or set of rules or regularities) which provides for the creation and interpretation of utterances.* Traditional explanations of language acquisition which are based upon learning theory cannot adequately account for our linguistic capabilities. Communication and language experiences provide the details from which we induce the linguistic and communication rules of our community.

An important practical implication is that if instruction in language is to parallel the natural development of the ability to learn it, then we need to present the learner with guided practical experiences from which he can induce the underlying rules—or perhaps we can teach him the rules themselves. In other words, rote exercise in the pronunciation of isolated sounds, the memorization of individual words, or the diagramming of sentence structures may not be the most efficient strategies for language instruction. Guided experiences may be most effective when the communication context and the function of language in it are taught along with the language forms. Some attempts are already underway to teach students the "new grammar" based on the underlying rules of a language (Jacobs and Rosenbaum, 1968). Although the college student is past linguistic maturity, he might benefit if he considers that every communication situation offers experiences from which to induce linguistic knowledge. Situations naturally offer information about both linguistic form and function. A sensitivity to these facets of social life should pay dividends in developing a student's own repertoire.

3. *Specific language and habits of communication are culturally bounded.* In short, although all humans develop language, the specific language and its uses are a function of social factors. Differences exist not only among language communities but, within such communities, among

different dialect groups. Dialectical differences are often related to social status, ethnicity and, within one person, even to the situation. All such differences are closely correlated with the demands of communication situations.

This has a practical implication. *People are different*, and the language differences we observe are a natural result of cultural differences in the developmental process. Social psychologists (e.g., Lambert, 1967) have found that, when a person lives in a relatively closed culture and hence lacks knowledge of the details of people and cultures other than his own, his attitudes will be ethnocentric—that is, he will view his own culture as superior and others as inferior. This same ethnocentricity is found particularly with regard to language, and it is reflected when persons talk about *sub*standard English rather than *non*standard English dialects. Elsewhere (Williams, 1970), we have argued that part of the aim in communication instruction should be to create an awareness in students of how and why dialects exist. You should capitalize upon this awareness in communicating with persons of other regions, social groups, and ethnicities. Unfortunately, more college students than teachers in this generation seem to have such an awareness.

4. *Linguistic form and function vary together according to the demands of different communication situations.* The social aspect of language is a practical matter; people typically talk the way they do because effectiveness in a given situation demands it. *Communicative competence* can be considered as the kind of knowledge of form-function that allows one to create and understand utterances in the light of the demands of specific communication situations.

It may be that college classes in English composition stress form at the expense of function. Speech classes stress function at the expense of form. Both, unfortunately, seem to concentrate their exercises within a generalized communication context that is relatively formal and in which only standard English is used. Such contexts represent a small share of the communication situations of our society; and further, they do not provide a picture of how form and function vary together in different contexts. As a college student you may be left to draw this over-all picture on your own. Putting on a tie the day of your speech, standing up straight, using 3-x-5 note cards, looking your audience in the eye, and employing only complete sentences (to borrow from the advice of many speech texts) is not the path to total communicative competence, although it *is* the thing to do in a small share of the communication situations in our society. Communicative competence is the ability to know the differences in communication situations, their demands, and the relation of linguistic form and function which meets those demands.

5. *The linguistic stages of the acquisition of the ability to communi-*

*cate may be ordered according to classes of communication situations.* Although we can describe how a child's language seems to develop, the functions that his language fulfills, or the kinds of situations he may find himself communicating in, all three facets can be combined and ordered, like form and function, in relation to the demands of different classes of communication situations. Such stages may then provide us with a development sequence.

Although the classes of communication situations may have a developmental sequence, the mature user of language will find himself exercising all the types of speech found within them. A sensitivity to the distinctions among these classes should benefit your performance within them. Such sensitivity is also beneficial in the understanding of the different strategies persons of different ages, social class, or ethnicity employ in given communication situations. If your ability to communicate must lie mainly in topic-centered discourse, knowing the form-function characteristics of this class should facilitate your efforts at improvement. That is, the message should transcend the communication context; meaning must be made explicit; maximal demands will be made upon lexical and syntactic repertoires; and so on.

## SOME FURTHER CONSIDERATIONS

It should be obvious there is much more to be said about the learning of language and communication behavior. Moreover, there are some hazards in what we have already said.

For one thing, research and theory in psycholinguistics and sociolinguistics are constantly being updated. The materials which we have discussed should provide you with accurate ideas of the kinds of questions asked in the two areas, but the answers to these questions are constantly being elaborated and refined.

More needs to be known about the development of nonverbal communication behavior, which plays a major role in our everyday lives and which may fit critically within the process learning to communicate. (It was noted in Table 1 that as speech is more context-bound, nonverbal forms of communication become more capable of meeting communicative demands.) Currently, we need research and theorizing in the development of nonverbal communication. The little research that has been done has been done largely apart from the ideas about language acquisition introduced in this chapter.

Finally, we will never have a complete picture of communication acquisition in the modern child until we know more about the role of the media in this process. More and more, children are reared in environments which are rich, perhaps overly rich, in communication experiences. Television, radio, motion pictures, recordings, print, and the telephone serve up a multiplicity of experiences to the young child. Considering the magnitude of the questions about the effect of these experiences on learning to communicate, even upon the future of man, it is odd that more people are not trying to answer them.

## *REFERENCES*

Baratz, Joan C. Teaching reading in an urban Negro school system. In Joan C. Baratz and R. W. Shuy (Eds.), *Teaching black children to read.* Washington, D.C.: Center for Applied Linguistics, 1969. Also reprinted in F. Williams (Ed.), *Language and poverty: Perspectives on a theme.* Chicago: Markham Publishing Co., 1970.

Bernstein, B. A sociolinguistic approach to socialization: with some reference to educability. In F. Williams (Ed.), *Language and poverty: Perspectives on a theme.* Chicago: Markham Publishing Co., 1970.

Birdwhistell, R. L. *Introduction to kinesics.* Washington, D.C.: U. S. Dept. of State, Foreign Service Institute, 1952.

Chomsky, N. *Aspects of the theory of syntax.* Cambridge, Mass.: M.I.T. Press, 1965.

Ekman, P. Body positions, facial expressions and verbal behavior during interviews. *Journal of Abnormal and Social Psychology,* 1964, 68, 295–301.

Fries, C. C. *American English grammar.* New York: Appleton-Century-Crofts, 1940.

Hall, E. T. *The silent language.* Garden City, N.Y.: Doubleday & Company, Inc., 1959.

Hymes, D. H. On communicative competence. In Renira Huxley and Elisabeth Ingram (Eds.), *Mechanisms in language development.* London: Center for Advanced Study in the Developmental Sciences, in press.

Jacobs, R. A. and Rosenbaum, P. S. *English transformational grammar.* Waltham, Mass.: Blaisdell Publishing Co., 1968.

Labov, W. *The social stratification of English in New York City.* Washington, D.C.: Center for Applied Linguistics, 1966.

________, *The study of nonstandard English.* Champaign, Ill.: National Council of Teachers of English, 1970.

Lambert, W. E. A social psychology of bilingualism. *Journal of Social Issues,* 1967, 23, 91–109.

Lenneberg, E. H. *Biological foundations of language.* New York: John Wiley & Sons, Inc., 1967.

McNeill, D. Developmental psycholinguistics. In F. Smith and G. A. Miller (Eds.), *The genesis of language.* Cambridge, Mass.: M.I.T. Press, 1966.

Miller, G. A. Some psychological studies of grammar. *American Psychologist,* 1962, 17, 764–782.

________, Some preliminaries to psycholinguistics. *American Psychologist,* 1965, 20, 15–20.

Osgood, C. E. On understanding and creating sentences. *American Psychologist,* 1963, 18, 735–751.

Sainsbury, P. Gestural movement during psychiatric interview. *Psychosomatic Medicine,* 1955, 17, 458–469.

Schlosberg, H. Three dimensions of emotion. *Psychological Review*, 1954, 61, 81–88.

Skinner, B. F. *Verbal behavior.* New York: Appleton-Century-Crofts, 1957.

Stewart, W. A. Urban Negro Speech: Sociolinguistic factors affecting English teaching. In R. W. Shuy (Ed.), *Social dialects and language learning.* Washington, D.C.: Center for Applied Linguistics, 1965.

Williams, F. Language, attitude and social change. In F. Williams (Ed.), *Language and poverty: Perspectives on a theme.* Chicago: Markham Publishing Co., 1970.

——— and Naremore, R. C. On the functional analysis of social class differences in modes of speech. *Speech Monographs*, 1969, 36, 77–102.

Williams, F. and Tolch, J. Communication by facial expression. *Journal of Communication*, 1965, 15, 17–27.

Wolfram, W. A. *A sociolinguistic description of Detroit Negro speech.* Washington, D.C.: Center for Applied Linguistics, 1969.

## SECTION TWO: READINGS

### *Introduction and Objectives for Reading One: "Some Preliminaries to Psycholinguistics"*

This essay by George Miller summarizes many of the objections that psychologists have had to learning-theory accounts of language acquisition. At the same time, it introduces some of the current research concerns of the psycholinguists.

After reading this paper you should be able to restate and describe Miller's seven theoretical considerations for psycholinguistic research.

George A. Miller

## *SOME PRELIMINARIES TO PSYCHOLINGUISTICS*[1]

The success of behavior theory in describing certain relatively simple correlations between stimulation and response has encouraged experimental psychologists to extend and test their theories in more complicated situations. The most challenging and potentially the most important of these extensions, of course, is into the realm of linguistic behavior. Consequently, in recent years we have seen several attempts to characterize human language in terms derived from behavioristic investigations of conditioning and learning in animals. These proposals are well known, so I will make no attempt to summarize them here. I will merely say that, in my opinion, their results thus far have been disappointing.

If one begins the study of a new realm of behavior armed with nothing but hypotheses and generalizations based on experience in some quite different area, one's theoretical preconceptions can be badly misleading. Trivial features may be unduly emphasized, while crucially important aspects may be postponed, neglected, or even overlooked entirely. These hazards are particularly dangerous when we generalize across species, or from nonverbal to verbal behavior.

The impulse to broaden the range of phenomena to which our concepts can be applied is commendable. But when this enthusiasm is not guided by a valid conception of the new phenomena to be explained, much intelligent enterprise can end in frustration and discouragement. Human language is a subtle and complex thing; there are many aspects that, if not actually unique, are at least highly distinctive of our species, and whose nature could scarcely be suspected, much less extrapolated from the analysis of nonverbal behavior.

It was with such thoughts in mind that I decided to take this opportunity to summarize briefly seven aspects of human language that should be clearly understood by any psychologist who plans to embark on explanatory ventures in psycholinguistics. The ideas are familiar to most people working in the field, who could no doubt easily double or treble their number. Nevertheless, the seven I have in mind are, in my opinion, important enough to bear repeating and as yet their importance does not seem to have been generally recognized by other psychologists.

Without further apologies, therefore, let me begin my catalogue of preliminary admonitions to anyone contemplating language as a potential subject for his psychological ratiocinations.

[1]This paper is based on research supported in part by funds granted by the Advanced Research Projects Agency, Department of Defense, Contract No. SD-187; by Public Health Service Research Grant No. MH-08083 from the National Institutes of Health; by National Science Foundation, Contract No. GS-192; and by Carnegie Corporation of New York Grant No. 8-3004, to the Center for Cognitive Studies, Harvard University.

From George A. Miller, "Some Preliminaries to Psycholinguistics," *American Psychologist*, XX (1965), 15–20. Copyright (1965) by the American Psychological Association, and reproduced by permission.

## A Point of View

It is probably safe to say that no two utterances are identical in their physical (acoustic and physiological) characteristics. Nevertheless, we regularly treat them as if they were. For example, we ask a subject to repeat something we say, and we count his response as correct even though it would be a simple matter to demonstrate that there were many physical differences between his vocal response and the vocal stimulus we presented to him. Obviously, not all physical aspects of speech are significant for vocal communication.

The situation is more complicated than that, however. There are also many examples—homophones being the most obvious—where stimuli that are physically identical can have different significance. Not only are physically different utterances treated identically, but physically identical utterances can be treated differently. It may often happen that the difference in significance between two utterances cannot be found in any difference of a physical nature, but can only be appreciated on the basis of psychological factors underlying the physical signal.

The problem of identifying significant features of speech is complicated further by the fact that some physical features are highly predictable in nearly all speakers, yet have no communicative significance. For example, when a plosive consonant occurs initially, as in the word *pen,* American speakers pronounce it with aspiration; a puff of air accompanies the *p* (which you can feel if you will pronounce *pen* holding the back of your hand close to your lips). When *p* occurs as a noninitial member of a consonant cluster, however, as in *spend*, this puff of air is reduced or absent. The same phoneme is aspirated in one position and unaspirated in the other. This physical feature, which is quite reliable in American speech, has no communicative significance, by which I mean that the rare person who does not conform is perfectly intelligible and suffers no handicap in communicating with his friends. Facts such as these, which are well known to linguists, pose interesting problems for psychologists who approach the acquisition of language in terms of laboratory experiments on discrimination learning.

In order to discuss even the simplest problems in speech production and speech perception, it is necessary to be able to distinguish significant from nonsignificant aspects of speech. And there is no simple way to draw this distinction in terms of the physical parameters of the speech signal itself. Almost immediately, therefore, we are forced to consider aspects of language that extend beyond the acoustic or physiological properties of speech, that is to say, beyond the objective properties of "the stimulus."

Since the concept of significance is central and unavoidable, it is important to notice that it has two very different senses, which for convenience, I shall call "reference" and "meaning."

For example, in most contexts we can substitute the phrase, "the first President of the United States" for "George Washington," since both of these utterances refer to the same historical figure. At least since Frege's time, however, it has been customary to assume that such phrases differ in meaning even though their referent is the same. Otherwise, there would be no point to such assertions of identity as "George Washington was the first President of the United States." If meaning and reference were identical, such an assertion would be as empty as "George Washington was George Washington." Since "George Washington was the first President of the United States" is not a pointless assertion, there must be some difference between the significance of the same "George Washington" and of the phrase "the first President of the United States," and, since this difference in significance is not a difference of referent, it must be a difference in something else—something else that, for want of a better name, we call its meaning.

This distinction between reference and meaning becomes particularly clear when we consider whole utterances. An utterance can be significant even though it might be extremely difficult to find anything it referred to in the sense that "table" refers to four-legged, flat-topped piece of furniture, etc. Sentences are meaningful, but their meaning cannot be given by their referent, for they may have none.

Of course, one might argue that psycholinguists should confine their attention to the significance of isolated words and avoid the complexities of sentences altogether. Such an approach would be marvelously convenient if it would work, but it would work only if words were autonomous units that combined in a particularly simple way. If the meaning of a sentence could in some sense be regarded as the weighted sum of the meanings of the words that comprise it, then once we knew how to characterize the meanings of individual words, it would be a simple matter to determine the meaning of any combination of words. Unfortunately, however, language is not so simple; a Venetian blind is not the same as a blind Venetian.

Perhaps the most obvious thing we can say about the significance of a sentence is that it is not given as the linear sum of the significance of the words that comprise it. The pen in "fountain pen" and the pen in "play pen" are very different pens, even though they are phonologically and orthographically identical. The words in a sentence interact.

In isolation most words can have many different meanings; which meaning they take in a particular sentence will depend on the context in which they occur. That is to say, their meaning will depend both on the other words and on their grammatical role in the sentence. The meanings to be assigned to word combinations can be characterized in an orderly way, of course, but not by some simple rule for linear addition. What is required is an elaborate description of the various ways in which words can interact in combination.

As soon as we begin to look carefully at the relations among words in sentences, it becomes obvious that their interactions depend on the way they are grouped. For example, in sentences like, "They are hunting dogs," one meaning results if we group "are hunting" together as the verb, but another meaning results if we group "hunting dogs" together as a noun phrase. We cannot assign meanings to words in a sentence without knowing how the words are grouped, which implies that we must take into account the syntactic structure of the sentence.

Moreover, when we consider the psychology of the sentence, the problem of productivity becomes unavoidable. There is no limit to the number of different sentences that can be produced in English by combining words in various grammatical fashions, which means that it is impossible to describe English by simply listing all its grammatical sentences. This fairly obvious fact has several important implications. It means that the sentences of English must be described in terms of *rules* that can generate them.

For psychologists, the implication of this generative approach to language is that we must consider hypothetical constructs capable of combining verbal elements into grammatical sentences, and in order to account for our ability to deal with an unlimited variety of possible sentences, these hypothetical constructs must have the character of linguistic rules.

Language is the prime example of rule-governed behavior, and there are several types of rules to consider. Not only must we consider syntactic rules for generating and grouping words in sentences; we must also consider semantic rules for interpreting word combinations. Perhaps we may even need pragmatic rules to characterize our unlimited variety of belief systems. Only on the assumption that a language user knows a generative system of rules for producing and interpreting sentences can we hope to account for the unlimited combinatorial productivity of natural languages.

Rules are not laws, however. They can be broken, and in ordinary conversation they frequently are. Still, even when we break them, we usually are capable of recognizing (under appropriate conditions) that we have made a mistake; from this fact we infer that the rules are known implicitly, even though they cannot be stated explicitly.

A description of the rules we know when we know a language is different from a description of the psychological mechanisms involved in our use of those rules. It is important, therefore, to distinguish here, as elsewhere, between knowledge and performance; the psycholinguist's task is to propose and test performance models for a language user, but he must rely on the linguist to give him a precise specification of what it is a language user is trying to use.

Finally, it is important to remember that there is a large innate component to our language-using ability. Not just any self-consistent set of rules that we might be able to invent for communicative purposes could serve as a natural language. All human societies possess language, and all of these languages have features in common—features that are called "language universals," but are in fact prelinguistic in character. It is difficult to imagine how children could acquire language so rapidly from parents who understand it so poorly unless they were already tuned by evolution to select just those aspects that are universally significant. There is, in short, a large biological component that shapes our human languages.

These are the seven ideas I wished to call to your attention. Let me recapitulate them in order, this time attempting to say what I believe their implications to be for psycholinguistic research.

## *Some Implications for Research*

*1. Not all physical features of speech are significant for vocal communication, and not all significant features of speech have a physical representation.* I take this to imply that the perception of speech involves grouping and interpreting its elements and so cannot be simply predicted from studies of our ability to discriminate among arbitrary acoustic stimuli. Such studies can be useful only in conjunction with linguistic information as to which distinctions are significant. Linguists seem generally agreed that the absolute physical characteristics of a particular phone are less important than the binary contrasts into which it enters in a given language. It is noteworthy that after many decades of acoustic phonetics, we are still uncertain as to how to specify all the physical dimensions of the significant features of speech, particularly those that depend on syntactic or semantic aspects of the utterance.

*2. The meaning of an utterance should not be confused with its reference.* I take this to imply that the acquisition of meaning cannot be identified with the simple acquisition of a conditioned vocalization in the presence of a particular environmental stimulus. It may be possible to talk about reference in terms of conditioning, but meaning is a much more complicated phenomenon that depends on the relations of a symbol to other symbols in the language.

*3. The meaning of an utterance is not a linear sum of the meanings of the words that comprise it.* I take this to imply that studies of the meanings of isolated words are of limited value, and that attempts to predict the meaning of word compounds by weighted averages of the meanings of their components—an analogy with the laws of color mixture—cannot be successful in general. In Gestalt terminology, the whole is greater than (or at least, different from) the sum of its parts.

*4. The syntactic structure of a sentence imposes groupings that govern the interactions between the meanings of the words in that sentence.* I take this to imply that sentences are hierarchically organized, and that simple theories phrased in terms of chaining successive responses cannot provide an adequate account of linguistic behavior. Exactly how concepts are combined to produce organized groupings of linguistic elements that can be uttered and understood is a central problem for psycholinguistics.

5. *There is no limit to the number of sentences or the number of meanings that can be expressed.* I take this to imply that our knowledge of a language must be described in terms of a system of semantic and syntactic rules adequate to generate the infinite number of admissible utterances. Since the variety of admissible word combinations is so great, no child could learn them all. Instead of learning specific combinations of words, he learns the *rules* for generating admissible combinations. If knowledge of these rules is to be described in our performance models as the language user's "habits," it is necessary to keep in mind that they are generative habits of a more hypothetical and less abstract nature than have generally been studied in animal learning experiments.

6. *A description of a language and a description of a language user must be kept distinct.* I take this to imply that psycholinguists should try to formulate performance models that will incorporate, in addition to a generative knowledge of the rules, hypothetical information-storage and information-processing components that can simulate the actual behavior of language users. In general, limitations of short-term memory seem to impose the most severe constraints on our capacity to follow our own rules.

7. *There is a large biological component to the human capacity for articulate speech.* I take this to imply that attempts to teach other animals to speak a human language are doomed to failure. As Lenneberg has emphasized, the ability to acquire and use a human language does not depend on being intelligent or having a large brain. It depends on being human.

In science, at least half the battle is won when we start to ask the right questions. It is my belief that an understanding of these seven general propositions and their implications can help to guide us toward the right questions and might even forestall ill-considered forays into psycholinguistics by psychologists armed only with theories and techniques developed for the study of nonverbal behavior.

## *A Critique*

I have now stated twice my seven preliminary admonitions. In order to make sure that I am being clear, I want to repeat it all once more, this time in the form of a critical analysis of the way many experimental psychologists write about language in the context of current learning theory.

For the purposes of exposition, I have chosen a sentence that is part of the introduction to the topic of language in a well-known and widely used textbook on the psychology of learning. After remarking that, "language seems to develop in the same way as other instrumental acts," the author says:

> Certain combinations of words and intonations of voice are strengthened through reward and are gradually made to occur in appropriate situations by the process of discrimination learning.

This, I believe is fairly representative of what can be found in many other texts. I have chosen it, not because I bear any malice toward the author, but simply because I think that all seven of my admonitions are ignored in only 27 words. Let me spell them out one by one.

First, since infants are not born with a preconception of what words are, they could hardly be expected to begin acquiring language by uttering combinations of words. Perhaps the author was not thinking of infants when he wrote this sentence. If he had been, he would probably have written instead that, "Certain combinations of *sounds* and intonations of voice are strengthened through reward and made to occur by the process of discrimination learning." In either case, however, he ignores my first admonition that not all physical features of speech are significant and not all significant features are physical.

A child does not begin with sounds or words and learn to combine them. Rather, he begins by learning which features are significant, and progressively differentiates his utterances as he learns. It is conceivable, though not necessary, that he might acquire those significant distinctions that have some physical basis "by the process of discrimination learning," but it would require an extensive revision of what we ordinarily mean by discrimination learning in order to explain how he acquires significant distinctions that are not represented in the physical signal, or why he acquires those features (such as aspiration only on initial plosives) that are not significant and are not systematically rewarded or extinguished.

Second, as I have already admitted (too generously, perhaps), it is possible to argue that a referential relation might be established between a visual input and a vocalization "by the process of discrimination learning." I deny, however, that it is reasonable to speak of acquiring meaning in this way.

Exactly what should be included in the meaning of a word is open to debate, but any interpretation will have to say something about the relation of this word's meaning to the meanings of other words and to the contexts in which it occurs—and these are complicated, systemic interrelations requiring a great deal more cognitive machinery than is necessary for simple discrimination. Since the author says specifically that *words* are acquired by discrimination learning, and since words have meaning as well as reference, I can only assume that he has ignored my admonition not to confuse reference and meaning. Perhaps a more accurate interpretation, suggested by the phrase "occur in appropriate situations," would be that he has not really confused reference and meaning, but has simply ignored meaning entirely. In either case, however, it will not do as a basis for psycholinguistics.

There is unfortunate ambiguity in the phrase, "Certain combinations of words and intonations of voice." I am not sure whether the author meant that each word was learned with several intonations, or that we learn several intonations for word combinations, or that we learn both to combine words and to modulate the pitch of our voice. Consequently, I have been forced to cheat on you by examining the context. What I found was no help, however, because all the formal propositions referred simply to "words," whereas all the examples that were cited involved combinations of words.

Perhaps I am being unfair, but I think that this author, at least when he is writing on learning theory, is not deeply concerned about the difference between words and sentences. If this distinction, which seems crucial to me, is really of no importance to him, then he must be ignoring my third admonition that the meaning of words are affected by the sentences in which they occur.

My fourth admonition—that the syntactic structure of a sentence imposes groupings that govern the interactions between the meanings of its words—is also ignored. No matter how I interpret the ambiguous phrase about, "Certain combinations of words and intonations of voice," it must be wrong. If I read it one way, he has ignored the problem of syntax entirely and is concerned only with the conditioning of isolated word responses.

Or, if I put a more generous interpretation on it and assume he meant that combinations of words are strengthened and made to occur by discrimination learning, then he seems to be saying that every word and every acceptable combination of words is learned separately.

By a rough, but conservative calculation, there are at least $10^{20}$ sentences 20 words long, and if a child were to learn only these it would take him something on the order of 1,000 times the estimated age of the earth just to listen to them. Perhaps this is what the word "gradually" means? In this interpretation he has clearly violated my fifth admonition, that there is no limit to the number of sentences to be learned, and so has wandered perilously close to absurdity. Any attempt to account for language acquisition that does not have a generative character will encounter this difficulty.

Sixth, from the reference to responses being "strengthened" I infer that each word-object connection is to be characterized by an intervening variable, along the lines of habit strength in Hull's system. This is a rather simple model, too simple to serve as a performance model for a language user, but it is all our author has to offer. As for keeping his performance model distinct from his competence model, as I advise in my sixth admonition, he will have none of it. He says—and here I restort to the context once more—that language "is a complex set of responses [*and*] also a set of stimuli." It may be defensible to talk about speech as a set of responses and stimuli, but what a language user knows about his language cannot be described in these performance terms.

A language includes all the denumerable infinitude of grammatical sentences, only a tiny sample of which ever have or ever will occur as actual responses or stimuli. The author would blush crimson if we caught him confusing the notions of sample and population in his statistical work, yet an analogous distinction between speech and language is completely overlooked.

Finally, we need to make the point that the kind of reinforcement schedule a child is on when he learns language is very different from what we have used in experiments on discrimination learning. No one needs to monitor a child's vocal output continually and to administer "good" and "bad" as rewards and punishments. When a child says something intelligible, his reward is both improbable and indirect. In short, a child learns language by using it, not by a precise schedule of rewards for grammatical vocalizations "in appropriate situations." An experimenter who used such casual and unreliable procedures in a discrimination experiment would teach an animal nothing at all.

The child's exposure to language should not be called "teaching." He learns the language, but no one, least of all an average mother, knows how to teach it to him. He learns the language because he is shaped by nature to pay attention to it, to notice and remember and use significant aspects of it. In suggesting that language can be taught "by the process of discrimination learning," therefore, our author has ignored my final admonition to remember the large innate capacity humans have for acquiring articulate speech.

In summary, if this sentence is taken to be a description of the fundamental processes involved in language acquisition, it is both incomplete and misleading. At best, we might regard it as a hypothesis about the acquisition of certain clichés or expressive embellishments. But as a hypothesis from which to derive an account of the most obvious and most characteristic properties of human language, it is totally inadequate.

This completes the third and final run through my list of preliminaries to psycholinguistics. If I sounded a bit too contentious, I am sorry, but I did not want to leave any doubt as to why I am saying these things or what their practical implications for psycholinguistic research might be.

My real interest, however, is not in deploring this waste of our intellectual resources, but in the positive program that is possible if we are willing to accept a more realistic conception of what language is.

If we accept a realistic statement of the problem, I believe we will also be forced to accept a more cognitive approach to it: to talk about hypothesis testing instead of discrimination learning, about the evaluation of hypotheses instead of the reinforcement of responses, about rules instead of habits, about productivity instead of generalization, about innate and universal human capacities instead of special methods of teaching vocal responses, about symbols instead of conditioned stimuli, about sentences instead of words or vocal noises, about linguistic structure instead of chains of responses—in short, about language instead of learning theory.

The task of devising a cognitive production model for language users is difficult enough without wearing blinders that prevent us from seeing what the task really is. If the hypothetical constructs that are needed seem too complex and arbitrary, too improbable and mentalistic, then you had better forgo the study of language. For language is just that—complex, arbitrary, improbable, mentalistic—and no amount of wishful theorizing will make it anything else.

In a word, what I am trying to say, what all my preliminary admonitions boil down to, is simply this: Language is exceedingly complicated. Forgive me for taking so long to say such a simple and obvious thing.

### *Introduction and Objectives for Reading Two: "Language and Cognitive Assessment of Negro Children Assumptions and Research Needs"*

In this provocative article, Joan Baratz argues directly against the notion of social pathology so often applied to the language and cognitive development of Negro children. Articles like this one have led many to question whether the so-called linguistic "deficits" of Negro populations are not in reality more a case of linguistic "differences."

Upon reading this paper you should be able to:

1. Describe the shortcomings of the notion of "deficit" in the description of children's language.
2. Give and describe at least five examples of Negro linguistic nonstandardization.

3. Summarize the main suggestions which Baratz makes for the future study of Negro children's language.

Joan C. Baratz

# *LANGUAGE AND COGNITIVE ASSESSMENT OF NEGRO CHILDREN: ASSUMPTIONS AND RESEARCH NEEDS*

The view of the black man as inherently inferior, an item of chattel rather than a person with human dignity, became a well-entrenched doctrine in American society. Even when the abolitionists were most vociferous in their insistence upon eliminating slavery in the United States (some 200 years after the initial importation of Negro slaves) they were not disputing the thought that the Negro was genetically inferior to the white man, but simply insisting that slavery was an immoral institution even if those held in bondage were inferior individuals.

The doctrine of genetic inferiority of the Negro was widely held and was responsible for many of the laws that created separate black and white communities after Emancipation. In fact, it was not until the 1954 Supreme Court decision concerning segregation in the public schools that the institutional tradition of regarding the Negro as genetically inferior was legally replaced by the idea that the Negro was not genetically inferior but rather that his behavior was pathological in the social sense, due to the history of slavery in this country.

## *The Professional Literature*

The replacement of the genetic inferiority theory with the social pathology theory encouraged a great deal of research in the social sciences which was interested in describing Negro behavior in terms of how it de-

From Joan C. Baratz, "Language and Cognitive Assessment of Negro Children: Assumptions and Research Needs," *American Speech and Hearing Association,* XI (1969), 87–91. Reprinted by permission of the publisher and author.

viated from the white norm. Thus an entire body of literature has been created that describes the Negro, not as he is, but in terms of how he does or does not conform to the modes of behavior that the white man has established as normative and appropriate. This body of knowledge (or, to look at it another way, this body of misunderstanding) might be termed the "myth of the Negro present."[1]

As Bernard (1966) has indicated, the use of white control groups to describe who the Negro is, actually results in "studies of the white population with emphasis on Negro or non-white data as representing deviance from a white norm." This unhappy state of affairs has led the social sciences to create a picture of the Negro as a "sick white man." A man for whom we, the white society, should feel great compassion and no little amount of guilt, for we have infected him with his current "disease," but a man who nevertheless, no matter the reason why, is ill.

This mythical illness can be easily identified with a brief glance at the "professional literature." There are several prominent symptoms that are continuously diagnosed—disintegration or "lack of" family structure (Moynihan, 1965, Schiefelbusch, 1967), poor motivation (Katz, 1967), inability to delay gratification (Klaus and Gray, 1968), and underdeveloped language and cognitive abilities (Deutsch, 1965; John, 1963; Bereiter and Engelmann, 1966; Klaus and Gray, 1968). All these alleged symptoms need to be examined more closely, but the focus of this paper is on the premise operating in research on language and cognitive assessment of the Negro. The kinds of research assumptions that are present in the literature concerning language can also be found in regard to the myths about family structure, motivation, etc.

When reviewing the literature one finds three major professions concerned with describing the language and cognitive abilities of black children: educators, psychologists (mainly child development specialists), and linguists.[2] The educators were the first to contribute a statement about the language difficulties of these children, a statement that amounted to the fact that these children were virtually verbally destitute—i.e., they couldn't talk and if they did, their speech was deviant and filled with "errors." The next group to get into the foray—the psychologists—reconfirmed initially that the children didn't talk, and then added the sophisticated wrinkle that if they did talk, their speech was such that it was a deterrent to cognitive growth. The last group to come into the picture was composed of linguists

[1]An obvious tribute to Herskovits' *Myth of the Negro Past* (1941), in which misunderstanding about the cultural background of Afro-Americans was first dealt with.

[2]Speech pathologists have been notably silent overall concerning language problems of subcultural groups. One can count on one hand the articles in our official journals concerning this topic.

who, though thoroughly impressed with the sophisticated research of the psychologist, were astonished at the naivety of his pronouncements concerning language. The linguist began to examine the language of black children and brought us to our current conceptions of the language abilities of these children—i.e., that they speak a well-ordered, highly structured, highly developed language system which in many aspects is different from standard English.

### *Assessing The Child's Language*

We have a fascinating situation here where three professions are assessing the same behavior—the child's oral language production and comprehension—but with varying assumptions so that they see different things. However, it is not merely another example of the parable of the six blind men describing the elephant and asserting an elephant equalled that portion of the elephant that the blind man happened to be touching—for in the parable all men were partially correct, and an elephant could be adequately described in the sum total of their "observation." But when we look at the assumptions of the educator, the psychologist, and the linguist, we find that there are some premises held by one profession (psychology)—that, for example, a language system could be underdeveloped—that another profession (linguistics) sees as completely untenable, and even absurd. The educator worked under the assumption that there is a single correct way of speaking and that everyone who does not speak in this grammar book fashion is in error. (Indeed, although the psychologist may not recognize it, he tacitly adheres to this principle when he defines language development in terms of "correct" standard English usage.) This assumption is also untenable to the linguist who is interested in the structure and function of an utterance. To him the discussion of a hierarchical system that says a double negative such as *they don't have none* is inferior to a single negative, *they haven't any*, is meaningless. The linguist simply wishes to describe the rules of the system that allow a speaker of that system to generate a negative utterance—or any other complex structure—that is considered grammatical and is understood as intended by the users of the system.

Let me briefly review the linguistic research on the assessment of language abilities of Negro children and then look back at the assumptions of the psychologist that led him astray and allowed him to build an elaborate, mythological body of literature concerning the linguistic incompetence of black children.

The linguist takes as basic that all humans develop language. After all, there is no reason to assume that black African bush children develop a language and black inner city Harlem children do not! Subsumed under this is that the language is a well-ordered system with a predictable sound pattern, grammatical structure, and vocabulary (in this sense, there are no "primitive" languages). The linguist assumes that any verbal system used by a community that fulfills the above requirements is a language and that no language is structurally better than any other language; French is not better than German, Yiddish is not better than Gaelic, Oxford English is not better than standard English, etc.

The second assumption of the linguist is that children learn language in the context of their environment—that is to say, a French child learns French not because his father is in the home or his mother reads him books, but because French is the language that he hears continually from whatever source and it is the language that individuals in his environment respond to.

The third assumption that the linguist works with is that by the time a child is five he has developed language—he has learned the rules of his linguistic environment.

## *Rules of The Linguistic Environment*

What are those rules and how have they been determined? By using ghetto informants, linguists such as Stewart (1964, 1965, 1967, 1968), Dillard (1965, 1967), Bailey (1965, 1968), Labov (1967a, 1967b), and Shuy, Wolfram, and Riley (1967) have described some of the linguistic parameters of Negro nonstandard English. Differences between standard English and Negro nonstandard occur to varying degrees in regard to the sound system, grammar, and vocabulary.

Although Negro nonstandard has many similar phonemes to those of standard English the distribution of these phonemes varies from standard English. For example /ɩ/ and /ɛ/ may not be distinguished before nasals, so that a "pin" in Negro nonstandard may be either an instrument for writing a letter or something one uses to fasten a baby's diaper. Sounds such as /r/ and /l/ are distributed so that *cat* may mean that orange vegetable that one puts in salads—standard English *carrot*—as well as the four legged fuzzy animal, or a "big black dude." The reduction of /l/ and /r/ in many positions may create such homonyms as *toe* meaning a digit on the foot, or the church bell sound—standard English *toll*. Final clusters are reduced in Negro nonstandard so that *bowl* is used to describe either a vessel for cereal or a very brave soldier—standard English *bold*.

These are but a few of the many instances where Negro nonstandard sound usage differs from standard English. It is no wonder, then, that Cynthia Deutsch (1964) should find in her assessment of auditory discrimination that disadvantaged black children did not "discriminate" as well as white children from middle class linguistic environments. She administered a discrimination task that equated "correct responses" with judgments of equivalences and differences in standard English sound usage. Many of her stimuli though different to the standard English speaker, i.e., *pin-pen,* are similar to the Negro nonstandard speaker. She attributed the difference in performance of disadvantaged children to such things as the constant blare of the TV in their homes and there being so much "noise" in their environment that the children tended to "tune out." However, black children make responses based on the kind of language they consider appropriate. In the same way that *cot* for sleeping and *caught* for ensnared, or *marry* for to wed, *Mary* for the girl, and *merry* for to be happy are not distinguished in the speech of many white people (so that they would say on an auditory discrimination test that *cot* and *caught* were the same), *pin* and *pen* are the same in the language of ghetto blacks. The responses that the black child makes are on the basis of the sound usage that he has learned in his social and geographical milieu, and do not reflect some difficulty discriminating—just watch how fast he picks out the scamper of a rat from the "noise" in his environment!

The syntax of low income Negro children also differs from standard English in many ways (unfortunately the psychologist, not knowing the rules of Negro nonstandard, has interpreted these differences not as the result of well learned rules, but as evidence of "linguistic underdevelopment"). Some examples of the differences are provided below:

1. When you have a numerical quantifier such as 2, 7, 50, etc., you don't have to add the obligatory morphemes for the plural:—*50 cent, 2 foot.*
2. The use of the possessive marker is different. For example, the standard English speaker says *John's cousin*; the nonstandard Negro speaker says *John cousin.* The possessive is marked here by the contiguous relationship of John and cousin.
3. Conditional is expressed by word order change rather than by *if.* Standard English: *I asked if he wanted to go.* Negro nonstandard: *I aks did he want to go.*
4. The third person singular has no obligatory morphological ending in nonstandard so that *she works here* is expressed as *she work here* in Negro nonstandard.
5. Verb agreement differs so that one says *she have a bike, they was going.*
6. The use of the copula is not obligatory: *I going, he a bad boy.*
7. The rules for negation are different. The double negative is used. Standard English *I don't have any* becomes *I don't got none* in Negro nonstandard.
8. The use of ain't in expression of the past: Negro nonstandard present tense is *he don't go*, past tense is *he ain't go.*
9. The use of the *be* to express habitual action: *he working right now* as contrasted with *he be working every day.*

These are but a few examples of the rules that the nonstandard speaker employs to produce utterances that are grammatical to other speakers in his environment.

Baratz and Povich (1967) assessed the language development of a group of five year old black Head Start children. They analyzed speech responses to photographs and to CAT cards using Lee's (1966) developmental sentence types model. A comparison of their data and Menyuk's (1964) restricted and transformational types of white middle-class children was performed. Results indicated that the Negro Head Start child is not delayed in language acquisition—the majority of his utterances are on the kernal and transformational levels of Lee's developmental model. His transformational utterances are similar to those described above—he has learned the many complicated structures of Negro nonstandard English.

## *Assessment by The Psychologist*

### LANGUAGE DEVELOPMENT

But how has the psychologist assessed language abilities of Negro children that led him to conclude erroneously that the black child has an insufficient or underdeveloped linguistic system? The psychologist's basic problem was his assumption that the development of language meant the development of his own form of standard English. Therefore, he concluded that if black children do not speak like white children they are deficient in language development. His measures of "language development" were measures based on standard English (Bereiter, 1965; Thomas, 1962; Deutsch, 1964; Klaus and Gray, 1968).

The illogical aspects of the psychologists' assumptions are evident if one realizes that using their criteria for "language development" one would have to say that a French child of five was linguistically underdeveloped because he did not speak standard English! Clearly in future assessment procedures the psychologist must distinguish between the questions: (1) has this child acquired language? and (2) has this child acquired competence in standard English? Only then can he make valid statements about the black child's linguistic abilities.

### LANGUAGE AND COGNITION

But what other faulty notions does the psychologist appear to be using to assess language and cognitive ability of black children? Perhaps one of the most blatant has been a confusion between hypotheses concerning language and ones concerning cognition. For this reason, superficial differences in language structures and language styles have been taken as manifestations of underlying differences in cognitive ability.

For example, Bereiter and Engelmann (1966) hold as one of the cardinal cognitive needs of the child the learning of conditionality as measured by the use of *if* constructions. They assume that the absence of *if* by a child indicates an instance in which the concept of conditionality is absent. However, Stewart and other linguists have described the fact that in some nonstandard dialects of English such as Negro nonstandard, conditionality may be expressed by the use of a word order inversion rather than with the vocabulary item "if." Thus, conditionality is expressed in the statement *I ask Alvin did he want to go* by changing *he* plus verb to *did he* plus verb, even though in standard English the same kind of conditionality would be expressed with *if* as in *I asked Alvin if he wanted to go.*

Different usages of vocabulary items may lead to confusion on the part of the examiner so that he feels the child is lacking in a particular concept. For example, the Peabody Picture Vocabulary Test has an item that asks children to identify *building*; the correct response being the picture of men constructing an edifice. However, in Negro nonstandard vernacular *building* is used only as a noun (one *makes* an edifice) so that the child will not respond to that item in the expected way. (There are other aspects about the PPVT which are culturally biased against the black child.)

The literature on cognitive abilities of black children comes mainly from two sources. One is the attempt of many child psychologists to adopt Basil Bernstein's postulates on differences in language styles between lower and middle class English speakers, and to concretize these hypotheses into categories of language behavior that directly imply restrictions in cognitive ability. Interesting as are Bernstein's ideas about language style differences of various socioeconomic groups, the relationship of particular linguistic usages to conceptual ability has yet to be determined. In fact, the preceding case of the confusion of the concept of conditionality with the presence or absence of the word *if* is an illustration of how misled one can become when relating specific speech forms with cognitive processes. Bernstein's writings appear to deal more specifically with the sociolinguistics of style variation than with the psycholinguistic implications of cognitive functioning.

The second problem with the cognitive assessment literature is that there has been a tendency to take Piaget's cognitive development formulations as a total definition of cognition, and to equate cognition with rationality. As Greenfield and Bruner (1966) have pointed out concerning cross-cultural studies of Piagetian psychology (in which I believe we can include the American studies with black ghetto children) the main effect has been to depict developmental lag through a tacit acceptance of white control group norms. Bruner et al. (1966) have several illustrations of cases where the experimenters' recognition of cultural differences affected the child's abilities to perform the task. In one instance involving a conservative task, the child was asked, "Why do you say they are different?" He could not answer the question. Then it was discovered that the use of "do you say," though grammatically correct, was inappropriate to that culture. When the child was asked instead, "Why are they different?" he answered the question immediately. The psychologist must take cultural differences of black ghetto children into consideration in the course of his assessment of their cognitive ability.

The last assumption of the psychologist that I wish to deal with briefly is the widespread notion that "some environments are better than others for stimulating general language and cognitive growth" (Deutsch and Deutsch, 1968). This assumption is, I believe, an attempt to deal with the psychologist's confusion of language development and the acquisition of standard English which were discussed earlier. His confusion causes him to think he must explain a "language deficit." According to these researchers, one set of factors that is most detrimental for language and cognitive development involves the "inadequacies" of the ghetto mothering patterns in that:

1. The ghetto mother is so taken up with survival ("subsistence behaviors") that she is too exhausted to talk to her children. Such a notion tells us more about the psychologist's lack of knowledge about the ghetto mother than it does about her actual role. It also assumes that there is a minimal amount of language that must be present for language to be learned and that Negro mothers don't give this to their children. Subsumed under this is the notion that language is only learned from one's mother (and that, of course, it can only be transmitted when there is a father in the home!). Also underlying such statements about the mother's role is the assumption that she is verbally immature (Raph, 1967), i.e., the language learned from her is underdeveloped.
2. It is presumed that the mother of a black child does not know how to stimulate or reinforce her child so that learning can occur. Subsumed under that assumption is the idea that such things as reading a book and singing to a child are essential behaviors for language to develop. The discussions on the inadequate reinforcements of verbal behavior on the part of the ghetto mother presumes that she encourages "passive, withdrawn behavior in her children" (Schiefelbusch, 1967) and that verbal ability is not highly valued in the ghetto community. One need only to look at the anthropological literature concerned with language behavior to find dozens of attestations of the importance of verbal skills—"rapping, playing the dozens, signifying, etc." to the ghetto community (Hannerz, 1968; Newman, 1968; Abrahams, 1964; Kochman, 1968).

The assumptions that the psychologist uses in assessing language and cognitive skills of the black ghetto community appear to have evolved because of misconceptions of what language is and how it functions. He has constructed elaborate ecological and psychological explanations of differences in language behavior which can be understood much more simply in terms of how linguistic and cultural systems operate. The assumptions have been used "after the fact" to erroneously explain data. The assumptions themselves have no observational/experimental base.

Clearly what the psychologist and speech pathologist need is some sense of the ghetto child's culture: how he organizes his world, what his language system is, what his learning patterns are, how they are similar to those of children in middle class white cultures, how they are different, and how these differences interfere with the child's learning in a society that uses white cognitive styles and linguistic patterns as a basis for instruction and assessment of ability.

## *References*

Abrahams, R., *Deep Down in the Jungle.* Hatboro, Pa.: Folklore Associates (1964).

Bailey, B., Linguistics on non-standard language patterns. Nat. Coun. Tchrs. English paper (1965).

Bailey, B., Some aspects of the impact of linguistics on language teaching in disadvantaged communities. *Elementary English,* 45, 570–579 (1968).

Baratz, J. C., and Povich, E. A., Grammatical constructions in the language of the Negro preschool child. ASHA Convention (1967).

Bereiter, C., Academic instruction and preschool children. In Corbin, R., and Crosby, M. (Eds.), *Language Programs for the Disadvantaged.* Champaign, Ill.: Nat. Coun. Tchrs. English (1965).

Bereiter, C., and Engelmann, S., *Teaching Disadvantaged Children in Preschool.* Englewood Cliffs, N.J.: Prentice-Hall (1966).

Bernard, J., *Marriage and Family among Negroes.* Englewood Cliffs, N.J.: Prentice-Hall (1966).

Bruner, J., Oliver, and Greenfield, P., *Studies in Cognitive Growth.* N.Y.: Wiley (1966).

Deutsch, C., Auditory discrimination and learning: social factors. *Merrill-Palmer Qu.,* 10, 277–296 (1964).

Deutsch, C., and Deutsch, M., Brief reflections on the theory of early childhood enrichment programs. In Hess, R., and Bear, R. (Eds.), *Early Education Current Theory, Research and Action.* Chicago, Ill.: Aldine (1968).

Deutsch, M., The role of social class in language development and cognition. *Amer. J. Orthopsychiat.,* 35, 78–88 (1965).

Dillard, J. L., The Urban Language Study of the Center for Applied Linguistics. *Linguistic Reporter,* 8, 1–2 (1967).

Dillard, J. L., Negro children's dialect in the inner city. *The Florida Foreign Language Reporter*, 2 (1967).

Greenfield, P., and Bruner, J., Culture and cognitive growth. *Int. J. Psychol.*, 1, 89–107, (1966).

Hannerz, U., What ghetto males are like: another look. In Szwed, J., and Witten, N. (Eds.), *Negroes in the New World: Problems in Theory and Method.* In press.

Herskovits, M., *The Myth of the Negro Past.* N.Y.: Harper (1941).

John, V., The intellectual development of slum children. *Amer. J. Orthopsychiat.*, 33, 813–822 (1963).

Katz, I., The socialization of academic motivation in minority group children. *Nebraska Symposium on Motivation,* Univ. Nebraska Press (1967).

Klaus, R., and Gray, S., The early training project for disadvantaged children: A report after five years. *Monogr. Soc. Res. Child Dev.*, 33 (1968).

Kochman, T., Language in the ghetto. Midwestern Anthropological Assoc., Detroit (1968).

Labov, W., Some suggestions for teaching standard English to speakers of non-standard urban dialects. In *New Directions in Elementary English.* Champaign, Ill. (1967a).

Labov, W., and Cohen, P., Systematic relations of standard rules in grammar of Negro speakers. Project Literacy #7 (1967b).

Lee, L., Developmental sentence types: a method for comparing normal and deviant syntactic development, *J. Speech Hearing Dis.*, 31, 311–330 (1966).

Menyuk, P., Syntactic rules used by children from preschool through first grade. *Child Dev.*, 35, 533–546 (1964).

Moynihan, D., *The Negro Family: The Case for National Action.* U.S. Dept. Labor, Washington, D.C. (1965).

Newman, S., The Goucher, Paper presented to Midwestern Anthropology Assoc., Detroit (1968).

Raph, J., Language and speech deficits in culturally-disadvantaged children. *J. Speech Hearing Dis.*, 32, 203–215 (1967).

Schiefelbusch, R., Language development and language modification. In Haring, N., and Schiefelbusch, R. (Eds.), *Methods in Special Education.* N.Y.: McGraw-Hill (1967).

Shuy, R., Wolfram, W., and Riley, W., *Linguistic Correlates of Speech Stratification in Detroit Speech.* Final Report, Coop. Res. Project 6, 1347, U.S. Off. Ed. (1967).

Stewart, W., Urban Negro Speech: sociolinguistic factors affecting English teaching. In R. Shuy (Ed.), *Social Dialects and Language Learning.* Champaign, Ill.: Nat. Coun. Tchrs. English (1964).

Stewart, W., Foreign language teaching methods in quasi-foreign language situations. In Stewart, W. (Ed.), *Non-standard Speech and the Teaching of English.* Washington, D.C.: Center for Applied Linguistics (1965).

Stewart, W., Sociolinguistic factors in the history of American Negro dialects. *The Florida Foreign Language Reporter,* 6, 3ff. (1967).

Stewart, W., Continuity and change in American Negro dialects. *The Florida Foreign Language Reporter*, 7, 1ff. (1968).

Thomas, D., Oral language sentence structure and vocabulary of kindergarten children living in low socio-economic areas. *Dissertation Abstracts,* 23, No. 3, 1014 (1962).

## *Introduction and Objectives for Reading Three: "A Sociolinguistic Approach to Socialization"*

In this introduction to a longer chapter, Basil Bernstein dispells some of the misapplication of his theory to the problems of language and social class in the United States. In so doing, he gives examples of his *restricted* and *elaborated* language codes.

After reading this selection you should be able to:

1. Describe the difference between the types of language deficits thought to be observed among the so-called "disadvantaged" in the United States, and Bernstein's conception of a restricted code.
2. Describe how Bernstein uses "context boundedness" to differentiate between restricted and elaborated language codes.

Basil Bernstein[1]

# *A SOCIOLINGUISTIC APPROACH TO SOCIALIZATION: WITH SOME REFERENCE TO EDUCABILITY*

Since the late 1950s in the United States there has been a steady outpouring of publications concerned with the education of children of low social class whose material circumstances are inadequate, or with the edu-

[1]Sociological Research Unit, University of London Institute of Education. The work reported in this paper was supported by grants from the Nuffield Foundation, Department of Education and Science, and from the Ford Foundation, to whom, gratefully, acknowledgement is made. A similar version of this paper is scheduled for publication under the same title in J. J. Gumperz and D. Hymes, *Directions in Sociolinguistics* (Holt, Rinehart & Winston).

From Basil Bernstein, "A Sociolinguistic Approach to Socialization: With Some Reference to Educability," in *Language and Poverty: Perspectives on a Theme,* ed. F. Williams (Chicago, Ill.: Markham Publishing Co., 1970), pp. 25–27. Reprinted by permission of the author and publisher.

cation of black children of low social class whose material circumstances are chronically inadequate. An enormous research and educational bureaucracy has developed in the United States, financed by funds obtained from federal, state, or private foundations. New educational categories have been developed—the *culturally deprived,* the *linguistically deprived,* the *socially disadvantaged*, and the notion of compensatory education was introduced as a means of changing the status of those children in the above categories. Ideas on compensatory education issued in the form of massive preschool programs (as in Head Start), large-scale research programs in the early 1960s (e.g., Deutsch and associates 1967), and a plethora of small-scale intervention or enrichment programs for preschool children (e.g., Bereiter and Engelmann 1966) or children in the first years of compulsory education (program Follow Through). Very few sociologists were involved in these studies. On the whole they were carried out by psychologists.

The focus of these studies and programs was on the child in the poverty family and on the local classroom relationship between teacher and child. In the last few years one can detect a change in this focus. As a result of the movements toward integration and the opposed movement toward segregation (the latter a response to the wishes of the various Black Power groups), more studies in the United States have shifted the focus to problems of the schools. Rosenthal and Jacobson's classic study, *Pygmalion in the Classroom* (1968) drew attention to the critical importance of the teacher's expectations of the child.

Most studies or programs along the lines discussed above have dealt directly with the language of children, and among these a number have incorporated with varying degrees of accuracy some of the concepts of language and socialization which appeared in the author's early writings of the late 1950s and the early 1960s (e.g., Bernstein 1958, 1959, 1960a, b, 1961). Most notably, the reference has often been to the differentiation between *restricted* and *elaborated* language codes, and the consequences that these codes hold for the people who use them. The use (or abuse) of this distinction has sometimes led to the erroneous conception that a restricted code can be directly equated with linguistic deprivation, linguistic deficiency, or being nonverbal.

The error here seems largely due to the superficial focus upon the spoken details of the two codes rather than the broader conception of the codes as referring to the transmission of the basic or deep-meaning structures of a culture or subculture. This broader conception links code with communication context, and both with social structure. To emphasize this broader concept, consider the distinction between uses of language which can be called context-bound and uses of language which are less context-bound. This distinction can be seen in two stories constructed by Hawkins

(1969), based upon his analyses of the speech of middle-class (story *A*) and working-class, (*B*), five-year-old children in London. The children were given a series of four pictures which portrayed the sequence of a story and they were invited to tell this story. The first picture shows some boys playing football near a house; the second shows the ball breaking a window; the third shows a man making a threatening gesture; in the fourth, the children are moving away, while watched by a woman peering out of the window.

> *(A)* Three boys are playing football and one boy kicks the ball—and it goes through the window—the ball breaks the window—and the boys are looking at it—and a man comes out and shouts at them—because they've broken the window—so they ran away—and then that lady looks out of her window—and she tells the boys off.
>
> *(B)* They're playing football—and he kicks it and it goes through there—it breaks the window and they're looking at it—and he comes out and shouts at them—because they've broken it—so they run away—and then she looks out and she tells them off.

With the first story the reader does not have to have the four pictures which were used as the basis for the story, whereas in the second story, the reader would require the initial pictures in order to make sense of the story. The first story is free of the context which generated it, whereas the second story is much more closely tied to its context. As a result the meanings of the second story are implicit, whereas the meanings of the first story are explicit. It is not that the working-class children do not have in their lexical repertoire the vocabulary used by the middle-class children. Nor is it the case that the children differ in their tacit understanding of the linguistic rule system. Rather what we have here are differences in the use of language arising out of a specific context. One child makes explicit the meanings which he is realizing through language for the person he is telling the story to, whereas the second child does not do this to the same extent. The first child takes very little for granted, whereas the second child takes a great deal for granted. Thus for the first child the task was seen as a context in which his meanings were required for explication, whereas the task for the second child was not seen as a task which required such explication of meaning. However, it would not be difficult to imagine a context where the first child would produce speech rather like that of the second.

What we are dealing with here are differences between children in the way they realize, in their language use, what is apparently the same context. We could say that the speech of the first child generated universalistic meanings in the sense that the meanings are freed from the context and so understandable by all. Whereas the speech of the second child generated particularistic meanings, in the sense that the meanings are closely tied to the context and would be only fully understood by others if they had access to the context which originally generated the speech. Thus universalistic meanings are less bound to a given context, whereas particularistic meanings are severely context-bound.

## *References*

Bereiter, C. and Engelmann, S. *Teaching disadvantaged children in the pre-school.* Englewood Cliffs, New Jersey: Prentice-Hall, 1966.

Bernstein, B. Some sociological determinants of perception. *British Journal of Sociology,* 1958, 9, 159–174.

Bernstein, B. A public language: some sociological implications of a linguistic form. *British Journal of Sociology,* 1959, 10, 311–326.

Bernstein, B. Socio-Kult urelle determunaten des lernens. *Kolner Keitschrift Soziologie und Sozial-Psychologie,* 1960, 4, 52–79. (a)

Bernstein, B. Language and social class. *British Journal of Sociology,* 1960, 11, 271–276. (b)

Bernstein, B. Social class and linguistic development: a theory of social learning. In A. H. Halsey, J. Floud, and A. Anderson (Eds.) *Economy, education and society.* New York: Harcourt, Brace and World, 1961.

Deutsch, M. and associates. *The disadvantaged child.* New York: Basic Books, 1967.

Hawkins, P. R. Social class, the nominal group and reference. *Language and Speech,* 1969, 12, 125–135.

Rosenthal, R. and Jacobson, Lenore. *Pygmalion in the classroom.* New York: Holt, Rinehart and Winston, 1968.

## *Introduction and Objectives for Reading Four: "Stages in the Acquisition of Standard English"*

In this portion of a larger paper, William Labov describes the forces which shape the stages of the development of standard English in the child. Such descriptions are classified under the broad heading of sociolinguistics.

Upon reading this selection you should be able to:

1. Describe what Labov means by linguistic acculturation of the child to adult norms.
2. List and describe the six stages which Labov defines for the acquisition process.
3. Describe obstacles to the acquisition of standard English, in general and in New York City in particular.

William Labov

# STAGES IN THE ACQUISITION OF STANDARD ENGLISH

## The Acquisition of Standard English by Children

A. The Gradual Development of Adult Norms. . . . We can now turn to the question of the acquisition of these [linguistic] norms and levels of behavior by children. The sample of informants under twenty years old was not as systematic as the sample of adults in the study of New York City; we depended primarily upon the children of our adult informants, and it was not possible to obtain a high percentage of the total sample population. Fifty-eight children of the New York City informants were interviewed, ranging from eight to nineteen years of age. The evidence brought forward in this section is consistent with that of the preceding, but the type of sampling used does not permit the same high level of confidence in the conclusions. We may consider the following outline of the acquisition of the levels of competence in Standard English as a series of tentative statements to be confirmed by further study in the New York City area.[1]

First of all, we may look at the overall performance of young people

[1]The data given in this paper as a whole apply primarily to New York City. There is reason to think that the behavior of the Lower East Side informants is characteristic of linguistic behavior within the city as a whole, and that regional differences within New York are minor. Several supplementary studies have given essentially the same results as the survey of the Lower East Side. On the other hand, it has been possible to show in great detail how New York City informants differ from those who were raised outside of the city. The two variables discussed here, (th) and (r), are the ones which are most general in their application, and which are essentially the same for the New York and non-New York informants. The principles of sociolinguistic organization illustrated here are therefore more general than the limitation to New York City would imply.

From William Labov, "Stages in the Acquisition of Standard English," in *Social Dialects and Language Learning*, ed. R. W. Shuy (Champaign, Ill.: National Council of Teachers of English, 1965) pp. 88–99. Reprinted with the permission of the National Council of Teachers of English and William Labov.

in all of the measures outlined above: their use of the linguistic variables in the various contextual styles, their subjective response tests, and their self-evaluation tests. The overall percentage of cases in which they follow the predominating pattern of the adult community climbs gradually as they approach adult status:

| *Age* | *% conformity with adult norms* |
|---|---|
| 8–11 | 52 |
| 12–13 | 50 |
| 14–15 | 57 |
| 16–17 | 62 |
| 18–19 | 64 |
| (20–39 | 84) |

We can view this process of acculturation most clearly if we examine families with more than one informant below the age of twenty. The table given above reflects a rather uneven distribution of informants in the various age groups; but if we take brothers and sisters within the same family, we can minimize fluctuations due to factors other than age. Figure 1 shows the percentage of agreement with adult norms shown by members of twenty-eight families. Here the horizontal axis represents the age of the informants, and the vertical axis the percentage of agreement. Points representing members of the same family are connected along straight lines.

Figure 1 shows graphically the process of acculturation which is often described in less specific terms. The linguistic indicators give us a precise measure of the extent to which the young person has grasped the norms of behavior which govern the adult community. It can be seen that some families begin this process relatively high in the continuum: middle class families are to be found near the top of the diagram, together with a few working class families. Some working class families, and all of the lower class families, are to be seen operating at a much lower level of conformity to adult norms. Despite this great variation in relative position, we see that the slope of most of the lines is similar. Some working class and most lower class families are apparently too far removed from the middle class norms to assimilate them efficiently, and we can see that those youngsters who are below 50 percent at eighteen or nineteen years old will probably not reach any significant degree of conformity while they still have the learning ability to match performance to evaluation. At the ages of thirty-five or forty, these individuals may be able to evaluate the social significance of their own and other speech forms, without being able to shift their own performance. At the same time, there is also a correlation between those families that expressed the most hostility to middle class norms of social behavior, and those who appeared low on Figure 1. We can infer that there are other values operating to produce the differential of Figure 1, beyond mere differences in familiarity with middle class patterns.

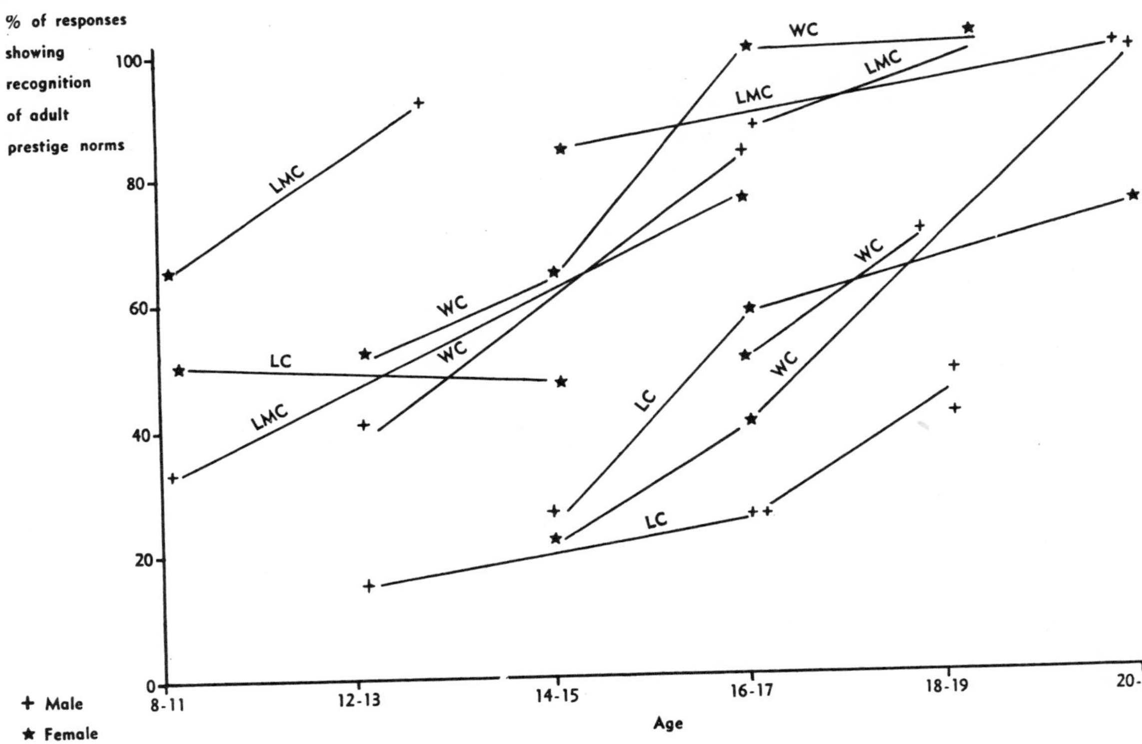


**Figure 1.** Acquisition of prestige norms in families with two or more children

B. Levels in the Acquisition of spoken English. From some of the evidence discussed above, and from other details obtained in the interviews with young people, we can construct a model of six stages of the acquisition of the full range of spoken English.

1) *The basic grammar.* The first level is the mastery of the main body of grammatical rules and the lexicon of spoken English, in such a form that the child can communicate his basic needs and experiences to his parents. This stage is normally achieved under the linguistic influence of the parents—that is the case with all of our younger informants, who are at least third generation New Yorkers.

2) *The vernacular.* The second stage is the most important one from the point of view of the evolution of the language. In the preadolescent years, roughly ages five to twelve, the child learns the use of the local dialect in a form consistent with that of his immediate group of friends and associates. At this stage, neighborhood dialect characteristics become automatically established responses in the pattern of everyday speech, and the influence of the parents is submerged under the influence of the peer group. It is during this period that the child begins to learn to read in school.

3) *Social perception.* The third stage begins with early adolescence, as the child begins to come into wider contact with the adult world. The social significance of the dialect characteristics of his friends becomes gradually apparent to him as he becomes exposed to other speech forms, even while he himself is still confined to the single style of his own vernacular. At the age of fourteen or fifteen children begin to respond to the subjective reaction test with patterns that resemble the adult pattern.

4) *Stylistic variation.* In the next stage, the child begins to learn how to modify his speech in the direction of the prestige standard, in formal situations, or even to some extent in casual speech. The great turning point seems to be exposure to a group larger than the neighborhood group in the first year of high school. In our sample, for instance, we find that the number of stops and affricates used for (th) differs greatly between those speakers who have never been to high school and those who have had at least one year.

5) *The consistent standard.* It is not enough to be able to use standard speech forms sporadically. The ability to maintain standard styles of speech for any length of time is often not acquired at all. At best, some New Yorkers may be able to add a few corrected forms to their speech patterns. The ability to switch to a consistent style of speech and maintain that style with reasonable consistency is acquired primarily by the middle class groups. . . .

6) *The full range.* Some speakers attain complete consistency, or something close to it, in range of styles appropriate for a wide range of

occasions. Comparatively few New Yorkers attain this level of skill in speaking, and those who do are mostly college educated persons with special interest in speech. In the case of (th), quite a few of our subjects did use the fricative form all of the time. We also found that there were many subjects who did not depart at all from standard syntax and word morphology. This mastery of the prestige forms seemed to accompany a certain rigidity of linguistic style: few of these speakers seem to have retained the ability to switch "downwards" to their original vernacular. On the other hand, there was a continual shift in the percentage of (r) used, but not one of our informants who was raised in New York City had achieved complete consistency in the use of the prestige form.[2]

From this outline, it is plain that the relations between learning to speak and learning to read are not as simple as they have been sometimes said to be. The pattern of the vernacular is not fully formed when the child first learns to read, and there are many further steps in the mastery of spoken English which are still beyond his horizon. And success or failure in learning to read may have a strong effect upon the development of these other verbal skills.

By examining linguistic changes in progress, we have seen that the ability to perceive the social significance of dialect differences precedes the acquisition of consistent prestige styles in Standard English. For example, in the subjective evaluation of (r), we find that there is a sudden increase in the recognition of the prestige status of (r) for the group of sixteen-seventeen year olds. For eighteen-nineteen year olds, there is almost the same total agreement in the recognition of (r) as for the young adults, the twenty to thirty-nine year olds. At the same time, only the upper middle class speakers show any ability to use (r) in their everyday speech. Since the great majority of the members of the adult community agree in the evaluation of speech forms, why then do most New Yorkers fail to acquire levels (5) and (6) in the series sketched above?

C. OBSTACLES TO THE ACQUISITION OF STANDARD ENGLISH. The regular patterns of social stratification in the use of linguistic variables reflect a balance of forces, rather than a simple, overall trend. On the one hand, the vernacular of the New York City speech community evolves in its own consistent pattern, following a mechanism that is not yet wholly

[2]Throughout this paper, I have used the conception of stylistic levels which is most commonly employed in the discussion of social variation. However, this approach in the New York City speech community leads to a multiplication of structural devices that seems increasingly unrealistic as we gather more data. It is possible to view the sociolinguistic structure as a single complex, within which continuous variation occurs along the social and the stylistic dimension. Cf. "The Linguistic Variable as a Structural Unit," paper given before the Washington Linguistics Club, Washington, D.C., November 1964.

understood. On the other hand, the New York City speech community has also maintained prestige patterns borrowed from other communities: from England, New England, or most recently, from (r)-pronouncing areas outside of the city. While almost everyone recognizes the middle class values inherent in his borrowed prestige pattern, there is a wide range of differences in the actualization of this pattern. We can consider the following bases for such a range of performance.

1) *Isolation.* It is possible that working class and lower class speakers are simply not as familiar with the prestige norms as middle class speakers —that they have less opportunity to hear the prestige dialect. At one time, this may have been an important factor, but it is clearly becoming less important with the development of the mass media. The great majority of prestige figures on radio and television in the New York City area use the prestige dialect consistently. Furthermore, the conditions of daily life in a large city permit a considerable amount of interaction between speakers of various levels.

2) *Structural interference.* It is also possible that there are mechanical constraints upon the linguistic performance of some speakers, proceeding from differences in the structure of their vernacular and the structure of the prestige pattern.

We can see in such interference in the case of a young New Yorker who enters the sixth grade speaking a vernacular in which *bad, bared,* and *beard* are completely homonymous, together with thousands of other words in these classes. If we add to this list the homonymy of *laud, lord,* and *lured; god* and *guard; dot* and *dart; pin* and *pen;* it is apparent that a great many new distinctions must be learned if the child is to master the Standard English spoken by the teacher.

In the case of the new population of in-migrants from the South who speak a nonstandard dialect, or in the case of the Puerto Rican group, such interference may be important. It is not as likely to be a strong factor in the speech of the main body of New Yorkers, who began to acquire early in life the pattern of stylistic shifting which carries them from their basic vernacular to the prestige forms.

Nevertheless, an important step in the study of any such system of social stratification is to attempt an analysis of the vernacular of each social group, showing the internal relations of the elements within each system. (See footnote 14.) This analysis will be essential for the understanding of linguistic change, and it will isolate the differences between systems which must be adjusted in the mastery of Standard English.

3) *Conflict of value systems.* It can easily be seen that any systematic differences between dialects of English in New York City are small in comparison with the similarities. One can hardly imagine a theory of mechanical constraints which could account for the dilemma proposed at the beginning of this paper: How is it that young people who are exposed

to the Standard English of their teachers for twelve years cannot reproduce this style for twelve minutes in a job interview? The problem is parallel to the more serious question as to how a student can sit through eight to ten years of school without learning to read more than a few words. Those who feel that they can solve this problem by experimenting with the machinery of the learning process are measuring small causes against large effects. My own feeling is that the primary interference with the acquisition of Standard English stems from a conflict of value systems.

Language may be looked upon as a system for integrating values. Linguistics has made the most progress in analyzing the cognitive component; but many elements of language (certainly not all) are imbued with noncognitive values as well, and the total information conveyed in these noncognitive functions may outweigh the cognitive information. In our subjective reaction tests we have studied only those values which follow the middle class patterns: the suitability of a speech form for various occupations. But there are other values, values which support the use of the vernacular style of the working class, and the social stratification of language. . . . There are many New Yorkers, for example, who feel no desire to be identified with middle class, white collar workers. They deliberately turn aside from white collar jobs in seeking lower skilled, lower paid manual work. Identification with the class of people that includes one's friends and family is a powerful factor in explaining linguistic behavior. Furthermore, I believe that we can establish that the working class style of casual speech has values strongly associated with masculinity. In the work now being carried on in Harlem and other parts of New York City, we plan to explore these value systems.

There are also negative factors in the conflict of value systems. The adolescent peer group exerts strong pressure against any deviation in the direction of middle class standards. This is a type of behavior that we would like to investigate in more detail; there is a great deal of anecdotal evidence of such pressure, but it consists mostly of recollections of striking incidents in the past. Evidence to the contrary—group approval of the verbal proficiency of a member—might not be so striking and therefore would not appear in anecdotal evidence. Therefore we need observations of group pressures upon language behavior as these pressures operate. If it is true that adolescent groups do not permit free experimentation with middle class language styles, and that they penalize members who try to put into practice the teaching of the schools,[3] then the practical problem of urban dialect engineering will have such group constraints as a major focus.

[3]The current program for research in Harlem among teenage speakers is designed to obtain further evidence on this point. No one would deny that such tendencies exist; the question is, to what extent do they influence behavior? Only quantitative methods can answer such questions; after a certain point, anecdotal evidence only confuses the issue.

It will be necessary to build into the community a tolerance for style shifting which is helpful in educational and occupational advancement.

Another negative factor undoubtedly exists in the conflict of values symbolized by the difference between the teachers' speech and the students. Although English teachers have been urged for many years to treat the nonstandard vernaculars as simply "different" from Standard English, it is clear that the prevailing attitude is that the students' vernacular is "bad English," "incorrect," and "sloppy" speech. It would be surprising if this were not so. The survey of New York City shows that such opinions of the teacher reflect an almost universal sentiment of the speech community.[4] The conflict is a covert one: both teacher and student may be only partly aware of the value systems which bring them into unyielding opposition.

. . . In casual speech, [most teachers in the New York City system] unconsciously use forms which they themselves stigmatize in the speech of others. When they pronounce words in isolation, they use an even higher percentage of prestige forms than those who use these forms naturally in casual speech. Their performance is governed by certain norms, and these norms are the sounds or images that they hear themselves use. Thus the teacher will frequently condemn students in strong, moralistic terms for the use of speech forms that she frequently uses herself without being aware of them. There are undoubtedly many nonstandard forms used by the students that the teacher does not use, but the essential fact is that the teacher has no more tolerance for style shift than the adolescent groups mentioned above. Neither teacher nor student is aware of the fact that they both follow the same pattern of style shifting in their language, though at different levels. The teacher struggles to impose a fixed standard, which she mistakenly believes she follows herself, upon youngsters who mistakenly believe that they also make no concession to the other side in daily life. In the data from the New York City survey, we see some evidence for the view that teachers may be transferring to the students their own inner conflicts; they recoil from a kind of behavior that is still very much a part of their own personalities. On the other hand, the student may rightfully feel that the teacher threatens him in trying to abolish completely the speech pattern that identifies him as a member of his own group: this is the group that he respects, that awards him prestige, that establishes his masculinity.

These comments suggest that the conflict of values should be investigated in the classroom itself. The foregoing remarks are merely extrapolations from observations made in a community study, and they are based on the least favorable case, in which a male student faces a female

[4]Again, one should note that this agreement extends only to those attitudes which reflect the middle class value system.

teacher. But the view given here becomes somewhat more plausible when we consider the even more serious problem produced by the new polarization within the New York speech community.

## *Opposing Value Systems within the New York City Speech Community*

The view of the speech community given so far is not complete. There are signs of a developing lower class group which is breaking away from the pattern shown, a group which has adopted other reference points and other values, and is drifting in a different direction from the main group.

Evidence for such a trend can be seen in some of the details of the phonological system. Whereas the traditional New York City system is continuing to evolve towards higher and higher in-gliding vowels in word groups such as *bad, ask, dance, where,* etc., and *off, talk, law,* etc., there is an opposing trend towards lower in-gliding vowels in these groups. Similarly, we find that the traditional New York City system shows a systematic backing of the first element in the diphthong of *my, side, why,* etc., while a separate trend exists towards the fronting of this element and the loss of the up-glide. These contrary directions are all the more striking when they are seen against a view of the overall structure of New York City speech.[5] The great majority of working class and middle class speakers follow the first direction mentioned, which continues the evolution which began in the nineteenth century. The second direction is characteristic of a sizeable group of Negro speakers, Puerto Ricans, and lower class white speakers who live in close contact with these other groups.

The differences in speech performance are matched by a new polarization of values developing in New York City. The old polarization of ethnic groups showed a number of equally balanced interest groups: Italians, Jews, Negroes, Irish, who determined the political character of the city as well as its informal social structure.[6] The newer pattern shows that a growing minority of Negroes, Puerto Ricans, and lower class whites reject the value system implied by the dominant speech pattern and adopt a new reference point in which southern Negro speech is central.

[5]William Labov, *The Social Stratification of English in New York City* (Washington, D.C.: Center for Applied Linguistics, 1966).

[6]The ethnic composition of New York City is described in N. Glazer and D. Moynihan, *Beyond the Melting Pot: The Negroes, Puerto Ricans, Jews, Italians and Irish of New York City* (Cambridge: M.I.T. and Harvard University Press, 1963).

This new development is best illustrated by considering the overt attitudes expressed by New Yorkers about speech itself. Most white New Yorkers do not like the sound of New York City speech. Almost all of our informants agree that they would be complimented if they were told that they did *not* sound like New Yorkers. As far back as we can go, the city's prestige patterns have always been borrowed from other regions. On the other hand, many white New Yorkers like the sound of white southern speech. The attitudes of most Negro informants are quite the reverse. They like almost any type of northern speech, and dislike southern speech intensely. Southern speech is considered "rough," "uneducated," "bad" speech. One excerpt from an interview with an older Negro informant in New York City will illustrate this value pattern vividly. Mr. Joseph McSorley was born and raised in New York City sixty years ago. He works as a guard at a YMCA building, and although he has had little formal education, he is a well-read, well-spoken man. In answer to the question on the danger of death, he told of an incident in which he was asked to investigate a report that someone had a gun in his room and had threatened some other tenant with it. In this narrative, Mr. McSorley used two very different voices: his own quiet, pleasant, and cultivated northern manner, and a rough, rapid style with many strongly southern characteristics and a tone of voice that was rasping and whining. The first style is indicated in regular type below—the second in capitals.

> I go up whistlin', let him know I'm comin', shakin' my keys, you know. "Hey, Bill! What are you doin'?"
>
> "WHADA YOU WANT?"
>
> I said, "What are you doin'?"
>
> "I AIN'T DOIN' NUTTIN', JOE."
>
> I said, "Well, they claim a little disturbance up here, somebody says you chased them with something. What did you chase them with?"
>
> "OH JOE, I AIN'T GOIN' BOTHER 'EM. I WASN'T DOIN' NOTHIN'."
>
> I said, "Open the door, Bill. Let me look." So he opened the door and I went in there. He did have a gun. So I said, "You better get rid of that because down at the desk, they're calling for the police department."
>
> "I GOT A P'MIT FO' IT."
>
> I said, "You better show it to the cops when they come."
>
> "O.K. JOE, O.K."

The voice that Mr. McSorley usually used is not easily identified as that of a Negro by most listeners, but the second voice was plainly that of a southern Negro. At the end of the interview, I complimented Mr. McSorley on his ability to sound like two different people. He was quite mystified by my remark. He had no idea that he had used any voice other than his usual one; yet his niece, who had been listening, agreed that he had done so, and she told him that he had sounded "just like a southern Negro."

Finally, I asked Mr. McSorley what sort of a man Bill was—what was his background. "I don't know," said Mr. McSorley, "some kind of a Hungarian, I think."

In this incident we see a process of unconscious substitution taking place in accordance with the value system of the speaker. The man Mr. McSorley was imitating used a speech pattern that was evidently rough and uneducated, but unfamiliar in detail to him. In representing this style, he automatically and unconsciously substituted the only rough uneducated low prestige dialect with which he was intimately familiar—that of non-standard southern Negro English.

Mr. McSorley is typical of the many Negro New Yorkers who are puzzled by the recent trend towards southern speech among the young people he knows. He finds it hard to understand why people would go out of their way to talk in a rough, uneducated way. In actual fact, this polarization of linguistic values about a new norm is a sign of a cultural split in New York City which goes beyond language. We find that even lower class whites who live in apparent hostility with Negroes have unconsciously adopted the Negro delinquent youth as a reference group for their own behavior.[7] This trend is dramatically evident in a section of another interview from the Lower East Side survey. The subjects were six brothers, from thirteen to nineteen years old, from an Irish-Italian family that would be rated on most indicators near the lower end of the socioeconomic scale. In their social attitudes and aspirations most of the Riley brothers show overt hostility to middle class values. The most vocal is the second oldest, Jimmy Riley, the natural joker and storyteller of the group. At eighteen, he had resisted all of the schools' efforts to teach him white collar skills, and more or less decided to become a longshoreman, like his father. In his account of a situation in which he was in danger of being killed, he told of being attacked by a group of Negroes. In the course of the narrative, he drifted into a style of speech which is remarkably like that of the Negro boys who are his immediate enemies:

> I went ice skatin' in Jersey—Hoboken. Came back two o'clock in the mornin'. Whole bunch of guys went—I come back, everybody says, "I'm hongry, I'm hongry." I say, "I'll be right back."
>
> I go next door for a pizza. I come out, and there's five big niggers standin' there. They say, "Gimme that!" I say, "Give you *wot*." Yerrr whop! I went down. They kicked me, everything. Boom!
>
> I got up, 'n' ran in the house, 'n' grabbed a steak knife and chased

[7]"Reference group" is used here in the technical sense introduced by Herbert Hyman in *The Psychology of Status,* 1942, and utilized by Robert Merton in *Social Theory and Social Structure* in 1949. When an individual or a group adopts the values of some other group outside of their own network of social contacts, that other group is said to serve as a reference group for them.

> them. A guy jumped into his car and chased them. Spanish guy named Rickey, he took out a bread knife, ran down the subway, and scared an old lady silly. Thought he was gonna kill her.
>
> Bright cop comes over—cullud ['k l d] cop. "Wha' happened?" I say. "Five of your bright people jumped me." He says, "What were dey?" I say, "Yeah, they were colored." He says, "Den they—they ain't my people." I said, "You cullud." He says, "They ain't my people." I say, "O.K., g'bye, f'get everyt'ing. Went t'the hospital."

Again, this stylistic behavior proved to be quite unconscious. When one of Jimmy Riley's own brothers told him that he sounded like a nigger himself when he was telling the story, he was quite surprised. Yet he had quoted himself saying "You cullud," a form of predication without the copula which is highly characteristic of Negro speech as opposed to other vernacular speech forms.

In the case of Jimmy Riley, we see a constellation of factors that seems to lead to low educational achievement, lack of occupational skills, and unemployment. His speech patterns are sensitive indicators of these trends. It is not likely that any change in the methods of teaching English will be powerful enough to cope with problems such as these. I think, however, that we must be aware of these problems, because they reflect social processes that will continue to operate to produce similar results in the future. No amount of research into the mechanism of language learning will remove these larger social forces from the scene. The polarization of linguistic behavior serves as an excellent indicator of the social processes that are occurring, but these indicators do not give us any immediate program for corrective action, or even for amelioration. The linguist is essentially an analyst, not an educator; it would seem that his goal in attacking the problems of the urban schools is to give the educators information with which they can build programs and check the results of their efforts.

### *Introduction and Objectives for Reading Five: "The Ethnography of Speaking: Speech in Socialization"*

In this selection from a larger paper, Dell Hymes tells us that a child's learning of the speech of his society is one of the main ways by which he internalizes the characteristics of that society.

Upon reading this selection you should be able to:

1. Define what is meant by the role of speech in socialization.
2. Distinguish "directive function" from "referential function" in speech.

3. Describe how speech may play varying roles in socialization.
4. Describe how speaking enters into the definition of the roles acquired or observed by children in a given social structure.

Dell H. Hymes

# THE ETHNOGRAPHY OF SPEAKING: SPEECH IN SOCIALIZATION

## Speech in Socialization

I now want to survey the role of speaking in socialization. In one sense this role is one part of the kind of descriptive analysis that has been proposed. In another sense, it is a question of the induction of new recruits into the ongoing adult system. Whichever perspective is chosen, and we often shift back and forth in ordinary thinking, it is worthwhile to single out speech in socialization because, from a comparative viewpoint, it has been entirely neglected; there is far too little attention to it in the study of individual groups; and it presumably underlies much of the variation in individual adult behavior.

Studies of the child's acquisition of speech have concentrated on mastery of the code for referential function. Far too few such studies have been informed by modern linguistics as to the structural nature of what it is the child learns, but the number is increasing. Adequate studies of the child's acquisition of the other functions of speech have been more or less unknown to American linguistics and anthropology, but recently the work of Russian psychologists on the directive function has gained recognition (Luria 1959; Luria and Yurovich 1959). The Russian scholars consider the child's acquisition of speech ("the secondary signalling system") in interaction with adults as fundamental to the child's development of control over its own behavior and of its picture of the world. Their experimental work has shown that the development of capacity to understand an utterance (referential function) does not have as automatic consequence the capacity to respond adequately, to have behavior directed by it. The capacity for the directive functioning of speech develops independently and by stages in the first years of life. Thus before the age of 1½ years a

From Dell H. Hymes, "The Ethnography of Speaking," pp. 39–44. Reproduced by permission of the Anthropological Society of Washington from *Anthropology and Human Behavior*, 1962. Reprinted also by permission of the author.

child responds to a verbal request for a toy fish by getting and handing the object, but is not able to do so if another toy (say a cat) is closer, and between it and the fish. It will orient toward the object named, but maintain the directive function of the word only until the external situation (the toy cat) conflicts, then grasp and offer the intervening toy. At 3 to 3½ years, if a child is to perform a certain task of pressing a ball, it will not achieve the necessary control over its responses if simply given preliminary verbal instructions, but if it gives itself the appropriate verbal commands, it will succeed. At this age, however, the success is only for positive commands. If the child gives itself the command "Don't press," it not only fails to stop pressing, but presses even harder. Only at the age of 4 to 4½ years does the verbal command "Don't press" actually acquire inhibitory effect, according to these studies.

Thus the directive function of speech depends partly upon maturation, and is partly independent of the dependence upon maturation of control of referential function. As for another salient function, the expressive, observations indicate that it begins to be acquired quite early. Expressive use of intonation and other features may precede referential control. In short, the three most prominent types of function (referential, expressive, directive) appear to develop in childhood in partial independence of each other and in varying relation to the process of maturation.

It also appears that mastery of these functions varies in education and adult life. The basic patterns of the referential function, of grammar and lexicon, are shared as prerequisites to the maintenance of communication at all. There are of course differences at some levels of control of resources for reference. And there seems to be a quite looser rein as to the other functions and greater individual variability. Individuals differ greatly, for example, in control of intonation patterns in our society; some never learn the right intonation for announcing a joke, and some, having learned a certain intonation as students, as part of a pattern of quick repartee, carry it in later life into situations in which it acts to cut off every conversational sequence. And if we extend our horizon from the usual scope of linguistic descriptions to the full repertoire of conventional linguistic habits, to the recurrent linguistic routines and situational idioms of daily verbal behavior, variation in individual mastery is even more apparent. The consequences range from social discomfort to exclusion from or failure in significant areas of activity, because ignorant or maladroit; or, on the other hand, recruitment for and success in certain areas, because adept. There may be a consequence for the possibility of psychotherapy. Such differences may characterize whole subcultures that in basic patterns share the same language.[1]

[1]Cf. the work now being done by Basil Bernstein. . . . He contrasts two modes of speech, *formal* and *public,* associated with the English middle-class and lower-class, respectively. Bernstein finds that the two modes arise because

Concern with differences in individual verbal behavior leads to concern with differences in the role of speech in socialization, and through that, to differences which obtain between groups, whether subcultures or whole societies. Russian psychologists emphasize that the vital functions of speech are acquired in interaction with adults, but seem not to consider the consequences for their experimental norms of different cultural patterns of interaction. This lack they share with most writers, who, if they point out the socialization importance of language, do so in a generic way.[2]

The role of speech in socialization, the context of its acquisition, may vary in every aspect of the patterning of speech events, factors, and functions. Some kinds of variation can be highlighted in a notes-and-queries way with respect to the speech materials and resources available, the processes often stressed in study of personality formation, social structure and organization, and cultural values and beliefs.

What are the cognitive and expressive resources of the linguistic codes of the community? What portion of these are available to children, to what extent and in what sequence? Among the Nupe there are few terms for sexual matters and most knowledge about them is acquired by observation and experience. If there is more than one linguistic code, which is learned first, if either is? (Among the Chontal of Oaxaca, children learn a "second language," Spanish, first, in the home, and Chontal and some other aspects of native culture only in adolescence.) Is there a specialized baby-talk? If so, what is its content (referential, expressive, directive)? Are there verbal games, perhaps metalinguistic in that they draw attention to features of the code as such? (Since much significance has been attached to the child's acquisition of personal pronouns, and means of self-reference, these should be singled out.) What are the *linguistic routines* which the child is taught or can acquire?

A linguistic routine is a recurrent sequence of verbal behavior, whether conventional or idosyncratic. Its pattern may be obvious and concrete, as in single sequences such as the numerals 1 to 10, the days of the week, the ABC's or as in antiphonal sequences such as many children's games, as well as adult games and ceremonies. Or the pattern may not be

---

two social strata place different emphases on language potential, that once this emphasis is placed, the resulting modes of speech progressively orient speakers to different types of relationships to objects and persons, and that this is reflected in differences of verbal intelligence test scores, of verbal elaboration of subjective intent, and otherwise.

[2]George Herbert Mead is one example. Another is A. Irving Hallowell, whose inventory article on "Culture, Personality, and Society" states: "A necessary condition for socialization in man is the learning and use of a language. But different languages are functionally equivalent in this respect, and one language is comparable with another because human speech has certain common denominators" (Hallowell 1953:612).

obvious because it is not concrete, but consists of some regular sequence of emotion or topic. Instruction may be couched as "Then he says . . . and then you say . . .," but often it is not a matter of the exact words. (In magic and instruction from supernatural helpers, of course, often it is.) Or it may be a formal pattern such as a limerick. Feedback may be involved, and the patterning of the routine resemble a branching tree diagram. (A good "line" or salesman's pitch has alternative ways of reaching the same goal.) A vast portion of verbal behavior in fact consists of recurrent patterns, of linguistic routines. Description has tended to be limited to those with a manifest structure, and has not often probed for those with an implicit pattern. Analysis of routines includes identification of idomatic units, not only greeting formulas and the like, but the full range of utterances which acquire conventional significance, for an individual, group, or whole culture. Description is usually limited to idioms of phrase length which, because their reference is not predictable from their parts, must be independently listed in a dictionary as lexical units (e.g., "kick the bucket"). Even for clear referential categories such as those of place and personal names, a carefully considered description of the status and formation of idioms is rare (see Hoijer 1948:182–3 for a fine example), and conventionalization in terms of other functions is important in behavior and personality formation. There are utterances conventionalized in metalinguistic and contextual function, but especially interesting here are those with directive or expressive function. A child's play in imitation of adult roles, as a girl with her dolls, may reveal many of the conventionalized sequences of her family—sequences which have recurred in situations until in some sense they "name," "stand for" the situation and carry a significance, expressive or directive, not predictable from their constituent parts. A mother may find herself using expressions to her child that her own mother had used to her, and with horror, having sworn as a child never to do so.

The number and range of such idioms varies between individuals, families, groups. These and linguistic routines play a great part in the verbal aspect of what Lantis (1960) points to as "vernacular culture," the handling of day-to-day situations, and they are essential in verbal art, in the oral performance of myths, sung epics, many speeches and lectures. The text of these is not identical from one performance to the next, but the general sequence is more or less constant, and most of the verbal content is drawn from a standard repertoire. They fill the slots of a speech, as words fill the slots of a sentence. (Their presence can sometimes be detected when a performer finds himself not communicating. Sequences which he has drawn on as ready coin may prove to have no conventional value for a new audience, which struggles for an interpretation of something intended merely as formulas or labels.) The acquisition of conventional sequences, both idioms and routines, is a continuous process in life, and herein resides some of the theoretical interest, for to a great extent these sequences exist in the cambium between idiosyncrasy and culture. They exhibit persisting effort toward the patterning and predictability of behavior. Some sequences become idiomatic for a person or group because of a memorable novelty (see Hockett 1958:304ff.), but more because sensed as appropriate or as needed. Most do not achieve generality or persistence, but some would lose value if they did, being intended or enjoyed as distinctive, or private to a few.

Turning to the formation of personality, how does speaking figure in the economy of punishment and reward, as alternative to physical acts (spanking, hugging) and to deprivation or giving of things such as candy? At what stage in psycho-sexual development is pressure about speech applied, if any is? How intensive is it? Autobiographical materials from Ghanian students reveal great childhood anxiety about speech. When is socialization pressure about weaning, toilet-training, self-feeding and the like applied in relation to the child's verbal development? In some groups it is after the demands can be verbally explained, in some not. What is the incidence of stuttering and other speech defects, if any? There is evidence that this depends upon socialization pressures, being absent in some groups, and perhaps among the Pilagá characteristic of girls rather than, as among us, of boys. If there is bilingualism, do speech defects appear in both or but one language? How much does speech figure in the transmission of skills and roles? Among some groups, such as the Kaska (Canada), it figures very little. Does a baby talk facilitate or retard acquisition of adult speech patterns? Is speaking a source of pleasure, of oral, perhaps erotic gratification? That some languages are extremely rich in vocabulary showing sound symbolism, some quite poor, suggests differential enjoyment of the phonic substance of language.

From the viewpoint of the social system of the group, how does speaking enter into definition of the roles acquired or observed by children? In what ways does this determine or reflect how speaking is acquired? How relatively significant is speaking in aggressive roles, such as that of warrior? of shaman or priest? (Perhaps the role of speaking in interaction with parents will correspond to the role of speaking in interaction with enemies or the supernatural.) How do residence rules, marriage rules, and the like affect the composition of the household in which the child learns to speak? In affecting the number and relative ages of children, these things affect the rate of mastery of adult speech patterns; there is evidence that singletons master speech more rapidly, children near the same age less rapidly, twins most slowly. Twins and children near the same age may develop and rely on their own verbal code vis-a-vis each other. If there is multilingualism, are the roles and settings of the languages kept distinct? If so, the child probably will acquire the languages without confusion, but if not, there may be personality difficulties. Are there situations and roles in which it is necessary to translate between two languages? If not, the child may very well master each without acquiring ability to do so. Such external factors have much to do with the effect of multilingualism on personality, including cognitive structure. In what settings are children required to speak, forbidden, permitted? What proportion of total behavior settings for the group permit the presence and speaking of children? A Russian visitor to France was astonished when the children of his host kept silent at the table; Russian children would have been reprimanded for *not* joining in the conversation with a guest.

The values and beliefs of the group of course pervade all this. What are the beliefs regarding children as participants in speech? Some believe neonates capable of understanding speech. The Ottawa believed the cries of infants to be meaningful, and had specialists in their interpretation. The Tlingit believed the talk of women to be the source of conflict among men, and an amulet was placed in a baby girl's mouth to make her taciturn. Are skill and interest in speech demanded, rewarded, ignored, or perhaps repressed? The Ngoni of Nyasaland value skill in speech, believing it part of what constitutes a true Ngoni, and so take pains to instill it in children and maintain it in adults. The remarkable polyglot abilities of Ghanian students in Europe perhaps reflect similar values in their own cultures. What values are held and transmitted with regard to the language or languages spoken? We have noted presence and absence of pride as between the Hopi-Tewa and Eastern Cherokee. The problem of bilingualism among immigrant children in the United States has been noted as one of the sense of inferiority associated with the non-English language. Concern for excellence of speech seems universal, but the degree and manifestation vary. Some groups tolerate sloppy pronunciation, some do not. If baby talk is present, is it believed easier for children? In sounds and forms it may in fact be as hard as the adult equivalents, and have the latent function of delaying the child's acquisition of these. What evidential status is accorded the statements of children? What degree and kind of intellectual awareness of speaking is present? What folk conceptions of a metalinguistic sort, as reflected in words for linguistic features or the abstraction of these for use in games and speech surrogates? Neighboring dialects may differ, as when one group of Mazatec abstract the tones of their language for a whistled code, while the Soyaltepec Mazatec do not. Bloomfield (1927) has ascribed the erroneous and sometimes injurious folk conceptions about language in our own culture to mistaken generalization from learning of writing, a later and conscious matter, relative to the largely unconscious learning of speech. Values and beliefs regarding speaking, or a language, may be interwoven with major institutions, and much elaborated, or peripheral and sketchy.

## *References*

Bloomfield, Leonard. 1927. "Literate and Illiterate Speech," *American Speech,* 2:432–39.

Hallowell, A. Irving. 1953. "Culture, Personality, and Society." In Kroeber, A. L. (ed.), *Anthropology Today*. Chicago: University of Chicago Press. Pp. 597–620.

Hockett, Charles F. 1958. *A Course in Modern Linguistics.* New York: Macmillan.

Hoijer, H.· 1948. "The Structure of the Noun in the Apachean languages," *Actes du XXVIIIe Congres International des Américanistes.* Paris: Société des Américanistes. Pp. 173–184.

Lantis, M. 1960. "Vernacular Culture," *American Anthropologist,* 62:202–216.

Luria, A. R. 1959a. "The Directive Function of Speech, I," *Word,* 15:341–52.

________. 1959b. "The Directive Function of Speech, II," *Word,* 15:453–64.

Luria, A. R. and Yuovich, F. Ia. 1959. *Speech and the Development of Mental Processes in the Child.* Translated by J. Simon. London: Staples Press.

## *QUESTIONS FOR DISCUSSION*

1. Select at least five speech situations where the English usage demanded is distinctly different—e.g., formal as against informal, specialized vocabulary, dialectal differences, and so on. For each, describe the relation between the demands for communication and the types of language necessary to meet these demands.
2. Describe your own experiences in the acquisition of the dialects and special usages of English. Do they fit into the sociolinguistic framework suggested by Labov or Bernstein?
3. Describe some of your own ideas about the verbal development of the child. If you were given the time and funds, how would you study such development?
4. Describe how, in view of these materials on language acquisition, you would design a communication skills course on the college level. What would be your objectives in this course, and how would you try to achieve them?
5. Discuss your ideas about how the mass media (newspapers, magazines, television, radio, recordings, movies, and so on) fit into the over-all pattern of a child's verbal development. How might the verbal development of a child in today's world differ from say, the early nineteenth century?

*chapter* **4**

# HUMAN INFORMATION PROCESSING AND DIFFUSION

## SECTION ONE: OVERVIEW AND PERSPECTIVE

### *Objectives for Section One*

After reading this section you should be able to:

1. Define in writing information and specify the circumstances in which information may be acquired.
2. Define in writing diffusion and describe the type of motivational characteristics that a communication source may have when engaging in diffusion.
3. Distinguish in writing between conditioning and reinforcement, and exemplify each.
4. List the selective tendencies that influence human information processing and identify in writing each in everyday communication transactions.
5. Explain in writing the concept of "multi-step flow" and describe how it may operate in the diffusion of information about a political candidate.
6. Define and distinguish in writing between "homophily" and "heterophily" in terms of your interaction with other people in an educational environment.
7. Specify in writing what a receiver can do to enhance his own acquisition of information.
8. Specify in writing what a source can do to enhance the acquisition of information of his receivers.

*James C. McCroskey*

# HUMAN INFORMATION PROCESSING AND DIFFUSION

Research on human processing and diffusion of information, undertaken by scholars from a number of academic fields, has resulted in a number of independent theories. There has been little attempt to integrate this body of research and theory. It will be the purpose of this essay to attempt such an integration and to suggest, as far as possible, the practical implications of this material for the communicator.

## *The Nature of Information and Its Diffusion*

### A MATTER OF DEFINITION

The term "information" is a part of almost everyone's vocabulary. In a sense, we all know what it means. But in another sense, the meaning of the term is most unclear. Engineers have reduced the definition to a mathematical formula, but for our purposes such a definition is inadequate. We shall define information as "knowledge about objects and events and about the relationships between objects and events."

James C. McCroskey *is Associate Professor and Director of Graduate Studies in Speech Communication at Illinois State University. His primary teaching and research interests are communication theory, persuasion, and communication education. He has published articles in these areas in the* Journal of Communication, Public Opinion Quarterly, Journal of Social Psychology, Journal of Broadcasting, Speech Monographs, Quarterly Journal of Speech, Speech Teacher, *and numerous regional and state journals. He is the author of a book entitled* An Introduction to Rhetorical Communication, *and coauthor of two other recently published books,* An Introduction to Interpersonal Communication *and* Elements of Debate.

"Knowledge" is a mentalistic term, and its use suggests a humanistic limitation of our definition of information. Knowledge cannot exist on its own. It only exists within the minds of people. Information, therefore, also exists in the minds of humans. When we say we wish to "communicate information" to another individual, what we are saying is that we wish to create knowledge about objects or events or about relationships between objects and events in the mind of the other person. We may accomplish this with verbal descriptions of the object or event, we may accomplish it nonverbally by bringing the other individual into proximity with an object, or we may employ both verbal and nonverbal means.

People also acquire information without the assistance of other people. If I walk into a room and see a wall, I can acquire information concerning the color of that wall by observation. The crucial thing to remember is that the acquisition of information is dependent upon mental associations within the individual acquiring the information. These mental associations may be stimulated by something in the external environment, or they may be stimulated either partially or exclusively by the internal state of the individual (thinking). Thus, information is acquired in some instances by an interaction of external stimuli and internal associations, and in other instances by purely internal associations.

It should be noted that at no point have we included the concept of "reality." Some people prefer to restrict the definition of information to "correct" perception of the external world, but such a restriction is unwarranted. If I walk into a room and look at a wall and perceive it to be painted gray when "in reality" it is painted green, I have nevertheless acquired information about the room, albeit incorrect information.

Defining "diffusion" is less difficult. Diffusion is the process of communicating information to other people. For diffusion to occur, at least one person must have acquired the information, and that person must be motivated by a desire to have other people acquire that information. It is important to consider for a moment the motivation for diffusion. Information seldom exists in a static state in an individual. Rather, information has a direct relationship to human behavior. To a large extent, we may be able to predict human behavior on the basis of the information which the individual has acquired. To diffuse information, therefore, is to influence behavior. In most instances the motivation which prompts diffusion of information is the motivation to modify human behavior. Diffusion of information, therefore, is closely related to the process of persuasion, which will be discussed in the next chapter. Although we will not consider persuasion further at this time, the close relationship between the material discussed in this and Chapter 5 should be kept clearly in mind while reading both.

## LEARNING THEORIES AND INFORMATION PROCESSING

The process of acquiring information is referred to as "learning." Thousands of experimental investigations of this phenomenon have resulted in several theories concerning how people learn, or acquire information. Two of these theories—conditioning and reinforcement—are particularly helpful for our purposes.

CONDITIONING. The work of Ivan P. Pavlov (1927) provided the foundation of conditioning theory. For Pavlov and other conditioning theorists, the basic process in learning is the formation of an association between a stimulus and a response because of their contiguity. Pavlov's research provides an example. Salivation is a natural response in dogs. In time a dog naturally learns to salivate when food is brought near him, although originally he salivated only when eating the food. He can then be taught to salivate in the presence of stimuli other than food, through the process of conditioning. Pavlov taught dogs to salivate in the presence of a ringing bell (stimulus), by ringing a bell on several occasions as food was brought before the dog. At the outset the dog would salivate because of the presence of food, but after a period of time he would salivate merely at the ringing of the bell, even if no food were present.

Humans also can be conditioned. A natural response in humans is for them to relax. The reverse response, a state of tension, is also a natural response. Which response will be made by an individual depends on what type of stimulus is present. This difference in human response may be compared to Pavlov's dogs: These dogs had two natural responses, to salivate and not to salivate, and which response was evoked depended, initially, on whether food was present. The conditioning of the dogs involved artificially inducing salivation in the presence of a stimulus that would not ordinarily produce salivation. A comparable technique has been used with humans to help them overcome debilitating anxiety. This technique, a behavior therapy referred to as "systematic desensitization," involves generating a relaxation response in people and then introducing a stimulus that would normally cause them to be tense and nervous. With repeated exposure, the individual is conditioned to respond with relaxation in the presence of a stimulus that previously would have produced tension.

The crux of conditioning theory is the relationship between stimulus and response on spatial and temporal dimensions. We learn that cloudiness and rain are associated, because it rains while it is cloudy and does not rain while the sun is shining. Much of our elemental learning can be explained by this process of conditioning.

REINFORCEMENT. Edward Lee Thorndike (1898, 1932) was the founder of reinforcement theory. He and his followers, particularly C. L. Hull (1943) and B. F. Skinner (1938, 1948), have assumed a dominant place in contemporary learning theory. The essence of reinforcement theory is that when a connection between a stimulus and response is made and this connection is followed by a satisfying result, the connection between the stimulus and response is strengthened. The important variable is reward. In short, organisms learn that which is rewarding and fail to learn that which is not. Thus, if a child raises his hand before he speaks in a classroom and is complimented for that by the teacher, he is likely to learn to raise his hand before speaking.

While learning theories are helpful in understanding human processing of information, there is an inherent problem with learning theory. Learning theory is the product of learning researchers—and these individuals, for the most part, have been rigid behaviorists. To them, "information," as we have defined it, would be meaningless. Their concern is whether or not the dog salivates or the child raises his hand, not what the child "thinks" or what the child "knows." A learning theorist would be likely to say that we know that a person has learned only when he behaves in such a manner that we can hypothesize that he must have learned in order to behave in that way. Most of the theory and research concerning learning which is based upon the conditioning and reinforcement traditions is highly mechanistic, not mentalistic. The theory does not depend upon "thinking" by the human who is learning. Nevertheless, it is possible to extrapolate from these theories and the mass of research which has supported them and to draw some conclusions about how humans acquire information.

If we assume that all living organisms seek desirable conditions for themselves and that man is not unique in this regard, we can describe human acquisition of information as the process of observing stimuli, relating those stimuli to previous information, determining whether or not the stimuli can increase the desirability of conditions for the individual, and either storing or discarding the stimuli from the memory. This procedure suggests that the individual engages in considerable selectivity in processing his information. This hypothesis is born out by considerable research.

## SELECTIVITY AND SCREENING IN INFORMATION PROCESSING

Because of the monumental number of stimuli that are constantly bombarding the individual, it almost goes without saying that the individual must select from all of these stimuli those to which he will attend and which he will process. While no two individuals are quite alike, research suggests four tendencies among people which affect the way that they select information for processing. It should be stressed that these are *tendencies*, rather than universal responses of individuals. While research has indicated that these tendencies exist, there is as yet insufficient information to describe precisely when they dominate a human's reactions.

Two bodies of theory have been drawn upon to explain how this selectivity comes to exist. The first is reinforcement. Briefly stated, the theory suggests that people will process information that promises to be rewarding, and that they will avoid selecting information which does not promise a reward. Another body of theory, often referred to as "consistency" theory, is also employed to explain selectivity. This theoretical position will be discussed further in the next chapter; but, briefly, consistency theory suggests that when an individual's cognitions are inconsistent, he will seek new information to resolve the inconsistency. This theoretical position also suggests that individuals will tend to avoid processing information which will create inconsistent cognitions.

The four tendencies in selectivity that lead to screening of information are selective exposure, selective attention, selective perception, and selective retention.

SELECTIVE EXPOSURE. Reinforcement theories suggest that people seek reinforcement for their attitudes, beliefs, values, and behaviors. Consistency theories suggest that people try to avoid a state of inconsistency such as would exist when information would be incompatable with prior or present behavior. Thus we should expect that people would seek information which is consistent with their own attitudes, beliefs, values, and behavior. The converse of this is that people will avoid conflicting information. Considerable research indicates that our expectations are correct (see Mills, Aronson, and Robinson, 1959). This tendency in people has been referred to as "selective exposure," by which is meant that people selectively expose themselves to information on the basis of whether they consciously or unconsciously believe that the information will be reinforcing. This tendency has important implications for communication behavior. We should expect people to seek interaction with other people whom they believe will provide consistent information. Similarly, usage of the mass media should be expected to be affected by this tendency. We should expect people with liberal tendencies to read the *New Republic* and people with more conservative tendencies to read the *National Observer*. Such choices would enable the individual to be reasonably assured that in most instances he will receive information that is consistent and reinforcing, rather than the reverse.

While this tendency in human processing of information has been observed in several research studies, it must be stressed that it is only a *tendency*. Researchers have not observed instances where everyone behaved in a manner consistent with such a tendency, and in some cases little or no trace of selective exposure has been found. Nevertheless, the tendency often is present and has an important bearing on the way humans process information (see Elihu Katz's article in this chapter).

SELECTIVE ATTENTION. Although people tend to avoid exposure to information which is inconsistent or unrewarding, it is not always possible to avoid such exposure. When exposure to inconsistent or unrewarding stimuli occurs, there is a tendency to pay selective attention. This is the tendency for people to pay close attention to information that is consistent with their attitudes, beliefs, values, and behaviors, and little attention to stimuli which are inconsistent (Gilkinson, Paulson, and Sikkink, 1955).

Of course, all attention is, in one sense, selective. Everything in our perceptual world makes some demand upon our attention. This maze of stimuli permits the operation of selective attention in the sense that we are discussing it here. Selective attention is not so much the conscious "tuning out" of inconsistent information as it is the unconscious "tuning in" of consistent information.

SELECTIVE PERCEPTION. Obviously, it is impossible always to avoid paying attention to nonreinforcing or inconsistent information. Some such information will be attended to. However, this does not mean that the individual necessarily will perceive that the stimulus is inconsistent. Research suggests that there is a tendency for people to perceive selectively what stimuli actually mean. We may see what isn't there, or we may fail to see what is there (Cooper and Johoda, 1947). People tend to perceive what they want to perceive or what they expect to perceive, whether or not such perceptions are in accord with what other people might consider reality. For example, a study was conducted, in which three messages with regard to bussing students to maintain racial balance in schools were variously attributed to the late Martin Luther King and Governor George C. Wallace of Alabama. One was a strongly worded message in favor of the bussing, one was clearly opposed, and one was a moderate statement expressing both favorable and unfavorable views about bussing. When the moderate position was read by college students, it made a considerable difference whether it was attributed to King or Wallace. Because the students expected King to be for bussing and Wallace to be opposed, the same message was perceived to be strongly supportive of bussing when attributed to King but to be strongly opposed to bussing when attributed to Wallace (Arnold and McCroskey, 1967). Thus, attention to stimuli does not guarantee that the stimuli will be perceived in accordance with what we might call "reality."

SELECTIVE RETENTION. Even though stimuli may survive the three preceding selective tendencies, there is still no assurance that they will be retained by the individual for any period of time. There appears to be a tendency for people to forget unrewarding or inconsistent stimuli and remember those which are rewarding and consistent (Levine and Murphy, 1954). It appears that humans tend simply to "process out" information that is inconsistent or unrewarding. They may not recall ever having been exposed to that information at any earlier time.

The conclusions from the research on selective tendencies may be summarized as follows: New information which is consistent with prior information or perceived to be potentially reinforcing is likely to be processed by the individual and retained; new information which is inconsistent with present information or is perceived to be potentially nonreinforcing is likely not to be processed or retained by the individual.

## SOURCES OF INFORMATION

Although the processes of selectivity and screening prevent us from acquiring much information which we could acquire, all of us do acquire new information. The question thus becomes, How do we acquire information? The answer to that question is both simple and complex. At the simple level, we acquire new information from the mass media, from contacts with other people, and from our direct observation of our environment. Or, to put it another way, we read, listen, and see. But this simple explanation of how we acquire information does not really explain why some information is acquired and other information is not.

Most people assume that if we were to desire to communicate information to a large number of people, the most efficient way of doing this would be the mass media. Research on the effect of the mass media on the acquisition of information provides some support for that assumption, but also indicates that it does not always hold. Briefly, the research suggests that people are very effectively exposed to information through the mass media, but that in many cases the information fails to become internalized The research suggests that the mass media are very effective in informing people about major news events, but have a minimal impact on the acquisition of other information. The research of Deutschmann and Danielson (1960) for example, indicates that 88 per cent of the population of the United States learned of the flight of Explorer I, President Eisenhower's first stroke, and Alaska's admission to statehood through the mass media. This research, and similar studies, lead to the conclusion that the mass media is a very effective instrument for informing the public. But while this may be true of information that is particularly newsworthy, it does not appear to be true of information with less news value. The mass media seem to be effective in diffusing information when the subject matter is new or relatively new to the receiver (e.g., a major news story), but they seem to have little effect when the receiver already knows quite a bit about the subject.

One of the assumptions that underlies most theory relating to information and attitude is that the acquisition of information will tend either to reinforce or modify attitudes and behavior. Thus, if the mass media is effective in dissemenating information there should be an observable effect on the relevant public attitudes and behavior. The research in this area tends to suggest that often no such effect occurs (Katz and Lazarsfeld, 1955). Simple exposure to the mass media does not necessarily mean that the information provided is internalized by the individual. Rather, it appears that often at least another step is necessary for this to occur. This has sometimes been referred to as the "two-step flow" of communication. By this is meant that one person, often called an "opinion leader," obtains the information through the mass media and then diffuses it to other people with whom he is acquainted. Hence the label, "two-step flow": mass media → opinion leader → person 2. Other research suggests that there may be more than two steps in the process. In short, the concept of a "multi-step flow" may be more appropriate (see van den Ban's article in this chapter).

To sum up, it appears that the acquisition of information by an individual is primarily dependent upon his own observation and his interaction with other people in his environment. The effect of the mass media seems to be only moderate.

## DIFFUSION OF NEW INFORMATION

Research on diffusion of new information points to the extreme importance of an individual's interacting with other people in his environment. The most significant research in this area falls under the category of "diffusion of innovations" research (Rogers, 1962). "Innovations" are new products or new procedures, and the acceptance of either requires the acquisition of new information. In most instances this new information will be inconsistent with old information and with old behavioral patterns, thus, the diffusion of innovations is particularly difficult because of the screening processes of individuals.

THE PRINCIPLE OF HOMOPHILY. One of the most important principles derived from research on the diffusion of innovations is the principle of homophily. "Homophily" is the degree to which pairs of individuals who interact are similar in certain attributes (beliefs, values, education, social status). Simply put, "the principle of homophily" is that acquisition of information most frequently occurs between a source and a receiver who are alike, i.e., homophilous. The reciprocal of this principle also holds: The more "heterophilous" (unlike) are source and receiver, the less likely there will be acquisition of information.

While the terms "homophily" and "heterophily" have only recently become common in the communication literature, the concepts which they represent are not new and are almost commonsensical. The concept is not a difficult one. It merely means that a plumber is more likely to acquire new information from another plumber than he is from a college professor; a teen-ager is more likely to acquire new information from a teen-ager than from a policeman; a black ghetto resident is more likely to acquire information from another black ghetto resident than from a white suburbanite.

THE CHANGE AGENT AND THE OPINION LEADER. Although all of us are motivated to attempt to diffuse information from time to time, some people find this to be a primary function in their professional career. Such people have been referred to as "change agents." The function of these people in society is to disseminate information in order to achieve behavioral change among people. Such people are normally vastly more informed on the subject under consideration than the people with whom they are concerned. In short, a highly heterophilous state normally exists in such transactions. Not only is the change agent more informed, he often holds higher social status, is better educated, and is much more secure economically. A fact of the change agent's life, therefore, is the extreme difficulty of accomplishing his communication objective. People normally do not turn to change agents for information because of the heterophilous state that exists between them; rather, they turn to what have been called "opinion leaders" for information. An "opinion leader" is a person who is essentially similar to the person who turns to him for information; however, he will normally have slightly more expertise. He may, but not necessarily, be slightly more educated, slightly higher in social status, and slightly more secure economically. We normally have considerable respect for our opinion leaders, and yet we feel comfortable with them. There is not complete homophily between us and our opinion leaders, but the heterophily that is present is not large.

The research in the area of diffusion of innovations suggests that the most expeditious way in which information can be diffused is through a process whereby the change agent diffuses the information to the opinion leader, who then diffuses the information to his followers. For example, a government agricultural specialist (change agent) may inform a leader of a small village (opinion leader), who may then inform the other villagers.

PROPOSITIONS DERIVED FROM DIFFUSION RESEARCH. Rogers and Bhowmik's paper explicates 12 propositions that have been derived from research on diffusion of innovations. Because their paper is reproduced in this chapter, we will not elaborate the propositions here. We would suggest that you read their article before continuing to the next section of this essay.

## IMPLICATIONS OF THE ACQUISITION, PROCESSING, AND DIFFUSION OF INFORMATION FOR THE COMMUNICATOR

Our concern in the foregoing part of this article, was with describing how humans process information and how information is diffused from one person to other persons. We have not attempted to summarize all the research in this area—which comes from diverse academic fields—but we have attempted to select that research upon which can be based meaningful suggestions to the practicing communicator. Since, as communicators, we function both as sources and receivers of information, we will divide the following recommendations into these categories.

THE COMMUNICATOR AS RECEIVER OF INFORMATION. It is essential for our intellectual growth and prosperity for us to acquire new information almost constantly. The person who ceases to acquire new information shortly becomes out of touch with the reality of his world. Meaningful acquisition of information requires effort on the part of the individual, if he is not to let valuable information slip by him. The acquisition of information, then, is an active rather than a passive process.

The first step is the identification of the information we already have. We must ask ourselves what we know about a given object or event. What information have we already internalized? This personal inventory is not an easy task, because much of the information that we have stored in our minds is not readily available at the conscious level. We tend to store information and only recall it when it seems relevant. Nevertheless, we must make this special effort to try to dredge up everything in our minds that is related to our current task or situation, in order to determine what we know.

Equally as important as determining what information we already possess is determining what reinforcers affect us. In short, you must ask yourself: What motivates me? What do I seek? What do I like? Since reinforcement appears to control the acquisition of information, it is important that we be aware of that which reinforces us. Thus we can maintain more control over our acquisition of information. As we watch television, for example, advertisers are attempting to get us to acquire certain information by reinforcing us for that behavior. Such acquisition may not be in our best interests, and our only defense against this attempt at influence is to be aware of what is motivating us and what influence is being attempted.

As we noted earlier, there appears to be a tendency in all human beings to screen information. This screening tends to block information which is inconsistent with information already acquired or with the desires of the individual. Screening can be overcome, and we often do overcome it, but in order to maximize our opportunity to acquire useful information, we must constantly be aware of our tendency to screen. Our tendency to expose ourselves selectively to consistent information must be overcome by a conscious effort to expose ourselves to information which we believe will be inconsistent. In the political scene, if we are liberals we should attempt to listen to conservative speakers and to others whose views differ from ours; if we are conservatives we should attempt to listen to liberal speakers as well as others' positions. If we are sincerely interested in acquiring information so that we can make intelligent decisions, we must always seek to hear the "other side." Similarly, when we are exposed to information, part of which is consistent and part of which is inconsistent with our present cognitions and motivations, we need consciously to avoid selective attention. We should try to pay as much attention to the information which we do not like as we do to the information which we do like. We probably will never be completely successful in such an attempt, but merely to make the attempt increases the probability of success.

Overcoming our own selective perception is particularly difficult, because this process occurs at such an unconscious level that we are very unlikely to be aware of its functioning. One way of overcoming this screening process is to check your perceptions against those of other people, particularly people with whom you disagree. If both those with whom you agree and those with whom you disagree perceive something the same way you do, it is likely your perceptions are correct. However, if your opponent perceives something differently than you, there is good reason to suspect that one, or both, of you are selectively perceiving the information.

Heterophily is probably the biggest barrier to our acquisition of new information, and it probably is the easiest to overcome. We tend to communicate mostly with our peers and avoid communicating with people holding a superior position. We should make every effort to communicate with the people who are heterophilous with us but are likely to have information which will be of use to us. Communication with people who know the same things we know does not provide much opportunity for the acquisition of new information. Communicating with heterophilous individuals does provide such opportunity.

We may summarize our suggestions for the practicing communicator as a receiver of information very simply: Be aware, and make an effort to acquire information. Such recommendations may sound platitudinous, but they are not. The barriers to our acquisition of new information are primarily within our own minds. The only way we can overcome those barriers is to be aware of them and to consciously attempt to control them.

THE COMMUNICATOR AS SOURCE OF INFORMATION. When we attempt to communicate information to another individual, we must be concerned with most of the same things that we must be concerned with as a receiver of information. However, we must be concerned with them on a different level. The best way to start is to presume that the receiver is not going to make an attempt to overcome the barriers to the acquisition of information, and that we have to help him.

First of all, we must determine as nearly as possible what information the receiver already has. If we are going to present information which is inconsistent with the information he already has we must be prepared to resolve that inconsistency for him. We know that if we don't, his tendency will be to screen our information out. One of the best ways of overcoming this problem is to know what reinforces the receiver. If our information is presented in a context which is reinforcing to the receiver, we increase the probability that he will acquire the information. Simply put, if you wish to communicate information to another person you need to know the person and adapt your communication to him and his needs.

However, even if we do know our receiver and attempt to adapt our communication to him, the process of screening may still get in our way. We must seek actively to overcome the tendency to screen on the part of the receiver. To begin with, we must concern ourselves with the tendency of receivers to selectively expose themselves to consistent information. If we wish to overcome this barrier, the best way is to present our information at a time and in such a way that the receiver would be expecting that information presented would be consistent, or at least when he is not expecting inconsistent information.

Let us assume that we are running a political candidate's campaign. We have *X* dollars to spend on television. We may spend that money for half-hour or hour speeches or presentations by our candidate, or we may choose to spend the money on spot announcements. The latter choice would appear to be the wiser: Because these spot announcements would occur without the receiver expecting them, he may be exposed to our information before he is fully aware of what is happening. Moreover, should the television listing for the evening indicate a half-hour's or hour's political presentation by our candidate, anyone who is not a supporter could easily screen out the information, merely by switching to another channel. Briefly, the best way to overcome the tendency toward selective exposure is to provide exposure under circumstances where it is not expected.

Overcoming the tendency to attend selectively to consistent information needs to be accomplished in a similar manner. If we know the receiver will tend to "tune us out" because our information is inconsistent, we need to place it into a context where it arouses attention. Providing reinforcement for attention is a good technique. Such reinforcement may take the form of entertainment, as when a newspaper columnist who wishes to provide new information to his audience may cloak that information in an entertaining or amusing style. The reader may read the column because it is entertaining, and acquire the information, whereas otherwise he might not read it at all.

Probably the best means of overcoming the tendency to perceive information selectively is to determine in advance what type of misperception is likely to occur and specifically point out that that perception is incorrect. As we have said, selective perception is almost completely at the unconscious level. When it is brought to the conscious level by a communicator it is effectively overcome in most instances.

Selective retention can be overcome in a similar, direct manner. Since information is likely to be forgotten, the surest way to insure that it will not be forgotten is to remind the individual of it continuously. This is a principle upon which much national advertising of products is based. Everybody who smokes has heard of Kent cigarettes, those who smoke another brand may forget all about Kent. The advertiser attempts to overcome this selective retention by constantly putting Kent in front of the individual through his billboard and magazine advertisements.

Screening on the part of the receiver can be overcome by the source if he makes a conscious attempt to do so. Most communicators do not effectively overcome their receivers' screening processes, either simply because they are unaware that they exist or because they make no effort to overcome them. The diffusion of information can be enhanced substantially by making such an effort.

The principle of homophily is a very powerful principle of effective communication. As sources of information, we need to be fully aware of the implications of this principle and consciously attempt to take advantage of them. The first step in making homophily work for, rather than against, us is to analyze the receiver with whom we hope to communicate. Such an analysis is designed to determine in what respects we are hetrophilous with our receiver and in what respects we are homophilous with him. If we observe that very little homophily exists, it is clear that we are not the appropriate person to attempt the communication. We must seek to communicate with an opinion leader. However, if some homophily does exist, we may attempt to communicate with the individual by stressing our similarities. We should remember that there is a natural cycle involving homophily and communication: The more homophilous with an individual we are, the more we communicate with him, and the more we communicate with him, the more homophilous with him we become. Thus, if sufficient homophily is not present today for us to convey effectively the information we desire to communicate, one of the ways of increasing the probability of success in the long run is simply to communicate with the individual more and more, in order to establish homophily. At a point sometime in the future, therefore, sufficient homophily may exist to enable us to communicate information to that individual.

### PRINCIPLES OF HUMAN INFORMATION PROCESSING AND DIFFUSION

1. People acquire information from external stimuli, from internal stimuli, and from combinations of the two.
2. People acquire information by being repeatedly exposed to contiguous stimuli and responses.
3. People tend to process information that is reinforcing and fail to process information that is nonreinforcing.
4. People tend to expose themselves to information that is consistent with their attitudes and beliefs but to avoid exposure to inconsistent information.
5. People tend to pay more attention to information that is consistent with their attitudes and beliefs than they do to inconsistent information.
6. People tend to perceive information as consistent with their attitudes and beliefs even when it is inconsistent.
7. People tend to remember information that is consistent with their attitudes and beliefs and forget information that is inconsistent.
8. Most of our information is acquired from interpersonal communication.
9. The mass media generally have a major impact on the diffusion of new information but have little impact on attitudes.
10. The major impact of the mass media in the diffusion of information is through a multi-step flow: mass media to opinion leader to person two to person three and so on.
11. Acquisition of information most frequently occurs between a source and a receiver who are homophilous.
12. Heterophily is the most serious barrier to human communication.

The communication of information from one individual to another is not a simple process. It is likely to be unsuccessful unless either the source or the receiver, or both, makes a conscious effort to facilitate the communication transaction.

## *REFERENCES*

Arnold, W. E. and McCroskey, J. C., Experimental studies of perception distortion and the extensional device of dating. Paper presented to the Speech Association of America convention, Los Angeles, 1967.

Cooper, Eunice and Johoda, Marie. The evasion of propaganda: how prejudiced people respond to anti-prejudice propaganda. *Journal of Psychology*, 1947, 23, 15–25.

Deutschmann, P. J. and Danielson, W. A., Diffusion of knowledge of the major news story. *Journalism Quarterly*, 1960, 37, 345–355.

Gilkinson, H., Paulson, S. F., and Sikkink, D. E. Conditions affecting the communication of controversial statements in connected discourse: Forms of presentation and the political frame of reference of the listener. *Speech Monographs,* 1953, 20, 253–60.

Hull, C. L., *Principles of behavior.* New York: Appleton-Century-Crofts, 1943.

Katz, E. and Lazarsfeld, P. F. *Personal influence.* New York: The Free Press, 1955.

Levine, J. M. and Murphy, G. The learning and forgetting of controversial material. *Journal of Abnormal and Social Psychology*, 1954, 49, 23–28.

Mills, J. Aronson, E., and Robinson, H. Selectivity in exposure to information. *Journal of Abnormal and Social Psychology,* 1959, 59, 250–53.

Pavlov, I. P. *Conditioned reflexes: An investigation of the physiological activity of the cerebral cortex.* Translated and edited by G. V. Anrep. London: Oxford University Press, 1927.

Rogers, E. M. *The diffusion of innovations.* New York: The Free Press, 1962.

Skinner, B. F. *Behavior of organisms.* New York: Appleton-Century-Crofts, 1938.

———, *Walden two.* New York: The Macmillan Company, 1948.

Thorndike, E. L. Animal intelligence: An experimental study of the associative processes in animals. *Psychological Monographs*, 1898, 2, No. 4.

———, *The fundamentals of learning.* New York: Teachers College, Columbia University, 1932.

# SECTION TWO: READINGS

## *Introduction and Objectives for Reading One: "On Reopening the Question of Selectivity in Exposure to Mass Communication"*

The author of this selection discusses a concept basic to theory and research concerning the flow of mass communications—selective exposure. Although the emphasis of the article is on research relevant to mass communication, it also relates directly to interpersonal communication.

After reading this selection you should be able to:

1. Define in writing the term "selective exposure" and describe its implications for research on the effect of media on audiences.
2. Specify in writing three hypotheses concerning supportive selectivity.

3. Identify in writing three factors that the author suggests need to be controlled in experiments (or field studies) investigating selective exposure.

Elihu Katz*

# ON REOPENING THE QUESTION OF SELECTIVITY IN EXPOSURE TO MASS COMMUNICATION

The notion of selective exposure is basic to theory and research on the flow of mass communications. It appears as a major explanatory factor in attempts to account for the repeatedly observed fact that the mass media do not easily persuade people to change their attitudes or practices. Communications campaigns—this argument holds—reach the already-converted; others simply tune out. Hence the generalization that the mass media typically reinforce people in their attitudes and practices, but rarely convert them.

In this sense, selectivity is one of a series of ideas that have led to a reformulation of the image of the relationship between the mass media and their audiences. Whereas the media had been thought capable of impressing their message on the defenseless masses, it now appears as if the audience has quite a lot of power of its own. Indeed, the fashion in research nowadays is not to ask "what the media *do to* people" but "what people *do with* the media," or at least to be sure to ask the second question before the first. This shift in emphasis represents a shift of interest away from the study of mass media 'campaigns' in favor of the study of the 'uses' or the 'gratifications' which people derive from exposure to the media. This shift makes the concept of selectivity all the more important, insofar as the attempt now is to explain selectivity in terms of the functional contribution

*I should like to thank Miss Mady Wechsler for research assistance in this project, and the Social Science Research Committee of the University of Chicago for financial aid.

Elihu Katz, "On Reopening the Question of Selectivity in Exposure to Mass Communications," in Robert P. Abelson, et al. (Ed.), *Theories of Cognitive Consistency: A Source Book*, © 1968 by Rand McNally and Company, Chicago, pp. 788–796. Reprinted by permission of the publisher.

of exposure to some social or psychological need, of which selectivity for the purpose of attitude-reinforcement may be only a particular case.

It is more than a little dissonance-producing, therefore, to read Freedman and Sears' (1965a) conclusion that neither experimental nor field studies provide convincing evidence of the operation of this sort of motivated selectivity. There is no question that selectivity exists—i.e., that individuals are disproportionately exposed to communications which are congenial to their attitudes. The question is whether there is a motivated choice involved, one that is specifically associated with the quest for reinforcement, as distinct from the expression of 'interest' or the search for 'utility,' or the like, and as distinct from de facto selectivity whereby circumstances, rather than motives, conspire to expose people to congenial communications.

The objective of what follows is to look again, in the light of the question raised by Freedman and Sears, at the evidence from mass communications studies. We shall try, at the same time, to respond to the Freedman-Sears call to go beyond the specific notion of selectivity-for-the-purpose-of-obtaining-support and to examine other bases of selective exposure. It is probably correct that some of these are considerably more important than 'supportive selectivity' and may set the conditions under which the latter does or does not take place. Nevertheless, we shall argue that 'supportive selectivity'—at least as far as field studies of mass communications bear witness—is still a factor to be reckoned with.

## *Supportive Selectivity Among Mass Media Audiences*

To restate the argument somewhat more carefully, we will be concerned with the hypotheses (a) that an individual self-censors his intake of communications so as to shield his beliefs and practices from attack; (b) that an individual seeks out communications which support his beliefs and practices; and (c) that the latter is particularly true when the beliefs or practices in question have undergone attack or the individual has otherwise been made less confident of them. Propositions (a) and (c) derive from Festinger's (1957) theory of dissonance. But, say Freedman and Sears, the "experimental evidence does not demonstrate that there is a general psychological tendency to avoid nonsupportive and to seek out supportive information" (p. 69), "nor the more specific hypothesis that whatever preference there is for supportive information will be greater under high than under low dissonance" (p. 75).

When Freedman and Sears turn from the laboratory evidence to the evidence from the (mostly nonexperimental) field studies of mass media campaigns, their argument necessarily changes. They do not say that these studies disprove the hypothesis of selectivity-for-the-purpose-of-obtaining-support but rather that other, more parsimonious, explanations have not been ruled out. Thus, they warn that field studies must take account of the relative availability of different kinds of information before concluding that supportive selectivity has taken place. Equally cogently, they insist that socioeconomic status be controlled before inferring supportive selectivity from findings such as that persons favorable to the United Nations were disproportionately exposed to a UN information campaign. This kind of finding, they rightly maintain, may reflect nothing more than the well-known fact that better-educated individuals are more likely to be in the audience for any communication in the field of public affairs and that better-educated individuals are probably more internationally minded.

While the criticism is sobering, a second look at the admittedly far-from-adequate evidence leaves one wondering whether it is really necessary to change one's bet.

The voting studies are the first to come to mind. Even after Freedman and Sears weight the selective exposure by Democrats and Republicans by the greater availability of Republican information in Erie County, Ohio (Lazarsfeld *et al.,* 1948), there remains very clear evidence of selectivity on the part of the minority party. The same thing holds true—if one weights selectivity by availability in the later Elmira study (Berelson, Lazarsfeld, & McPhee, 1954, p. 245), though the authors do not make the claim themselves. A similar finding turns up in an English election study (Trenaman & McQuail, 1961, p. 87).

The latter, it should be pointed out, presents a stronger case for de facto than for 'motivated' selectivity inasmuch as the correlation between partisanship and selective exposure to party *broadcasts* is only very weak while the relationship between partisanship and choice of partisan *newspapers* is strong. Our inference that this makes a better case for de facto selectivity is based on the assumption that the newspaper can be selected for a large variety of reasons other than political compatibility while the choice of a political broadcast is much more likely to reflect a desire to hear what one of the political parties has to say. Still, it is quite possible—and an interesting subject for comparative study—that Britons seek partisanship in print but fair-play and neutrality in radio and television. It is possible, in other words, that certain arenas are expected to be partisan while others are defined in terms of the expectation of 'equal time.'

Altogether, one must beware—as Mills also points out in Chapter 77—of the bias introduced in the search for selectivity in precisely those arenas where fair play and the hearing of both sides is a fundamental norm, such as in elections, jury trials, debates, and the like. Indeed, these institutions were virtually created to ensure exposure to both sides. Perhaps we should be surprised, therefore, to find any selective exposure at all.

The televised series of Kennedy-Nixon debates is a good example of this. The evidence from several studies (summarized in Katz and Feldman, 1962) indicates that an equally high proportion of members of both parties were in the audience—at least for the first debate. (Subsequent debates tended to include greater numbers of Nixon supporters, probably by virtue of their higher education.) It is particularly interesting, therefore, that there were proportionately more Catholics than Protestants in the audience despite the generally higher educational and occupational status of the Protestants. Indeed, one of the studies (Deutschmann, 1962) found that those Protestants who mentioned religion as "the most important issue of the campaign" were far less likely to be in the viewing audience. This seems to be a real example of selective avoidance, though the number of cases involved is very small. Moreover, this same study demonstrates that after listening to the debate, listeners sought out somebody to talk with, and, overwhelmingly, this was somebody who shared the listener's initial political predisposition. While it is quite likely that this is another case of 'de facto' selectivity, it is interesting to see how people move back and forth—within the same substantive realm—between partisan and non- or bipartisan exposures.

But if the audiences for political communications tend to be affected by norms of fair-play and de facto selectivity, neither of these factors seems important in the area of religious communications. It is almost too obvious to point out that not only do people attend the church of their choice, they also attend, very selectively, the religious broadcasts of their choice. In a study of the audience for religious broadcasting in New Haven, Parker, Barry, and Smythe (1955, p. 207) found that the audience for 5 Catholic programs was predominantly Catholic while the audience for 11 Protestant programs was mostly Protestant.[1] Or, to tell the story more exactly, the Catholics are strongly oriented to religious radio broadcasts, the Protestants are not. To the extent that Protestants listen at all (14 per cent do), they listen in equal numbers to Protestant and to Catholic programs while a very large proportion of Catholics (41 per cent) listen to Catholic programs, and only a small proportion (4 per cent) to Protestant programs. Yet, since the total audience of the Protestant programs is small, and the number of religious listeners among the Catholics is very large, the small proportion of Catholics which listens to Protestant programs is enough to constitute a sizable minority. Note that the religious listeners among the Protestants act something like the Republicans in Erie County and Elmira, exposing themselves almost equally to both 'parties,' while the Catholics, like the Democrats, are much more strongly selective. There is a suggestion

[1]The Catholic programs were not all explicitly such; content analysis confirmed the arbitrary assignment to categories (i.e., the programs designated Catholic had more Catholic content). Although the local audience for Protestant programs was quite small, there were a large number of such programs on the air.

here that the 'minority group' (in terms of the availability of supporting messages, not in terms of numbers in the population) exercises greater selectivity.

Are these people seeking support for their beliefs? It is difficult to imagine why else they are listening and, in the case of the Catholics, why they focus their attention on their own programs. Freedman and Sears say that church attendance may be motivated by factors other than the desire for reinforcement of belief, but even if this is so, the latent functions of attending to religious broadcasts are surely fewer. It is quite likely that such listening partakes of the feeling that one is in touch with one's 'own' and that the mass media are duly recognizing one's belief culture, but these nations are very difficult to separate from the notion of seeking reinforcement.

Another of the studies on which the evidence for selective exposure rests is the classic field experiment reported by Hyman and Sheatsley (1947) in "Some Reasons Why Information Campaigns Fail." Respondents on a national survey were asked whether they had heard a given piece of news (the joint English-French-American announcement denouncing the Franco regime, and the proposal of an Anglo-American Committee that the United States aid in keeping order in Palestine). All respondents—whether they said they had heard or not—were given the substance of the news items by the interviewer (preceded by "As you remember . . ." in the case of those who claimed they had heard). Respondents were then asked whether or not they favored each of the proposals. The finding that those who had heard previously were more favorable than those who had not is presented in support of the selective exposure hypothesis. It may be rightly objected that educational level should have been controlled since it is possible that persons of higher education would have been more likely both to have heard the news and to agree with these two policies. But assuming—and it is not unreasonable—that the finding would stand up under controls, it represents rather strong evidence in support of the 'supportive' hypothesis whether one chooses to regard it as selective exposure or selective retention.

But the notion of selectively seeking support does not appear only in studies of the diffusion of information; it appears in studies of other uses of the mass media as well. A well-known example, though it is based on impressionistic evidence, is Warner's (1948) study of the soap opera, *Big Sister*. Warner argues that the program was so successful among its housewife listeners because it offered them reinforcement for their status in the person of an effective and influential housewife-heroine. In a world in which the housewifely role is challenged as uncreative and unworthy, these programs—so the argument goes—help to reduce the dissonance.

The evidence presented to this point is full of shortcomings and is certainly not conclusive, but it does seem to offer good reason for keeping the hypothesis alive. These studies and the ones criticized by Freedman and Sears (Star & Huges, 1950; Cartwright, 1949; and others) were not designed, in general, to test the hypothesis that support is sought selectively in the mass media, and they cannot really prove it. The relationships are often weak, the formulations are not really tight, alternative explanations have not been ruled out, and the prevailing norms governing exposure are typically overlooked. These shortcomings are exacerbated by the fact that the kind of selective exposure in evidence in these studies is associated with the second, and least interesting, of the three hypotheses listed at the head of this section. In other words, the studies deal primarily with the observed correspondence between a person's attitudes and the communications to which he exposes himself and are virtually silent on whether individuals actively avoid communications that negate their beliefs, and whether the search for reinforcement is accelerated under conditions of dissonance. But the situation need not remain this way. The methodological possibilities of the panel (repeated interviews with the same respondents) or the field experiment, both of which add a time dimension to mass communications research, would certainly lend themselves to the design of more conclusive research in this area.

## *Utility As a Basis of Selectivity*

Even if the hypothesis of supportive selectivity stands up to genuine testing, as I suspect it will, it is very likely that other factors will prove more important as bases for selectivity in exposure to mass communications. Freedman and Sears are correct in calling for more serious attention to some of these other factors and to the psychological dynamics implicit in them.

Thus, Freedman and Sears emphasize the motive of "utility," suggesting that people want information when it answers a felt need or serves a practical purpose. When nonsupportive information is useful, the authors suggest, people will prefer it to less useful information that is supportive.

Freedman and Sears appear to mean by utility any piece of information that helps in the performance of a role or the successful completion of a task. In other words, the notion of utility in this broader sense is nothing short of a functional approach to mass media exposure. It asks, "What do people do with the media?" or, more exactly, "What patterns of communications behavior can be predicted from a knowledge of the needs of different kinds of people?"

Thus, Feldman (1965), for example, indicates that women are more exposed than men to health information—particularly the sort of information that has to do with symptoms of disease—and this despite the lower interest of women in many other substantive areas. Indeed, the difference in the degree of health knowledge between women and men is already evident in the ninth grade. Feldman suggests that these differences in knowledge, interest, and exposure have to do with the fulfillment of role expectations: health information is 'useful' to women in anticipating and carrying out their roles. The same sorts of expectations are directed to educated people and constitute one of the explanations why education is so consistently related to high levels of exposure to all sorts of information, particularly in the realm of public affairs. It also explains why opinion leaders selectively attend to those media which bring information in their own spheres of influence but not to others (Katz, 1958).

Some kinds of exposure, however, are 'useful' precisely because they are 'useless' in that they permit people to avoid, or escape, the performance of a task or a role (cf. Katz & Foulkes, 1962). For example, the less one has of whatever it is that one's schoolmates happen to value (grades, athletic prowess, money), the more heavily one is exposed to the media, particularly to popular expressions of adolescent protest and alienation (Johnstone, 1961).

But 'useful' information can also be rejected—even when it seems to answer an objectively defined need—if one perceives oneself as useless. Thus, in an extremely interesting series of studies, Seeman (1966) has demonstrated that individuals who rank themselves near the 'powerlessness' end of a scale manage to avoid learning information which would be of use to them in their specific situations (reformatory, hospital, workers' organizations) although they do not differ from others on the learning of information unrelated to the exercise of control in their environments. These are studies of selective learning rather than selective exposure, but their import seems very much the same. Indeed, they are very closely related to the finding (Schramm, Lyle, & Parker, 1961) that the greater the disparity between a child's own aspirations and the perceived aspirations for him of parents and peers (where the latter are higher than the former), the greater the exposure to "fantasy-oriented" media and the lower the exposure to "reality-oriented" media. In other words, it appears as if beliefs can sometimes override utility as a selective factor in exposure, bringing the argument full circle.

### *Interest As a Basis of Selectivity*

Apart from the quest for support and for utility, mere interest would seem to be an important factor in selectivity. The desire to see one's self-reflection is part of this. So is the desire to keep watch over things in which one has invested one's ego. Thus, moviegoers identify with screen stars of similar age and sex (Handel, 1950; Maccoby & Wilson, 1957); one reads in the newspaper about an event in which one personally participated; one reads advertisements for the product one purchased (Ehrlich *et al.*, 1957; Mills, 1965a); political partisans immerse themselves in political communications regardless of its source; smokers choose to read material supporting the smoking-lung cancer relationship no less than material disclaiming the relationship, and much more avidly than nonsmokers (Feather, 1963); after one has been introduced to a celebrity one notices (or 'follows') his name in print even more frequently.

But while the examples just cited suggest that 'interest' as a basis of selective exposure is a different sort of thing than exposure on the basis of seeking support (interest leads to exposure to *both* sides of the argument), it is not as easy as it sounds to separate interest from utility and support-seeking. Indeed, some of the examples themselves are used as arguments for supportive selectivity. The problem of distinguishing between the two processes arises as soon as one postulates that interest is, or leads to, ego-involvement. And, if one then hypothesizes—in the spirit of dissonance theory—a continual quest for assurance that one's ego is worthy or well-cathected, the seeing of oneself or one's interests reflected and validated in the mass media is a kind of supportive selectivity—even when such communications are negative.[2] The famous public relations slogan sums this up very well: "Don't mind what they say about you, just as long as they mention your name." Narcissism, in other words, may have some built-in dissonance, and the consequent quest for external validation may not be easily distinguishable from ego-involvement. But this, of course, is simply another example of the overall problem of isolating the supportive motive in selective exposure. In principle, however, the distinction is clear: interest, or investment of the ego, may be followed by the desire for validation, and either or both of these may lead to selective exposure.

There is another aspect to the relationship between interest and support as bases of selectivity. We tend to think of opinions as consisting of a component of general interest in a subject, and a component of specific partisanship. Thus, we think of political partisans as having interest in politics in general and a specific partisan commitment. But many opinions or commitments do not work this way. It may well be, for example, that individuals do not have much interest in religion in general, but only in their own denominations. Or, to take another example, it may well be that

[2] I assume here that we are dealing with persons who have high self-esteem (highly positive self concepts) in the area under discussion. This would exclude situations such as those in the Aronson and Carlsmith (1962) study where subjects were purportedly behaving so as to obtain information confirming their low opinions of themselves (see also McGuire, 1966a, pp. 498–500. . . .

general interest in a subject—Franco Spain, for example, to hark back to the Hyman-Sheatsley (1947) example—is manifested only by those who are on one side (opponents of the regime, in this case) and that there simply is no 'other side' among those who are interested. There are many issues which have enthusiasts on only one side, while all the rest are disinterested (and, by definition, nonpartisan). Studies of selective exposure on a given issue should take account of the empirical relationship between interest and partisanship. Thus, the pro-Franco respondents who had missed the anti-Franco message, according to Hyman and Sheatsley, may have missed the message not because they disagreed but because they were uninterested. And the anti-Franco people, for their part, may have caught the message because they were interested rather than because they were partisan, and would have been equally aware of a pro-Franco communiqué. Methodologically, this argument is exactly analogous to Freedman and Sears' call for holding educational level constant in tests of the supportiveness hypothesis. Interest and utility must be added to the list of factors to control. In any given case, however, it may turn out that selective exposure on the basis of interest and selective exposure on the basis of seeking support may be indistinguishable because interest in a subject may be identical with partisanship.

## *Additional Notes and Conclusions*

The hypothesis that individuals seek information that will support their beliefs and practices and avoid information that challenges them still seems viable from the vantage point of mass communications research. Reexamination of the evidence in the wake of the objections raised by Freedman and Sears, however, reveals how little evidence is required for an hypothesis to be accepted as 'proven.'

Studies are cited from the fields of public affairs, voting, religion, etc., in support of the hypothesis, though none of them can be considered conclusive or a really strict test. Echoing Freedman and Sears, we have been underlining the importance of holding certain other factors constant before concluding that partisanship is the motivating factor in selective exposure.

But it is not easy to test the hypothesis, especially in a field situation. An ideal test requires (a) the taking account of time, in order to demonstrate that partisanship causes selective exposure rather than vice versa; and (b) a situation in which communications are available on both sides of an issue, and where there is a coresponding division of opinion. But this does not solve the problem of how to demonstrate in the field that people avoid uncongenial information, independent of their preference for congenial information. Some adaptation of the Hyman-Sheatsley (1947) method to include 'neutral' communications might prove effective here, in much the way that Mills (1965a) compares the degree of interest expressed by respondents in reading about accepted and rejected products and other products which are neither accepted nor rejected.

Further thought must also be given to field-testing the hypothesized relationship between the extent of support-seeking and the magnitude of dissonance. An attempt in this direction was made by Troldahl (1963) in a field experiment which predicted, among other things, that there would be greater advice-giving and greater advice-seeking in interpersonal communication under conditions of inconsistency between a message and previous beliefs. Unfortunately, however, the experimental message, 'planted' in an agricultural bulletin directed to suburban farmers, failed to arouse much interest, and consequently there was hardly enough interpersonal communication to test the hypothesis.

An even more basic methodological problem to which attention must be given in field studies has to do with the operational definition of selective exposure itself. What are the mechanisms by means of which individuals recognize that they are in the presence of supportive or discrepant information: Do they scan headlines? Do they anticipate what the content of a communication is likely to be from its source? How, in other words, does an individual select among communications according to the supportiveness principle without being exposed to them? In the laboratory, the subject is asked, typically, whether he would like to read a pamphlet or an advertisement taking a stand for or against his opinion or behavior, or he is shown a list of titles from which to choose. Intuitively, this would seem to be the rough equivalent of headline-reading as a means of selectivity, but is it? And how does this work in the case of TV programs? or conversation?

Altogether, this paper argues that the supportive selectivity hypothesis is, in part, a special case of an approach to the problem of exposure in terms of 'uses' or 'gratifications,' i.e., in functional terms. Some of the evidence for selective exposure on the basis of utility is reviewed, and the concept of 'use' is considerably broadened. It is suggested that a conflict over whether to attend to a communication which includes both nonsupportive and useful elements may be resolved either way. Interest, or ego-involvement, is also discussed as a basis for selective exposure.

The discussion of utility and interest, and to a certain extent, the discussion of supportiveness itself, indicates that the problem of selectivity is not limited to the sphere of mass media information. It relates equally to entertainment and other forms of mass media content, and, indeed, to exposure to the mass media per se (regardless of content). Concern with the notion of utility reflects the overall shift in mass media research away from studies of short-run changes of information and attitude as a result of mass media campaigns to studies of different ways in which mass media messages serve the social and psychological needs of their audiences.

## References

Aronson, E. & Carlsmith, J. M. Performance expectancy as a determinant of actual performance. *Journal of Abnormal and Social Psychology*, 1962, *65*, 178–182.

Berelson, B. R., Lazarsfeld, P. F., & McPhee, W. N. *Voting*. Chicago: University of Chicago Press, 1954.

Cartwright, D. Some principles of mass persuasion. *Human Relations*, 1949, *2*, 253–267.

Deutschmann, P. Viewing, conversation, and voting intentions. In S. Kraus (Ed.), *The great debates*. Bloomington, Indiana: University of Indiana Press, 1962.

Ehrlich, D., Guttman, I., Schonbach, P., & Mills, J. Post-decision exposure to relevant information. *Journal of Abnormal and Social Psychology*, 1957, *54*, 98–102.

Feather, N. T. Cognitive dissonance, sensitivity, and evaluation. *Journal of Abnormal and Social Psychology*, 1963, *66*, 157–163.

Feldman, J. J. The dissemination of health information: A case study of adult learning. Unpublished doctoral dissertation, University of Chicago, 1965.

Festinger, L. A theory of cognitive dissonance. Evanston, Ill.: Row, Peterson, 1957.

Freedman, J. L. & Sears, D. O. Selective exposure. In L. Berkowitz (Ed.) *Advances in experimental social psychology*, Vol. 2. New York: Academic Press, 1965. Pp. 58–98. (a)

Handel, Leo. *Hollywood looks at its audience*. Urbana, Illinois: University of Illinois Press, 1950.

Hyman, H. & Sheatsley, P. B. Some reasons why information campaigns fail. *Public Opinion Quarterly*, 1947, *11*, 412–423.

Johnstone, J. W. C. Social structure and patterns of mass media consumption. Unpublished doctoral dissertation, University of Chicago, 1961.

Katz, E. The two-step flow of communication: An up-to-date report on an hypothesis. *Public Opinion Quarterly*, 1958, *21*, 61–78.

Katz, E. & Feldman, J. J. The Kennedy-Nixon debates: A survey of surveys. In S. Kraus (Ed.), *The great debates*. Bloomington, Indiana: University of Indiana Press, 1962.

Katz, E. & Foulkes, D. On the use of the mass media as "escape": Clarification of a concept. *Public Opinion Quarterly*, 1962, *26*, 377–388.

Lazarsfeld, P., Berelson, B., & Gaudet, H. *The people's choice*. New York: Columbia University Press, 1948.

Maccoby, E. E. & Wilson, W. C. Identification and observational learning from films. *Journal of Abnormal and Social Psychology*, 1957, *55*, 76–87.

McGuire, W. J. Attitudes and opinions. *Annual Review of Psychology*, 1966, *17*, 475–514, (a)

Mills, J. Avoidance of dissonant information. *Journal of Personality and Social Psychology*, 1965, *2*, 589–593, (a)

Parker, E. C., Barry, D. W., & Smythe, D. W. *The television-radio audience and religion*. New York: Harper, 1955.

Schramm, W., Lyle, J., & Parker, E. B. *Television in the lives of our children*. Stanford: Stanford University Press, 1961.

Seeman, M. Alienation, membership, and political knowledge. *Public Opinion Quarterly*, 1966, *30*, 353–367.

Trenaman, J. & McQuail, D. *Television and the political image.* London: Methuen and Co., 1961.

Troldahl, V. C. Mediated communication and personal influence. Unpublished doctoral dissertation, University of Minnesota, 1963.

Warner, W. L., The radio daytime serial: A symbolic analysis. *Genetic Psychology Monographs,* No. 37, 1948.

## *Introduction and Objectives for Reading Two: "A Revision of the Two-step Flow of Communications Hypothesis"*

This selection is concerned with the two-step flow theory of communication. The author suggests that the theory be revised on the basis of new research findings which indicate a more complex relationship between individuals and information flow than the present theory suggests.

After reading this selection you should be able to:

1. Draw a diagram of the two-step flow of communication, name its components, and describe the relationships among them.
2. Describe in writing how the studies reported in the article suggest a revision in the two-step flow of communication hypothesis.

A. W. van den Ban*

# *A REVISION OF THE TWO-STEP FLOW OF COMMUNICATIONS HYPOTHESIS*

Some unpredicted findings have been discovered in a study on voting habits made twenty years ago by a group of research workers of Columbia University who formulated their discovery thus: 'Ideas often flow *from*

*I am indebted to Dr. H. H. Felstehausen, of the University of Wisconsin, and to Prof. F. F. H. Kolbé, of the University of Pretoria, for their valuable criticism of an earlier draft of this article.

A. W. van den Ban, "A Revision of the Two-Step Flow of Communications Hypothesis," *Gazette*, X (1964), 237–49. Reprinted by permission of the publisher and the author.

radio and print *to* the opinion leaders and *from* them to the less active sections of the population.' This statement, known as the two-step flow of communications hypothesis, has attracted wide attention in communication literature. At present, however, most research workers agree that the situation in real life is more complicated than this hypothesis suggests. Research on the diffusion of new ideas, techniques, etc., and especially a recent study on the diffusion of new farming methods in the Netherlands, shows that both opinion leaders and their followers are influenced by mass media as well as by personal influence. Farmers usually hear for the first time of the existence of a new method through the mass media, but the decision to adopt an innovation is mainly influenced by personal contacts. However, the kinds of mass media influencing opinion leaders and the kinds of personal contacts influencing them differ from those which influence their followers.

The conclusions drawn from various studies of communication processes differ with regard to the question whether people are mainly influenced by persons of a higher social status or by persons of the class they themselves belong to. The Dutch study suggests that this depends upon the need people feel for new information. If they are badly in need of information, they will turn to well-informed persons who often belong to a higher social status, but they are likely to receive most information on new ideas they do not very badly want to know about through casual conversations with people of their own status group.

## *Review of Literature*

Few findings in communications research have aroused so much interest as the 'two-step flow of communications hypothesis'. This hypothesis originated from an analysis of the 1940 presidential election campaign in the United States which unexpectedly revealed that the majority of the voters were not only influenced by mass media, but that they were even more influenced by other people. These findings led to the hypothesis: 'Ideas often flow *from* radio and print *to* the opinion leaders and *from* them to the less active sections of the population.'[1] Later research showed that communication processes are often more complicated than this hypotheis indicates. In an up-to-date test of this hypothesis published in 1957,[2] Katz found that 'despite their greater exposure to the (mass) media, most opinion leaders are primarily affected not by the comunication media but by still other people.' Katz mainly used the studies of the Bureau of Ap-

[1]P. F. Lazarsfeld, B. Berelson and H. Gaudet, *The People's Choice,* 2nd ed. New York, Columbia University Press, 1948, p. 151.

[2]*Public Opinion Quarterly,* 21, pp. 61–78.

plied Social Research of Columbia University for his 'up-to-date test', but he did not give much attention to the analyses made by rural sociologists of the adoption of new farming methods.

In the tradition of this rural sociological research, Ryan and Gross published their famous study on the adoption of hybrid seed corn already twenty years ago.[3] Subsequent research confirmed their findings that the adoption of new farming methods is usually a rather lengthy process during which people become aware of new ideas mainly through mass media, but where the decision to adopt the new idea is predominantly made as a result of personal influence.[4] It was also found that, as a rule, opinion leaders are better informed than their followers.[5] In the study which forms the subject of this article, we tried to combine these findings by analysing which sources of information were used by opinion leaders and which by their followers during the various stages of the adoption process.

A student of journalism, Mason, had made an attempt to study the same problem. He is rather critical of rural sociological research in this field, but in my opinion his study is only of limited value because of some weaknesses in his methodology.[6] Rural sociologists had asked farmers, subsequent to their having adopted a new idea, about their sources of information while they went through the various stages of the adoption process. Mason, however, asked the farmers at different stages of the adoption process questions such as: 'How much have you talked to someone at the State College about a community drainage project? A lot, quite a bit, a little, or not at all?' This method has two weaknesses. In the first place, in the case of those who had already adopted the new method, the replies related not merely to the sources of information which influenced them during the period which led to their final decision to adopt the new method, but also to the sources from which they got their initial information about this project. In the second place, the differences in the use of the sources of information found in the different stages of the adoption process are partly due to the well known fact that innovators use different sources of information than people do who lag behind in adopting anything new. In addition, it seems doubtful to me whether all those who said that they

[3]B. Ryan and N. Gross, "The Diffusion of Hybrid Seed Corn in Two Iowa Communities," *Rural Sociology,* 8 (1943) pp. 15–24.

[4]This research is summarized in E. M. Rogers, *The Diffusion of Innovations,* Free Press, New York, 1962, ch. IV.

[5]Summarized in Rogers, Ibid, ch. VIII.

[6]R. Mason, "Information Source Use in the Adoption Process," Ph.D. dissertation, Dept. of Communication, Stanford University, Stanford, Cal. R. Mason, "The Use of Information Sources by Influentials in the Adoption Process," *Public Opinion Quarterly*, 27 (Fall 1963), pp. 455–466, and R. Mason, "The Use of Information Sources in the Adoption Process," *Rural Sociology,* 29 (March 1964), pp. 40–52.

had used a certain source of information quite a bit, had actually made use of this source to the same extent.[7]

In a study of an election campaign in the United States, Deutschmann and Pinner found that over 80% of the informed people got their initial information on two major campaign events from mass media. Personal conversations usually take place subsequent to people having been informed by these media. Such conversations usually exert a greater influence on the intention how to vote than mass media do. However, a large number of people who were only influenced by mass media also changed their intention how to vote to some extent.[8] These findings confirm the two-step flow hypothesis. This is also true of the studies on the diffusion of the news of the death of Senator Taft[9] and on that of the assassination of President Kennedy.[10] In the case of the shooting of President Kennedy, it was found that over half the population had got their information from personal sources, but that they had usually turned to the mass media for confirmation and additional information. In the less sensational case of Senator Taft, far fewer people were found to have got their initial information from personal sources, but here too, many had turned to the mass media for additional information, although over half of the total sample were found not to have consulted any other medium for additional information.

These studies give one the impression that people usually get their news first from the mass media, except in cases of very important and unexpected events which cause a lot of excitement and comment. If they are interested in the event, they may consult mass media for additional factual information, but they are perhaps more inclined to listen to personal sources for interpretation and evaluation of these events. The correctness of the hypothesis that one group of people is informed through mass media, and another group through personal contacts, is, therefore, very doubtful.

## *Research Methods*

In the case of our study in the Netherlands, interviews were conducted with all of the approximately one hundred farmers in each of three

[7]Perhaps this is an indication of the rather weak interviewing techniques Mason has used throughout his study. Among other things he reports that out of 97 farmers who had not tested their soils, 38 incorrectly claimed that they had done so (Ph.D. dissertation, table 7, p. 59).

[8]J. Deutschmann and F. A. Pinner, "A Field Investigation of the Two-stage Flow of Communication," paper read for the Association for Education in Journalism, mimeograph, Communication Research Center Michigan State University, East Lansing, 1960.

[9]O. N. Larsen and R. J. Hill, "Mass Media and Interpersonal Communication in the Diffusion of a News Event," *American Sociological Review,* 19 (1954), pp. 426–433.

[10]B. S. Greenberg, "Diffusion of News of the Kennedy Assassination," mimeograph, Institute of Communications Research Stanford University, 1964.

communities with widely different cultural patterns.[11] In order to establish opinion leadership, three sociometric questions were asked:

1. Which two farmers do you ask for advice when you are not sure of the merits of new farming methods?
2. Which two farmers do you consider to be good farmers?
3. Which two farmers do you talk to most frequently?

This method enabled us to count how often each farmer was mentioned in the replies to each of these questions. In addition, in each community, six or seven 'judges', mostly influential farmers, were asked to give each farmer a rating, ranging from a low zero to a high ten, according to the farmer's influence during discussions on farm management. These ratings were then averaged. A factor analysis showed that each of these four 'measures' mainly gave an indication of the same dimension: social status.

In order to measure the information sources used, each farmer was given a card with seven different sources: mass media; meetings and lectures; excursions, demonstrations and experimental plots; the local agricultural advisory officer (in the U.S.: county agent of the extension service); other farmers; salesmen; personal experience.[12] They were then asked which of these sources was usually the most important to them with regard to learning for the first time about a new farming method. The next question was: 'Many farmers await the effect of a new method before deciding whether to apply it themselves. If you make such a decision, which of the information sources on this card is usually the most important to you?' The replies showed that some farmers chose one of the mass media and said that to them the radio or their farming paper was the most important. These replies were also coded. The main reason why these questions were not asked with regard to specific methods was that it would then have been difficult to get any idea about the information sources influencing the late-comers who usually follow in the wake of the opinion leaders.

In addition to the questions on the importance farmers attached to the different information media, questions were also asked about the extent to which farmers used the major information sources.[13]

[11]Except 2% refusals and not-at-homes.

[12]T.V. has not been included, because television is not (yet) used by the agricultural advisory service in the Netherlands. Dutch television programmes only give an agricultural programme for people living in towns; half an hour a month. There are no commercials on the Dutch T.V.

[13]A more complete discussion of these research methods and of the research findings is given in A. W. van den Ban, *Boer en Landbouwvoorlichting; De Communicatie van Nieuwe landbouwmethoden* (The Communication of New Farm Practices in the Netherlands, English summary), Assen. Netherlands, Van Gorcum, 1963.

## *Information Sources Used by Leaders and Followers*

According to the two-step flow hypothesis one would expect leaders to make more use of mass media than their followers. Table 1 shows that this is true with regard to the number of farming papers received by the farmers, but not with regard to listening to farming programmes on the radio, with the exception—to some extent—in the Noord Beveland community. The other information media too, including personal contacts with the local advisory officer, were used more frequently by the opinion leaders than by their followers.

TABLE 1. THE AVERAGE 'JUDGE'S' RATING OF THE INFLUENCE OF FARMERS USING INFORMATION MEDIA TO VARIOUS EXTENTS—SCALE: 0–10

| | *Average Influence Rating* | | |
|---|---|---|---|
| *Information Media Used* | *Noord-Beveland*[1] | *Milheeze*[2] | *Dwingeloo*[3] |
| Number of farming papers | | | |
| None | | [4] | 6.0 |
| 1 | 5.5 | | 6.3 |
| 2 | 6.0 | | 7.6 |
| 3 or more | 7.0 | | 7.6 |
| Listening to radio farming programmes | | | |
| Never | 5.8 | 5.8 | 6.5 |
| Sometimes | 5.9 | 5.9 | 6.8 |
| Nearly always | 6.4 | 5.7 | 6.3 |
| Number of agricultural meetings attended | | | |
| None | 5.1 | 4.9 | 6.1 |
| 1–5 | 5.8 | 5.1 | 6.7 |
| 6 or more | 6.8 | 6.6 | 7.2 |
| Number of farm visits by agricultural advisory officer last year | | | |
| None | 5.3 | 5.0 | 5.4 |
| 1–3 | 6.1 | 6.0 | 6.6 |
| 4 or more | 6.5 | 7.1 | 6.8 |
| Demonstrations attended | | | |
| None | 5.6 | 5.3 | 6.5 |
| Some | 6.3 | 6.2 | 6.6 |

[1]A community with modern farm management and many contacts with urban culture.
[2]A community with modern farm management and few contacts with urban culture.
[3]A community with traditional farm management and few contacts with urban culture.
[4]All farmers in this community receive a farming paper, but only 7% more than one.

## STAGES IN THE ADOPTION PROCESS

A second reason to revise the two-step flow of communications hypothesis is based on the results of Table 2, showing the sources of information used during the different stages of the adoption process.

TABLE 2. THE PERCENTAGE OF FARMERS CONSIDERING VARIOUS SOURCES OF INFORMATION TO BE THE MOST IMPORTANT

| *Source of Information* | *To Learn*[1] | *To Decide*[2] |
|---|---|---|
| Farming papers | 16 | 1 |
| Radio | 13 | 0 |
| Mass Media in general | 41 | 3 |
| Mass Media plus some other source | 5 | [3] |
| Demonstrations, meetings, etc. | 6 | 12 |
| Advisory officer | 3 | 20 |
| Other farmers | 11 | 43 |
| Other farmers plus some other source | [3] | 8 |
| Salesmen | 3 | 4 |
| Personal experience | 0 | 3 |
| Other combination of sources | 2 | 3 |
| No answer | 0 | 4 |

[1]Initial information about new farming methods.

[2]On the adoption of those methods.

[3]Coded as other combination.

For initial information about new methods 75% of the farmers mentioned mass media as their most important source of information, but these media have hardly any importance when it comes to decide to adopt the new method. During the decision stage of the adoption process, personal contacts with other farmers, advisory officers and salesmen were mentioned as the major information sources by 75% of the respondents. Under these conditions it is hardly possible for opinion leaders to have been exclusively influenced by mass media, or for their followers to have been influenced only by personal contacts.

In accordance with the two-step flow hypothesis we found that those farmers who usually first hear from other farmers about new methods, exert very little influence themselves. However, there are so few of these farmers—only 33 out of 303 respondents—that this can hardly be considered sufficient evidence for the correctness of the hypothesis. Furthermore, the eleven farmers who mentioned mass media as their major source of information in the decision stage of the adoption process were not exceptionally influential.

We may therefore conclude that opinion leaders as well as their followers are influenced both by mass media and by other people, but during different stages of the adoption process.

### *Who Influences Whom?*

According to the original two-step flow hypothesis there is one group of opinion leaders who influence all others. Later research has shown, however, that there may actually be a hierarchy of leaders. How this process works is not quite clear from previous research. Some authors say that 'opinion leaders and the people whom they influence are very much alike and typically belong to the same primary groups.'[14] But other studies showed that 'farmers were generally inclined to look up the status scale for advice on matters related to farming.'[15]

The replies to our three sociometric questions enable us to analyze how this process worked within one community. We do not possess any information on the farmers outside this community who may influence farmers within, or vice versa.[16] In order to analyze who influences whom within a community, the farmers were first divided into four groups ('quartiles') according to the scores showing their contacts with the advisory service.[17] It was then possible to calculate how many choices had been made for farmers in the same quartile according to their contact with 1, 2 or 3 quartiles more or less contact and, also, how many choices would have been made if each farmer had chosen two other farmers at random. By dividing these two sets of figures we obtained Table 3.

The last line of this table shows that not all farmers made the two choices they were requested to make; if they had done so, all the figures on this line would have been 100. More interesting are the columns showing that there is a tendency to choose as friends, farmers with a little more contact with the advisory service than the respondents maintain themselves; but to choose as 'good farmers', farmers who maintain much more

[14]Katz, *op. cit.*

[15]H. F. Lionberger, *Adoption of New Ideas and Practices,* Iowa State University Press, 1960, p. 86.

[16]Rogers found that the innovators, that is the first 2.5% to adopt new methods, have many contacts with colleagues outside their community. E. M. Rogers, "Characteristics of Innovators and Other Adopter Categories," *Ohio Agr. Exp. Station, Research Bull.* 882. Columbus, 1961.

[17]These scores included not only the personal contacts with the local advisory officer, but also the readership of farming papers and publications of the advisory service, visits to farm demonstrations and meetings, etc.

contact, whereas the choice for the advisor lies between the two others. The reason for this difference between the people chosen in reply to the three sociometric questions probably is, that the contact with the advisory service is correlated with social status, especially in the communities with modern farm management. It is a well known fact that people tend to spend their leisure with people belonging more or less to the same social status, but that people prefer to work together with group members of higher social status.[18] If this is the case here too, we should find this tendency more clearly expressed by dividing the farmers, not according to their contact with the advisory service, but according to their social status. For this reason a table, similar to Table 3, was made for the "judges" rating of the farmers' influence.[19]

TABLE 3. THE NUMBER OF SOCIOMETRIC CHOICES MADE ACCORDING TO THE DIFFERENCE IN SCORES FOR CONTACT WITH THE ADVISORY SERVICE BETWEEN THE CHOOSER AND THE FARMERS CHOSEN, IN PERCENTAGES OF THE NUMBER OF CHOICES WHICH WOULD HAVE BEEN MADE IF EVERY FARMER HAD MADE TWO CHOICES AT RANDOM

| *Number of Quartile Differences* | *Adviser* | | | *Good Farmer* | | | *Friend* | | |
|---|---|---|---|---|---|---|---|---|---|
| | *N. Bev.*[1] | *Mlh.*[2] | *Dw.*[3] | *N. Bev.* | *Mlh.* | *Dw.* | *N. Bev.* | *Mlh.* | *Dw.* |
| −3 Farmer chosen, far less contact | 0 | 17 | 0 | 0 | 9 | 9 | 9 | 43 | 17 |
| −2 | 8 | 21 | 26 | 31 | 13 | 37 | 42 | 73 | 59 |
| −1 | 41 | 27 | 42 | 62 | 27 | 35 | 77 | 60 | 66 |
| 0 as much contact | 61 | 84 | 47 | 90 | 100 | 69 | 74 | 98 | 79 |
| +1 | 94 | 87 | 75 | 108 | 108 | 97 | 113 | 90 | 87 |
| +2 | 111 | 111 | 66 | 138 | 158 | 117 | 126 | 94 | 80 |
| +3 Farmer chosen, much more contact | 112 | 69 | 43 | 197 | 248 | 103 | 84 | 69 | 52 |
| Total | 62 | 64 | 49 | 87 | 88 | 69 | 82 | 80 | 71 |

[1] = Noord-Beveland [2] = Milheeze [3] = Dwingeloo

For the communities with modern farm management—Noord-Beveland and Milheeze—this table shows a strong tendency to select as 'good farmers', farmers with much more influence than the respondents exerted themselves. In the community with traditional farm management this was shown to be true to a lesser extent. Moreover, the tendency to select as

[18]G. C. Homans, *Social Behaviour; Its Elementary Forms,* New York, Burlingame, Harcourt, Brace and World, 1961, Ch. 15.

[19]The ratings 2, 3 and 4 and the ratings 8 and 9 have been combined, because few farmers received such an extreme rating. Otherwise, some percentages in Table 4 would have been calculated on the basis of very small numbers of observations.

friends, farmers of about the same social status, is more pronounced in Table 4 than in Table 3.[20]

TABLE 4. NUMBER OF SOCIOMETRIC CHOICES MADE ACCORDING TO THE DIFFERENCE IN THE 'JUDGE'S' RATING OF THE INFLUENCE EXERTED BY THE CHOOSER AND THE FARMERS CHOSEN, EXPRESSED IN PERCENTAGES OF THE NUMBER OF CHOICES WHICH WOULD HAVE BEEN MADE IF EVERY FARMER HAD MADE TWO CHOICES AT RANDOM

| Points Difference in 'Judge' Rating | *Adviser* | | | *Good Farmer* | | | *Friend* | | |
|---|---|---|---|---|---|---|---|---|---|
| | *N. Bev.* | *Mlh.* | *Dw.* | *N. Bev.* | *Mlh.* | *Dw.* | *N. Bev.* | *Mlh.* | *Dw.* |
| −4 Farmer chosen had far less influence | 0 | 0 | 19 | 0 | 0 | 0 | 0 | 0 | 58 |
| −3 | 0 | 0 | 0 | 0 | 0 | 7 | 0 | 32 | 14 |
| −2 | 0 | 0 | 8 | 23 | 0 | 15 | 8 | 31 | 30 |
| −1 | 18 | 37 | 39 | 26 | 3 | 18 | 49 | 96 | 83 |
| 0 Farmer chosen had about as much influence | 54 | 85 | 73 | 77 | 83 | 101 | 112 | 110 | 101 |
| +1 | 120 | 93 | 49 | 109 | 120 | 72 | 148 | 102 | 60 |
| +2 | 107 | 114 | 49 | 145 | 184 | 110 | 107 | 83 | 76 |
| +3 | 157 | 150 | 107 | 278 | 221 | 165 | 100 | 79 | 79 |
| +4 Farmer chosen had much more influence | 98 | 0 | 96 | 343 | 407 | 154 | 74 | 41 | 115 |
| Total | 62 | 64 | 49 | 87 | 88 | 69 | 82 | 80 | 71 |

These findings show, in accordance with the opinion of Katz, that opinion leaders sometimes belong to the same primary groups as their followers, but that at other times people prefer to ask advice from others with a higher social status, and probably belonging to quite different primary groups, in accordance with Lionberger's findings. Katz is correct with regard to information gathered in casual conversation, probably on subjects like films one wants to see, or about the qualities of the different candidates in an election. Few people feel an urgent need for information on such subjects. On the other hand, for information on new farming methods—the problem studied by Lionberger—many farmers badly need this information because they know that this may have a considerable influence on their income. In the latter case, therefore, they will turn for advice to farmers they consider more competent than themselves, in spite of the fact that crossing such a social barrier may further diminish the social status of the farmer asking for advice, as has been shown by Homans.[21]

[20]The exceptions in Dwingeloo, for farmers with 4 points more or less influence, are probably caused by chance because of the small number of observations in these cells.

[21]*Op. cit.*, p. 324.

This indicates that the question as to whether or not the diffusion of new ideas is a two-step process, does depend on the need for information people feel. When they urgently need information about a new idea, a two-step process within the community will occur most frequently. Certainly our data show that in these Dutch farming communities most farmers know which farmers are best informed about new methods. However, as long as people believe that they can get along quite well without specific information, as is often the case, new ideas have to pass along a rather long chain of people before they have moved from the top to the bottom of the social status scale.

## *Characteristics of Opinion Leaders Depend upon the Progressiveness of Their Community*

The analysis of three communities, differing in their willingness to adopt new ideas, enabled us to study the influence on opinion leadership of the community norms. In this study, community norms have not merely been inferred by means of the average adoption and contact-with-advisory-service scores, but also with the aid of the interview question: 'What is the general opinion in this village about farmers who are always among the first to try new methods?' Table 5 shows that the community norms are much less favourable in the Dwingeloo area than in Noord-Beveland, and

TABLE 5. THE GENERAL OPINION IN THE VILLAGE ABOUT FARMERS WHO ARE ALWAYS AMONG THE FIRST TO TRY NEW METHODS, EXPRESSED IN PERCENTAGES OF INTERVIEWEES PER COMMUNITY

| *Opinion* | *Noord-Beveland* | *Milheeze* | *Dwingeloo* |
|---|---|---|---|
| Favourable | 31 | 45 | 10 |
| Favourable with qualifications | 12 | 5 | 12 |
| No general opinion | 29 | 30 | 20 |
| Unfavourable | 26 | 14 | 49 |
| No answer | 3 | 5 | 8 |

most favourable in the Millheeze area. The figures relating to the contact with the advisory officer and the adoption scores show about the same tendency.

While trying to formulate a general theory on opinion leadership, Homans presented the hypothesis that a person becomes an opinion leader by 'providing rare but valuable services to others.'[22] In progressive communities like Milheeze and Noord-Beveland, farmers are apt to put a much higher value on information about new methods than farmers in tra-

[22]*Op. cit.*, p. 314.

ditional communities like Dwingeloo. We would, therefore, expect opinion leaders at Dwingeloo to be less well informed about new methods than in the other two communities. Table 1 and 3 have already shown some indications that this is indeed the case. Table 1 shows that the difference in influence between the farmers who do and those who do not use various sources of information, often is smaller in the Dwingeloo area than in the other, more progressive communities. Similarly, Table 3 shows that Dwingeloo farmers are least inclined to select as good farmers or advisers, farmers who maintain a closer contact with the advisory service than they do themselves. These indications become clearer when we correlate the contact-with-advisory-service scores of Table 6 with the four different measures of opinion leadership.

TABLE 6. CORRELATION COEFFICIENT OF CONTACT WITH ADVISORY SERVICE SCORES AND FOUR MEASURES OF OPINION LEADERSHIP

| *Measure of Opinion Leadership* | *Noord-Beveland* | *Milheeze* | *Dwingeloo* |
|---|---|---|---|
| Number of times chosen as: | | | |
| adviser | 0.480 | 0.506 | 0.371 |
| good farmer | 0.336 | 0.528 | 0.253 |
| friend | 0.394 | 0.355 | 0.218 |
| Judges' rating of influence | 0.482 | 0.707 | 0.280 |

This table shows indeed that the correlation coefficients between opinion leadership and contact with extension are higher in the Noord-Beveland and Milheeze communities, where more farmers are interested in information about new methods than in a traditional community like Dwingeloo.

Similar conclusions have been drawn from investigations on opinion leadership among farmers in Kentucky[23] and in another part of the Netherlands.[24]

## *Conclusions*

On the basis of the research reported in this article, it seems necessary to replace the two-step flow of communications hypothesis by a more complicated set of hypotheses:

[23]C. P. Marsh and A. L. Coleman, "Farmers' Practice-adoption Rates in Relation to the Adoption Rates of 'Leaders'," *Rural Sociology*, 19 (1954) pp. 180–181.

[24]A. W. van den Ban, *op. cit.*, p. 168.

1. The adoption of a new idea usually takes quite a long time, certainly in the case of methods which imply many changes in related spheres.
2. Mass media are major agents in arousing the interest in new methods early in the adoption process, but during a later stage personal contacts are especially influential in the decision to adopt a new method. Basically, this process is the same for opinion leaders and for their followers.
3. The first persons to adopt a new idea make intensive use of all sources which can provide reliable information about the idea including mass media as well as personal contacts with qualified informants.
4. Often these innovators and early adopters are also the opinion leaders of their group, but the relationship between pioneering and opinion leadership is much closer in progressive than in traditional groups.
5. Problems, about which more information is badly needed, will often make people turn for advice to the best informed people in the community. These are usually people of a high social status.
6. On most new ideas, however, people will not feel an urgent need for information. In this case, people will get their information personally through casual conversations, mainly with people of about the same social status.

Considerable evidence for these hypotheses is found in a study on the diffusion of new farming methods in the Netherlands whereas the study of other innovations also offers some evidence, especially the study on new farming methods in the United States. There is no certainty, however, that these hypotheses will also be found to be true for different cultures and different new ideas. Further research will be needed to test the validity of these hypotheses, for instance with regard to ideas about political candidates in Latin America.

## *Introduction and Objectives for Reading Three: "Homophily—Heterophily: Relational Concepts for Communication Research"*

This selection discusses a relatively new approach to the study of communication. The reader will find several fresh ideas for research in communication and several applications to everyday communication events.

After reading this selection you should be able to:

1. Distinguish in writing between the individual and relational analysis-research approaches in communication studies.
2. Define in writing the terms "homophily" and "heterophily."
3. List in writing 6 of the 12 propositions about homophily–heterophily discussed in the article.

Everett M. Rogers and Dilip K. Bhowmik

## *HOMOPHILY-HETEROPHILY: RELATIONAL CONCEPTS FOR COMMUNICATION RESEARCH**

The purpose of the present article is to synthesize a special type of communication research, in which source-receiver relationships are the units of analysis, in terms of a propositional inventory about homophily-heterophily in communication behavior.

### *Relational Analysis*

Most communication research to date has focused on individuals as units of analysis, largely ignoring the importance of communication *relationships* as units of analysis. Relations between source and receiver account for many aspects of communication, such as credibility, empathy, attraction, etc., and ultimately the effectiveness of communication. Pointing to the need for relational analysis, Coleman[1] asserted that survey research approaches were, in part, responsible for the past focus on the individual as the unit of analysis. "Samples were random, never including (except by accident) two persons who were friends, interviews were with one individual as an atomistic entity, and responses were coded onto separate IBM cards, one for each person." The net result, says Coleman: "Aggregate psychology."

This methodological cul-de-sac often focused content interests in communication research improperly on *intrapersonal characteristics* of sources or receivers, leaving the *interactive process* of communication

[1]James S. Coleman, "Relational Analysis: The Study of Social Organizations with Survey Methods," *Human Organization*, 1958, 16: 28–36.

Everett M. Rogers and Dilip K. Bhowmik, "Homophily-Heterophily: Relational Concepts for Communication Research," *Public Opinion Quarterly*, in press. Reprinted by permission by publisher and author.

*Paper presented at the Association for Education in Journalism, Berkeley, California, August 24–27, 1969. The authors acknowledge the influence of Richard Joyce of Western Michigan University on the present article.

flows from a source to a receiver largely neglected. This point is illustrated in the voluminous research completed on the diffusion of innovations. The field began in the late 1930's when social scientists were asked by extension services to study the diffusion of agricultural research results to farmers; surveys of the receivers focused upon the individual as the unit of analysis.[2] Now, 40 years and 1,800 publications later, we know a great deal about the individual characteristics of farmers, physicians, and teachers who are relatively earlier or later to adopt new ideas. But we know precious little about the communication relationships involved in innovation diffusion.[3] A similar point can be made in the case of persuasion research, studies of media institution gatekeepers, mass media effects, and cross-cultural communication.

We erroneously have assumed that if individuals are the units of *response,* they must also be the units of *analysis.* However, certain recent communication research (to be reviewed in this article) demonstrates that even when the individual provides the response data, the dyadic communication relationship, a communication network, or a sociometrically-determined communication clique within a larger system, can be the unit of analysis.[4]

In the past, communication research has dealt with how to optimize various combinations of source variables, message variables, channel variables, and receiver variables, in order to produce desired effects. But we can often pursue the research objective of determining communication effects[5] more efficiently with various types of relational analysis, as we intend to demonstrate shortly.

[2]Diffusion research also illustrates another implicit "bias" in much communication research: It is usually sponsored by the source, conducted by scientists who gather data from the receivers for eventual utilization by the sources in order to bring about desired behavioral modification by the receivers. Thus, diffusion researchers seem to unwittingly "side" with change agents, not clients, just as persuasion investigators seem to identify with the persuaders, and modernization scholars with development planners, not peasants.

[3]A content analysis of 1,084 empirical diffusion studies in the Michigan State University Diffusion Documents Center shows only about 136 (or 12 percent) utilized a dyadic approach, the most common type of relational analysis. See Everett M. Rogers with F. Floyd Shoemaker, *Communication of Innovations: A Cross-Cultural Approach*, 1970, New York, Free Press of Glencoe.

[4]"Most social research . . . treats social relationships, if at all, as attributes of individuals or groups. . . . An alternative approach, which has not been sufficiently explored, is to treat not the individual, but the interpersonal relationship, as the unit of analysis." Peter M. Blau, "Patterns of Choice in Interpersonal Relations," *American Sociological Review,* 1962, 27: 41–56.

[5]De Fleur points out that effects are the dependent variable in almost all communication research. See Melvin L. De Fleur, *Theories of Mass Communication,* 1965, New York, McKay.

*Relational analysis* is a research approach in which the unit of analysis is a relationship between two or more individuals. Consider an example of how relational analysis differs from individual analysis: Say that we wish to explain the role of a change agent in diffusing agricultural innovations among peasants. We can determine that peasants of higher social status are more likely to adopt innovations; this is individual analysis in that the individual is the unit of analysis (we determine the association or covariance of two intrapersonal variables, individuals' status and innovativeness). In relational analysis, we would determine the similarity or difference in a villager's status and the status of a change agent with whom he interacts, as a predictor of the peasant's innovativeness. Now the change agent-villager dyad has become our unit of analysis; it is the nature of their communicative relationship that is used to explain the effects of their interaction.

The relational approach can be followed in either laboratory or field research. In the case of survey methods, which are often essential for gathering large-scale amounts of data as a basis for generalization, various techniques of conceptualization, measurement, data-gathering, and data-analysis can be utilized to provide a focus upon communication relationships rather than on individuals. So while survey methodology has focused communication research on monadic analysis, as Coleman[6] claims, it need not necessarily be so. We have lacked appropriate concepts (like homophily-heterophily, for instance) to guide our analysis of dyadic or other types of relational data, and these new concepts must be created, explicated, and measured. The measurement devices may include some type of sociometric or quasi-sociometric question.[7] The data-gathering techniques consist of sampling intact groups (or sub-systems) or pairs of individuals, as with so-called "snowball sampling."[8] The data-analysis methods amount to using the dyad, network, or the sub-system as the unit of analysis.[9]

[6]*Op. cit.*

[7]An example of such a quasi-sociometric query is when individual A is asked if he perceives individual B, with whom he interacts, as similar or different from himself on a specified dimension.

[8]Leo A. Goodman, "Snowball Sampling," *Annals of Mathematical Statistics,* 1961, 32: 148–170.

[9]Network or clique identification and analysis is often facilitated by computer matrix multiplication procedures. This method consists of reducing the sociometric data about interpersonal communication to a "who-to-whom" matrix in which the source individuals are located on one dimension of the matrix and the receivers on the other. The matrix is squared, cubed, etc., usually by computer techniques. Cliques and networks soon become apparent within the total matrix of interpersonal relationships. For details on methods of matrix analysis and dyadic analysis, see: David Lingwood, *An Analysis of Communication Patterns Among Scientists,* Ph.D. dissertation, 1969, Department of Communi-

We conclude that *future inquiry should utilize relational analysis as a means of probing the nature of communication behavior.* We hope to demonstrate the potential profit of this recommendation in the remainder of the present article, in our relational analyses of homophily-heterophily.

## *Homophily-Heterophily*

One of the most obvious and fundamental principles of human communication is that the exchange of messages most frequently occurs between a source and a receiver who are alike, similar, homophilous. *Homophily* is the degree to which pairs of individuals who interact are similar in certain attributes, like beliefs, values, education, social status, etc. The term homophily derives from the Greek word *homoios,* meaning alike or equal. *Heterophily* is the degree to which pairs of individuals who interact are different in certain attributes.

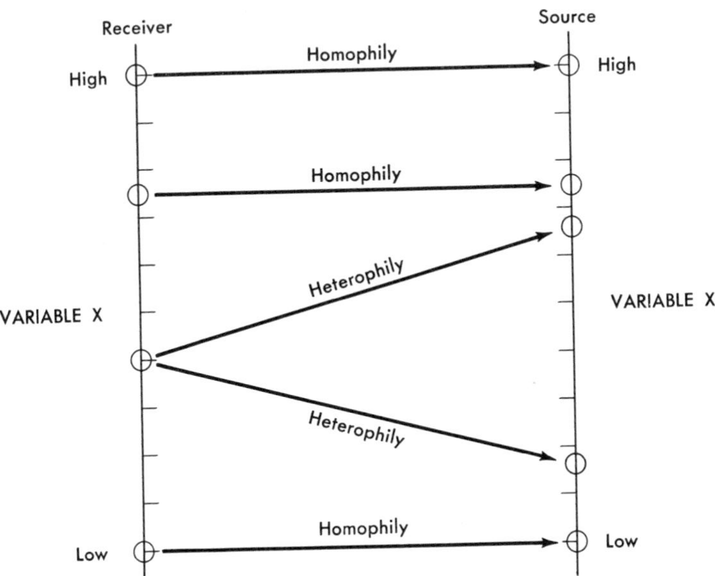


**Figure 1.** Homophilous and Heterophilous Communication between a Source-Receiver Dyad.

---

cation, Stanford University; Lytton Guimarães, *Matrix Multiplication in the Study of Interpersonal Communication*, M. A. Thesis, 1968, Department of Communication, Michigan State University; Leon Festinger, "The Analysis of Sociograms Using Matrix Algebra," *Human Relations,* 1949, 2: 153–158; and Charles H. Hubbel, "An Input-Output Approach to Clique Identification," *Sociometry*, 1965, 12: 377–399.

While a conceptual label—homophily—has only been assigned to this phenomenon in recent years by Lazarsfeld and Merton,[10] the existence of homophilic behavior was noted over a half century ago by Tarde:[11] "Social relations, I repeat, are much closer between individuals who resemble each other in occupation and education." Many synonyms for homophily and heterophily have been used by contemporary social scientists: Similarity and dissimilarity,[12] segregating and differentiating,[13] co-linear and non-linear,[14] "social closeness" and "social distance,"[15] and similarity and complementarity.[16] Seemingly, these authors have not fully recognized the basic commonality of these various polar concepts. Certain of these researchers have specified the variables or dimensions on which homophily-heterophily are measured, for example, "value homophily," "status homophily," "cognitive similarity". Further, homophily-heterophily have been operationalized with the individual,[17] the dyad, and the social system[18] as the unit of analysis.

[10]Paul F. Lazarsfeld and Robert K. Merton, "Friendship as a Social Process: A Substantive and Methodological Analysis," in Monroe Berger and others (eds.), *Freedom and Control in Modern Society,* 1954, New York, Van Nostrand.

[11]Gabriel Tarde, *The Laws of Imitation,* 1903, New York, Holt, Rinehart and Winston.

[12]The numerous researches using these concepts are summarized by A. J. Lott and B. E. Lott, "Group Cohesiveness as Interpersonal Attraction: A Review of Relationships with Antecedent and Consequent Variables," *Psychological Bulletin,* 1965, 64: 259–309; Ellen Berscheid and Elaine Hatfield Walster, *Interpersonal Attraction,* 1969, Reading, Massachusetts, Addison-Wesley, pp. 69–91; and Herbert W. Simons and others, "Similarity, Credibility, and Attitude Change: A Review and a Theory," *Psychological Bulletin,* 1970, 73: 1–16.

[13]Blau, *op. cit.*

[14]Philip J. Runkel, "Cognitive Similarity in Faciliatating Communication," *Sociometry,* 1956, 19: 178–191.

[15]Dean C. Barnlund and Carroll Harland, "Propinquity and Prestige as Determinants of Communication Networks," *Sociometry*, 1963, 26: 467–479.

[16]E. E. Jones and B. N. Daugherty, "Political Orientation and the Perceptual Effects of an Anticipated Interaction," *Journal of Abnormal and Social Psychology,* 1959, 59: 340–349; Theodore M. Newcomb, "The Prediction of Interpersonal Attraction," *American Psychologist,* 1956, 11: 575–586; Paul Watzlawick and others, *Pragmatics of Human Communication*, 1967, New York, Norton, pp. 66–67. The latter authors use the term "symetrical" rather than similiar.

[17]At the individual level, an homophily-heterophily index indicates the degree to which an individual communicates with several others who are either similar or dissimilar to himself on certain variables. There are few studies of homophily-heterophily at the individual level, and they are not reviewed in the present article.

[18]Yung Chang Ho, *Homophily in the Diffusion of Innovations in Brazilian Communities*, M. A. Thesis, 1969, Department of Communication, Michigan

Homophily-heterophily is conceptualized at two levels, on the basis of measurement: (1) *subjective*, the degree to which a source or receiver perceives the dyad as similar or dissimilar in attributes, and (2) *objective*, the degree of observable similarity-dissimilarity between source and receiver.[19] Most past researches on relational analysis dealt with objective homophily-heterophily, but the study of subjective homophily-heterophily is also needed. In the process of communication both the source and receiver behave according to their perceptions of each other and of the message being transmitted. Obviously, the effects of a message on a receiver's behavior depend upon how that receiver perceives the communication situation (including the degree of homophily or heterophily), in addition to how some observers measure dimensions of that situation.

Past investigations generally indicate that (1) the degree of subjective homophily is positively correlated with the degree of objective homophily, although not perfectly, (2) the degree of subjective homophily is perceived to be higher by members of dyads than the degree of objective homophily,[20] and (3) subjective homophily is more closely related than objective homophily to such other variables as interpersonal attraction and frequency of interaction.[21]

Now we turn to a propositional inventory of the role of homophily-heterophily in communication behavior. Much past communication research of a relational nature can be summarized in the present propositions, even though the concepts of homophily-heterophily were not explicitly utilized by many of the orginal authors. Certain of these propositions are

---

State University; Guimarães, *op. cit*; Everett M. Rogers with Lynne Svenning, *Modernization Among Peasants: The Impact of Communication,* 1969, New York, Holt, Rinehart and Winston, p. 238.

[19]Objective homophily-heterophily is usually measured by computing the correspondence of a source's and a receiver's scores on some variable; the scores are obtained by questioning both members of the dyad.

[20]For instance, Bender and Hastorf found that respondents perceived themselves as rather homophilous to specified other individuals on certain personality dimensions ($r=.71$), while objective homophily was low ($r=.15$). I. E. Bender and A. H. Hastorf, "The Perception of Persons: Forecasting Another Person's Responses on Three Personality Scales," *Journal of Abnormal and Social Psychology*, 1950, 45: 556–661.

[21]The most comprehensive investigation providing support for this statement is Newcomb's (*op. cit.*) study, in which he arranged for previously-unacquainted college students to live together in a rooming house for several semesters. Rokeach summarized the results of over a dozen studies by concluding that perceived homophily-heterophily of beliefs is a more powerful determinant of interpersonal attraction than objective homophily-heterophily on racial or ethnic variables. Milton Rokeach, *Beliefs, Attitudes, and Values: A Theory of Organization and Change*, 1968, San Francisco, Jossey-Bass, p. 63.

more like hypotheses than generalizations, and mainly offer suggestion for future inquiry.

### The Homophily Principle

In a free-choice situation, when a source can interact with any one of a number of different receivers, there is a strong tendency for him to select a receiver who is like himself.[22] "Birds of a feather flock together." Empirical evidence of the homophily principle is available from studies of a great variety of communication situations: Political influence patterns in a Presidential election were homophilous in age and social status,[23] interactions among members of a legislature were between those of equal age, partisanship, and prestige;[24] Iowa farmers talked about agricultural innovations with those of similar attitudinal disposition;[25] communication patterns in formal organizations are mostly horizontal (that is, between individuals of similar hierarchical status) rather than vertical;[26] Chicago ghetto dwellers share family planning ideas with others of like social status, age, marital status, and family size;[27] and Indian peasants interact mostly with other villagers of similar caste ranking, education, and farm size.[28]

[22]Homans noted: "The more nearly equal in social rank a number of men are, the more frequently they will interact with one another." George C. Homan, *The Human Group,* 1950, New York, Harcourt, Brace and World, p. 184. A recent review of social psychological studies concludes: "Undoubtedly, the most prominant assertion in group research is that people . . . interact with those who are most similar to them." Karl E. Weick, *The Social Psychology of Organizing*, 1969, Reading, Massachusetts, Addison-Wesley, p. 14.

[23]Paul F. Lazarsfeld and others, *The People's Choice,* 1948, New York, Columbia University Press, pp. 137–139.

[24]John C. Wahlke and others, *The Legislative System: Exploration in Legislative Behavior*, 1962, New York, Wiley.

[25]Rex Hovey Warland, *Personal Influence: The Degree of Similarity of Those Who Interact*, M. S. Thesis, 1963, Ames, Department of Economics and Sociology, Iowa State University.

[26]R. L. Simpson, "Vertical and Horizontal Communication in Formal Organizations," *Administrative Science Quarterly*, 1959, 4: 188–196.

[27]James Palmore, "The Chicago Snowball: A Study of the Flow and Diffusion of Family Planning Information," in Donald J. Bogue (ed.), *Sociological Contributions to Family Planning Research,* 1967, University of Chicago, Community and Family Study Center.

[28]Santi Priya Bose, "Social Interaction in an Indian Village," *Sociologia Ruralis*, 1967, 7: 156–175.

We could go on and on. In summary, we suggest Proposition I: *Communication patterns frequently tend to be homophilous.*[29]

## *Communication Effectiveness*

Why is homophily so frequent in human communication? One reason is suggested by Proposition II: *More effective communication occurs when source and receiver are homophilous.*[30] When the sources(s) and receiver(s) share common meanings, attitudes and beliefs,[31] and a mutual code, communication between them is likely to be more effective. Most individuals enjoy the comfort of interacting with others who are similar in social status, education, beliefs, etc. Interaction with those quite different involves more effort to make communication effective. Heterophilic interaction is likely to cause message distortion,[32] delayed transmission, restriction of communication channels, and may cause cognitive dissonance, as the receiver is exposed to messages that may be inconsistent with his existing beliefs and attitudes, an uncomfortable psychological state.

Homophily and effective communication breed each other; they have an interdependent relationship[33] in that a little increase in one leads to a little increase in the other, etc. An homophilous source-receiver pair interact more (Proposition I), this communication is relatively more effective (Proposition II), and hence create greater consensus and similarity between them, this is rewarding, which leads to a higher rate of interaction,

[29]Our Proposition I is a more general case of Collins and Guetzkow's proposition 9–5, which states: "Communication will be directed toward (a) persons in close physical proximity (b) persons in the same work group, and (c) the same socio-economic status." Barry E. Collins and Harold Guetzkow, *A Social Psychology of Group Processes for Decision Making*, 1964, New York. John Wiley and Sons, Inc., p. 178.

[30]Tarde recognized that the more "distant" (in a geographical, psychological, or sociological sense) the source of communication, the less strong its influence. See Terry N. Clark, *Gabriel Tarde on Communication and Social Influence,* 1969, University of Chicago Press, p. 60.

[31]Runkel (*op. cit.*) stated: "Since the effects of a communication depend on the manner in which it 'meshes' with an existing cognitive map, we might entertain the notion that these effects will take place more readily when the cognitive maps of the communicators are similar in structure."

[32]Numerous small group laboratory studies demonstrate that heterophily leads to message distortion, one type of ineffective communication. For an example and a summary of past work, see Barnlund and Harland, *op. cit.*

[33]A detailed discussion of the interdependence relationship between two variables is found in Hans L. Zetterberg, *On Theory and Verification in Sociology* 1965, Totowa, New Jersey, Bedminister Press, p. 70.

etc.[34] So homophily may be (1) the basis of *choice* of those individuals with whom one interacts, or (2) the *result* of previous interaction.[35] For instance, the Erie County Presidential election study[36] led to the conclusion: "The changes in vote intention increase group homogeniety. . . . the majority of voters who change at all, change in the direction of the prevailing vote of their social group."

These findings and logic suggest that our Proposition II about effective communication and homophily can be reversed in the implied time-order of antecedent and consequent, so that interaction leads to "homophilization". Proposition III states: *Effective communication between source and receiver leads to greater homophily in knowledge, beliefs, and overt behavior.*[37]

### *Homophily on Relevant Variables*

We have shown that effective communication and homophily are generally positively related (Propositions II and III). Yet there are many important communication situations where heterophily on certain variables is a necessary ingredient: The white, middle class teacher in a ghetto classroom, a father and son dyad, a change agent diffusing innovations to his peasant clients, international communication between two individuals, such as diplomats, who do not share a common culture. If these communication events involved participants who were *completely* homophilous (obviously an impossible occurrance), such interaction would be facil, but totally redundant. The receiver would already know the message content, and it would contain no information for him. If the participants in a communication event were completely heterophilous, source and receiver would not share a common code, and no communication would occur. The source's symbols and meanings would not correspond to those in the mind of the receiver, and the messages would go unheeded.

Most communication situations, of course, are somewhere between these two extremes, and usually, closer to the homophilous end of the continuum (Proposition I). But it is a gross oversimplification to limit our

[34]This reasoning is described in Harry C. Triandis, "Cognitive Similarity and Communication in a Dyad," *Human Relations*, 1960, 13: 175–183; and is supported with data from a laboratory experiment by William J. Chambliss, "The Selection of Friends," *Social Forces*, 1965, 43: 370–380.

[35]Lazarsfeld and Merton, *op. cit.*

[36]Lazarsfeld and others, *op. cit.*

[37]But of course it could not lead to greater homogeneity on such demographic variables as age, formal education, etc. But even such a relatively static variable as status was homophilized by effective communication, Larsen and Hill report (Otto N. Larsen and Richard J. Hill, "Social Structure and Interpersonal Communication," *American Journal of Sociology*, 1958, 43: 497–505).

conception of homophily-heterophily to any single variable, as we have seemed to do so far in the present article. A source and a receiver are usually homophilous on certain variables and heterophilous on certain others. So source-receiver homophily or heterophily is not one variable, but a whole class of variables. For example, Katz and Lazarsfeld[38] studied communication dyads for consumer purchases and movie attendance decisions by Illinois housewives. The dyads were homophilous on social class, but heterophilous on age; the older women told the younger wives about consumer products, but the younger women told the older women about what movies to attend.

So one needs to ask: Homophily with respect to what? The relevant[39] variables on which homophily and heterophily occur, and their consequences on communication effectiveness, depend on who the source and receiver are, the message content, and other considerations. Given that members of a dyad cannot be homophilous on all variables, they should be homophilous on as many as are relevant to the situation, in order for effective communication to occur, and they may be heterophilous on all others. For example, source-receiver blood types would be irrelevant in most communication situations.[40]

There is research evidence that more effective change agents are those who are most like their average client on all variables except for technical competence about the innovations promoted. For instance, the Allahabad Agricultural Institute[41] found that village-level change agents in India with only an elementary education were more effective in reaching villagers (who were mostly illiterate) than were change agents with high school or university education. But all of the change agents were quite heterophilous from their clients in competence with agricultural innovations.

Likewise, the most effective change agents in the Madras (India) vasectomy adoption campaign[42] were those equally as poor, uneducated, and low in status as the target audience, but heterophilous in that they had previously had the vasectomy operation (that is, had adopted the innovation).

[38]Elihu Katz and Paul F. Lazarsfeld, *Personal Influence: The Part Played by People in the Flow of Mass Communication*, 1955, New York, Free Press of Glencoe.

[39]"Relevant" in the present sense depends on the way in which the receiver perceives the communication situation. For example, if a change agent's technical competence affects a receiver's acceptance of his message, then competence is a relevant variable to their interaction.

[40]Newcomb, *op. cit.*

[41]Allahabad Agricultural Institute, *Extension Evaluation,* 1957, Allahabad, India, Allahabad Agriculture Institute Report.

[42]Robert Reppetto, "India: A Case Study of the Madras Vasectomy Program," *Studies in Family Planning*, 1969, 31: 8–16.

In Taiwan, it was found that effective extension agents were better educated and more technically competent than their farmer clients, but were perceived as homophilous on most other variables because they operated farms, and adopted innovations on their farms, before they recommended them to their clients.[43]

Further evidence on the importance of relevant homophily to communication effectiveness comes from survey studies of opinion leadership. Researches show that opinion leaders (defined as those members of a system sought by their peers for opinions and advice) possess social characteristics, beliefs, and conformity to norms that mark them as "super-representative", that is, they are very homophilous with their average follower. But opinion leaders also tend to be more competent (on the issue being communicated) than their followers, although not *too* much so.[44]

Perhaps one reason why change agents often concentrate their efforts on opinion leaders is to "halve" the heterophily gap with their average clients.[45] But if opinion leaders are *too* much more innovative than the average clients, the heterophily (and accompanying ineffective communication) that formerly existed between the change agents and their clients, now exists between the leaders and their fellow clients. This is why innovators are poor opinion leaders in traditional systems; they are too elite and change-oriented. They serve as an unrealistic model for the average client, and he knows it. Sometimes change agents identify appropriate and potentially effective opinion leaders among their clients, but they concentrate their change efforts too much on the leaders, who soon become innovators and hence lose their following.[46] The homophilization of the ex-leaders by the change agents led them to become too heterophilous from their former followers for effective communication to occur.

Laboratory studies also support our central notion that homophily is important in effective communication only if it occurs on relevant variables.

[43]Herbert F. Lionberger and H. C. Chang, *Farm Information for Modernizing Agriculture: The Taiwan System,* 1970, New York, Praeger.

[44]The present summary of numerous opinion leadership studies is based on Rogers with Shoemaker (*op. cit.*) and Elihu Katz, "The Two-Step Flow of Communication: An Up-to-Date Report on an Hypothesis," *Public Opinion Quarterly*, 1957, 21: 61–78.

[45]A related method is to employ non-professional "aides" to the change agent, who are essentially paid opinion leaders. The emphasis during the 1960's in the U. S. on reaching poor clients has led to use of aides in each of the helping professions: Education, mental health, public health, community development, and the extension service. For details about the use of aides, see Arthur Pearl and Frank Riessman, *New Careers for the Poor: The Nonprofessional in Human Service*, 1965, New York, Free Press of Glencoe.

[46]Support for this idea comes from the Rogers with Svenning (*op. cit.*, pp. 219–220) study of opinion leaders in Colombian villages, and from Charles M. Hardin, "'Natural Leaders' and the Administration of Soil Conservation Programs," *Rural Sociology*, 1951, 16: 279–281.

Simons and others[47] synthesize a number of persuasion studies with their proposition that "Attitude change toward the position advocated by the source depends on the extent to which interpersonal similarities or dissimilarities are perceived as having instrumental value for the receiver". If the variables are not instrumental, they are irrelevant to effective persuasion.

We conclude the present discussion with Proposition IV: *For maximum communication effectiveness, a source and receiver should be homophilous on variables relevant to the situation, but they may be heterophilous on irrelevant variables.*

### *Status Inconsistency*

We have argued that source-receiver homophily-heterophily must be considered on several dimensions rather than just on one variable. The multi-dimensionality of most communication situations is also involved in another way. *Status inconsistent*[48] individuals are "internally heterophilous," which allows them the potential to be homophilous on different variables with different sets of receivers, and hence to bridge heterophily gaps in a system. They may tend to be "liaison individuals"[49] in linking two or more heterophilous cliques within the system, and hence are able to play an important communication role. In the case of cross-cultural communication, members of the "third culture"[50] are status inconsistants

[47] *Op. cit.*

[48] *Status inconsistency* is the relative lack of similarity in an individual's ranking on various indicators of social status. The concept, originally referred to as "status crystallization," was called to scientific attention by G. E. Lenski, "Status Crystallization: A Non-Vertical Dimension of Social Status," *American Sociological Review*, 1954, 19: 405–413.

[49] See Eugene E. Jacobson and Stanley E. Seashore, "Communication Practices in Complex Organizations," *Journal of Social Issues,* 1951, 7: 28–40; Dharam P. Yadav, *A Comparative Analysis of Communication Structure and Innovation Diffusion in Two Indian Villages,* Ph.D. thesis, 1967, Department of Communication, Michigan State University; R. S. Weiss and Eugene E. Jacobson, "A Method for the Analysis of the Structure of Complex Organizations," *American Sociological Review,* 1955, 20: 661–68; Donald F. Schwartz, *Liaison Communication Roles in Formal Organization,* Ph.D. thesis, 1968, Department of Communication, Michigan State University.

[50] The third culture is composed of individuals living in a second culture to their own, who possess elements from both their original and host culture, and, as such, share certain communalities with other such individuals in other cultures, thus constituting a third culture. The concept is explicated by John Useem, "The Community of Man: A Study in the Third Culture," *Centennial Review*, 1963, 7: 481–498; and John Useem," Work Patterns of Americans in India," *The Annals,* 1966, 368.

in a cultural sense, and hence are in an advantageous position to facilitate effective international communication. Although there is little direct evidence to support this notion, we suggest Proposition V: *Heterophilous communication is more effective when source and/or receiver are status inconsistents.*[51]

## *Credibility*

One reason often given[52] for the greater communication effectiveness of homophilous sources with receivers is that such homophily leads to greater *credibility*, defined as the degree to which a source is perceived to be more trustworthy and reliable. Recently, Simons and others[53] have questioned this doctrine: "Contrary to prevalent formulations, it appears that certain dissimilarities have positive effects on attitude change".

We feel that the relationship of homophily-heterophily, through credibility, to communication effectiveness may be more complex than previously conceptualized, and may depend on the *type* of credibility involved. Factor analyses of semantic differential data show at least two subdimensions of source credibility: (1) "qualification", or expertness, and (2) "safety".[54] A source who is perceived as possessing qualification credibility is usually heterophilous from his receivers; for instance, a change agent must know more about the innovations he is introducing than his clients, or they will not view him as especially qualified. But a source perceived as possessing safety credibility often is highly homophilous with his receivers; peers usually have this type of credibility, while a change agent does not, in the eyes of his clients. This logic is supported by research on

[51]Barnlund and Harland (*op. cit.*) found some evidence for this proposition in their study of communication patterns among college sororities. Most of the communication patterns were very homophilous on the basis of sorority prestige. The one sorority whose members displayed a high degree of heterophily in their interaction patterns had recently been upwardly mobile in the campus prestige hierarchy, and was thus characterized by status inconsistency (as a social system).

[52]E. Berscheid, "Opinion Change and Communicator-Communicatee Similarity and Dissimilarity," *Journal of Personality and Social Psychology*, 1966, 4: 670–680; and T. E. Brock, "Communicator-Recipient Similarity and Decision Change," *Journal of Personality and Social Psychology*, 1965, 1: 650–654.

[53]*Op. cit.*

[54]David K. Berlo and others, "Dimensions for Evaluating the Acceptability of Message Sources," *Public Opinion Quarterly*, 1969, 33: 563–576.

sources/channels utilized most frequently in the innovation-decision process:[55] At the knowledge stage in this process, when the individual is gaining information about the innovation, heterophilous sources/channels are most frequently consulted because they possess qualification credibility. But at the persuasion stage, when the individual is forming a positive attitude toward the innovation, homophilous sources/channels are most frequent because they are perceived as possessing safety credibility.

In one study,[56] a highly respected sergeant was found to be less effective than a civilian social psychologist in convincing Army trainees to use such foods as irradiated meats, instant coffee, and grasshoppers. The explanation in this case maybe that although the sergeant was homophilous on certain variables (he shared the same occupation with his receivers), the civilian psychologist had both qualification (because of his higher education) and safety (because of his not being in the military) credibility. Thus, heterophily in some cases, can lead to both qualification and safety credibility.

A shift in both safety and qualification credibility from more homophilous to more heterophilous individuals may occur as a social system modernizes. For instance, one researcher[57] found that in a traditional Indian village, peasants attached greatest credibility to the fellow villagers. As new communication channels entered the village and tranformed it to a more open system, qualification credibility shifted to agricultural scientists, extension agents, and radio, but safety credibility remained with homophilous peers. Eventually, the innovators in the system might even perceive such heterophilous channels/sources as change agents and the mass media, as having safety credibility.

We summarize this section with Proposition VI, which is an hypothesis needing empirical study: *An heterophilous channel/sources is perceived by a receiver as having qualification credibility, while an homopilous channel/source is perceived by a receiver as having safety credibility.* This proposition does not account for shifts in the nature of credibility as a system becomes more open, although such further specification may become necessary in the face of further evidence.

[55]Which is synthesized by Rogers with Shoemaker, *op. cit.* The *innovation-decision process* is defined as the mental process an individual goes through in becoming aware of a new idea, forming an attitude toward it, and deciding to adopt or reject it.

[56]Ewart Smith, "The Power of Dissonance Techniques to Change Attitudes," *Public Opinion Quarterly*, 1961, 25: 626–629.

[57]C. Shankariah, *A Study of Differentiated Communication Patterns in a Progressive and a Non-Progressive Village*, Ph.D. thesis, 1969, New Delhi, Indian Agricultural Research Institute, p. 128.

## *Instrumental and Consummatory Communication*

All communication events can be classified as either (1) instrumental, or (2) consummatory.[58] *Instrumental* communication is intended to achieve effects. It is a means, rather than an end in itself. Examples are the diffusion of a new idea from a change agent to a client, most classroom communication, and the use of mass media channels by development experts to modernize traditional receivers. *Consummatory* communication is rewarding in itself and is initiated without a specific intent to achieve effects. Illustrations are interaction between friends or listening to a musical radio program for pleasure.

Consummatory communication is most frequently homophilous. Of course, both consummatory and instrumental communication are more effective when homophilous, as we stated earlier (Proposition II). But

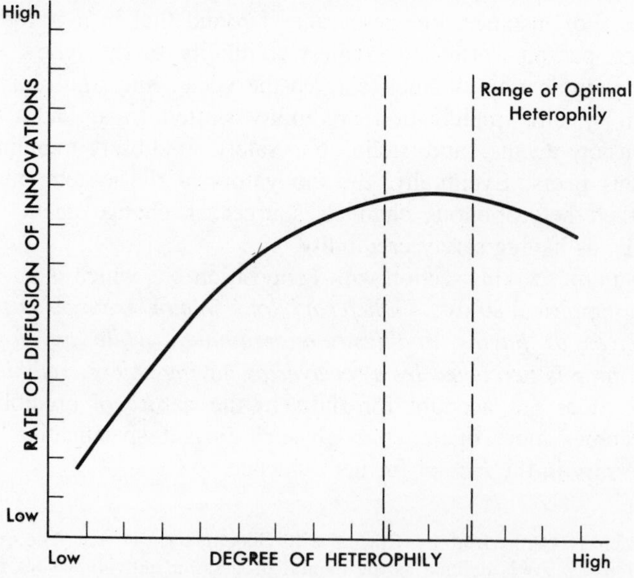


**Figure 2.** Optimal Heterophily and the Rate of Diffusion of Innovations.

[58]Leon Festinger, "Informal Social Communication," *Psychological Review,* 1950, 57: 271–292; and David K. Berlo, *The Process of Communication,* 1960, New York, Holt, Rinehart and Winston, pp. 17–20. A somewhat related classification of "immediate" and "delayed rewards" for communication is made by Wilbur Schramm, "The Nature of News," *Journalism Quarterly,* 1949, 26: 259–269; and Jack Lyle, "Immediate vs. Delayed Reward Use of Newspapers by Adolescents," *Journalism Quarterly,* 1962, 39: 83–85.

Proposition VII states that: *Some degree of heterophily is more likely to occur when communication is instrumental rather than consummatory.*[59] Friendship and other kinds of consummatory communication usually occur between alikes. But for instrumental communication to take place (that is, to have communication effects), the source must be more knowledgeable about an idea, more favorable toward it, or more likely to have experience with it. This heterophily, whether objectively present or not, must at least be perceived as such by the receiver for him to see the source as having more qualification credibility.

## *Empathy and Heterophilous Communication*

Much heterophilous communication is ineffective, as we have pointed out. Yet *some* teachers do "get through" to their ghetto pupils, some change agents reach their peasant clients very effectively. Why? One reason is the empathic ability of the source.

*Empathy* is the ability of an individual to project himself into the role of another. When an heterophilous source or receiver is able to empathize with the other, effective communication is more likely. If one can perceive how one's receiver is feeling and share these feelings, it is possible to better suit the message to the receiver. When a source has high empathy with an heterophilous receiver, they are *really* "homophilous" in a social-psychological sense. This point suggests that our earlier proposition (II) about heterophily and effective communication now needs modification. Proposition VIII is largely an untested hypothesis that: *Heterophilous communication is more effective when the source has a high degree of empathy with the receiver.* Of course, empathy with a dissimilar (heterophilous) role than one's own is more difficult, in part because effective communication is unlikely to have occurred with such roles in the past, and so we usually lack much knowledge of such roles.[60]

[59]Relatively inconclusive tests of this proposition, which yielded only partial confirmation, are Teresa Kang Mei Chou, *Homophily in Interaction Patterns in the Diffusion of Innovations in Colombian Villages,* M.A. thesis, 1966, Department of Communication, Michigan State University; and Narsinhbhai Bhikhabhai Patel, *Status Determinants of Interpersonal Communication: A Dyadic Analysis,* Ph.D. thesis, 1966, Department of Rural Sociology, University of Kentucky.

[60]In fact, one explanation for the relatively low empathy of traditional individuals is that they were socialized in systems with a high degree of homophily (a "restricted environment"), and hence never learned to take the roles of different others. For a discussion of the socialization explanation of individual differences in empathic capacity, see Don Stewart and Thomas Hoult, "A Social-Psychological Theory of the Authoritarian Personality," *American Journal of Sociology,* 1959, 65: 274–279.

Receivers also may possess some degree of empathy with sources. Gans[61] found that most social workers in a Boston slum had relatively low empathy with their clients, whereas the ghetto residents were able to take the role of the change agents with greater ease. This provided the clients with a manipulative advantage; they understood the social workers' objectives and strategies, and acted accordingly. One result was that the change agents' programs were largely unsuccessful in changing clients' behavior. This experience suggests Proposition IX, which is an hypothesis for future study: *Heterophilous communication is more effective when the source has greater empathy than the receiver.*

### *Feedback*

Proposition X: *Heterophilous communication is more effective when the source attends to feedback from his receivers.* Feedback is more necessary for effective communication when source-receiver pairs are heterophilous. If a source lacks information about his receivers, who are actually heterophilous from him, the source may assume they are homophilous (or should be), and thus communication is ineffective. If the source, through feedback, realizes that his receivers are heterophilous rather than homophilous from him, communication may become more effective. Through attending to feedback and gaining information about his receivers, a source may be able to empathize more fully with them, understand their language, symbols and meanings, and ultimately he may become more "homophilous" (social-psychologically), leading to more effective communication.

The amount of feedback that occurs depends in part on the norms governing communication in the system in which the source and receiver interact. For example, in certain traditional systems the norms discourage a lower status receiver from sending feedback to a higher status source. Likewise, in a formal organization where negative feedback from lower hierarchical levels to superiors is often discouraged by negative sanctions, hierarchically heterophilous communication messages are especially ineffective.

[61]Herbert J. Gans, *The Urban Villagers: Group and Class in the Life of Italian Americans*, 1962, New York, Free Press of Glencoe.

## *Homophily and Interpersonal Attraction*

Newcomb[62] suggests that attraction between persons is a function of the extent to which reciprocal rewards are present in their interaction; these rewards frequently derive from interaction in which source and receiver attitudes toward message content are homophilous. Byrne[63] found that individuals with attitudinal homophily are better liked than heterophilous individuals, as did Smith[64] and Broxton,[65] especially in the case of subjective attitudinal homophily. These researches plus numerous others,[66] suggest Proposition XI: *Source-receiver homophily is positively related to interpersonal attraction, both of which are related to more effective communication.*

## *Homophily-Heterophily in Modern and Traditional Systems*

The concepts of homophily-heterophily may be studied at the system level as well as at the individual or dyadic level. This type of relational analysis requires an index of system homophily-heterophily. System homophily, indicating the degree to which members of the system interact, on the average, with others like themselves, can act as a barrier to the rapid flow of ideas within a system. New ideas usually enter via higher status and more innovative members of a system. When a high degree of homophily is present, these elite individuals interact mainly with each other and there

[62]Newcomb (*op. cit.*) also reports from his study of friendship and interaction among college students: "If and when increased attraction between pairs of persons does occur with opportunity for communication, it will be associated with increased similarity of attitude" (this is homophilization).

[63]Donn Byrne, "Interpersonal Attraction and Attitude Similarity," *Journal of Abnormal and Social Psychology*, 1961, 62: 713–715.

[64]Anthony J. Smith, "Similarity of Values and Its Relation to Acceptance and the Projection of Similarity," *Journal of Psychology*, 1957, 43: 251–260.

[65]June A. Broxton, "A Test of Interpersonal Attraction: Predictions Derived from Balance Theory," *Journal of Abnormal and Social Psychology*, 1963, 63: 394–397.

[66]Which are summarized by Lott and Lott, *op. cit.*; Berscheid and Walster, *op. cit.*; and Simons and others, *op. cit.*

is little "trickle down" of the innovations to non-elites. A series of researches have analyzed the degree of homophily in contrasting pairs of relatively modern and traditional agricultural villages:[67] Rogers with Svenning[68] in Colombia, Yadav[69] and Shankariah[70] in India, Guimarães[71] in Brazil, van den Ban[72] in the Netherlands. All but the letter reported evidence for Proposition XII: *More traditional systems are characterized by a greater degree of homophily in interpersonal communication.* Only when the norms of the villages become more modern did diffusion become more heterophilous. And this breakdown of homophilous patterns acted to make the system even more modern, by facilitating the trickle-down of innovative messages within the village.[73] As a system becomes more modern, the possession of information about new ideas becomes more widely shared and is less the monopoly of the system elites.

## QUESTIONS FOR DISCUSSION

1. Discuss the implications of the concept of "homophily" in human acquisition of information.
2. What role does selectivity play in regular classroom learning?
3. Which is a better description of the process of diffusion of information: two-step flow or multi-step flow? Why?
4. Who are your opinion leaders? For whom do you serve as an opinion leader? Does any name appear on both lists?
5. It is often said that in our society Blacks know a lot more about whites than whites know about Blacks. Presuming that this is true, what principles of human acquisition and processing of information that have been discussed in this section might account for this?
6. Are learning and the acquisition of information the same thing? Why or why not?

[67]In these investigations a relatively modern system was characterized by a more rapid rate of social change, a more complex technology and social organization, and higher levels of living.

[68]*Op. cit.*, pp. 234–238.

[69]*Op. cit.*

[70]*Op. cit.* Shankariah reported that in his modern village all the peasants were aware of a new wheat variety after two interpersonal "steps" (in the sense of the two-step flow of communication), while some peasants were still not aware after five "steps" in the traditional village.

[71]*Op. cit.*

[72]A. W. van den Ban, *Boer en Landvoorlichting: De Communicatie over Nieuwe Landouwmethoden*, 1963, Assen, Netherlands, Van Gorkum.

[73]Bose (*op. cit.*) found a very high degree of homophily among the residents of an Indian village on the basis of caste ranking. In the nearby city of Calcutta, however, caste was unimportant in structuring interaction patterns, but income was very important. So the exact attributes on which homophily-heterophily occurs also seem to vary with whether the system is traditional or modern.

## *Conclusions*

In communication research, more attention is due relational analysis, rather than continuing to utilize the individual as the unit of analysis. Relationships of the source and receiver should more often be the unit of analysis, an approach which would better explain communication effectiveness.

Homophily-heterophily is the degree to which pairs of individuals who interact are similar or dissimilar in certain attributes like beliefs, values, education, social status, etc. It can be conceptualized as subjective or objective, and it can be measured at the dyadic or at the system level.

The 12 propositions detailed in this article utilize homophily-heterophily as "sensitizing concepts" in that we expect the exact dimensions of homophily-heterophily to vary with different communication situations; these remain to be specified in future analyses. Further, future research should concentrate on subjective measures of homophily-heterophily, rather than the objective measure utilized in most past research, in order to raise the predictive power of our propositions. Perhaps with improved operations of homophily-heterophily[74] and the resulting greater precision of our results, we shall gain a clearer picture of the role of homophily-heterophily in communication flows. We are only at the introductory phase of such investigation, but the potential, both conceptually and empirically, is promising.

[74]Many of the researches reviewed in this article used zero-order Pearsonian correlation to index homophily-heterophily (examples are Chou, *op. cit.,* and Rogers with Svenning, *op. cit.*) or Robinson's measure of agreement (for example, Patel, *op. cit.*). Coleman (*op. cit.*) proposed an homophily index, h, for dichotomous variables, and a test of significance for h is available (Vito Signorile and Robert M. O'Shea, "A Test of Significance for the Homophily Index," *American Journal of Sociology*, 1965, 70: 467–470).

# chapter 5

# PERSUASION AND ATTITUDE CHANGE

## SECTION ONE: OVERVIEW AND PERSPECTIVE

*Objectives for Section One*

After reading this article, you should be able to:

1. Illustrate the modes and functions of persuasive communications in social and political settings.
2. Distinguish the behavioral approach to persuasion from other methods and objectives.
3. Define persuasion, differentiate between coactive and coercive persuasion, and distinguish both from other forms of influence.
4. List the major components of attitudes.
5. Indicate how the premises of various *general* theories of persuasion lead to different *minature* theories about "prestige suggestion."
6. On the basis of the model presented in Figure 2, indicate how the author's mediational theory derives from learning, perception, and balance theories of persuasion.
7. Define what is meant by a contingent generalization, and illustrate.
8. Enumerate and illustrate some or all of the major findings on persuasion.
9. Illustrate how persuasive techniques must be adapted to different audiences and social settings.
10. List several stages in the preparation of persuasive communications.

*Herbert W. Simons*

# PERSUASION AND ATTITUDE CHANGE

## *The Study and Practice of Persuasion*

Look back over the Sixties and you will see that persuasion came in many forms. On a public level, one recalls the influential symbols of the era in a panoply of disjointed images: the vigorous gestures of a President, his forefinger almost protruding through the television tube; a mighty Papal doctrine issuing from a fragile old man; "We shall overcome" and "Hell no, we won't go"; Excedrin headaches, Marlboro Country and "Maybe you've got bad breath"; a picture of a napalmed child and the promise of a Great Society; Love beads and peace buttons, Afro haircuts and raised fists, Silent Majorities and Forgotten Americans.

Less dramatic but even more pervasive are the private instances of persuasion, the daily exchanges between husband and wife, buyer and seller, worker and boss, teacher and student. It has been estimated that about 90 per cent of a business executive's working day is spent issuing or receiving communications. Some scholars have argued that all communications are ultimately designed to persuade, but let us at least grant that the bulk of the executive's time is spent in such pursuits; furthermore, that whether by design or not, all communications may have persuasive im-

Herbert W. Simons *has taught Speech Communication at Temple University since 1960. He received an M.S. (in 1958) and a Ph.D. (in 1961) in Speech from Purdue University. Active as a protestor, mediator, and target of confrontations, he has written several articles on persuasion theory and on strategies of protest. In 1970, Professor Simons studied at Berkeley's Law and Society Center and that summer was also a guest lecturer at the University of Washington. His book on persuasion (Addison-Wesley Publishing Company, Inc.) is scheduled for 1973.*

pact. The "soap opera" on radio, the Western movie, the comic strip in the newspaper, the subtle nuance in a professor's question—all may persuade.

For some, "persuasion" is a dirty word, evoking pictures of confidence artists and Hitlerian propagandists. In ancient days, Plato branded teachers of the art as "sophists," claiming that they were more concerned with effect than with truth. Most of us resent being "manipulated" into buying popcorn; even more, we resent the growing trend toward packaging Presidential candidates as though they were popcorn.

The first selection following this article is an account by Joe McGinniss (1969) of how Richard Nixon employed the advertising man's techniques to market his own "image." McGinniss's account raises serious ethical questions which we hope you will consider thoughtfully. Despite our own ethical concerns, however, our focus in this chapter will be descriptive rather than prescriptive; with what works rather than with what ought to work. Lest the reader compare us with the objects of Plato's wrath, let us remind him that one of the best guarantors of resistance to persuasion is an awareness of the means by which it may be achieved. Some may decline to participate actively in the persuasive process—though there is hardly a "people profession" (law, teaching, social work, and so on) in which persuasion is not a mainstay. In any event, all of us spend hours each day as consumers of persuasive messages. We might as well learn how the art is practiced.

The study of persuasion—still referred to by traditionalists as "rhetoric"—might be reduced to the question: What works, on whom, in what settings, and under what conditions? The first book in recorded history dealt with that question; even Plato took a stab at it. So profound was Aristotle's *Rhetoric* that Lord Welldon characterized it as "the solitary example of a book which not only begins a science but completes it."

Lord Welldon's claim is exaggerated. As befits a tool which serves saints and sinners equally, modern conceptions of persuasion have been flavored by the diverse contributions of the ages. Historical shifts in the primary concerns of rhetoricians have reflected changes in man's view of himself as a political animal. Some periods have been marked by a fascination with "mere rhetoric": the intricacies of stylistic figures or the roundness of a pear-shaped tone, for example. At other times, rhetoricians have been preoccupied with whatever would bring power or personal success to the persuader; at still others, with persuasion as a means of managing conflict through reasoned discourse.

Contemporary contributions to our knowledge of persuasion come from a variety of quarters. In search of the keys to persuasive effectiveness, historically minded rhetorical critics have scrutinized the great speeches of the past. Others in the Speech profession and in allied fields have examined persuasion in protest movements and advertising campaigns, in bargaining sessions and in cooperative decision-making groups, in psychiatric interviews and in the graffiti on bathroom walls. Persuasion is indeed everywhere.

Only in the past 30 years or so has persuasion been subjected to rigorous scientific study, but researchers seem to be making up for lost time. More contributions to speech-communication and social-psychology journals are annually written on persuasion than on any other topic. Most of the research reflects our own *behavioral orientation*: *a systematic attempt to subject theoretically derived hypotheses to experimental tests.*

In this chapter we will sketch the broad outlines of persuasion as a behavioral area of study: its key concepts and variables, its major theories and research findings, the implications of these findings for the practitioner. The readings which follow should serve to illustrate relationships among theory, research, and practice.

## *What is Persuasion? Some Definitions, Distinctions and Variables*

Persuasion may be defined as a process of *communication* designed to *influence* receivers by modifying their *attitudes* in *intended directions.* Before we examine the key (italicized) terms of our definition and distinguish persuasion from other processes, it is well to keep in mind that since definitions are assigned by men, they must always be to some extent arbitrary. Definitions ordinarily should be consistent with conventional usage but, as you saw in Chapters 1 and 2, there are always several conventional usages for abstract terms such as "communication," "attitude," and "influence." The best one can hope for is that these terms will be used clearly and consistently within any given context; furthermore, that the user of a term will not act as though he had discovered its "real" meaning.

We concede that our own definition of persuasion is somewhat arbitrary; moreover, that we are prepared to shift our definition of the term in different contexts. At times we will speak of persuasion, not as a process, but as a quality of a communication ("persuasive message") or as an intention ("an attempt at persuasion," whether successful or not), or as a result which has actually been achieved. The context should make the meaning clear.

### PERSUASION AND ATTITUDES

So great is the conceptual confusion surounding the term "attitude" that several authorities have all but abandoned the task of defining it.

After reviewing the numerous and often conflicting distinctions drawn between attitudes and opinions, it has occurred to McGuire that they may be "names in search of distinctions" (1969, p. 152). Berelson and Steiner (1964) gave up their attempt to distinguish opinions, attitudes, and beliefs and settled for a single term, "OAB," to designate all three.

Attitudes have been variously defined as perceptual or cognitive processes, as affective or emotive tendencies, and as forms of behavior or action. We prefer to think of them as having cognitive, affective and behavioral *components*. We define attitude as a predisposition to respond favorably or unfavorably toward an object; for purposes of verbal persuasion, as agreement or disagreement with an advocated proposition. We make no distinction between attitudes and opinions but, following Fishbein (1963), we do find it useful to distinguish attitudes from beliefs and values.

As viewed here, beliefs and values are the cognitive and affective components of attitudes, respectively. Beliefs exist on a scale of *probability*, values on an *affective* or *feeling* scale. With respect to capital punishment, for example, we may believe it probable that capital punishment does not reduce crime, that it prevents criminals from being rehabilitated, and that it violates our humanistic ethic. We may also assign high values to crime reduction, rehabilitation, and humanistic ethics. Our attitudes toward capital punishment may be thought of as a joint product of the probabilities we assign to our statements of belief about the topic and the affective ratings we assign to key value terms in those statements.

More important, perhaps, than any definition of attitudes, is an understanding of the continua along which attitudes may vary. Attitudes may be felt intensely or held with relative indifference. *Salient* attitudes, those which are characterized by ego-involvement, are held more intensely than those which are peripheral to the self. Attitudes may also be public or private, or both. Like the Sabbath-day believer, we may express one attitude for public consumption while privately entertaining a quite different one. Attitudes may reflect behavioral readiness or be intellectual substitutes for action. Finally, they may be held in isolation or logically related to broader attitudes and values and to subsidiary beliefs.

For purposes of persuasion, the key variable is obviously the receiver's attitude toward the position expressed by the communicator. In varying degrees, the communicator may find that receivers are with him, against him or "on the fence," the last being a rather ambiguous category which includes the uninformed, the indifferent, and the conflicted. Figure 1 shows a hypothetical continuum representing the positions a receiver might hold and, below it, the types of persuasive effects a communicator might intend.

| Initial Attitudes: | | Disagreement | | | On the Fence | | Agreement | | | |
|---|---|---|---|---|---|---|---|---|---|---|
| | | | | | | | | | | Ready |
| Hostile | !!!! | !!! | !! | ! | ????? | ! | !! | !!! | !!!! | To Act |
| | −4 | −3 | −2 | −1 | 0 | +1 | +2 | +3 | +4 | |

Intended
Effects:* ——→Reduced Hostility——→Conversion——→Intensification——→

*Reduced hostility involves any decrease in disagreement with the source, up to the point where receivers are "on the fence." When receivers "hurdle" or "climb off" the fence, they experience conversion. Intensification involves any increase in the strength of agreement for receivers who are already in some agreement with the source.

**Figure 1.** Initial Attitudes and Intended Effects: A Model

## PERSUASION AND INTENDED EFFECTS

The ultimate aim of persuasive communication is to modify overt behavior. Any one communication may fall far short of that goal, however, and still be quite successful. Depending on his audience, the persuader may seek to reduce hostility, to convert his hearers, or to reinforce or intensify favorable attitudes. Any favorable shift in direction along the continuum represented in Figure 1 may be considered successful persuasion. It may involve creating conflict where none existed previously or resolving conflict by changing a single belief. At times, the process of making allies may require only that the receiver be made more aware or more interested; at other times, that he surrender a cherished value.

All of this underscores the importance of accurate audience analysis as a condition for successful adaptation. The problem is magnified by the fact that in an age of mass media, messages addressed to one audience are likely to reach others. Within any one audience, moreover, there are likely to be wide differences of opinion. The same communication might be effective with one group of receivers and "boomerang" with another. Often as not, the persuader must forsake one segment of his audience in order to be effective with other segments.

## COMMUNICATION AND PERSUASION

Persuasion is a type of communication. Hence, everything that you have read until now about the communication process should be applicable to persuasion as well. The following principles deserve special mention.

1. *Persuasion proceeds in stages. The process is as strong as its weakest link.* Persuasive attempts may be doomed to failure even before

the message is encoded. Unless the communicator has analyzed his audience and the social setting within which he will operate, unless he has clarified his own objectives and has conceived strategies and tactics consistent with those objectives, he is unlikely to have the effect he intends. Beyond that, attempts at influence may be betrayed by the speaker's words or gestures or by the physical or psychological "noise" that intervenes between him and the receiver. Listeners may not attend to the message; or they may hear it but distort it, or they may comprehend it but forget it or refuse to accept it. Small wonder that we often seem to be speaking to ourselves.

2. *Persuasive communications are instrumental acts, not ends in themselves.* A coyote's howl may have persuasive impact but it is an emotive expression, not a persuasive act. Similarly, the poet who "writes for himself" is not a persuader; his act is its own reward. One possible distinction between information and education on the one hand, and persuasion or propaganda on the other, is that comprehension by a receiver is regarded by the teacher as an end in itself, whereas the persuader or propagandist regards comprehension as only a means to an end. By our definitional ground rules, then, messages must be designed to modify attitudes in order for persuasion to take place. Shifts in attitude should themselves be instrumental in modifying overt behavior; these behavioral changes may in turn be viewed as preliminary results.

3. *Persuasion is an adaptive process; it takes place on the recipient's terms.* Strictly speaking, the teacher has not communicated that "Two plus two are four" if Johnny hears, "Lou and Sue are sore." In the same way, the clever debater who wins arguments but not belief has not persuaded; nor has the mutual-funds salesman who cannot translate monetary income into psychic income for the prospective purchaser. In a real sense, we do not persuade others at all; we only provide the stimuli with which they can persuade themselves.

## PERSUASION AND INFLUENCE

Varying degrees of pressure may be exerted to influence attitudes or behavior. At one extreme, an individual may be influenced by unintended messages or by direct experience; at the other, he may be compelled, by raw physical coercion or by other stimuli which trigger automatic, involuntary responses, to modify his behavior. In a gray area between these two poles—its geography only vaguely mapped—lies the domain of persuasion. Persuasion is a manipulative act, but it also leaves receivers with at least the perception of choice.

Within persuasion's domain, we distinguish two broad classes of influence: *coactive persuasion* and *coercive persuasion.* Persuasive strategies range from those involving minimal pressure on the receiver to those stopping just short of raw coercion.

Coactive persuasion is that pattern of communication with which persuasion theorists are most familiar. Often represented as the whole of persuasion, it involves shaping the attitudes of receivers as a condition for changes in their behavior. The mechanism for coactive persuasion is *attitudinal convergence.* Persuaders are advised to "move toward" the receiver—to "reduce psychological distance"—by adapting their dress styles, manners, arguments, and so on, to the receiver's frame of reference. Having achieved "common ground," the persuader is in a position to reconcile differences between himself and the receiver. Coactive persuasion is *coactive* in the sense that the receiver is expected to move toward the persuader's position as a consequence of the persuader's apparent movement toward the receiver's frame of reference.

Coactive persuasion may be accomplished by the apparent logic of an argument or appeal, or through identification by the receiver with the source of a message. Most of us recognize coactive persuasion in platform speeches and newspaper columns. We are as often persuaded, however, by coactive messages that are less directive. Through persuasion in the guise of an orientation session, a classroom lecture, or a documentary film, we may be consciously indoctrinated or "socialized" by employers, fraternity presidents, teachers, ministers, and others. These same authority figures may lead us to form new attitudes or to modify old ones, not so much by what they say as by what they do; by the modeling functions which they perform.

From Aristotle onward, persuasion has been viewed as the antithesis of force; hence, our own concept of coercive persuasion might well be viewed as a contradiction in terms. Still, we would maintain that there are patterns of persuasion—quite different from the traditionally conceived pattern—which fall just short of outright coercion.

In contrast to coactive persuasion, coercive persuasion involves shaping the *behavior* of receivers as a condition for changes in attitudes. Whereas coactive persuasion presumes an ultimate identity of interests between sender and receiver, coercive persuasion presumes, at the very least, that differences cannot be reconciled by talk alone. Thus, whereas coactive persuaders use communication as an alternative to force, coercive persuaders employ symbols as an expression, instrument, or accompaniment of force.

Behind the use of coercive persuasion is the assumption that behavioral compliance creates discrepancies between actions and attitudes. Under certain conditions, the receiver is expected to bring his attitudes into line with his actions through a process of self-persuasion. One explanation of the process is Festinger's theory of forced compliance (1964), a derivative of his more general theory of cognitive dissonance (1957).

A rough distinction may be drawn between coercive persuasion and raw coercion on two counts. First, coercive persuasion has at least the theoretical advantage of not requiring constant threat, surveillance, and punishment for noncompliance. By eventually changing attitudes, and not just behavior, the persuader has created the impetus for self-reinforced compliance by the receiver. Second, for reasons that Festinger and his associates have explored in a number of experimental studies, coercive persuasion is likely to modify attitudes in intended directions only when minimal degrees of coercive pressure are employed.

Coercive persuasion is most clearly seen in the symbolic confrontations staged by militant protest movements (Simons, 1969a, 1969b). It is by no means confined to such protests, however. The college debater who is ordered to defend a position contrary to his own may well modify his attitudes as a consequence of his actions. A governmental authority figure may issue a directive as a *fait accompli*; rather than wait for the citizenry to be influenced coactively, the President or Governor may sign an executive order, the effect of which may be to cause those affected to bring their attitudes into line with the behavior expected of them. Executives, teachers, even parents, employ a subtle blend of coactive and coercive persuasion with those subordinate to them. Some protest leaders, such as Martin Luther King, Jr., have also managed to combine coactive and coercive strategies. As we have indicated elsewhere (Simons, 1970), the strengths and limitations of each approach create important dilemmas for the leaders of any protest movement. Research findings bearing on the relative advantages of each approach are discussed briefly in the sections of this chapter on source-message variables and on action-attitude balancing.

## *Behavioral Theories of Persuasion*

A theory is like a funnel. Into the funnel come findings about phenomena which the theory attempts to summarize and explain; out of the funnel come deduced hypotheses which, when tested, add new grist for the theoretical mill. The heart of a theory—the narrow part of the funnel—is a systematized set of concepts, definitions of those concepts, and general statements or theorems which relate the concepts to each other. (For a more comprehensive discussion of the nature of theory, see Chapter 2.)

Behavioral theories of persuasion may be general or specific. General theories serve as the links between even broader conceptualizations about human behavior and miniature theories about such specific phenomena as the nature of source credibility, the effect of appeals to fear, and the consequences of counterattitudinal advocacy. In this section we shall compare general theories. For purposes of illustration we shall give special emphasis to the miniature theories, about a phenomenon known as "prestige suggestion," that the general theories have given rise to. Other miniature theories will be discussed within the context of our review of research findings.

### LEARNING THEORIES OF PERSUASION

Persuasion may be viewed as a form of learning. Just as a caged rat in a laboratory may learn to approach some stimuli and avoid others, so may a human being learn that Nationalist China is "good" and Communist China "bad." Just as the rat may modify its behavior as a result of the experimenter's "message," so may the human modify his attitudinal responses toward the two Chinas on the basis of persuasive communications. Learning theorists have developed principles governing the acquisition of responses to new stimuli, their transfer to new situations, their extinction, and so on. Theoretically, at least, these same principles should be applicable to the process of persuasion.

Learning theories of persuasion range from those *S-R* (Stimulus–Response) models which view man as a passive entity to those *S-O-R* (Stimulus–Organism–Response) models which view persuasive learning as a joint product of the messages an individual receives and the mediating forces within him which act upon those messages to determine persuasive outcomes. *S-R* theorists attempt to predict behavior strictly from a knowledge of observable stimuli and responses. *S-O-R* theorists find it necessary to hypothesize the existence of forces within the organism, directly linkable to external stimuli and responses, which help to predict behavior.

Among the dozens of *S-R* learning theories which are applicable to persuasion (see Hill, 1963), several hold that attitudinal responses may be modified through either operant or classical conditioning. We can presumably be conditioned, not just by characteristics of a message, but also by associations between a source and the position he advocates. Pavlov's dog, you will remember, was *classically conditioned* to salivate at the sound of a bell after the bell was linked to the presence of meat powder. In the same way, a listener might be conditioned to respond to an advertised product after the product is linked to a prestige source. The already favorable source might be akin to the meat powder; the more neutral product analogous to the bell. The process of "prestige suggestion," is commonly defined by learning theorists as a mechanism for inducing "uncritical acceptance" of a proposition by linking it to a prestigious source.

If the *S-R* account seems unsatisfactory, it may be because it says nothing about the internal state of the receiver at the time he is persuaded. What prompts him to listen to the commercial in the first place? Why does he want the product at all, let alone the brand being advertised? What, in short, are the motivational bases for his behavior?

At a minimum, *S-O-R* learning theories posit some internal state of motivation which must be "triggered" in order for persuasion to take place (Hovland, Janis, and Kelley, 1953). The motivational state is generally described as painful or unpleasant; it *drives* the organism to seek relief from his discomfort. Biological drives such as hunger and thirst are said to be *primary*, and quite powerful. Others, such as curiosity, social approval, and acquisition are said to be *secondary* or acquired drives, learned by association with primary drives. Why might the viewer want a given product, such as tea or ginger ale? Because his thirst drive has been activated? Why might he want Lipton's or Canada Dry in particular? Perhaps because he is driven to seek the approval of the source who has been linked to the brand name.

As evidence has accumulated to challenge the simple "trigger-action" theories of drive reduction, other *S-O-R* theories have been developed which say a good deal more about internal states of attention and comprehension and which introduce new and more complex accounts of motivational processes. Note that the paradigm presented in Figure 2, p. 241 reflects a mediational, *S-O-R* theory of persuasion.

## PERCEPTION THEORIES OF PERSUASION

Whereas *S-R* theories focus on external inputs and outputs, theories of perception are primarily concerned with the world of inner experience, the way the world looks to the individual doing the perceiving. Attitudes are not so much behavioral responses as they are "pictures in our heads," evaluative frames of reference which may *predispose* us toward behavioral responses. Persuasion is viewed as a process of reordering perceptual categories based on organized cues from the environment and on internal needs and values.

In order to demonstrate further how theory and research may be brought to bear on a particular phenomenon, linkages between source and position continue to occupy center stage in several of the readings which follow this chapter. Solomon Asch's (1952) account of prestige suggestion contains a blistering critique of experiments designed to demonstrate the validity of *S-R* theories or narrowly circumscribed *S-O-R* interpretations. Far from picturing prestige suggestion as automatic conditioning, Asch holds that some linkages between prestige sources and the positions they advance are not at all persuasive; moreover, those that do have impact are persuasive precisely because they lead the receiver to *restructure his perceptions* of the object. Thomas Jefferson's call for "revolution every twenty years" would have quite another meaning to a receiver if he attributed the utterance to Karl Marx.

Other perception theorists are similarly critical of accounts which treat prestige suggestion as relatively automatic and predictable. Robert Merton (1946) has theorized that, to be maximally effective, the source must appear to have *symbolic fitness*; what he represents to his audience as a person must somehow mesh well (form a "good *gestalt*") with the product he advertises. Still another theory would challenge the ability of persuaders to sell all products equally well. According to Sherif, Sherif, and Nebergall (1965), there is, for each of us, a range of propositions we can accept, another range of statements to which we are noncommittal, and still another range we will reject. Especially when there is ego-involvement, positions on issues tend to be either *assimilated* (perceived as more similar to our own than they really are) or *contrasted* (seen as more unlike our own than they really are). Moreover, when there is ego-involvement, our "latitudes of rejection" tend to be considerably larger. Thus, however prestigious the source might be, should he attempt to sell a daytime TV audience on the merits of a pornographic novel, his efforts will probably boomerang.

Perception theorists are equally loath to grant the *S-O-R* view that audiences are "driven" to accept testimonials uncritically. Although much of their own research on perception has convinced them that man's efforts to make sense of the world are not always "sensible" by external standards, they would nevertheless insist that it is not necessarily unreasonable to lean on the cues provided by a prestige source, especially when—as so often happens—there is little other information to go on.

If they do nothing else, perception theorists perform a valuable service by reminding us that it is the receiver's *psychological reality* which counts in persuasion, not the physical reality of sounds and light waves emitted by the persuader. No matter how well-intentioned the source may be, no matter how reasonable his message, it is the receiver's perceptions of these qualities which affect his attitudes.

The third selection following this article contains three excerpts from an important article by a well-known functional theorist, Daniel Katz (1960). In the first excerpt, Katz offers a conciliatory view of the conflict between the learning theorists and the perception theorists about prestige suggestion. Like the rabbi confronted with an irate husband and an equally irate wife, Katz argues that both Asch and the learning theorists are right, but each under certain conditions.

Space prohibits a detailed account of Katz's theory or of other functional theories, for that matter (see Smith, Bruner, and White, 1956; Kelman, 1961). Suffice it to suggest that, according to Katz, appropriate strategies of persuasion cannot be developed until one knows whether a particular attitude held by a receiver serves an instrumental, an ego-defensive, a value-expressive, or an informational function, or some combination thereof. An ego-defensive listener, for example, will not be persuaded by arguments which link a given proposal with his self-interest. Nor will he be persuaded by group pressures or by "information campaigns" of the kind often employed in extolling the virtues of brotherhood. As Katz's chart on page 275 suggests, it is a lot easier to reinforce prejudiced attitudes than to change them. Whereas attitudes serving an instrumental function may be modified by picturing the rewarding consequences of adopting another position or the unpleasant consequences of not adopting it, ego-defensive attitudes can only be changed through a process akin to psychotherapy. Katz provides a useful reconciliation of learning and perception theories as well as of other competing formulations.

## BALANCE THEORIES OF PERSUASION

The assumption that man seeks a psychologically consistent view of the world—first articulated by perception theorists—serves as the major premise for a number of "balance" theories (Cartwright and Harary, 1956; Heider, 1946; Newcomb, 1953). Like the *S-R* learning theorists, some balance theorists (e.g., Osgood and Tannenbaum, 1955) maintain that attitudinal changes following communications are automatic and predictable. For many balance theorists, in fact, the need for psychological consistency is a drive, perhaps as basic as the drive to reduce hunger. Like Katz's functional theory, balance theories help to effect a reconciliation between learning and perception theories.

The best known and most provocative of the balance theories (it has generated over 300 research studies) is Festinger's theory of cognitive dissonance (1957). According to Festinger, cognitions (used loosely to include beliefs, attitudes, values—any bits of knowledge) may be mutually dissonant, mutually consonant, or mutually irrelevant. Whether *logically inconsistent* with each other or *psychologically inconsistent*, dissonant cognitions create pressures to reduce the resulting discomfort.

For purposes of relating Festinger's theory to our own model of persuasion, we distinguish four types of discrepancy, each of which may create cognitive dissonance: (1) *Action-attitude discrepancies*. [These were discussed in the section on Persuasion and Influence.] As we have already indicated, an administrator's public approval of a Black Studies program may be dissonant with his private attitudes toward the program. Similarly, knowledge that one smokes is dissonant with the cognition that smoking is harmful to health. The decision to purchase one product is dissonant with favorable cognitions about other products, and so on. (2) *Source-position discrepancies* are generated by prestige suggestions or by the pressures exerted on a deviant group member by other members of his group. Knowledge that our favorite newspaper columnist prefers our choice of political candidates is cognitively *consonant* and thus reinforcing. Knowledge that he disagrees with us on the candidate is cognitively *dissonant.* Unless we also value him as a football expert, knowledge that he disagrees with us on the merits of the Green Bay Packers is likely to be cognitively *irrelevant.* (3) *Belief-attitude discrepancies* and (4) *value-attitude discrepancies* are inconsistencies between our general positions on issues and the cognitive or affective basis for the attitudes embodied in these positions. It is cognitively consonant to promote the reelection of an incumbent governor on grounds that he has run a liberal administration. Should we be convinced, however, that our *beliefs* about his past record are ill-founded or that we err in *valuing* liberal administrations, a state of cognitive dissonance would now exist.

Festinger emphasizes that modifications of attitudes do not follow automatically from cognitive dissonance. Although pressures to reduce dissonance are increased as the number or importance of dissonant cognitive elements increases, all of us manage to live with some dissonance. Moreover, attitudinal shifts are only one means of relieving dissonance. In the case (once again) of a prestige source urging a position discrepant from our own, we may: (1) derogate the source; (2) decide that our disagreement is not very important, or rationalize it in some other way; (3) seek social support or supportive evidence for our own viewpoint; (4) misperceive the source's position; (5) compartmentalize (ignore or forget that the cognitions are discrepant); (6) attempt to convince the source of his error (if he is available); or (7) modify our own attitudes.

What happens when a disliked candidate states a position consistent with our own? For many "doves" and others who were hostile toward Nixon in 1968, perhaps a state of dissonance was created as they heard Nixon campaigning for election on a platform to Vietnamize the war and "bring American boys home." The first selection following this chapter presents an account by Joe McGinnis (1969) of how Nixon employed TV commercials to link himself with favorable positions. Whether the commercials enhanced Nixon's image among "doves" is not clear. From Festinger's theory, it would follow that "doves" could have reduced dissonance in other ways: by misperceiving Nixon's position, by rationalizing, by compartmentalizing, and so on. Festinger's theory serves as a warning that persuaders must do more than "unbalance" cognitions by creating cognitive dissonance. They must also "rebalance" cognitions by directing the receiver in specified ways and by closing off alternative methods of reducing dissonance.

### TOWARD A RECONCILIATION OF PERSUASION THEORIES: THE AUTHOR'S OWN VIEW

From our brief survey of general persuasion theories, we have already seen both the desirability and the possibility of reconciliation among them. *S-R* theories have advanced our understanding of the relationships between external inputs and outputs and have clarified key concepts by assigning them operational definitions. *S-O-R* theories have shown us how organismic variables may be lawfully related to external stimuli and responses, especially when the theories have included internal factors of attention and comprehension along with motivational factors. Albeit with admittedly fuzzy concepts like "symbolic fitness," perception theorists have led us into the inner world of the receiver and have shown us how decoding processes may affect persuasion. Katz and other functional theorists have reminded us that any theory of persuasion must begin with an analysis of the functions that attitudes perform for a given audience in a given social settting. The balance theorists—and especially Festinger—have tickled our imaginations by deriving non-obvious miniature theories from their general theories (such as the forced-compliance formulation mentioned in our discussion of coercive persuasion). Moreover, they have enabled us to see "unbalancing" and "rebalancing" as the heart of the persuasive process.

No general theory can include all the major variables of persuasion or account for the complex relationships among them. Figure 2 is our own model of the persuasive process—drawn, as you can see, from the theories we have reviewed. The model should serve as a framework for integrating other theories and for reviewing major research findings.

## *Principles of Persuasion*

What conclusions can be drawn about persuasion on the basis of experimental research? Is it a common-sense process, reducible to a few simple rules, or is it a hopelessly complex process for which no rules can reliably be established?

The answer is somewhere inbetween. Simplistic hypotheses have been belied in research on scores of communication variables. Rarely can we state *without qualification* that one technique is more effective than its opposite (e.g., that one-sided messages are more persuasive than those giving both sides, or that "emotional" appeals are more effective than "logical" appeals). Contrary to common-sense expectations, for example, the forewarned listener may not be better armed against attempts at influence than the unsuspecting listener. Surprisingly enough, there may even be some occasions when speakers with little credibility are more persuasive than those with much credibility!

| Stimulus (*S*) | | Organism (*O*) | | Response (*R*) |
|---|---|---|---|---|
| Antecedent Factors | Input Factors | Mediators: Preliminary Effects | | Output Factors |
| | | Decoding | Balancing | |
| Receiver<br>Social setting | Source<br>Message<br>Medium | Attention<br>Comprehension | Source-position<br>Belief-attitude<br>Value-Attitude<br>Action-attitude | Reduced hostility<br>Conversion<br>Intensification<br>Others |

**Figure 2.** A Mediational Model of Persuasion

Does this mean that persuasion, like love, will unyieldingly defy any attempts to comprehend it? An interesting art but never a science? The answer is yes, *but*! Scientists will never unearth all the complex contingencies which regulate the relationship between a given communication variable and its effects on attitudes. They *can* identify some of the most significant contingencies, however, and can indicate how they facilitate or inhibit persuasive effects. Although we cannot say that one-sided messages are more effective than two-sided messages, we can say that the former are more effective with predisposed audiences, the less well-educated, and those who will not be exposed to counterarguments. These are contingent generalizations, true, but, *the aim of the behavioral approach to persuasion is to develop contingent generalizations.*

In this section we list some of the major research findings on persuasion, drawn largely from recent reviews of experimental literature (Higbee, 1969; Insko, 1967; McGuire, 1969; McCroskey, 1969; Simons, Moyer, and Berkowitz, 1970; Zimbardo and Ebbeson, 1969). The reader is referred to these sources for additional findings as well as for references to original work. Our review is organized around the model presented in Figure 2.

## A SUMMARY OF RESEARCH FINDINGS

I. *Antecedent Factors*

A. Receivers

1. Attitudes are learned and can therefore be unlearned.
2. The cognitive, affective, and behavioral components of attitudes are highly correlated.

a. Beliefs, expectations, predictions, and so on are highly correlated with wishes, desires, values, and so on.

b. Although attitudes and behavior are positively correlated, attitudes do not predetermine behavior. Receivers can decide to call attitudes into play. Moreover, what one *would* do and what he *says* he would do are not correlated.

3. General tendencies to resist or to be receptive to persuasive appeals are determined by a number of personal characteristics.

a. Receivers whose egos are involved are more resistant than uninvolved listeners. Persons who take extreme positions generally have more ego-involvement.

b. Public attitudes are more resistant than private attitudes, especially when they have group support.

c. Attitudes which are solidly anchored to a large number of beliefs, values, and other attitudes are highly resistant to change. The simpler the receiver's cognitive structure, the easier it is to change it.

d. Dogmatic persons, those low in self-esteem, and those labeled as authoritarians tend to be highly persuasible on peripheral issues and highly resistant to change on ego-involving issues.

e. It is generally easier to persuade females than males, children than adults, unintelligent people than intelligent people, those who characteristically cope with anxiety than those who characteristically avoid anxiety. These findings tend to be somewhat inconsistent, however.

B. Social Setting

1. The same individual may hold or reflect different attitudes in different social settings and in different roles (at home, as a boss, and so on).

2. Groups, organizations, and cultures each impose ritualized norms (sanctions and taboos) of behavior for different social settings.

3. The physical characteristics of a social setting (room temperature, degree of crowding, and so on) affect persuasion.

II. *Input Factors*

A. Source-Message Variables[1]

1. Credibility, Attractiveness, Power

[1]Since source and message generally interact, we have chosen to group source and message variables together in this review.

a. Credibility, attraction, and power are affected by judgments of the source prior to his presentation as well as by what he says and does when presenting his message. Credible persons are those viewed as having expertise and trustworthiness. Specifically, those seen as knowledgeable, prestigious, objective, sincere, and interested in their receivers are considered most credible. Attraction is based on attitudinal and membership-group similarities, liking, and familiarity, each of which probably reinforces the other. Power rests with a source when he is able to control a receiver's rewards and punishments, is perceived as desirous of the receiver's compliance, and can check on the compliance of the receiver.

b. Credibility, attractiveness, and power are in some respects antithetical. Attraction rests on the perception of near equality, of psychological proximity between the source and receiver. Credibility requires psychological distance, a perception that the source is more expert and possibly more trustworthy than the receiver, at least with respect to the contents of his message. Power divides sender and receiver, rendering the source less trustworthy and less attractive.

c. Perceptions of source credibility, especially of expertise, or prestige, lead to attitudinal change.

    (1). Although expertise and prestige do not significantly affect comprehension, they probably cause receivers to accept the source's opinions more uncritically.

    (2). Sources perceived as reliable or objective may not be as effective as sources perceived as anxious to persuade. Trustworthy speakers have not been found to be more persuasive than untrustworthy speakers except where trustworthiness has been confounded with expertise, a high level of involvement by the audience, or intensity of language. In most studies, warnings of intent have not impeded persuasion.

    (3). Sources who indicate agreement with receivers on at least some issues, even when these issues are irrelevant to the proposition being advocated, are more likely to win acceptance of that proposition.

(4). With the passage of time, receivers tend to dissociate the source from the message, unless the source is reinstated.

d. Attraction contributes to changes in attitude.

(1). Perceived similarities in attitude are more likely to effect attitudinal change than perceived membership-group similarities, except among highly prejudiced people or under other special circumstances.

(2). Opinion leaders in communities tend to be members of the groups they influence, but they are better informed, somewhat better off financially, more conformist, more interested, and more gregarious.

e. Whereas credibility and attraction lead directly to changes in attitudes, power affects compliance, which in turn may affect attitudes.

2. Magnitude of Discrepancy

a. The more a persuader asks for, the more he is likely to get. Up to rather extreme levels of discrepancy, the greater the distance between the receiver's position and the position of the communicator, the greater is the attitudinal change.

b. Discrepant messages delivered to highly involved audiences or to hostile audiences tend to have no effect or to boomerang, especially when delivered by sources low in credibility.

3. Message Structure

a. Organized messages do not seem to produce greater attitudinal change than disorganized messages, although they may increase the source's credibility.

b. Giving equal weight to both sides of a controversial issue or stating "the facts" impartially does not persuade. Two-sided messages that draw conclusions are more effective than one-sided messages when the receivers are more intelligent and better educated, are initially opposed or undecided, or will later be exposed to counterarguments.

c. Stating an explicit conclusion at the outset of a communication is generally more effective than implying it or saving it for the end. Exceptions may include communications addressed to highly intelligent or hostile audiences.

4. Evidence, Arguments, and Appeals
    a. Good evidence is generally persuasive over the long run, but it is not necessarily persuasive over the short run if the source is credible, if the message is delivered poorly, or if the audience is already familiar with the evidence.
    b. There is little consistent basis for claims that logical or emotional appeals are relatively more effective. Given conventional definitions of these terms, judges find it difficult to distinguish between them.
    c. Strong threats are generally more effective than weak threats, especially when the source is credible. When either strong or weak appeals to fear are accompanied by recommendations that are specific and easy to implement, their effectiveness increases.

B. The Medium
    1. Informal face-to-face communications are generally more persuasive than mass media presentations.
    2. The relative persuasiveness of the mass media varies widely from topic to topic.

III. *Mediating Factors*

A. Decoding: Attention and Comprehension
    1. Antecedent factors and input factors affect attention and comprehension.
        a. On the basis of internal needs and wants, as well as of structural characteristics of the message, receivers selectively attend to, perceive, recall, and utilize information. In general, however, receivers do not selectively avoid discrepant information.
        b. Organized messages are generally not better comprehended or retained than disorganized messages.
    2. Attention and comprehension usually facilitate the acceptance of messages, but not always. Deliberate ambiguity may facilitate persuasion. On the other hand, intelligent people may well be more resistant to change, despite the fact that they comprehend and retain messages with greater ease.

B. Balancing
    1. Source-Position Discrepancies
        a. In the absence of evidence, or when issues are complex, people tend to lean on social sources of influence.
        b. When source and position are discrepant, attitudes toward both are modified so as to be made more congruent.

2. Belief-Attitude and Value-Attitude Discrepancies
   a. When beliefs or values change, attitudes tend to be modified.
   b. It is easier to change beliefs than values.
3. Action-Attitude Discrepancies
   a. Changes in behavior lead to changes in attitudes more readily than the reverse.
   b. Forced compliance is most likely to lead to "self-persuasion" when receivers cannot justify their own decisions to comply on extraneous grounds. This is likely to happen under conditions of minimal pressure to comply and minimal justification for compliance, when compliers exert maximal effort and when sources have little credibility.

IV. *Output Factors*

A. Types of Effect
1. The effects of persuasive communications tend to be exaggerated. When conversion occurs, it is usually as a result of a protracted campaign or because persuasive messages have combined with a number of other forces to produce the effect.
2. It is easier to reinforce or intensify existing attitudes than it is to convert others or to reduce their hostility.
3. Most persuasive communications are addressed to already sympathetic audiences and are designed to reinforce existing attitudes.

B. Duration of Effect
1. The effect of persuasive communications tends to wear off gradually, although "sleeper" effects (increases in effect after a lapse of time) have been noted, especially when messages were presented by sources of little credibility.
2. Periodic restatement of a persuasive communication tends to prolong its influence.

## *Implications for the Persuader*

On the basis of everything that has been said so far, what general steps might a communicator follow who wants to persuade?

1. Determine whom you want to persuade, why you want to persuade, and what effects you want to achieve.
2. In light of your objectives, analyze your audience (or audiences), especially their attitudes toward your position.

3. For purposes of coactive persuasion, present yourself as a "super-representative" of your audience.
4. For purposes of coercive persuasion, induce compliance through positive rather than negative reinforcements, so as to retain some credibility and attractiveness.
5. Structure your message for psychological impact. Do not worry much about logical orderliness, but use strong appeals and good evidence.
6. Get attention and comprehension, preferably by adapting your message to your audience's needs and wants but, if need be, by forcing it upon your audience.
7. Create dissonance or imbalance. Then specify to your audience the means by which they may reduce their imbalance.
8. Remember that, although the practice of persuasion may be greatly informed by the findings of research, it is still very much an art and an elusive one at that.

## *REFERENCES*

Asch, S. E. *Social Psychology.* Englewood Cliffs, N.J.: Prentice-Hall, Inc., 1952.

Berelson, B., & Steiner, G. A. *Human behavior: an inventory of scientific findings.* New York: Harcourt, Brace & World, Inc., 1964.

Cartwright, D., & Harary, F. Structural balance: A generalization of Heider's theory. *Psychological Review*, 1956, 63, 277–293.

Festinger, L. *A theory of cognitive dissonance.* Stanford: Stanford University Press, 1957.

Festinger, L. (Ed.) *Conflict, decision and dissonance.* Stanford: Stanford University Press, 1964.

Fishbein, M. An investigation of relationships between beliefs about an object and the attitude toward that object. *Human Relations*, 1963, 16, 233–239.

Heider, F. Attitudes and cognitive organization. *Journal of Psychology*, 1946, 21, 107–112.

Higbee, K. L. Fifteen years of fear arousal: Research on threat appeals: 1953–1968. *Psychological Bulletin*, 1969, 72, 426–444.

Hill, W. F. *Learning: A survey of psychological interpretations.* San Francisco: Chandler, 1963.

Hovland, C., Janis, I., & Kelley, H. *Communication and Persuasion.* New Haven: Yale University Press, 1953.

Insko, C. *Theories of attitude change.* New York: Appleton-Century-Crofts, 1967.

Katz, D. The functional approach to the study of attitudes. *Public Opinion Quarterly*, 1960, 24, 163–205.

Kelman, H. Processes of opinion change. *Public Opinion Quarterly*, 1961, 25, 57–58.

McCroskey, J. C. A summary of experimental research on the effects of evidence in persuasive communication. *Quarterly Journal of Speech*, 1969, 55, 169–176.

McGinniss, J. *The selling of the president, 1968.* New York: Trident, 1969.

McGuire, W. J. The nature of attitudes and attitude change. In G. Lindzey and E. Aronson (Eds.) *The handbook of social psychology*. Vol. 3. Reading, Mass: Addison-Wesley, 1969.

Merton, R. *Mass persuasion*. New York: Harper, 1946.

Newcomb, T. An approach to the study of communicative acts. *Psychological Review*, 1953, 60, 393–404.

Osgood, C., & Tannenbaum, P. The principle of congruity in the prediction of attitude change. *Psychological Review*, 1955, 62, 42–55.

Sherif, C., Sherif, M., & Nebergall, R. *Attitude and attitude change*. Philadelphia: Saunders, 1965.

Simons, H. Patterns of persuasion in the civil rights struggle. In J. J. Auer (Ed.), *The rhetoric of our times*. New York: Appleton-Century-Crofts, 1969a.

Simons, H. Confrontation as a pattern of communication in university settings. *Central States Speech Journal*, 1969b, 20, 163–170.

Simons, H., Moyer, R. J., & Berkowitz, N. N. Similarity, credibility and attitude change: A review and a theory. *Psychological Bulletin*, 1970, 73, 1–18.

Simons, H. W. Requirements, problems and strategies: a theory of persuasion for social movements. *Quarterly Journal of Speech*, 1970, 56, 1–12.

Smith, M., Bruner, J., & White, R. *Opinions and personality*. New York: Wiley, 1956.

Zimbardo, P., & Ebbeson, E. *Influencing attitudes and changing behavior*. Reading, Mass.: Addison-Wesley, 1969.

## SECTION TWO: READINGS

### *Introduction and Objectives for Reading One: The Selling of the President, 1968*

The following excerpts from Joe McGinniss' best-seller deal with Richard Nixon's use of TV in his 1968 election campaign. The first excerpt describes Nixon's rhetorical problem; the second illustrates the methods he employed to solve that problem.

After reading this selection you should be able to:

1. Discuss the ethical questions raised by Nixon's approach to persuasion. Consider questions such as the following: If Nixon had grown to the point of meriting the Presidency, was he not entitled—even obligated—to accomplish his objectives by any means possible? Since the press had systematically demolished the "natural" Nixon, was he not justified in running a contrived and deceptive campaign? Since Humphrey and Wallace were also playing the advertising man's game, could Nixon be blamed for playing it better?
2. Indicate, by using one or more theories about prestige suggestion, how the juxtaposition of source and message may serve to bolster the source's image.

Joe McGinniss

## *THE SELLING OF THE PRESIDENT: 1968*

Politics, in a sense, has always been a con game.

The American voter, insisting upon his belief in a higher order, clings to his religion, which promises another, better life; and defends passionately the illusion that the men he chooses to lead him are of finer nature than he.

It has been traditional that the successful politician honor this illusion. To succeed today, he must embellish it. Particularly if he wants to be President.

"Potential presidents are measured against an ideal that's a combination of leading man, God, father, hero, pope, king, with maybe just a touch of the avenging Furies thrown in," an adviser to Richard Nixon wrote in a memorandum late in 1967. Then, perhaps aware that Nixon qualified only as father, he discussed improvements that would have to be made—not upon Nixon himself, but upon the image of him which was received by the voter.

That there is a difference between the individual and his image is human nature. Or American nature, at least. That the difference is exaggerated and exploited electronically is the reason for this book.

Advertising, in many ways, is a con game, too. Human beings do not need new automobiles every third year; a color television set brings little enrichment of the human experience; a higher or lower hemline no expansion of consciousness, no increase in the capacity to love.

It is not surprising then, that politicians and advertising men should have discovered one another. And, once they recognized that the citizen did not so much vote for a candidate as make a psychological purchase of him, not surprising that they began to work together.

The voter, as reluctant to face political reality as any other kind, was hardly an unwilling victim. "The deeper problems connected with advertising," Daniel Boorstin has written in *The Image,* "come less from the unscrupulousness of our 'deceivers' than from our pleasure in being deceived, less from the desire to seduce than from the desire to be seduced. . . .

"In the last half-century we have misled ourselves . . . about men . . . and how much greatness can be found among them. . . . We have

Excepts from J. McGinnis, *The Selling of the President: 1968* (New York: Trident Press, 1969), pp. 26–39, 87–92. Copyright 1969 by Joemac Incorporated. Reprinted by permission of Trident Press, division of Simon and Schuster, Inc.

become so accustomed to our illusions that we mistake them for reality. We demand them. And we demand that there be always more of them, bigger and better and more vivid."

The Presidency seems the ultimate extension of our error.

Advertising agencies have tried openly to sell Presidents since 1952. When Dwight Eisenhower ran for re-election in 1956, the agency of Batton, Barton, Durstine and Osborn, which had been on a retainer throughout his first four years, accepted his campaign as a regular account. Leonard Hall, national Republican chairman, said: "You sell your candidates and your programs the way a business sells its products."

The only change over the past twelve years has been that, as technical sophistication has increased, so has circumspection. The ad men were removed from the parlor but were given a suite upstairs.

. . . . . . . . . . . . . . . . . . . .

Television seems particularly useful to the politician who can be charming but lacks ideas. Print is for ideas. Newspapermen write not about people but policies; the paragraphs can be slid around like blocks. Everyone is colored gray. Columnists—and commentators in the more polysyllabic magazines—concentrate on ideology. They do not care what a man sounds like; only how he thinks. For the candidate who does not, such exposure can be embarrassing. He needs another way to reach the people.

On television it matters less that he does not have ideas. His personality is what the viewers want to share. He need be neither statesman nor crusader; he must only show up on time. Success and failure are easily measured: how often is he invited back? Often enough and he reaches his goal—to advance from "politician" to "celebrity," a status jump bestowed by grateful viewers who feel that finally they have been given the basis for making a choice.

The TV candidate, then, is measured not against his predecessors—not against a standard of performance established by two centuries of democracy—but against Mike Douglas. How well does he handle himself? Does he mumble, does he twitch, does he make me laugh? Do I feel warm inside?

Style becomes substance. The medium is the massage and the masseur gets the votes.

In office, too, the ability to project electronically is essential. We were willing to forgive John Kennedy his Bay of Pigs; we followed without question the perilous course on which he led us when missiles were found in Cuba; we even tolerated his calling of reserves for the sake of a bluff about Berlin.

We forgave, followed, and accepted because we liked the way he looked. And he had a pretty wife. Camelot was fun, even for the peasants, as long as it was televised to their huts.

Then came Lyndon Johnson, heavy and gross, and he was forgiven nothing. He might have survived the sniping of the displaced intellectuals had he only been able to charm. But no one taught him how. Johnson was syrupy. He stuck to the lens. There was no place for him in our culture.

"The success of any TV performer depends on his achieving a low-pressure style of presentation," McLuhan has written. The harder a man tries, the better he must hide it. Television demands gentle wit, irony, understatement: the qualities of Eugene McCarthy. The TV politician cannot make a speech; he must engage in intimate conversation. He must never press. He should suggest, not state; request, not demand. Nonchalance is the key word. Carefully studied nonchalance.

Warmth and sincerity are desirable but must be handled with care. Unfiltered, they can be fatal. Television did great harm to Hubert Humphrey. His excesses—talking too long and too fervently, which were merely annoying in an auditorium—became lethal in a television studio. The performer must talk to one person at a time. He is brought into the living room. He is a guest. It is improper for him to shout. Humphrey vomited on the rug.

It would be extremely unwise for the TV politician to admit such knowledge of his medium. The necessary nonchalance should carry beyond his appearance while *on* the show; it should rule his attitude *toward* it. He should express distaste for television; suspicion that there is something "phony" about it. This guarantees him good press, because newspaper reporters, bitter over their loss of prestige to the television men, are certain to stress anti-television remarks. Thus, the sophisticated candidate, while analyzing his own on-the-air technique as carefully as a golf pro studies his swing, will state frequently that there is no place for "public relations gimmicks" or "those show business guys" in his campaign. Most of the television men working for him will be unbothered by such remarks. They are willing to accept anonymity, even scorn, as long as the pay is good.

Into this milieu came Richard Nixon: grumpy, cold, and aloof. He would claim privately that he lost elections because the American voter was an adolescent whom he tried to treat as an adult. Perhaps. But if he treated the voter as an adult, it was as an adult he did not want for a neighbor.

This might have been excused had he been a man of genuine vision. An explorer of the spirit. Martin Luther King, for instance, got by without being one of the boys. But Richard Nixon did not strike people that way. He had, in Richard Rovere's words, "an advertising man's approach to his work," acting as if he believed "policies [were] products to be sold the public—this one today, that one tomorrow, depending on the discounts and the state of the market."

So his enemies had him on two counts: his personality, and the convictions—or lack of such—which lay behind. They worked him over heavily on both.

Norman Mailer remembered him as "a church usher, of the variety who would twist a boy's ear after removing him from church."

McLuhan watched him debate Kennedy and thought he resembled "the railway lawyer who signs leases that are not in the best interests of the folks in the little town."

. . . . . . . . . . . . . . . . . . . . . . .

America still saw him as the 1960 Nixon. If he were to come at the people again, as candidate, it would have to be as something new; not this scarred, discarded figure from their past.

He spoke to men who thought him mellowed. They detected growth, a new stability, a sense of direction that had been lacking. He would return with fresh perspective, a more unselfish urgency.

His problem was how to let the nation know. He could not do it through the press. He knew what to expect from them, which was the same as he had always gotten. He would have to circumvent them. Distract them with coffee and doughnuts and smiles from his staff and tell his story another way.

Television was the only answer, despite its sins against him in the past. But not just any kind of television. An uncommitted camera could do irreparable harm. His television would have to be controlled. He would need experts. They would have to find the proper settings for him, or if they could not be found, manufacture them.

. . . . . . . . . . . . . . . . . . . . . . .

So this was how they went into it. Trying, with one hand, to build the illusion that Richard Nixon, in addition to his attributes of mind and heart, considered, in the words of Patrick K. Buchanan, a speech writer, "communicating with the people . . . one of the great joys of seeking the Presidency"; while with the other they shielded him, controlled him, and controlled the atmosphere around him. It was as if they were building not a President but an Astrodome, where the wind would never blow, the temperature never rise or fall, and the ball never bounce erratically on the artificial grass.

. . . . . . . . . . . . . . . . . . . . . . .

And it worked. As he moved serenely through his primary campaign, there was new cadence to Richard Nixon's speech and motion; new confidence in his heart. And, a new image of him on the television screen.

. . . . . . . . . . . . . . . . . . . . . . .

Everyone was excited about the technique and the way it could be used to make people feel that Richard Nixon belonged in the White House. The only person who was not impressed was Nixon. He was in a hotel room in San Francisco one day, recording the words for some of the early commercials. The machine was turned on before Nixon realized it and the end of his conversation was picked up.

"I'm not sure I like this kind of a . . . of a format, incidentally,"

Nixon said. "Ah . . . I've seen these kinds of things and I don't think they're very . . . very effective. . . ."

Still, Nixon read the words he had been told to read:

"In recent years crime in this country has grown nine times as fast as the population. At the current rate, the crimes of violence in America will double by nineteen seventy-two. We cannot accept that kind of future. We owe it to the decent and law-abiding citizens of America to take the offensive against the criminal forces that threaten their peace and security and to rebuild respect for law across this country. I pledge to you that the wave of crime is not going to be the wave of the future in America."

There was nothing new in these words. Harry Treleaven had simply paraphrased and condensed the standard law and order message Nixon had been preaching since New Hampshire. But when the words were coupled with quickly flashing colored pictures of criminals, of policemen patrolling deserted streets, of bars on storefront windows, of disorder on a college campus, of peace demonstrators being led bleeding into a police van, then the words became something more than what they actually were. It was the whole being greater than the sum of its parts.

. . . . . . . . . . . . . . . . . . . .

The first spot was called simply *Vietnam*. Gene Jones had been there for ninety days, under fire, watching men kill and die, and he had been wounded in the neck himself. Out of the experience had come *A Face of War*. And out of it now came E.S.J. [for Eugene S. Jones] #1, designed to help Richard Nixon become President. Created for no other purpose.

| *Video* | *Audio* |
|---|---|
| 1. Opening network disclaimer: "A political announcement." | |
| 2. Fadeup of fast paced scenes of helo assault in Vietnam. | SFX and under |
| 3. Wounded Americans and Vietnamese. | *R.N.* Never has so much military, economic, and diplomatic power been used as ineffectively as in Vietnam. |
| 4. Montage of facial CU's of American servicemen and Vietnamese natives with questioning, anxious, perplexed attitude. | And if after all of this time and all of this sacrifice and all of this support there is still no end in sight, then I say the time has come for the American people to turn to new leadership—not tied to the policies and mistakes of the past. |
| 5. Proud faces of Vietnamese peasants ending in CU of the word "love" scrawled on the helmet of American G.I. and pull back to reveal his face. | I pledge to you: we will have an honorable end to the war in Vietnam. |
| | Music up and out. |

. . . . . . . . . . . . . . . . . . . . . .

Dead soldiers and empty words. The war was not bad because of insane suffering and death. The war was bad because it was *ineffective*.

So Richard Nixon, in his commercial, talked about new leadership for the war. New leadership like Ellsworth Bunker and Henry Cabot Lodge and U. Alexis Johnson.

*Vietnam* was shown across the country for the first time on September 18. Jack Gould did not like this one any more than he had liked Connie Francis.

"The advertising agency working in behalf of Richard Nixon unveiled another unattractive campaign spot announcement," he wrote. "Scenes of wounded GIs were the visual complement for Mr. Nixon's view that he is better equipped to handle the agony of the Vietnamese war. Rudimentary good taste in politics apparently is automatically ruled out when Madison Avenue gets into the act."

The fallen soldiers bothered other people in other ways. There was on the Nixon staff an "ethnic specialist" named Kevin Phillips, whose job it was to determine what specific appeals would work with specific nationalities and in specific parts of the country. He watched *Vietnam* and sent a quick and alarmed memo to Len Garment: "This has a decidely dovish impact as a result of the visual content and it does not seem suitable for use in the South and Southwest."

His reasoning was quite simple. A picture of a wounded soldier was a reminder that the people who fight wars get hurt. This, he felt, might cause resentment among those Americans who got such a big kick out of cheering for wars from their Legion halls and barrooms half a world away. So bury the dead in silence, Kevin Phillips said, before you blow North Carolina.

Another problem arose in the Midwest: annoyance over the word "Love" written on the soldier's helmet.

"It reminds them of hippies," Harry Treleaven said. "We've gotten several calls already from congressmen complaining. They don't think it's the sort of thing soldiers should be writing on their helmets."

Len Garment ordered the picture taken out of the commercial. Gene Jones inserted another at the end; this time a soldier whose helmet was plain.

This was the first big case of "political" guidance, and for a full week the more sensitive members of the Gene Jones staff mourned the loss of their picture.

"It was such a beautiful touch," one of them said. "And we thought, what an interesting young man it must be who would write 'Love' on his helmet even as he went into combat."

Then E.S.J. Productions received a letter from the mother of the soldier. She told what a thrill it had been to see her son's picture in one of Mr. Nixon's commercials, and she asked if there were some way that she might obtain a copy of the photograph.

The letter was signed: Mrs. William Love.

*Introduction and Objectives for Reading Two:*
*"The Doctrine of Suggestion"*

This selection is concerned with "the doctrine of suggestion" and its influence in research on attitudes and human persuasion. The author examines a number of studies investigating social influence in the light of some basic premises underlying hypnotic suggestibility.

After reading this selection you should be able to:

1. Indicate the bases for Asch's critique of early prestige suggestion experiments.
2. Show how the hypotheses in early prestige suggestion experiments derive from simple *S-R* and *S-O-R* learning theories.
3. Describe the basic paradigm used by researchers in experimental studies of social influence.
4. Describe the significance of the motif of indirectness.

Solomon E. Asch

# THE DOCTRINE OF SUGGESTION

## THE DOCTRINE OF SUGGESTION

"Social man is a somnambulist." In these words the French sociologist Tarde [1903] summarized a psychological doctrine of social interaction in the second half of the nineteenth century. A view that concludes (or, to be more accurate, which starts with the assumption) that men in society are akin to sleepwalkers is at least of historical interest. It becomes worthy of examination when it is adopted by sociologists and finds its way

Excerpts from Solomon E. Asch, *Social Psychology* © 1952. (Englewood Cliffs, N.J.: Prentice-Hall, Inc., 1952), pp. 398–414. Reprinted by permission of Prentice-Hall, Inc., Englewood Cliffs, New Jersey.

to the very center of social psychology. Its importance increases still further in light of the fact that it has guided the formulation of problems, the procedure of investigations, and even the interpretation of results.

. . . . . . . . . . . . . . . . . . . .

The interest that attached to waking suggestibility seemed warranted for a number of reasons. It was first of all a social effect, one induced in one person by another. Second, it appeared to be not only a normal phenomenon, but also possibly the fundamental form of interaction between person and person. Finally, it possessed an astonishing property that was probably the principal reason for the interest it commanded. What struck observers most was that one person could induce effects in another *without* introducing corresponding changes in the environment. The heart of the phenomena of suggestion, the property that made them unique, was the ability to produce changes in individuals in the absence of appropriate objective conditions. By means of commands it was apparently possible to produce experiences and beliefs to which nothing in the environment corresponded. Here was an effect produced by purely "psychological" means, one that short-circuited the workings of real conditions and had no foundation in fact or reason. By the same token the effects obtained marked a blind, uncritical acceptance of choices and beliefs. This became the defining characteristic of suggestion. According to McDougall's [1926] representative definition, suggestion was the acceptance of a proposition "in the absence of logically adequate grounds," a characterization that has remained unaltered to the present.[1]

. . . . . . . . . . . . . . . . . . . .

It is a matter of considerable import that there should have grown up in psychology a view that described social action generally in terms of passivity and equated group influence with arbitrary control. The model was an individual deprived of autonomy, one whose actions stemmed not from an inner direction but from external influences forcing themselves upon him and taking control away from him. The initiative belonged to an autocratic suggestor who was either a person in authority or a multitude of persons. The phenomena that were said to be central in social action were characterized by thoughtlessness and unreasonableness. In fact, it was the intent of the suggestion movement to describe social behavior as "irrational" in its roots and branches, as synonymous with manipulation. It became an

[1]Consider F. H. Allport's definition: "Suggestion is a process involving elementary behavior mechanisms in response to a social stimulus; the nature of the process being that the one who gives the stimulus controls the behavior and consciousness of the recipient in an immediate manner, relatively uninfluenced by thought, and through the method of building up motor attitudes, releasing them, or augmenting the released response as it is being carried out." ([1924,] p. 251.) See also Cantril and Frederiksen. [1939]

accepted proposition that as a rule men can be induced to believe and act according to dictation and to hold opposed views with equal conviction.

Discussions of suggestion did refer to "critical" factors that limit its operations. But the role assigned to thinking was mainly that of an inhibitory process, serving as a brake upon the more primitive and permanent forces of suggestion. Some writers went as far as to state a thesis of "primitive credulity," to the effect that there is a fundamental tendency in the human mind to believe immediately *any* idea presented to it provided no contradictory idea is allowed to intrude—a view that advertisers and propagandists came to practice seriously.

It was this view of social processes that was transposed and applied to the entire region of social events—to the behavior of crowds, the role of leaders (of all leaders, from statesmen to parents), the spread of fashions, the growth of religious beliefs and of taste in art.[2] In the more recent period it has become the basis for accounts of propaganda[3] and advertising and of the formation of attitudes. It appears as the hard core of apparently different psychological ideas such as "prestige" and "imitation"; these are minor variations on the idea of suggestion to which they can be reduced without difficulty.

Up to the present we have spoken of suggestion entirely in a descriptive sense. Although discussions of suggestion have been generally loose and inexact, they were nevertheless guided by a theoretical idea. At bottom the facts of suggestion were derived from the classical concept of association; they were a straightforward application of the associationistic postulate to social processes. The suggestion proceeding from another person was a stimulus (older writers called it an "idea") that starts a process in the subject. As a result of past experience the stimulus had become connected in the subject with a given response, say a movement or image. Whenever the stimulus reappears it automatically produces in the subject a habitual response in the form of an action or another idea. A suggestion is simply an external impression that exerts an automatic effect on the basis of previous experience. Viewed in this way suggestion is not a special psychological phenomenon. To be sure, it is of consequence that another person can become the source of stimulation and that he can control another's reactions in this manner. But this is an added fact that poses vir-

[2]"One of the most important single concepts in the field of social relations is that of suggestion, for it is largely by means of suggestion that the individual acquires the stereotyped norms of his community, his religion, his politics, his racial prejudices, his ethical and esthetic standards" [Cantril and Frederikson, 1939].

[3]"Propaganda is an organised and public form of the process which the psychologist calls 'suggestion.'" (Bartlett, F. C., *Political Propaganda.* Cambridge: The University Press, 1940, p. 51.)

tually no new problem for theory. When Bernheim [1888] declared that "every impression, every mental picture, every conscious phenomenon is a suggestion," he was restating, although in an inexact way, the associationist principle that each element of consciousness appears only by virtue of its association with another.[4] This characterization of suggestion has remained unchanged to the present, as the following statement of Pavlov testifies: "We can therefore, regard 'suggestion' as the most simple form of the typical conditioned reflex in man." ([Pavlov, 1927,] p. 407.) Early accounts of suggestion, because they based themselves on the postulate of association, were almost wholly devoid of reference to motivational conditions. But there was no difficulty in assimilating the facts of suggestion to the schema of learning under the guidance of reward and punishment. The reader can readily see that the stimulus-response account of imitation . . . requires no alteration when applied to actions said to be the result of suggestion.

## EXPERIMENTAL STUDIES OF SOCIAL INFLUENCE

The ideas just described have formed the basis of an attempt to study experimentally the effects of group forces on the formation and change of opinions and judgments. We shall here examine some representative investigations to see what they establish factually and in what relation they stand to theory. Generally they have followed a simple and forthright procedure. One establishes first how an individual evaluates a given matter. The second step consists of informing him about the evaluation of the same matter by others. If we find the individual altering his position in the suggested direction, we have obtained a definite social effect, the result of a reaction to the evaluation of others. In brief, one determines the views of individuals before and after they have been subjected to the views of others; the latter is the experimental factor, the effect of which is measured.

THE INVESTIGATION OF MOORE. One of the earliest investigations in this region is that of Moore (1921). Although not the most significant of

[4]The basis of the phenomena of suggestion in the fact of association was clearly stated by Freud in the introduction to his translation of Bernheim's work on suggestion: ". . . die Bezeichnung 'Suggeriren' wird gleichbedeutend mit der gegenseitigen Erweckung psychischer Zustände nach den Gesetzen der Association. Der Verschluss der Augen führt den Schlaf herbei, weil er als eine der constantesten Begleiterscheinungen mit der Vorstellung des Schlafes verknüpft ist; das eine Stuck der Phänomene des Schlafes suggerirt die anderen Phänomene der ganzen Erscheinung. Diese Verknüpfung liegt in der Beschaffenheit des Nervensystems, nicht in der Willkür des' Arztes, sie kann nicht bestehen, ohne sich auf Veränderungen in der Erregbarkeit der betreffenden Gehirnpartien, in der Innervation der Gefässcentren u.s.w. zu stützen und bietet ebensowohl eine psychologische, wie eine physiologische Ansicht." (p. xi.)

the studies we shall examine, it has a certain historical interest since it has served as a model for subsequent work. Moore asked a group of subjects, all college students, to state their judgments individually on a number of matters. They read pairs of ungrammatical statements under instructions to judge which member of a pair was less grammatical ("He never studies nights" and "She sort of avoided him"). The same groups also read pairs of statements describing ethical infringements, the task being to decide which was the more serious ("disloyalty to friends" or "willingness to get rich by questionable financial methods"). Finally, they were to judge which of two resolutions of the dominant seventh chord was the more consonant. Each of the categories of items was represented by a series of 18 pairs. In the first step of the investigation the subjects stated their evaluations. A few days later they judged the identical items again to establish how stable their reactions were in the absence of special external influences. After a lapse of time sufficient to obscure the recall of the earlier judgments (two and a half months), the same materials were again presented for judgment. This time each item was preceded by a statement of how the majority had judged it. (Some of the "majority judgments" were identical with those actually obtained; others were in the opposed direction.) The last step consisted of a repetition of the experiment, this time preceded by announcements of the way experts had judged the matters. With this procedure one can determine the reversals of choices in response to the conditions of "majority influence" and "expert influence." When these results are compared with the frequency of reversals that occur spontaneously, a measure is obtained of the strength of the experimentally introduced factors.

The results showed a large and statistically significant number of reversals in response to the opinions of the majority and of the experts. We learn, for example, that the majority opinion led the subjects to reverse 62 per cent of their linguistic, 50 per cent of their ethical, and 43 per cent of their musical judgments. Similar results were obtained in response to the expert opinions. How are these findings to be interpreted? Moore concluded that the results represent *modifications of judgment* in response to the pressure of majority and expert opinion.

To understand the purport of this investigation one needs to scrutinize more closely its procedure and assumptions. The opinions of the majority (and of "experts") were introduced as brute facts, without attempt to justify them by appeal to reason. All factors involving discrimination or thinking were deliberately excluded. The point of the investigation was to demonstrate that one can alter evaluations sheerly as a result of knowledge about the evaluations of others. The guiding assumption was that the effects to be studied were those of an uncritical process of suggestion; majority and expert opinion were conceived as "stimuli" that have been connected in the past with conforming responses and which now push the subjects in the suggested direction. The investigation presupposed the process and considered the sole remaining problem to be that of measuring it. "The general fact is beyond dispute but those who would like to see Social Psychology multiply its experimental findings are tempted to ask more specifically just how great this influence may be expected to be in any given situation. Can we hope to measure it?" (1921, p. 16.)

Are we seriously to suppose that the group scuttled 50 per cent of a set of ethical convictions under the stress of this experimental onslaught? Shall we conclude that there has finally been discovered a technique with which "to influence people," a means of changing ideas about the good, the true, and the beautiful and one that works with such absurd ease? To put these questions is to raise doubt about the meaning of the results. We need to ask: What does the investigation establish factually?

To answer this question it would be necessary to ascertain the sense of the subjects' reactions. Did the observed changes correspond to any change of conviction? Were the subjects convinced at one point that one alternative was right and later that they had been wrong? Did they say to themselves: "This is the majority opinion; majorities are usually right; therefore I now know what to believe?" At this point the investigation fails us; it provides no evidence about the sense of the reactions. We do not know whether the tasks touched off any conviction or whether they were taken seriously or in an off-hand way. It is possible that the latter occurred, since the judgments called for were artificial and often ambiguous. Whether one of two grammatical distortions is the more flagrant may not only be difficult to state; it is also a question one would not ordinarily put to oneself or to others. It would not be surprising if the subjects decided that the questions were trivial and lacking in reality and therefore took the easiest way out. The latter reaction, if it occurred, would be of interest but it would no longer have much in common with the problem with which the investigation started—the modification of evaluations. When Hamlet leads Polonius to agree that a cloud has in turn the shape of a camel, a weasel, and a whale, we understand that he is extracting a response of expediency and not necessarily producing the corresponding contents in the mind of the courtier.

Even within the limits of the investigation a more rigorous examination of the results would have pointed to certain problems. (1) The experimentally introduced factors of majority and expert opinion fell short of complete effectiveness; some judgments remained unaltered. The alleged suggestions must therefore have been limited by the operation of other factors and should have raised a question about their character. (2) The results were reported in averages. This leaves undecided the question whether all evaluations were equally affected by the experimental conditions or whether there were some that successfully resisted them. (3) A similar question arises about the contribution of the individual subjects to the mass results. Were all subjects equally affected? This does not seem likely. Were there perhaps some who refused to participate? Such "negative" reactions might be of consequence for theory. (4) Finally, no mention is made of changes in a direction contrary to majority and expert opinion. If such changes occurred, they would be of considerable importance and by no means consonant with the initial presuppositions. On these issues we remain in the dark.

SHERIF'S INVESTIGATION OF PRESTIGE. A more interesting investigation is that of Sherif [1936], who undertook to demonstrate by an ingenious technique that the factor of prestige can alter the evaluation of literary materials. Groups of college students read a set of 16 brief prose passages, each consisting of two or three sentences; each passage was accompanied by the name of a well-known author. The task was to rank the passages in an order of merit. On a previous occasion the same group had ranked the 16 authors for their merit. Now there was a hidden feature in the experiment: the passages were all taken from the writings of one author, R. L. Stevenson; in addition, they were selected so as not to differ in quality. In other words, there was no relation between the passages and their presumed authors. Would the evaluations of the passages be equally independent of the authorship imputed to them?

They were not. Although there was no intrinsic relation between the passages and the authors attached to them, the subjects showed a tendency (though only moderate) to rank the passages in the same directions as the arbitrarily coupled authors (the average correlations ranging from .30 to .53). Passages identified with more favored authors ranked more highly. In further work Sherif also showed that the same passage was ranked differently depending on the authors with whom it was paired.

This result, which is of definite interest, seems again in accordance with the assumption that one can alter evaluations arbitrarily. This was the interpretation of Sherif, who concluded that "authors rated high tended to push up the rating of the passages attributed to them. Conversely, authors rated low tended to pull down the ratings of passages attributed to them . . . Not the intrinsic merits of the passages but the familiar or unfamiliar frame of reference explained the findings." ([Sherif, 1936,] p. 122.) According to this interpretation the "prestige" of an author automatically transferred to the passage and altered its level. Did it?

To become clear about the results it is again necessary to ask what happened to the subjects in this situation. The investigation provides no answer since it was limited to the external results. It is to be noted that the task was a difficult and, indeed, an insoluble one. The subjects were asked to make a discrimination between materials that were deliberately selected so as not to differ substantially. There was no objective basis for fulfilling the task. Under the circumstances the subjects could reject the task. This, however, they did not do. They did not acknowledge (or perhaps know) that they had no basis for judgment. This is perhaps the most interesting aspect of the investigation, and one would like to understand the reason. Possibly because the social setting constrained them by placing them under the necessity of arriving at a judgment, the subjects tried to make the best of it and in the process fell into the experimental trap. Is it necessary to conclude that they did so by altering their evaluation? Elsewhere [Asch, 1948] the writer has suggested another possibility. Once the subject has accepted the task he feels the need to arrive at a judgment. Not having a clear basis to go on he leans on the clues the experimenter has placed in his path. But his concern may no longer be that of reaching a clear conclusion but to respond in a way to escape censure or ridicule. The result may be that his expressions of judgment do not carry conviction to himself and no longer represent actual evaluations. Were this so the results would be of interest for a reason that was not investigated, but they would not support the assumption they were intended to prove. One should note also that the results, although positive, were moderate; apparently there were factors at work resisting the experimental condition and stronger than it.

. . . . . . . . . . . . . . . . . . . . .

The studies described here have touched upon a problem and pointed to an effect of undoubted importance. Starting from the observation that we are sensitive to the opinions of others, they have demonstrated in different ways that under certain conditions there takes place a movement toward agreement, a result the implications of which we shall consider later. . . . On the technical side the procedures leave much to be desired. In particular, they have not inquired into the phenomenal aspect of the situation, with the result that the meaning and significance of the findings have not become clear. They did not reveal, because they did not explore, the processes responsible for the observed effects. This oversight was primarily the result of the confident assumption that a certain process, itself not subjected to investigation, represented the sole alternative. It should be the task of subsequent investigation to correct this one-sidedness.[5]

Finally it should be noted that the effects to which the term suggestion was first applied are obtained under special conditions that differ from the

[5]It is of interest to note that the authors of the investigations in question were in practice aware of the problems they ignored in their theory. Without exception they took care to hide the purpose of investigation from their subjects. Yet it is not clear that the notion of suggestion need predict that persons who are gullible under experimental conditions will also find it repugnant to "be influenced."

conditions prevailing in the experiments just described. In a suggestion experiment the individual is placed in a monotonous environment and is instructed to adopt a passive attitude. He is asked to fixate a particular stimulus, to make his mind a blank, and to refrain from thinking about other matters. Other impressions are deliberately excluded, and the individual is asked also to cooperate by limiting his voluntary movements. When the experimenter tells his subject: "Your arm is stiff and you cannot straighten it," the subject is expected to concentrate solely on the arm and the announcement. Typically the effects are obtained under conditions that create *a narrowing of the mental field.* A small segment of the environment is isolated from the stream of life, and the connection of the individual with ongoing events is momentarily suspended or reduced to the dwindling point. Suggestion refers to a stunted form of action lacking the characteristics of give-and-take that prevents the individual from testing the situation. Also contrary to a usual interpretation, which takes the facts of suggestion as irreducible, it presupposes an already established social relation with the person who is taking the initiative. The relation is one of trust; the subject places himself in the hands of the experimenter whose competence and intentions he does not question. Still more, there is a relation of cooperation; before any suggestion is made the subject has agreed to follow instructions, to do what he is told even when he does not fully understand, because to do otherwise would be to disrupt the common purpose. Effects obtained under these conditions are transient, as a rule not surviving the short span of the experiment. To understand the operations of suggestion it will be necessary to introduce rather than exclude reference to the properties of social interaction. Far from providing a foundation for understanding other phenomena, the facts of suggestion have not been satisfactorily clarified. An adequate theory of suggestion will require more searching knowledge than we possess at present of the changes attendant upon a narrowed mental field, of the dynamics of trust, of the reality-properties of experiences, and of the amenability of objects to perceptual change.

## *Sensible and Arbitrary Social Influence*

At best the suggestion movement dealt with a special problem in social influence—with factors that work *against* adequate judgment and evaluation. It failed to bring its observations into relation with social influences that are enlightening. It is obvious but necessary to say that we are not simply victims of one another, that others can help us to think more intelligently and to feel more deeply, that there are sensible ways of relying on others. By generalizing its findings it adopted the radical position that in the social sphere arbitrariness is the rule. It therefore came near to identifying the psychology of social thought and feeling with the study of misconceptions and illusions, and of likening the social process to a form of drug action that converts black into white. It came near to forgetting that discussion and co-operation have properties opposed to sheer imitation and conformity. Since this is not an isolated trend within psychology, it is important to understand its technical grounds.

## THE MOTIF OF INDIRECTNESS

In common sense, to judge means to look at a situation, to weigh its merits and shortcomings, or to get at the root of a matter. This notion of common sense is inverted in the approach and studies under discussion. This approach supposes that the object and its properties are not of primary importance; what matters is how the object has become connected with (or conditioned to) the response to another object, the qualities of which are again of no concern. It has virtually become a canon of method to say: If one wants to understand why a person evaluates a situation in a given way, do not try first to find out what of the situation he has grasped, how it looks here and now; one must first look to the way he has been conditioned to it, to the way his response happened to become connected with the situation in past experience. Our vision must be indirect, for that which we experience as the character or meaning of a thing is usually the result of its connection to something else.

This is a well-nigh inescapable feature of the associative position. If a child jumps in fright at the sight of a dog, the reason is not that the dog reveals fearful qualities, such as readiness to pounce and bite and a fierce look. The reason is that in the past the dog was accompanied by another stimulus that was frightening, such as an expression of fright in the mother. But when we turn to the past situation and repeat the question, we repeat the problem. We are forced to look for still another stimulus to which that one was connected, until we finally reach an "unlearned" fear reaction. Should the child subsequently lose his fear this is accounted for by the connection of the dog with another stimulus, this time a pleasant one, not by inquiring whether the child has found in the dog some likeable qualities and possibilities he had not noted before. Throughout, the dog with his qualities does not figure. The stimulus is an X which may be connected with an indefinite number of reactions.[6] . . .

The motif of indirectness often has the consequence of reducing psychological phenomena that possess meaning to phenomena lacking in meaning. The following statement of Thorndike about the establishment of a learned response is illustrative:

[6]No theory can, of course, escape the requirement that the stimulus be recognizable or identifiable on successive occasions. It is a question whether the minimum requirement of identifiability does not already presuppose the perception of the very qualities that the preceding formulation so sedulously avoids.

> When it is impossible or very difficult to contrive that $S_1$ shall evoke $R_x$ directly, we have recourse to learning by associative shifting, wherein we find some situation (call it $S_2$) that does evoke $R_x$ and change $S_2 \rightarrow R_x$ over to $S_1 \rightarrow R_x$ (by additions until we have $S_2 + S_1 \rightarrow R_x$, and later subtractions until we have $S_1 \rightarrow R_x$). Thus suppose that the aim is to link the attitude of liking to Uncle Jonas, who is not intrinsically able to arouse it in his nephew, aged five. We first present Jonas dressed as Santa Claus doing amusing tricks and bearing gifts, and interest is aroused. The Santa Claus disguise is taken off gradually, without destroying the liking. Uncle Jonas stops performing his tricks and still retains his nephew's liking. He is divested of the gifts and still retains it, the originally unattractive Uncle Jonas being now able alone to arouse the response originally aroused only by $S_2$. Rewards for the $S_1 \rightarrow R_x$ when it is obtained as a result of the shift may be used to maintain and strengthen it. ([Thorndike, 1935,] p. 191.)

This statement excludes the operation of intrinsic factors of judging and discovering, substituting for them manipulations of connection-bonds. Is there not another way to solve the problem? It is conceivable that the child is repelled by a quality he perceives *in* the uncle. The latter may be a gloomy person, one who does not laugh nearly enough; or he may be too loud and brusque: children are known to be quite sensitive to such qualities. The uncle may also be at heart a kindly man, a fact which his surface qualities unfortunately hide. If he wishes to come nearer to his nephew perhaps he should allow the child to see that he—not the mask or the candy—has likeable qualities and that he can be playful and friendly. In this way he might win the child. To play tricks and bring gifts might help, but only if the child is able to see that these acts are an expression of the uncle's character. Otherwise the child might continue to like the candy and despise the uncle.

The preceding discussion has a bearing on a problem of wide import for social psychology. We cannot understand beliefs and convictions unless we can see how they appear sensible. This holds also for beliefs that are objectively unfounded; the latter too are based on reasons. Only if we proceed in this way can we clarify how inadequate or wrong data form the compelling ground for conclusions at variance with fact.

## *References*

Allport, F. H., *Social Psychology*. Boston: Houghton Mifflin, 1924.

Bernheim, H. *Die Suggestion und Ihre Heilwirkung*. Leipzig und Wien: Franz Deuticke, 1888.

Cantril, H. and Frederiksen, N., "Social Functions of the Individual," in Boring, E. G., Langfeld, H. S., and Weld, H. P., *Introduction to Psychology*. New York: John Wiley, 1939.

McDougall, W., *An Introduction to Social Psychology*. Boston: John W. Luce, 1926.

Moore, H. T., "The comparative influence of majority and expert opinion," *American J. Psychology*, 1921, 32, 16–20.

Pavlov, I. P., *Conditioned Reflexes*. New York: Oxford University Press, 1927.

Sherif, M., *The Psychology of Social Norms*. New York: Harper, 1936.

Tarde, G., *The Laws of Imitation* (trans. from 2nd French ed. by E. C. Parsons). New York: Henry Holt, 1903.

Thorndike, E. L., *The Psychology of Wants, Interests and Attitudes*. New York: copyright by D. Appleton-Century, 1935.

## *Introduction and Objectives for Reading Three: "The Functional Approach to the Study of Attitudes"*

The author of this article expresses the view that most theoretical descriptions of the basis of human attitudes assume that man is either totally rational or totally irrational. The author offers a position which represents aspects of both these extremes.

After reading this article you should be able to:

1. Describe the two traditional approaches used to account for the basis of man's attitudes.
2. Describe the basic position of the functional approach to understanding the nature of attitudes.
3. List and describe briefly four functions which attitudes perform for individuals.

Daniel Katz

# *THE FUNCTIONAL APPROACH TO THE STUDY OF ATTITUDES*

## *Early Approaches to the Study of Attitude and Opinion*

There have been two main streams of thinking with respect to the determination of man's attitudes. The one tradition assumes an irrational model of man: specifically it holds that men have very limited powers of

Excerpts from D. Katz, "The Functional Approach to the Study of Attitudes," *Public Opinion Quarterly*, XXIV (1960), 163–92. Reprinted by permission of the publisher and author.

reason and reflection, weak capacity to discriminate, only the most primitive self-insight, and very short memories. Whatever mental capacities people do possess are easily overwhelmed by emotional forces and appeals to self-interest and vanity. The early books on the psychology of advertising, with their emphasis on the doctrine of suggestion, exemplify this approach. One expression of this philosophy is in the propagandist's concern with tricks and traps to manipulate the public. A modern form of it appears in *The Hidden Persuaders,* the use of subliminal and marginal suggestion, or the devices supposedly employed by "the Madison Avenue boys." Experiments to support this line of thinking started with laboratory demonstrations of the power of hypnotic suggestion and were soon extended to show that people would change their attitudes in an uncritical manner under the influence of the prestige of authority and numbers. For example, individuals would accept or reject the same idea depending upon whether it came from a positive or a negative prestige source.[1]

The second approach is that of the ideologist who invokes a rational model of man. It assumes that the human being has a cerebral cortex, that he seeks understanding, that he consistently attempts to make sense of the world about him, that he possesses discriminating and reasoning powers which will assert themselves over time, and that he is capable of self-criticism and self-insight. It relies heavily upon getting adequate information to people. Our educational system is based upon this rational model. The present emphasis upon the improvement of communication, upon developing more adequate channels of two-way communication, of conferences and institutes, upon bringing people together to interchange ideas, are all indications of the belief in the importance of intelligence and comprehension in the formation and change of men's opinions.

Now either school of thought can point to evidence which supports its assumptions, and can make fairly damaging criticisms of its opponent. Solomon Asch and his colleagues, in attacking the irrational model, have called attention to the biased character of the old experiments on prestige suggestion which gave the subject little opportunity to demonstrate critical thinking.[2] And further exploration of subjects in these stupid situations does indicate that they try to make sense of a nonsensical matter as far as possible. Though the same statement is presented by the experimenter to two groups, the first time as coming from a positive source and the second time as coming from a negative source, it is given a different meaning dependent upon the context in which it appears.[3] Thus the experimental

[1]Muzafer Sherif, *The Psychology of Social Norms,* New York, Harper, 1936.

[2]Solomon E. Asch, *Social Psychology,* New York, Prentice-Hall, 1952.

[3]*Ibid.,* pp. 426–427. The following statement was attributed to its rightful author, John Adams, for some subjects and to Karl Marx for others: "those who hold and those who are without property have ever formed distinct inter-

subject does his best to give some rational meaning to the problem. On the other hand, a large body of experimental work indicates that there are many limitations in the rational approach in that people see their world in terms of their own needs, remember what they want to remember, and interpret information on the basis of wishful thinking. H. H. Hyman and P. Sheatsley have demonstrated that these experimental results have direct relevance to information campaigns directed at influencing public opinion.[4] These authors assembled facts about such campaigns and showed conclusively that increasing the flow of information to people does not necessarily increase the knowledge absorbed or produce the attitude changes desired.

The major difficulty with these conflicting approaches is their lack of specification of the conditions under which men do act as the theory would predict. For the facts are that people do act at times as if they had been decorticated and at times with intelligence and comprehension. And people themselves do recognize that on occasion they have behaved blindly, impulsively, and thoughtlessly. A second major difficulty is that the rationality-irrationality dimension is not clearly defined. At the extremes it is easy to point to examples, as in the case of the acceptance of stupid suggestions under emotional stress on the one hand, or brilliant problem solving on the other; but this does not provide adequate guidance for the many cases in the middle of the scale where one attempts to discriminate between rationalization and reason.

. . . . . . . . . . . . . . . . . . . . .

## *Four Functions which Attitudes Perform for the Individual*

The major functions which attitudes perform for the personality can be grouped according to their motivational basis as follows:

1. *The instrumental, adjustive, or utilitarian function* upon which Jeremy Bentham and the utilitarians constructed their model of man. A modern expression of this approach can be found in behavioristic learning theory.
2. *The ego-defensive function* in which the person protects himself from acknowledging the basic truths about himself or the harsh realities in

---

ests in society." When the statement was attributed to Marx, this type of comment appeared: "Marx is stressing the need for a redistribution of wealth." When it was attributed to Adams, this comment appeared: "This social division is innate in mankind."

[4]Herbert H. Hyman and Paul B. Sheatsley, "Some Reasons Why Information Campaigns Fail," *Public Opinion Quarterly*, Vol. 11, 1947, pp. 413–423.

his external world. Freudian psychology and neo-Freudian thinking have been preoccupied with this type of motivation and its outcomes.

3. *The value-expressive function* in which the individual derives satisfactions from expressing attitudes appropriate to his personal values and to his concept of himself. This function is central to doctrines of ego psychology which stress the importance of self-expression, self-development, and self-realization.
4. *The knowledge function* based upon the individual's need to give adequate structure to his universe. The search for meaning, the need to understand, the trend toward better organization of perceptions and beliefs to provide clarity and consistency for the individual, are other descriptions of this function. The development of principles about perceptual and cognitive structure have been the contribution of Gestalt psychology.

Stated simply, the functional approach is the attempt to understand the reasons people hold the attitudes they do. The reasons, however, are at the level of psychological motivations and not of the accidents of external events and circumstances. Unless we know the psychological need which is met by the holding of an attitude we are in a poor position to predict when and how it will change. Moreover, the same attitude expressed toward a political candidate may not perform the same function for all the people who express it. And while many attitudes are predominantly in the service of a single type of motivational process, as described above, other attitudes may serve more than one purpose for the individual. A fuller discussion of how attitudes serve the above four functions is in order.

1. THE ADJUSTMENT FUNCTION. Essentially this function is a recognition of the fact that people strive to maximize the rewards in their external environment and to minimze the penalties. The child develops favorable attitudes toward the objects in his world which are associated with the satisfactions of his needs and unfavorable attitudes toward objects which thwart him or punish him. Attitudes acquired in the service of the adjustment function are either the means for reaching the desired goal or avoiding the undesirable one, or are affective associations based upon experiences in attaining motive satisfactions.[5] The attitudes of the worker favoring a political party which will advance his economic lot are an example of the first type of utilitarian attitude. The pleasant image one has of one's favorite food is an example of the second type of utilitarian attitude.

In general, then, the dynamics of attitude formation with respect to the adjustment function are dependent upon present or past perceptions of the utility of the attitudinal object for the individual. The clarity, consist-

[5]Daniel Katz and Ezra Stotland, "A Preliminary Statement to a Theory of Attitude Structure and Change," in Sigmund Koch, editor, *Psychology: A Study of a Science*, Vol. 3, New York, McGraw-Hill 1959, pp. 434–443.

ency, and nearness of rewards and punishments, as they relate to the individual's activities and goals, are important factors in the acquisition of such attitudes. Both attitudes and habits are formed toward specific objects, people, and symbols as they satisfy specific needs. The closer these objects are to actual need satisfaction and the more they are clearly perceived as relevant to need satisfaction, the greater are the probabilities of positive attitude formation. These principles of attitude formation are often observed in the breach rather than the compliance. In industry, management frequently expects to create favorable attitudes toward job performance through programs for making the company more attractive to the worker, such as providing recreational facilities and fringe benefits. Such programs, however, are much more likely to produce favorable attitudes toward the company as a desirable place to work than toward performance on the job. The company benefits and advantages are applied across the board to all employees and are not specifically relevant to increased effort in task performance by the individual worker.

Consistency of reward and punishment also contributes to the clarity of the instrumental object for goal attainment. If a political party bestows recognition and favors on party workers in an unpredictable and inconsistent fashion, it will destroy the favorable evaluation of the importance of working hard for the party among those whose motivation is of the utilitarian sort. But, curiously, while consistency of reward needs to be observed, 100 per cent consistency is not as effective as a pattern which is usually consistent but in which there are some lapses. When animal or human subjects are invariably rewarded for a correct performance, they do not retain their learned responses as well as when the reward is sometimes skipped.[6]

2. The Ego-Defensive Function. People not only seek to make the most of their external world and what it offers, but they also expend a great deal of their energy on living with themselves. The mechanisms by which the individual protects his ego from his own unacceptable impulses and from the knowledge of threatening forces from without, and the methods by which he reduces his anxieties created by such problems, are known as mechanisms of ego defense. A more complete account of their origin and nature will be found in Sarnoff's article.[7] . . . They include the devices by which the individual avoids facing either the inner reality of the kind of person he is, or the outer reality of the dangers the world holds for him. They stem basically from internal conflict with its resulting insecurities. In one sense the mechanisms of defense are adaptive in temporarily removing the sharp edges of conflict and in saving the individual

[6]William O. Jenkins and Julian C. Stanley, "Partial Reinforcement: A Review and Critique," *Psychological Bulletin,* Vol. 47, 1950, pp. 193–234.

[7]*Public Opinion Quarterly*, XXIV (1960), pp. 251–279.

from complete disaster. In another sense they are not adaptive in that they handicap the individual in his social adjustments and in obtaining the maximum satisfactions available to him from the world in which he lives. The worker who persistently quarrels with his boss and with his fellow workers, because he is acting out some of his own internal conflicts, may in this manner relieve himself of some of the emotional tensions which beset him. He is not, however, solving his problem of adjusting to his work situation and thus may deprive himself of advancement or even of steady employment.

Defense mechanisms, Miller and Swanson point out, may be classified into two families on the basis of the more or less primitive nature of the devices employed.[8] The first family, more primitive in nature, are more socially handicapping and consist of denial and complete avoidance. The individual in such cases obliterates through withdrawal and denial the realities which confront him. The exaggerated case of such primitive mechanisms is the fantasy world of the paranoiac. The second type of defense is less handicapping and makes for distortion rather than denial. It includes rationalization, projection, and displacement.

Many of our attitudes have the function of defending our self-image. When we cannot admit to ourselves that we have deep feelings of inferiority we may project those feelings onto some convenient minority group and bolster our egos by attitudes of superiority toward this underprivileged group. The formation of such defensive attitudes differs in essential ways from the formation of attitudes which serve the adjustment function. They proceed from within the person, and the objects and situation to which they are attached are merely convenient outlets for their expression. Not all targets are equally satisfactory for a given defense mechanism, but the point is that the attitude is not created by the target but by the individual's emotional conflicts. And when no convenient target exists the individual will create one. Utilitarian attitudes, on the other hand, are formed with specific reference to the nature of the attitudinal object. They are thus appropriate to the nature of the social world to which they are geared. The high school student who values high grades because he wants to be admitted to a good college has a utilitarian attitude appropriate to the situation to which it is related.

All people employ defense mechanisms, but they differ with respect to the extent that they use them and some of their attitudes may be more defensive in function than others. It follows that the techniques and conditions for attitude change will not be the same for ego-defensive as for utilitarian attitudes.

Moreover, though people are ordinarily unaware of their defense

[8]Daniel R. Miller and Guy E. Swanson, *Inner Conflict and Defense,* New York, Holt, 1960, pp. 194–288.

mechanisms, especially at the time of employing them, they differ with respect to the amount of insight they may show at some later time about their use of defenses. In some cases they recognize that they have been protecting their egos without knowing the reason why. In other cases they may not even be aware of the devices they have been using to delude themselves.

3. THE VALUE-EXPRESSIVE FUNCTION. While many attitudes have the function of preventing the individual from revealing to himself and others his true nature, other attitudes have the function of giving positive expression to his central values and to the type of person he conceives himself to be. A man may consider himself to be an enlightened conservative or an internationalist or a liberal, and will hold attitudes which are the appropriate indication of his central values. Thus we need to take account of the fact that not all behavior has the negative function of reducing the tensions of biological drives or of internal conflicts. Satisfactions also accrue to the person from the expression of attitudes which reflect his cherished beliefs and his self-image. The reward to the person in these instances is not so much a matter of gaining social recognition or monetary rewards as of establishing his self-identity and confirming his notion of the sort of person he sees himself to be. The gratifications obtained from value expression may go beyond the confirmation of self-identity. Just as we find satisfaction in the exercise of our talents and abilities, so we find reward in the expression of any attributes associated with our egos.

Value-expressive attitudes not only give clarity to the self-image but also mold that self-image closer to the heart's desire. The teenager who by dress and speech establishes his identity as similar to his own peer group may appear to the outsider a weakling and a craven conformer. To himself he is asserting his independence of the adult world to which he has rendered childlike subservience and conformity all his life. Very early in the development of the personality the need for clarity of self-image is important—the need to know "who I am." Later it may be even more important to know that in some measure I am the type of person I want to be. Even as adults, however, the clarity and stability of the self-image is of primary significance. Just as the kind, considerate person will cover over his acts of selfishness, so too will the ruthless individualist become confused and embarrassed by his acts of sympathetic compassion. One reason it is difficult to change the character of the adult is that he is not comfortable with the new "me." Group support for such personality change is almost a necessity, as in Alcoholics Anonymous, so that the individual is aware of approval of his new self by people who are like him.

The socialization process during the formative years sets the basic outlines for the individual's self-concept. Parents constantly hold up before the child the model of the good character they want him to be. A good boy eats his spinach, does not hit girls, etc. The candy and the stick are less in evidence in training the child than the constant appeal to his notion of his own character. It is small wonder, then, that children reflect the acceptance of this model by inquiring about the characters of the actors in every drama, whether it be a television play, a political contest, or a war, wanting to know who are the "good guys" and who are the "bad guys." Even as adults we persist in labeling others in the terms of such character images. Joe McCarthy and his cause collapsed in fantastic fashion when the telecast of the Army hearings showed him in the role of the villain attacking the gentle, good man represented by Joseph Welch.

A related but somewhat different process from childhood socialization takes place when individuals enter a new group or organization. The individual will often take over and internalize the values of the group. What accounts, however, for the fact that sometimes this occurs and sometimes it does not? Four factors are probably operative, and some combination of them may be necessary for internalization. (1) The values of the new group may be highly consistent with existing values central to the personality. The girl who enters the nursing profession finds it congenial to consider herself a good nurse because of previous values of the importance of contributing to the welfare of others. (2) The new group may in its ideology have a clear model of what the good group member should be like and may persistently indoctrinate group members in these terms. One of the reasons for the code of conduct for members of the armed forces, devised after the revelations about the conduct of American prisoners in the Korean War, was to attempt to establish a model for what a good soldier does and does not do. (3) The activities of the group in moving toward its goal permit the individual genuine opportunity for participation. To become ego-involved so that he can internalize group values, the new member must find one of two conditions. The group activity open to him must tap his talents and abilities so that his chance to show what he is worth can be tied into the group effort. Or else the activities of the group must give him an active voice in group decisions. His particular talents and abilities may not be tapped but he does have the opportunity to enter into group decisions, and thus his need for self-determination is satisfied. He then identifies with the group in which such opportunities for ego-involvement are available. It is not necessary that opportunities for self-expression and self-determination be of great magnitude in an objective sense, so long as they are important for the psychological economy of the individuals themselves. (4) Finally, the individual may come to see himself as a group member if he can share in the rewards of group activity which includes his own efforts. The worker may not play much of a part in building a ship or make any decisions in the process of building it. Nevertheless, if he and his fellow workers are given a share in every boat they build and a return on the proceeds from the earnings of the ship, they may soon come to identify with the ship-building company and see themselves as builders of ships.

4. THE KNOWLEDGE FUNCTION. Individuals not only acquire beliefs in the interest of satisfying various specific needs, they also seek knowledge to give meaning to what would otherwise be an unorganized chaotic universe. People need standards or frames of reference for understanding their world, and attitudes help to supply such standards. The problem of understanding, as John Dewey made clear years ago, is one "of introducing (1) *definiteness* and *distinction* and (2) *consistency* and *stability* of meaning into what is otherwise vague and wavering."[9] The definiteness and stability are provided in good measure by the norms of our culture, which give the otherwise perplexed individual ready-made attitudes for comprehending his universe. Walter Lippmann's classical contribution to the study of opinions and attitudes was his description of stereotypes and the way they provided order and clarity for a bewildering set of complexities.[10] The most interesting finding in Herzog's familiar study of the gratifications obtained by housewives in listening to daytime serials was the unsuspected role of information and advice.[11] The stories were liked "because they explained things to the inarticulate listener."

The need to know does not of course imply that people are driven by a thirst for universal knowledge. The American public's appalling lack of political information has been documented many times. In 1956, for example, only 13 per cent of the people in Detroit could correctly name the two United States Senators from the state of Michigan and only 18 per cent knew the name of their own Congressman.[12] People are not avid seekers after knowledge as judged by what the educator or social reformer would desire. But they do want to understand the events which impinge directly on their own life. Moreover, many of the attitudes they have already acquired give them sufficient basis for interpreting much of what they perceive to be important for them. Our already existing stereotypes, in Lippmann's language, "are an ordered, more or less consistent picture of the world, to which our habits, our tastes, our capacities, our comforts and our hopes have adjusted themselves. They may not be a complete picture of the world but they are a picture of a possible world to which we are

[9]John Dewey, *How We Think,* New York, Macmillan, 1910.

[10]Walter Lippmann, *Public Opinion,* New York, Macmillan, 1922.

[11]Herta Herzog, "What Do We Really Know about Daytime Serial Listeners?" in Paul F. Lazarsfeld and Frank N. Stanton, editors, *Radio Research 1942–1943,* New York, Duell, Sloan & Pearce, 1944, pp. 3–33.

[12]From a study of the impact of party organization on political behavior in the Detroit area, by Daniel Katz and Samuel Eldersveld, in manuscript.

DETERMINANTS OF ATTITUDE FORMATION, AROUSAL, AND CHANGE IN RELATION TO TYPE OF FUNCTION

| *Function* | *Origin and Dynamics* | *Arousal Conditions* | *Change Conditions* |
|---|---|---|---|
| Adjustment | Utility of attitudinal object in need satisfaction. Maximizing external rewards and minimizing punishments | 1. Activation of needs<br>2. Salience of cues associated with need satisfaction | 1. Need deprivation<br>2. Creation of new needs and new levels of aspiration<br>3. Shifting rewards and punishments<br>4. Emphasis on new and better paths for need satisfaction |
| Ego defense | Protecting agains internal conflicts and external dangers | 1. Posing of threats<br>2. Appeals to hatred and repressed impulses<br>3. Rise in frustrations<br>4. Use of authoritarian suggestion | 1. Removal of threats<br>2. Catharsis<br>3. Development of self-insight |
| Value expression | Maintaining self identity; enhancing favorable self-image; self-expression and self-determination | 1. Salience of cues associated with values<br>2. Appeals to individual to reassert self-image<br>3. Ambiguities which threaten self-concept | 1. Some degree of dissatisfaction with self<br>2. Greater appropriateness of new attitude for the self<br>3. Control of all environmental supports to undermine old values |
| Knowledge | Need for understanding, for meaningful cognitive organization, for consistency and clarity | 1. Reinstatement of cues associated with old problem or of old problem itself | 1. Ambiguity created by new information or change in environment<br>2. More meaningful information about problems |

adapted."[13] It follows that new information will not modify old attitudes unless there is some inadequacy or incompleteness or inconsistency in the existing attitudinal structure as it relates to the perceptions of new situations.

. . . . . . . . . . . . . . . . . . . .

## *QUESTIONS FOR DISCUSSION*

1. Is it always possible in persuasion to distinguish what is effective from what is ethical? Explain.
2. What are the relative advantages and disadvantages of coactive and coercive persuasion? Are militant confrontations most effective with the man on the street or with persons already in positions of power? Why?
3. Which general theory of persuasion is the most scientific? Which one gives you the best understanding of how persuasion works?
4. Is it possible to be credible, attractive, and powerful at the same time? If you had to choose, which would be your preference?
5. Are persuasive effects more or less predictable than your professor's grades? In what respects are his grades one type of persuasive effect?

[13]Lippmann, *op. cit.*, p. 95.

chapter 6

# PSYCHOPHYSIOLOGICAL APPROACHES TO STUDYING COMMUNICATION

## SECTION ONE: OVERVIEW AND PERSPECTIVE

*Objectives for Section One*

After reading this article, you should be able to:

1. Enumerate and illustrate some of the findings relating physiological arousal to changes in attitude or opinion.
2. List several physiological responses which have served as indices of arousal or activation level. Indicate which of these are the most popular measures.
3. Define psychophysiological research.
4. List and explain several theoretical and technical problems which underlie psychophysiological research.
5. Indicate the contribution of radio telemetry to psychopnysiological research.
6. List and explain two sources of spontaneous physiological response which must be controlled.
7. Illustrate how psychophysiologists have studied learning. Cite some of their research findings.
8. List some of the major disciplines which contribute to the study of psychophysiology.
9. List five communication settings in which psychophysiological research has been conducted. Cite one finding in each.

*Ralph R. Behnke*

# PSYCHOPHYSIOLOGICAL APPROACHES TO STUDYING COMMUNICATION

It can be successfully argued that as modern society increases its productivity, mobility, and general complexity, it will place more importance than ever before on effective communication. This being the case, those who study communication will be increasingly challenged to improve and extend the research methods by which they advance an understanding of successful communication. In this chapter we will demonstrate how psychophysiological technology makes it possible for the student of communication to learn about some of the covert or "hidden" responses generated in the communication process, and the significance of these responses.

Our space-age technology has provided some new and exciting tools for the psychophysiologist. As it turns out, the procedures for measuring the heart rate (and other physiological responses) of astronauts during space travel are equally useful in the communication research laboratory. Later, we will see some applications of this technology to the study of communication.

We should point out early in this article that psychophysiological research is still in an early stage of development. Presently, much of its

Ralph R. Behnke *is presently assistant professor and director of the Communication Research Laboratory in the Department of Communication at the Florida State University. He received his B.A. degree from the University of Missouri at Kansas City, his M.S. from the University of Wisconsin, and his Ph.D. from the University of Kansas. He has written chapters in two textbooks, as well as several journal articles on the psychophysiological study of human communication. Dr. Behnke has been awarded numerous research grants to develop and improve instrumentation systems for measuring speech communication behavior.*

energy is focused upon improving its technology. To date, it probably has been more concerned with *basic* rather than applied research. In order to cover the bases, we will examine the techniques, applications, findings, and implications of psychophysiology. Our effort is to determine its present and potential contributions to our understanding of human communication.

In this chapter we will examine: (1) the nature of psychophysiology; (2) some of its underlying theoretical concepts; (3) examples of psychophysiological research in communication settings; and (4) the probable implications of psychophysiological research for human communication behavior.

## *Review of Theory and Research*

### WHAT IS THE NATURE OF PSYCHOPHYSIOLOGY?

Later on in this chapter, in an essay by Sternbach (1966), a general introduction to psychophysiological research will be provided. He suggests the following definition: "Psychophysiology is the study of the interrelationships between the physiological and psychological aspects of behavior. It typically employs human subjects whose physiological responses are usually recorded on a polygraph while stimuli are presented which are designed to influence mental, emotional, or motor behavior; and the investigator need not be a psychologist (p. 3)."

Physiological responses have been employed in communication studies both singly and in combinations. Among these responses are blood pressure, muscular tension, blood volume, skin conductance, heart rate, pupillary dilation, and the electrical activity of the brain. Depending upon the type of study in which they are employed, each of these responses has served as an index of the level of activation or arousal of the individual.

A review of the research literature demonstrates that psychophysiologists are interested in a variety of problems. Some are concerned with the development of suitable research instrumentation for measuring physiological responses. Others are attempting to improve their techniques of measurement so that their procedures can become increasingly reliable and meaningful. Still others are interested in determining the most appropriate physiological measure for a given research problem.

Each physiological response presents its own measurement problems. For example, changes in the heart rate may be too slow to follow the rapid stimulus changes occurring in a particular communication situation. In another instance, the mechanical equipment necessary to monitor continuous changes in blood pressure may be cumbersome enough to preclude its use. Sensitive measures of muscular activity, requiring the insertion of needle electrodes, offer further problems. Although they also have their own problems of measurement, quantification, and interpretation, electrical skin resistance and heart rate are probably the two most commonly used physiological variables today.

The popularity of psychophysiological technology in communication research is on the upswing. At present physiological responses serve as measures of anxiety, attractiveness, alertness, attention, difficulty, stress, interest, and "emotion." The expectation is that physiological information, coupled with psychological and behavioral data, will provide a more complete understanding of the communication process.

### WHAT THEORETICAL AND TECHNICAL PROBLEMS UNDERLIE PSYCHOPHYSIOLOGICAL RESEARCH?

We have already seen that although many insights into the human communication process are afforded us through the use of psychophysiological measurement, a great many specialized research problems remain to be solved. The sources of contamination must be brought under control before major theories can be produced from these data. Let us examine a few of these sources.

Although physiological measurement systems have been vastly improved in recent years, one source of contamination is the instruments themselves. Assuming that a given instrument has been properly designed and is appropriate for the measures to which it will be applied, it still must be well maintained, and its accuracy continually tested. The operator's control of a measuring system is crucial to the success of the research and, of course, to the nature and quality of descriptive and prescriptive statements as a result of the research.

Some critics object to laboratory studies which use mechanical, electrical, and electronic "hardware." They suggest that these studies are too far removed from a "real" communication situation. These critics point out that the cold, sterile, and sometimes threatening environment necessitated by the physiological measuring devices preclude the possibility of a normal human response. This objection is well taken. The research of Maslow and Mintz (1956) on the effect of esthetic surroundings on experimental subjects clearly indicates that environmental factors can affect the outcome of a study.

However, recent advances in bioelectric instrumentation have significantly reduced the impact of this criticism. Research may now be conducted in natural settings—that is to say, settings much like those in which communication normally takes place. Laboratories no longer have to look like laboratories. They may now be furnished so as to make the subjects as comfortable as possible.

For example, a telemetry system makes a strong contribution toward improving the "naturalness" of a psychophysiological experiment. Prior to the beginning of an experiment, small transmitters are attached to the participants so that physiological changes may be radioed back to the laboratory where they can be conveniently recorded and analyzed. These miniature devices in no way cause discomfort to the subjects; in fact, they frequently report having forgotten that they were wearing the device. In this way, radio telemetry makes a vital contribution to the naturalness of the laboratory setting.

Another problem which restricts the inferences we can make from physiological data is that each individual subject is a distinctly different biological animal. When comparing human beings, we find that individual differences exist—in height, weight, appetite, intelligence, and various other characteristics. Physiological responses are no exception. Alexander, Roessler, and Greenfield (1963) demonstrate that people tend to differ in their responsiveness to certain stimulus situations and that they also tend to differ in the basic biological rhythms upon which their response patterns are superimposed. It is easy to see that each of these factors increases the difficulty of making generalizations and of replicating past research.

Wilder (1957) discusses still another basic problem of interpretation. In studies which employ a physiological variable of arousal one must account for the *law of initial values*. Basically, this law states that the ability to have a physiological response to a communication stimulus, or any other stimulus, is dependent upon the level of arousal immediately preceding the introduction of that stimulus. This seems reasonable enough, even on an intuitive level. A human organism has limited response capabilities. Therefore, the closer the subject is to his maximum response level, the more difficult it will be for him to make a large response. In many instances, unless the pre-stimulus or basal level of arousal is taken into account, the interpretation of the data is very difficult and in some cases meaningless.

Yet another interesting possible contaminator in psychophysiological studies is spontaneous arousal. We tend to label responses "spontaneous" when we cannot directly attribute them to the stimulus of the experiment or any other known or controlled source.

The sources of these spontaneous responses are varied. However, for the most part, they can be accounted for in two ways: (1) gross physical movement of the subject, such as scratching, yawning, taking an excessively deep breath or engaging in some other major bodily movement; and (2) "self-stimulation," instances in which the subject's attention strays from the experiment. He may be thinking about his date after class or the size of the fish he hopes to catch over the weekend. Obviously, physical activity is much easier to control than the stimulating thoughts which the subject might produce.

In the preceding discussion we have seen that very careful controls are necessary if the data from psychophysiological studies are to have meaning and utility. Our intention is not to overemphasize the problems of this kind of research, but rather to indicate clearly at the outset that it is essential to control the quality of the methods under which data are being collected if we are to be able to have confidence in our findings. When this is done, it appears that psychophysiological procedures make a unique and enlightening contribution to our understanding of human communication behavior and processes.

## WHAT ARE SOME EXAMPLES OF PSYCHOPHYSIOLOGICAL RESEARCH WHICH HAS BEEN CONDUCTED IN COMMUNICATION SETTINGS?

So far we have examined the general nature of psychophysiology, some of the physiological responses with which it deals, and some of the theoretical and technological problems which it faces. In this section we will look at some examples of this line of research and some of the pertinent findings. The studies will be grouped according to five basic communication settings: intrapersonal, interpersonal, and small-group communication, public speaking, and mass communication.

Probably one of the best examples of intrapersonal communication may be found in psychophysiological studies of learning. A considerable body of research relates arousal to effective learning. Germana and Pavlik (1964), for example, studied galvanic skin responses to learning materials presented on film. They found that skin responses were related to the students' ability to recall the filmed materials.

R. N. Berry has conducted a series of investigations on this topic. In an early study (1957), he found that the mean volume of the finger pulse of subjects was related to their ability to perform a simple rote learning task. In another experiment (1960), he found a relationship between a decrease in finger volume and mental problem-solving ability. Finally, in a recent study (1962), Berry found that skin conductance levels were associated with students' ability to recall memorized information. From Berry's research it is apparent that changes in the volume of the finger pulse and skin conductance are suitable physiological indices of learning.

Harleston, Smith, and Arey (1965) measured the effects of test-anxiety and physiological arousal on problem solving. They found that students who reported having high test-anxiety also had significantly higher heart rates. Moreover, large increases in heart rate were related to poor problem solving.

Certainly we would agree that the effect of various levels of arousal on the effectiveness of learning requires further study. However, the research literature does suggest that optimal ranges of arousal, within which learners will perform most effectively, can be described. The intrapersonal communication setting employed in the studies cited above is one framework within which psychophysiological studies have been conducted.

Levels and patterns of physiological events have also been examined in interpersonal communication settings. Studies of this nature are frequently concerned with measuring periods of stress or the release of tension. These measures are considered indices of the significance which the subject assigns to an event. Simultaneous recordings of arousal have been used to indicate the physiological interaction of two conversational partners.

Malmo, Boag, and Smith (1957) examined physiological covariation during a dyadic, or two-person, conversation. They measured the rise and fall of muscular tension during periods of praise and criticism. During periods of praise, both participants manifested a decrease in muscular tension which was not noted during periods of criticism. Coleman, Greenblatt, and Soloman (1956) studied the physiological covariation of a patient and a therapist during a series of therapy sessions. They found that physiological interaction varied from session to session. During sessions wherein the therapist was reportedly preoccupied with his own problems, low levels of physiological relationship were observed. When he was not preoccupied, covariation increased. Physiological covariation is thought to reflect an empathic exchange between the correspondents. Low levels of physiological covariation or interaction may be interpreted as self-stimulation, or at least dissimilar interpretations of the environment.

The results of these studies suggest that physiological measures of arousal in interpersonal communication provide a measure of the significance of the experience for the communicator. When the levels of arousal covary between conversational partners, the covariation is said to reflect the similarity of feelings and emotions over a period of time.

The nature of physiological functioning has also been studied in the small-group setting. A basic question posed in such research is, "What effect does the presence of other group members have on the activation level of an individual?" Zajonc (1965) found that individual arousal levels were elevated in the presence of others. The interpretation of this increased arousal depends upon the nature of the exprimental situation. For example, Kaplan (1967) found that the activation level was related to the amount of participation in group activity and to how well the individual was liked by the other group members.

Costell and Leiderman (1968) measured the arousal of a group member who attempted to maintain an independent opinion under group pressure to conform to the opinion of the majority. They found that students who maintained the independent opinion exhibited increased arousal, and that those who gave in experienced less activation. We might say that students who did not give in to the majority had to "work harder" to maintain their own point of view.

Further group research, an investigation of the autonomic correlates of attitude change, has been reported. Lawson and Stagner (1957) found that the presence of and discussion with an opposing majority produced only a nominal shift in attitude. They divided students into "nationalists" or "internationalists" on the basis of attitude scales. Their most interesting finding was that students who were classed as "nationalists," and who also were physiologically aroused during the discussion, changed their attitudes significantly afterward. Students classed as "internationalists" did not exhibit arousal patterns which could be associated with attitude change resulting from group discussion.

We hesitate to generalize from these data until a good deal more research has been conducted. The attitudinal patterns of participants, the specific topics being discussed, and individual differences in physiological functioning are variables which deserve special attention in psychophysiological research in group communication.

Psychophysiological studies in a public-speaking setting are less numerous. One interesting area which is gaining increasing attention, however, is the problem of anxiety, or stage fright. This is an old problem, and one which still plagues students in public-speaking classes.

The level of stage fright is usually measured in one of three ways: (1) by behavioral ratings from teachers or other audience members; (2) by the speaker's own assessment of his anxiety; and (3) by analyzing his physiological responses.

Clevenger, Carlile, and Motley (1967) studied the heart rates of students during classroom public-speaking assignments. They discovered that dramatic increases and decreases in heart rate were associated with critical moments in the speech. The sharpest rise in heart rate occurred when the student's name was called to go to the front of the class and begin speaking. In a later study, Behnke and Carlile (1970) investigated the relationship between the salient features of these heart-rate patterns and self-reported anxiety. In this study, the heart rates were telemetered from the classroom back to the laboratory, where they were recorded and analyzed. Significant correlations were found between the heart-rate patterns and the students' self-reported anxiety.

Physiological measures of anxiety in various communication settings are clearly in an early stage of development. They will probably increase in popularity, since they are reliable measures and do not direct the student's attention to what is being measured.

The effectiveness of messages presented via the mass media seems to be a topic of major concern today. Advertising agencies have long been on the lookout for techniques which would allow them to predict the impact or sales success of a commercial announcement. In some cases, the effectiveness of the message is determined by the sales volume which it ultimately generates. This method of testing effect is inefficient and expensive, especially when an advertisement fails to sell the product.

Because some methods of determining the impact of commercial messages had little validity and still others were very expensive, psychophysiologists became interested in this problem. Eckstrand and Gilliland (1948) investigated the usefulness of skin responses as predictors of the effectiveness of advertising material. Their subjects viewed and listened to persuasive and informative announcements about a number of products. During the sessions, skin responses were recorded and converted to a measure of total arousal for each ad. Since the advertisements employed in this experiment were later used in local advertising campaigns, the arousal responses of subjects could be compared to the product sales generated by the commercials. The information about product sales was provided by a professional agency.

The results showed a close relationship between the subjects' activation level and the sales effectiveness of the advertisements. The conclusion reached by the experimenters was that arousal levels are useful predictors of the impact of a message to be presented via mass media. The method appears to be an objective technique which reduces the cost of pre-testing commercial messages.

So far we have discussed the nature of psychophysiology and some examples of its research in communication settings. We will now examine the implications of this line of research for the individual and for society.

## IMPLICATIONS OF PSYCHOPHYSIOLOGICAL RESEARCH FOR COMMUNICATION

Earlier in this article we stated that psychophysiology is a relatively young science. Consequently, a rather high proportion of time is still being used to develop appropriate instrumentation and research methods for studying a widening range of research questions. Many of the published studies use selected groups of subjects and deal with very specialized problems. As a result, few practical generalizations or broadly applicable principles have emerged. With these limitations in mind, let us examine some of the implications of psychophysiological findings for the individual and for society.

The research literature in psychophysiology supports the following principles:

1. *There is probably an optimal level of activation for each individual in each communication activity in which he is engaged.* If such optimal

levels of activation can be reliably determined, then efforts could be made to attempt to condition or control the individual's arousal in order to improve his performance. Moreover, if arousal levels can in fact be experimentally controlled, it is possible that the procedures for accomplishing such control can be learned and used by the communicator himself.

The implications for society are closely related to the implications for the individual. An exciting area in which psychophysiological techniques might be profitably employed is in the improvement of educational procedures. If it should be possible to optimize and control levels of individual or group activation, then this procedure could be applied to students in classes. Continuous monitoring of arousal could indicate to instructors the relative effectiveness of the learning of a single individual or an entire class at any given moment in time. Furthermore, the arousal levels could serve as a "test" of information gained *during* the lectures, discussions, or classroom demonstrations, rather than waiting until after the educational experience is over to administer a conventional test.

In advertising, the effectiveness of an informative presentation or a persuasive appeal might be physiologically pre-tested in order to improve the quality of these messages. If physiological findings prove to be rather widely generalizable, then physiological pre-testing of mass media messages could be carried out on relatively small numbers of subjects, thereby reducing the normally expensive and time-consuming processes of data collection and analysis.

Clearly the social-psychological implications of psychophysiological research indicate the need for further investigation. More precise specification of the physiological differences among normal, neurotic, and psychotic individuals, for example, could lead to major scientific breakthroughs in the health sciences.

2. *Autonomic arousal is a useful index of deception.* The second general principle supported by the information in this chapter has some very practical applications.

The detection of deception plays an important role both in the validation of various types of paper-and-pencil tests and in criminological investigations. In the effort to validate self-reported psychological states and in the attempt to determine the "true" attitude of individuals, for example, psychophysiological data have already provided some interesting insights. Later in this chapter you will read about some of the techniques used by criminologists and psychologists to detect deception.

In the study of deception, as well as in other areas, it is hoped that psychophysiological research will shed light upon the little-understood interaction between body and mind.

Although the relatively youthful science of psychophysiology as yet offers few definitive instructions which individuals can apply in daily communication settings, it promises to provide new information about covert communication behavior which could not be gathered in any other way. As this science progresses in both functional and theoretical competence, we may expect it to offer many useful instructions for optimizing the communication process.

## *REFERENCES*


Alexander, A., Roessler, R., & Greenfield, N. S. Periodic nature of spontaneous nervous system activity. *Nature*, 1963, 197, 1169–1170.

Behnke, R. R., & Carlile, L. W. Heart rate as an index of speech anxiety. A paper read at the convention of the International Communication Association, Minneapolis, May, 1970.

Berry, R. N. The relationship of the magnitude of volume pulse to speed of rote learning. *American Psychologist,* 1957, 12, 414.

________, Changes in finger volume during a single addition task. *Psychological Reports*, 1960, 8, 446.

________, Skin conductance levels and verbal recall. *Journal of Experimental Psychology*, 1962, 63, 275–277.

Clevenger, T., Carlile, L. W., & Motley, M. Heart rate patterns during public speaking. A paper read at the convention of the Speech Association of America, Los Angeles, December, 1967.

Coleman, R., Greenblatt, M., & Solomon, H. C. Physiological evidence of rapport during psychotherapeutic interviews. *Disorders of the Nervous System*, 1956, 17, 2–8.

Costell, R. M., & Leiderman, P. H. Psychophysiological concomitants of social stress: The effects of conformity pressure. *Psychosomatic Medicine*, 1968, 30(3), 298–310.

Eckstrand, G., & Gilliland, A. R. The psychogalvanic method of measuring the effectiveness of advertising. *Journal of Applied Psychology*, 1948, 32, 415–425.

Germana, J. J., & Pavlik, W. B. Autonomic correlates of acquisition and extinction. *Psychonomic Science*, 1964, 1(5), 109–110.

Harleston, B. W., Smith, G. M., & Arey, D. Test-anxiety level, heart rate and anagram problem solving. *Journal of Personality and Social Psychology*, 1965, 1(6), 551–557.

Kaplan, H. B. Physiological correlates of affect in small groups. *Journal of Psychosomatic Research*, 1967, 11(2), 173–179.

Lawson, E. D., & Stagner, R. Group pressure, attitude change, and autonomic involvement. *Journal of Social Psychology*, 1957, 45, 299–312.

Malmo, R. B., Boag, T. J., & Smith, A. A. Physiological study of personal interaction. *Psychosomatic Medicine*, 1957, 19, 105–119.

Maslow, A. H., & Mintz, N. L. Effects of esthetic surroundings: I. Initial effects of three esthetic conditions upon perceiving "energy" and "well-being" in faces. *Journal of Psychology*, 1956, 41, 247–254.

Sternbach, R. A. *Principles of psychophysiology*. New York: Academic Press, 1966.

Wilder, J. The law of initial value in neurology and psychiatry: Facts and problems. *Journal of Nervous and Mental Disorders*, 1957, 125, 73–86.

Zajonc, R. B. Social facilitation. *Science*, 1965, 149, 269–274.

## SECTION TWO: READINGS

*Introduction and Objectives for Reading One:*
*"The Nature of Psychophysiology"*

In the following reading Richard Sternbach, a leading psychophysiologist, discusses his view of the general nature of psychophysiology, some important events in its historical development, and the questions which it attempts to answer.

After reading this article, you should be able to:

1. Distinguish between the fields of psychophysiology and physiological psychology.
2. List several measures of autonomic functioning which may be recorded on a polygraph.
3. List two major scientific developments which have greatly advanced the discipline of psychophysiology.
4. Enumerate the important questions in psychophysiology as Sternbach sees them.

Richard A. Sternbach

## *THE NATURE OF PSYCHOPHYSIOLOGY*

Psychophysiology, as we will be using the term, is not the same as physiological psychology. Both refer to the study of the relationships between mental and bodily events, but the means of studying them and the kinds of relationships studied are different. It is probably not possible to

Excerpts from R. A. Sternbach, *Principles of Psychophysiology* (New York: Academic Press, Inc., 1966), pp. 1–10. Reprinted by permission of the author and publisher.

make a formal definition of either field that will delimit it from the other, but since in the end the disciplines are defined by the activities of those who call themselves psychophysiologists and physiological psychologists, let us examine these activities.

Physiological psychology is the older of the two fields in the sense that it was "founded" a century ago; the term has been used for laboratories, texts, journals, and college courses. Although physiological psychologists originally used humans as subjects, it is now far more common that other animals are used. This is because many of the answers to questions asked require procedures which cannot be employed on humans, and because since Darwin it has been assumed that there is an essential continuity between man and the lower animals which makes the animal findings applicable to humans. Most psychophysiological studies, however, use humans as subjects. Yet because there is some overlap in each field in the kinds of subjects used, this cannot be the differentiating criterion.

Most traditional physiological psychology has proceeded by manipulating some physiological variable, observing changes in behavior, and then postulating an intervening internal event to account for the results. For example, animals trained to run a maze or press a lever may be deprived of food or water, or given a drug, or have some operation performed on their nervous system, and then the effects of this procedure on their performance will be noted. Although this experimental routine is not without exceptions, it is a good example of traditional physiological psychology. On the other hand, the usual psychophysiological experiment has reversed the process. Mental or emotional or behavioral activities are made to occur while physiological events are being observed; correlations between these activities and the observed physiological events are noted, and then some intervening internal event is postulated. Stern has listed examples of these differences, which are shown in Table I (Stern, 1964). This comparison of typical experimental methods comes a little closer to differentiating the fields, but it is possible to show that there are exceptions on both sides, in the activities of those who call themselves physiological psychologists or psychophysiologists.

Another difference which exists in emphasis, but which also has exceptions, has to do with the technique of recording observations. Physiological psychologists may use a wide variety of recording techniques depending upon the behavior and the species they are observing. Psychophysiologists, on the other hand, typically have employed a polygraph, or some similar device, to record the physiological activity in which they are interested. Although there are exceptions, as we have said, it is interesting to note that the journal *Psychophysiology*, which is the official organ of the Society for Psychophysiological Research, was preceded by the Society's *Psychophysiology Newsletter* and that, in turn, began as the *Polygraph*

TABLE 1.* SOME EXPERIMENTAL VARIABLES USED IN TWO DISCIPLINES

| | Independent variable | Dependent variable |
|---|---|---|
| Physiological psychology | Brain lesion | Learning—behavioral |
| | Brain stimulation | Performance |
| | Drug administration | Conditioning |
| | Diet manipulation | Food selection |
| Psychophysiology | Auditory stimulation | Habituation of orienting response |
| | Vigilance experiment | EEG evoked response |
| | Sleep deprivation | Background EEG |
| | Psychologic or psychiatric state (fear, anxiety, depression, etc.) | Conditionability of physiological system |
| | Dreaming | Physiological correlates |

*From J.A. Stern, "Toward a Definition of Psychophysiology," *Psychophysiology*, I (1964), 90–91. © 1964, The Williams & Wilkins Co., Baltimore, Md. 21202, U.S.A. Reprinted also by permission of the author.

*Newsletter*. Yet because of the exceptions, this polygraphic recording technique also cannot be the differentiating criterion.

A final difference in emphasis may be considered. By definition and tradition, a physiological psychologist is a psychologist, that is, one who has his degree (Ph.D.) from a department of psychology. Now, anyone else who is interested in the relationships between the physiological and psychological aspects of behavior, and who does research in the field, cannot call his work physiological psychology. Whether he has his Ph.D. in physiology, or he has an M.D., he cannot call himself a psychologist, even if he does feed drugs to rats and watch them run a maze. Consequently many investigators who do what physiological psychologists do have taken to calling themselves psychophysiologists in order to indicate that they are not psychologists. Yet this criterion is obviously an unsatisfactory one for differentiating the two fields. Some nonpsychologists are performing research that is physiological psychology, and perhaps half of those in psychophysiology *are* psychologists.

Although our failure to find a single criterion that defines psychophysiology may be confusing or discouraging, we can clarify things somewhat by putting together the several attributes we have been considering. *Psychophysiology is the study of the interrelationships between the physiological and psychological aspects of behavior. It typically employs human subjects, whose physiological responses are usually recorded on a polygraph while stimuli are presented which are designed to influence mental, emotional, or motor behavior; and the investigator need not be a psychologist.* This description covers the great majority of the research studies in psychophysiology to date. Although it is not an adequate formal definition, it is rather fair operational [one].

. . . . . . . . . . . . . . . . . . . . .

[Now] we come to a topic that might have been mentioned earlier in describing the field of psychophysiology. Most psychophysiological research has been concerned with the factors that influence autonomic functioning and this has usually involved recording (on the polygraph) peripheral effects of this functioning. Some of the measures commonly used are the sweating and temperature of the skin, the rate and force of cardiac contractions, blood pressure and gastric contractions, etc. However, many psychophysiologists also record measures of central nervous system activity, either in the form of the electroencephalogram (EEG; brain wave) or in the form of its peripheral effects on the electromyogram (EMG; muscle tone). Some workers have attempted to correlate these measures, recording ANS [Autonomic Nervous System]; EEG and EMG activity simultaneously in order to understand the ways in which such functions are integrated or coordinated in the body. We will discuss some of this work in the section on Activation. Yet it is true that most psychophysiological research has involved only ANS activity, and the principles which we will be discussing apply primarily to the ANS. For this reason we make no extensive mention of the other measures. . . .

## *Some Historical Developments*

Although psychophysiology has been a formal scientific discipline for only a short time, psychophysiological observations are as old as recorded history. Whenever we note that someone blushes with embarrassment, or flushes with anger, this is a psychophysiological observation. So it is, too, when you note that your palms get so sweaty during an examination that you make the test papers damp. In these instances, the observations establish a relationship between certain physiological (autonomic) changes, and some inferred emotion. The inference about the emotion is usually based on a knowledge of the stimulating conditions that produced the observed changes; yet our experience with many such situations and responses in everyday life often enables us to use only the physiological events themselves to infer the emotion. For example, when a person blushes, we assume embarrassment, and are the more convinced the louder the person protests otherwise.

Even experimental attempts to discover the relationships between emotions and physiology are not new. The remarkable Emperor Frederick

II performed the following study (among others) as reported by the historian Salimbene in the 13th century:

> . . . the sixth curiosity and folly of Frederick, as I have said in my other chronicle, was that at a certain luncheon he had two men very well beaten, and then sent one of them to sleep and the other to hunt, and on the following evening, he had them defecate in his presence, because he wanted to know which of them had digested the better. And it was decided by the doctors that he who had slept had enjoyed the better digestion. [Ross, J. B. and McLaughlin, M. M. (eds.), A Portable Medieval Reader. New York: Viking, 1949, p. 366.]

However, two developments were necessary to turn psychophysiological experimentation into the discipline it is today. The first was the development of the polygraph as an instrument of research. By the 1920's, the old Einthoven string galvanometer had been developed into a sensitive and precise instrument for recording a number of bioelectric potentials simultaneously. The impetus for this came from the electroencephalographers; once Hans Berger had demonstrated, in the 1930's, the feasibility and usefulness of recording the EEG, the demand for such a technique became quite strong from the clinical neurology services. Clinical EEG machines came to be standard equipment in hospitals everywhere, and with some slight modification for recording DC changes (skin resistance, temperature) these machines could serve very well as polygraphs.

What was important about the availability of polygraphs was that for the first time it was possible to record permanently and to measure objectively a number of physiological systems at the same time. For example, the electrocardiogram (EKG), galvanic skin response (GSR), skin temperature, the EEG, etc., could all be made to appear as simultaneous squiggles on a moving strip of paper. This chart became an objective and permanent record of the subject's physiological activity at the time. And since it was possible to calibrate the sensitivity of the polygraph's amplification system and to record at a known and constant paper speed, then quite precise determinations of the amplitude and rate of physiological activity could be made. A disadvantage of the system was that it required the subject to lie or sit quietly, in order not to disturb the pickup electrodes or entangle the many wires on him, which might produce artifacts or "noise" on the record. Figure 1 illustrates the appearance of a typical record.

Some recent developments have changed somewhat the traditional polygraph usage. One is the use of telemetering devices which do away with the need for wires, permitting the subject to move around and thus making possible the use of more "real life" experimental situations. Another is the use of data-recording magnetic tape which can be converted into digital data and fed into a computer for analysis, greatly simplifying and making more objective the handling of data, and making the paper record superfluous except for display purposes. Also, there is now an increased sensitivity, reliability, and range of response variables available, due to advances in electronic technology.

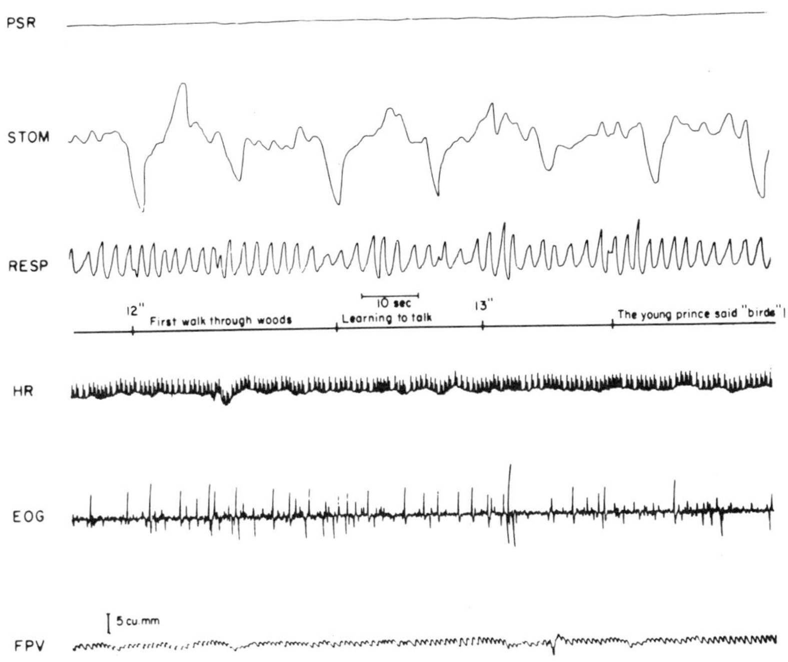


**FIGURE 1.** Sample polygraph tracings. The top tracing is palmar skin resistance, followed by gastric motility, respiration, signal pen (used to identify scenes in a movie being watched by the subject), heart rate, eye blinking, and finger pulse volume. A magnetometer was used to pick up the peristaltic movements of an ingested magnet. [Reprinted with permission from Richard A. Sternbach, "Assessing Differential Autonomic Patterns in Emotions," *Journal of Psychosomatic Research*, 6, (1962), 88, © 1962 Pergamon Press.]

The second development which enabled psychophysiology to become a scientific discipline was the availability of statistical techniques for analyzing the data obtained. Previously, physiological research had to be satisfied with demonstrating the existence of a phenomenon (such as the relationship between felt hunger pangs and stomach contractions) on a few subjects. However, when psychophysiologists asked questions such as, What is the *degree* of the relationship? or, To what *extent* do individual differences exist? then more sophisticated forms of experimental designs and data analysis became necessary. At about the same time answers were being provided to similar questions raised by those working with individual differences in intelligence and aptitude testing. Methods for obtaining correlations, testing for significance of obtained differences, and performing factor analyses were developed, and quickly adopted by psychophysiologists for use on their physiological data.

With polygraph instrumentation and statistical data analysis, psychophysiological publications began to appear in the 1930's and 1940's. Only a few workers consistently made this kind of research their full-time endeavor—most notably C. W. Darrow, R. C. Davis, and M. A. Wenger. After World War II, A. F. Ax and J. I. Lacey made important contributions, and in 1955 Ax began to circulate the *Polygraph Newsletter* among laboratories as a vehicle for an informal exchange of ideas and solutions to technical problems. In a few years this led to the founding of the Society for Psychophysiological Research (1960) which held its first annual meeting in 1961, and the journal *Psychophysiology* appeared under Society sponsorship in 1964. These latest developments reflect not only the increased interest in the field, but also the burgeoning of research findings which necessitated a new journal, and which make it important now to have an introductory text which surveys the major developments.

While we have described the nature of psychophysiology in a general way, and the typical form of the research, there remains to be specified the kinds of questions usually asked by psychophysiologists. In stating these we will be pointing out at the same time some of the historical factors which, along with technological and methodological innovations, have contributed to the formation of the field of psychophysiology.

## *Some Important Questions*

Perhaps the most basic question, implict in the definition of the field, is: What is the relationship between the mind and the body? This is a philosophical problem which has engendered metaphysical speculation for centuries, and about which there is little agreement. In the field of psychophysiology, however, we have virtually the only *experimental* attempt to find answers. When physiological psychology abandoned human for animal subjects in order to obtain better methodological controls, the possibility of dealing with the "mind" was also abandoned.

However much the mind-body problem may exist in the back of the minds of psychophysiologists, it is not the sort of question which can be formulated directly as an experimental hypothesis. More specific kinds of questions have been raised, however. For example, What are the physiological differences among the emotions? This question draws on traditional interests of both psychology and physiology, both with respect to the nature of emotions and to the adequate stimuli for physiological changes. Similarly with another common question: To what extent do individuals differ in their physiological functioning? Here the traditional interest of the psychologist in individual differences unites with the interest of the physiologist in normal functioning. However, another discipline is also interested in this question: medical researchers have been concerned with the problem of where normal functioning leaves off and pathological functioning appears. That is, the whole question of whether abnormal conditions differ from normal in kind or in degree can find a focus in the study of individual differences in physiological activity. Another series of questions also have a primarily medical source: What are the psychosomatic diseases? How do they occur? What information about normal functioning can we obtain from the study of these abnormal conditions? This last question has led psychologists and physiologists to the study of the psychosomatic disorders, just as the question about individual differences has led physicians to study normal physiological responses.

The crossing over of disciplinary boundaries is one of the interesting (and rewarding) aspects of psychophysiological research. Psychologists, physiologists, psychiatrists, and internists are all involved with similar problems and projects and find it useful to exchange information and ways of thinking about these things. But there is another group whose participation in this area may surprise you: bioelectronic and computer engineers. These physical scientists originally became involved to help solve the problems of recording and analyzing hard-to-get-at physiological activity. But quickly they became intrigued with questions of how to duplicate human functions in certain kinds of hardware, for example, in computers and in space systems. Remembering, problem-solving, learning, and perceiving are some of the functions which have been built into machinery, and now the other disciplines have become interested in these models as potentially fruitful ways of thinking about human functions, and this has led to the development of a new field—cybernetics. This constant information exchange is proving useful to all involved.

## *References*

Stern, J. A. Toward a definition of psychophysiology. *Psychophysiology*, 1964, 1, 90–91.

### *Introduction and Objectives for Reading Two: "Lie Detection"*

The final reading in this chapter deals with a very practical and useful application of psychophysiology, lie detection. Woodworth and Schlosberg describe several techniques for employing changes in level of activation as indices of deception.

After reading this article, you should be able to:

1. Explain the basic assumption underlying the use of physiological responses in lie detection.
2. List several physiological responses useful in detecting deception.
3. Illustrate two methods of questioning used in lie detection.

Robert S. Woodworth and Harold Schlosberg

## *LIE DETECTION*

The various indices of level of activation have been widely used in lie detection. In . . . the basic method [t]he suspect is asked to respond to words or questions, some of which are related to the details of the crime, while others are neutral. If he is guilty, he probably has knowledge of details that are not generally known, and he should show evidences of any attempts to cover up this knowledge. In the association method, these evidences show up as (1) significant or unusual verbal responses to the critical words or (2) increased or (3) variable associative reaction times on the critical words. The association time method works fairly well, but is cumbersome and not too dependable. Hence, a number of attempts have been made to improve the method by adding various indices of emotion, the assumption being that the effort to avoid incriminating responses will show up as an increase in the level of activation. . . .

THE GSR. One of the most impressive demonstrations one can make before a lecture group is to detect deception with the aid of the GSR. The galvanometer should be so arranged that the whole class can see the deflection. A volunteer is hooked into the electrodes, and asked to select one of 10 cards, remember it, and return it to the pack. *O* is then told to try to keep *E* from finding out which card *O* saw. The cards are shown to him, one at a time, and he says "No" to each. There will be a GSR with each reply, but the biggest deflection will usually be to the card he has seen. Although it sometimes fails, the GSR is a fairly effective method of

From Chapter 7 from *Experimental Psychology*, Revised Edition, by Robert S. Woodworth and Harold Schlosberg. Copyright 1938, 1954 by Holt, Rinehart and Winston, Inc. Copyright © 1966 by Mrs. Greta Woodworth Herron, Svenson Woodworth, William Woodworth, and Virginia Woodworth. Reprinted by permission of Holt, Rinehart and Winston, Inc.

detecting even such mild deception as this demonstration involves. Ruckmick (1938) reported 83 percent success in detection of cards.

In practical lie detection the GSR appears to be less satisfactory. Summers (1939) was quite successful with it, and considered it almost infallible *in the hand of an experienced interpreter.* But others find it somewhat uncertain (Marston, 1938; Inbau, 1942). Perhaps the trouble is that GSR is too responsive to incidental stimuli, thus obscuring the changes involved in deception. A GSR unit may be attached to the Keeler polygraph . . . and is so used by some operators, but only in conjunction with other indices of level of activation, as breathing and blood pressure. Inbau mentioned one practical use; if all the indices indicate a lie on a given question, the GSR record is usually striking enough to convince the suspect that he has given himself away so that he confesses. Confession is usually the chief aim as well as the validating criterion in lie detection.

RESPIRATORY SIGNS OF DECEPTION. Breathing would seem to offer good promise in lie detection for two reasons: (1) it is an extremely rapid and sensitive indicator of increase in activation level; and (2) it is intimately associated with the act of replying to the questions. Sharp catches, breaks, and other changes in the pattern of breathing do pick up many cases of deception . . . but psychologists are apt to look for some quantitative index such as the I/E ratio [the ratio of inspiration time to expiration time in the breathing cycle.] Benussi (1914) arranged an experiment as follows. The subject is placed in the situation of a witness in court. He is handed a card containing letters, numbers or both, arranged in a regular way, and he is to give either true or false testimony regarding the contents of that card, according to a secret sign placed upon it. Oral questions are put to him by the examining "lawyer" as to whether the card contains letters or numbers, how many, and in what arrangement; finally, he must read the letters in order; but if his task is to lie he must answer every question falsely, trying however to appear truthful to a"jury" sitting there before him. The jury tries to judge from the witness's general behavior whether he is lying or telling the truth, while the experimenter judges entirely by the pneumograph record.

The jurymen in Benussi's experiment did no better than chance, but Benussi from the breathing records made nearly 100 percent of correct judgments in over a hundred trials. He used entirely the I/E ratio (the I-fraction would of course have served him just as well). [The I-fraction is the ratio of inhalation time to the time of the total breathing cycle.] He compared the ratio before and after each answer, measuring 3–5 cycles immediately before *O*'s response and 3–5 cycles immediately after it. In a sample of 10 double experiments, half with lying and half with truth-telling, the median I-fraction was as follows:

| | *Before answer* | *After answer* |
|---|---|---|
| Truth told | .39 | .32 |
| Lies told | .40 | .50 |

The difference between the breathing of the truthful and lying witness might be attributed to the harder intellectual task of the liar who must make his false statements consistent to escape detection by the jury. To check on this possibility, Benussi tried a modified experiment in which it was understood in advance between the witness and the jury whether the report on a given card was to be true or false. The intellectual task remained as before, but the emotional situation was flattened out. The result was that the I/E ratio behaved the same in this pretended lying as in truth-telling. Benussi concluded that the breathing in genuine lying was dominated by the emotional situation. Since the I-fraction is essentially the same before either true or false statements, what we have to explain is the difference *after* the testimony. The increased I-fraction after lying can be explained as the result of (suppressed) excitement. The decreased I-fraction after a true statement might mean that *O* immediately became attentively expectant of the next question.

Benussi found that voluntary control of breathing did not eliminate the index of lying, and he hoped the test would prove practical. Those who have repeated the experiment (Burtt, 1921; Landis & Gullette, 1925) have not obtained very satisfactory results. It is possible that the exact conditions of Benussi's experiment have not been duplicated. It would make a difference how rapidly the questions were fired at *O* and how promptly he was forced to reply.

. . . . . . . . . . . . . . . . . . . .

Blood Pressure in Deception. Soon after Benussi had introduced his respiration test of lying, Marston (1917) performed a similar experiment with blood pressure as the indicator. Ten students served as subjects, testifying before a "jury." *O*'s friend was supposed to be accused of a crime, and *O* tried to save his friend by establishing an alibi. *O* could choose whether to follow a ready-made "true" alibi or to invent a "false" one. He was examined before the jury who rendered a verdict according to their impressions of *O*'s truth or falsity. At intervals before and during the examination *O*'s blood pressure was measured by the experimenter who rendered a verdict based entirely on rise of blood pressure and was correct in 103 out of 107 judgments. The true witnesses showed only a small rise, not over 5 mm, while the liars gave a gradual increase amounting to 16 mm on the average. These American students like the Europeans in Benussi's experiment proved themselves fairly competent liars so that the jury had only a 50-50 chance of reaching a correct verdict. The students preferred lying (under the experimental conditions) to the rather humdrum task of telling the truth. Their reported emotions included interest in deceiving the jury, a feeling of adventure, fear, and occasionally anger on being cornered by the "lawyer."

Marston attributed the blood pressure rise to this emotional state of the lying witness rather than to the intellectual activity involved. In control experiments with intense mental work—arithmetic, studying a lesson, inventing a story—his *O*s showed no large rises but usually a decline in blood pressure. In a later experiment (1923) he studied the blood pressure changes in a variety of situations, more or less exciting, and got considerable rises in most of them as shown in the table:

| | *Average rise for* | |
|---|---|---|
| | *10 Men (in mm)* | *10 Women (in mm)* |
| Resting with eyes covered | 11 | 19 |
| Reading story | 9 | 15 |
| Reading difficult psychological book | 8 | 14 |
| Reading newspaper | 5 | 19 |
| Conversing with one of opposite sex, met for the first time | 14 | 28 |
| Narrating story read 2 weeks previously | 7 | 15 |
| Narrating exciting personal experience | 9 | 20 |
| Narrating own actions for last 24 hours | 6 | 24 |
| Cross-examination on story read | 7 | 13 |
| Cross-examination on exciting experience | 7 | 16 |
| Cross-examination on own actions for last half day | 12 | 28 |

Results equally favorable for the blood pressure test of deception, at least under laboratory conditions, were obtained by Chappell (1929) in a true-or-false-alibi experiment similar to Marston's but without any jury. Chappell's truth tellers showed an average rise of 5 mm with very few going above 12 mm increase, while his liars averaged 19 mm with very few less than 12 mm. The use of 12 mm as a critical value separated the sheep from the goats in 87 percent of the individual cases.

In control experiments Chappell found: (1) a blood pressure rise in an intelligence test which worried the subjects; (2) no rise in mental arithmetic free from all worry; and (3) no rise in making false statements where there was no test situation involved. Chappell concludes that the blood pressure rise, where it occurs, is due to excitement rather than to lying. The test can therefore be used successfully "when the deception situation gives rise to excitement and when other causes of excitement are eliminated." (See the Keeler Polygraph, below.)

THE LURIA TECHNIQUE. The Russian psychologist Luria (1932) found that involuntary finger movements were a valuable adjunct to the association word method of lie detection. He reasoned that the act of lying involved conflict between two responses, the true word and the lie. This conflict should disorganize behavior. But to obtain a good measure of this disorganization there should be some simple behavior pattern that could be disorganized. Luria set up such a pattern by instructing *O* to press a key simultaneously with the response word, and to keep the other hand on a duplicate key. The keys were actually rubber bulbs, so arranged that they would record all changes of pressure, as well as the major stroke. A signal marker was also added to permit measurement of associative reaction time —it was presumably operated by *E*, who signaled the moments of stimulation and of response. . . . several types of clues . . . show up in various records. Perhaps the most obvious clue is a premature stroke on the reaction key, indicating a word that almost slipped out. There may also be marked irregularity in key pressure during the reaction period. Tremors frequently show up. The "inactive" hand may also show irregular pressure on its key, or tremor, or even strokes like those which *O* is instructed to give only with the other hand. The Luria method is properly a clinical technique; it involves the combination and evaluation of many . . . separate clues to conflict so that success or failure depends largely upon the skill of the investigator who examines the records. (Cf. Morgan & Ojemann, 1942.)

POLYGRAPHIC RECORDING. When the newspapers report the use of a "lie detector," they usually refer to the *Keeler polygraph.* In this connotation a polygraph is simply a portable ink-writing instrument that records breathing, fluctuations in blood pressure (but see p. 161 and Chappell, 1931), and associative reaction time. Some polygraphs include the GSR. Of course, the polygraph is not a "lie detector" any more than the microscope is a "germ detector"—in each case the instrument merely furnishes clues that must be interpreted by the expert. This is more than a mere quibble, for it must be emphasized that the interpretation of polygraph recordings requires specialized training and experience.

The development of the polygraph as an instrument suitable for routine investigation of deception goes back to Larson (1923; see also 1932). In 1926 Keeler (see Inbau, 1942) made some improvements; the Keeler Polygraph is the usual instrument in police work. An excellent description of the actual techniques is given by Inbau (1942).

*The use of the polygraph.* There are a number of different ways in which the interrogation may be set up. Perhaps the most dramatic is the peak-of-tension method, which we have illustrated with a record from Inbau (Fig. 1). This method is designed so that the suspect watches the critical question "creep up on him," and builds up tension; that is, he shows a steady increase in level of activation. Once the critical question is passed, he gradually relaxes. The peak may be picked up from the blood pressure curve, and it sometimes shows in breathing.

Another method is the relevant-irrelevant question method. Here the suspect is asked a series of questions, some of which are unrelated to the crime. Deception is indicated by various disturbances in the record, as suppressed breathing and an increase in blood pressure immediately after an (unthruthful) answer. As a matter of fact, this method was used to pick out the suspect who later gave the peak-of-tension record shown in Figure 1; before he was tested, the relevant-irrelevant question method had cleared two other people who were originally under greater suspicion than was the guilty man.

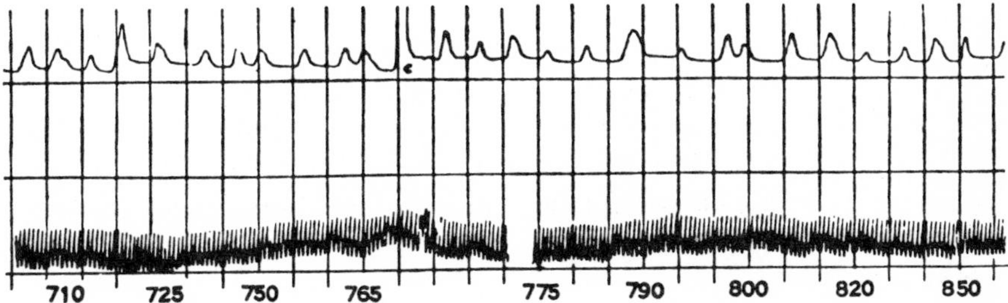


**FIGURE 1.** (Inbau, 1942.) The peak-of-tension method of lie detection. A man was suspected of having stolen a roll of bills containing about $750. (The man from whom it was stolen was not certain of the exact amount.) The polygraph was attached to the suspect, and he was asked if he knew the amount that had been stolen—"Was it $710?" "Was it $725?" etc., as shown below the blood pressure (lower curve). Note that the general level of blood pressure rises up to the $765 question, and then starts to fall on higher sums. (Disregard the blank space just before $775; the pen ran dry.) The respiration record (upper line) shows an unusually deep inhalation (marked C) at the $765 question. Later it was found that the amount stolen was exactly $765! The record is abbreviated here; the whole series ran from $650 to $850. [F. E. Inbau, *Lie Detection and Criminal Interrogation* (Baltimore: Williams & Wilkins Co., 1942). Used with permission of the author and publisher.]

*The practical utility of the lie detector test.* The first question is with regard to its accuracy. We should limit the question to its use in the hands of a trained operator rather than someone who has merely read an instruction manual. The need for such training and experience is recognized by the distributor of the Keeler polygraph, who arranges for training as part of the transaction. In the hands of a competent person, Inbau estimates that 70 percent of the cases will be correctly judged innocent or guilty. Another 20 percent will show so little response, or such inconsistent ones, that a cautious investigator would not make a judgment. The remaining 10 percent represent true errors, and they are largely in favor of the suspect.

This brings up the question of what one does with the results. Perhaps it is not too important whether they are admissible as court evidence, which is a complex legal problem. A more important function of the test is to clear innocent suspects; leaving aside the human values, this saves a lot of police time that can be devoted to other aspects of a crime. The test is also useful in picking up clues, accomplices, etc., which will strengthen the case. Finally, the suspect will often confess after he has seen how the record gives him away. A symposium by Wicker, Cureton & Trovillo (1953) is devoted to the legal and other practical aspects of lie detection.

SUMMARY. In all methods of lie detection the questions are set up so that the guilty person—and *only* the guilty person—will show an increase in level of activation ("emotion") in answering relevant questions, but *not* on control questions. Any index of level of activation may be used to measure the increase; several indices are better than one. Finally, it takes special training and experience to interpret the records; lie detection is an art, and not a laboratory science.

But lie detection is a fitting topic with which to end the chapters on emotion, for it shows that the laborious and sometimes discouraging experiments on bodily changes in emotion have turned up at least one very practical and useful technique. Lie detecting puts level of activation to work!

## *References*

Benussi, V. Die atmungssymptome der Lüge. *Arch. ges. Psych.*, 1914a, 31, 244–273.

Burtt, H. E. The inspiration-expiration ratios during truth and falsehood. *Journal of Experimental Psychology*, 1921, 4, 1–23.

Chappell, M. N. Blood pressure changes in deception. *Archives of Psychology of New York*, 1929, 105.

Feleky, A. The influence of emotions on respiration. *Journal of Experimental Psychology*, 1916, 1, 218–241.

Inbau, F. E. *Lie detection and criminal interrogation*. Baltimore: The Williams & Wilkins Co., 1942.

Landis, C., & Gullette, R. Studies of emotional reactions. III. Systolic blood pressure and inspiration-expiration ratios. *Journal of Comparative Psychology*, 1925, 5, 221–253.

Larson, J. A. The cardio-pneumo-psychogram in deception. *Journal of Experimental Psychology*, 1923, 6, 420–454.

————, *Lying and its detection*. Chicago: Chicago University Press, 1932.

Luria, A. R. *The nature of human conflicts*. New York: Liveright Publishing Corp., 1932.

Marston, W. M. Systolic blood pressure symptoms of deception. *Journal of Experimental Psychology*, 1917, 2, 117–163.

————, Sex characteristics of systolic blood pressure behavior. *Journal of Experimental Psychology*, 1923, 6, 387–419.

————, *The lie detector test*. New York: R. E. Smith, 1938.

Morgan, M. I., & Ojemann, R. H. A study of the Luria Method. *Journal of Applied Psychology*, 1942, 26, 186–179.

Ruckmick, C. A. The truth about lie detection. *Journal of Applied Psychology,* 1938, 22, 50–58.

Summers, W. G. Science can get the confession. *Fordham Law Review*, 1939, 8, 334–354.

Wicker, W., Cureton, E. E., & Trovillo, P. V. The polygraph truth test. A symposium report in the *Tennessee Law Review*, 1953, 22, 1–64.

## *QUESTIONS FOR DISCUSSION*

1. What are the relative advantages and disadvantages of physiological measurement in communication studies?
2. Can you propose some new areas of psychophysiological research which would make significant contributions to our understanding of human communication?
3. Do physiological responses provide any unique insights into the communication process?
4. Can you generate some new applications of the physiological measurement of deception in communication?

chapter **7**

# INTERPERSONAL COMMUNICATION WITHIN TRANSRACIAL CONTEXTS

## SECTION ONE: OVERVIEW AND PERSPECTIVE

### *Objectives for Section One*

Upon reading this chapter you should be able to:

1. List the peculiar constraints on interpersonal communication in transracial contexts.
2. Explain how ethnic perspective can act as a barrier to transracial communication.
3. Define interpersonal communication in transracial contexts.
4. List the elements of interpersonal communication and describe their functions in an inter-ethnic setting.
5. Distinguish between minority and majority codification in a typical Black-white communication and in a typical Spanish-speaking–English-speaking communication situation.
6. List some elements of Black community language.
7. Explain nonverbal communication in terms of effective interracial communication and cite examples.
8. Define sender-and-receiver proximity in transracial contexts and explain its role in communication.
9. Explain how codification systems may and may not overlap.

*Arthur L. Smith*

# INTERPERSONAL COMMUNICATION WITHIN TRANSRACIAL CONTEXTS

Assuming that in the next few years you will interact verbally with many persons of a different racial background than yours, we have prepared this chapter on the premise: *The understanding of transracial communication barriers and the will to interact will greatly facilitate your ability to communicate meaningfully across ethnic and racial lines.*

## *Transracial Communication*

We use "transracial communication," either dyadic or mass, to refer to the understanding that persons from different ethnic or racial backgrounds can achieve in a situation of verbal interaction. By defining "transracial" as including both *racial* and *ethnic* groups, we have sought to differentiate it from the much used term, "interracial," which usually denotes race only. After all, significant problems in communication exist between ethnic groups that may be anthropologically classified as of the same race.

Arthur L. Smith *is presently an associate professor in the Department of Speech at the University of California, Los Angeles. He received his B.A. degree from Oklahoma Christian College, his M.A. from Pepperdine College, and his Ph.D. from U.C.L.A. Of particular interest to Dr. Smith is research in the rhetoric of Black Power and in transracial communication. Four books and several scholarly journal articles reflect his expertise and interest in these very relevant communication problems of today's society. In addition to applying his knowledge of Black culture and problems to his academic work in the field of speech communication, Dr. Smith serves as a consultant to several universities and organizations that are attempting to establish better interacial communication among members of various communities.*

"Transracial" communication is also delineated from "intercultural" communication, which usually refers to political goals and diplomatic missions in an international context. "Transracial," in this chapter, refers, for the most part, to communication intra-nationally. You should also note that when we use the word "race" without also using "ethnic," and vice versa, both terms are meant, inasmuch as both "race" and "ethnic" are encompassed in our definition of *transracial communication.*

Such communication, more often than not, simultaneously takes place interculturally and intraculturally, in the sense that two or more ethnic cultures meet under the umbrella of what is for the most part a general culture, even though it might be synonymous with one of the ethnic cultures. Referring to minority ethnic groups as "culturally deprived" has been shown to be exceedingly erroneous (Allen and Hernandez, 1969), especially when groups such as Afro-Americans and Mexican-Americans consider themselves to be culturally advantaged.

The term "ethnic group" usually refers to those who possess a shared tradition, an idea of common destiny, and a feeling of spiritual togetherness, all of which may exist even if they possess no common territory or political organization. It has probably occurred to you that America is a nation of varied ethnic groups: Mexican-Americans, Afro-Americans, Jewish-Americans, Armenian-Americans, and so on. These groups tend to express an inner unity which often has semibiological undertones. In Black communities the term "soul" has come to express what is felt but cannot be transmitted to others. Growing out of a feeling of shared traditions and aspirations, this concept seems to name the semibiological experience of Black people.

Intra-ethnic expressions and aspirations identify common goals, beliefs, and anticipations which serve to cement the group. But group solidarity based on shared experiences need not become a barrier to intergroup communication. Sensitivity to others dissolves most walls that humans erect to keep from talking to others. Feeling into the peculiar set of experiences which sets another person apart from us can help to eliminate barriers while providing both parties with a shared experience: communication. This requires a concentrated effort.

An essential quality for the would-be transracial communicator is what Rokeach (1960) calls "open-mindedness." This is not a new concept to you. How many times have you responded to a friend's refusal to "see" your point with the words, "Oh, why can't you be open-minded?" Opposite to open-mindedness is close-mindedness, and both are pervasive character traits found in varying degrees in each person, depending upon his system of beliefs. There are certain things that we are more open-minded about than others. Each person has a "central–intermediate–peripheral" continuum which structures his beliefs (Rokeach, 1960). "Central beliefs" are the fundamental beliefs a person has about himself, the physical world and the "generalized other." These beliefs are characterized by the intensity with which they are held. "Intermediate beliefs" are those which are based upon a person's view of authority, and upon the persons he depends for a picture of his world. These beliefs are usually strongly held, but not so strongly maintained, as central beliefs. Finally, "peripheral beliefs" are those derived from authority, which help a person complete his idea of the world. The openness of a person's system of beliefs can be determined by discovering his interest in and willingness to assess new information. This is particularly relevant in transracial communication, inasmuch as persons might hold central or intermediate beliefs about interaction between different racial or ethnic groups.

Open-mindedness in an individual produces an optimistic outlook (Bettinghaus, 1968) about the way things happen in society, and causes a person to view information from an historical perspective. In contrast, a closed-minded person compartmentalizes the beliefs he holds and is reluctant to compare various beliefs. While it is nearly impossible to always predict the responses of persons involved in transracial communication, it can be asserted that open-minded individuals will enter into more harmonious interpersonal communication with persons of a different race than dogmatic or closed-minded individuals. This does not mean, however, that other factors will not affect the interactive process. Again, a person might be less open-minded about some issues than about many others, which means that the content of the communication will influence the communicators. When two closed-minded individuals confront each other, the possibility of effective communication is substantially reduced.

On the other hand, open-minded persons will receive and evaluate messages on their merit. This means that it is possible for two open-minded persons to disagree about the merit of an idea. In fact, transracial communication is only truly accomplished when verbal interaction is normalized to the extent that people of different races can disagree, evaluate each other, and express deep feelings without the matter of their racial difference entering into the conversation. *Normalization* is the end of effective interracial communication. It is not normal for Blacks and whites to be denied the opportunity of communicating their disagreements and dissatisfactions with each other as individuals. Abnormal interaction is characterized by dishonesty and lack of candor; normal interaction is characterized by openness and maturity. Thus, the *normalization* of interpersonal relations through verbal interaction is the end of effective transracial communication.

The selection following this essay is an article which demonstrates the diversity of language in the American society. Our approach to these different styles of language and communication should be based upon a mature respect for effective interaction. In a multi-ethnic society it is essential that we understand and accept diversity. Perhaps Gittler (1956, p. 139) puts the issue best when he states:

> The basic problem is not diversity, but acceptance of diversity. Most thoughtful men realize that group diversity is a part of our world. How we learn to live with and accept diversity will determine the future of civilization as we have known it.

In fact, a more harmonious society than we have known can be based upon the acceptance of American diversity while simultaneously reaching across barriers to communicate with persons of different ethnic backgrounds.

In preparing this chapter we have assumed that most people, particularly college students, freed from some of the encapsulating racial stereotypes and prejudices of a few years ago, will want to know how they can have more harmonious communication with persons of another racial group. Obviously many of the obstacles to this type of communication are fundamental to all communication. Yet there is evidence (Ratcliffe and Steil, 1970) which suggests that race may be a more important determinant of attitudinal differences toward social issues than sex, class rank, age, or geographical location. On the basis of this analysis we believe that race can play a potent role in how you interact verbally with persons of another racial background, even though it does not have to. The traditional communication barriers are often amplified in a transracial context, particularly when you have already based an opinion or a judgment of the other person upon his race.

We have organized this chapter under three basic headings: (1) an overview of theory and research; (2) principles derived from theory; and (3) a selected reading. The first section is an attempt to put interpersonal communication between persons of different races into focus by viewing related theoretical formulations and research. Under the heading of Principles Derived from Theory we discuss some of the key concepts of interpersonal communication in transracial contexts and demonstrate their applicability to your own communication with persons of other races. Finally, the reading provides you with additional discussion of our subject.

## *Overview of theory and research*

It is generally accepted by communication scholars (Westley and MacLean, 1957; Schramm, 1954; Berlo, 1960; and Bettinghaus, 1968) that interpersonal communication is liable to be more difficult to achieve, and is less likely to occur, the greater the contextual differences between source and receiver. This is to say, when communicators share a similar verbal code, are mutually available, and have similar values, their chances for understanding each other are immensely increased.

The paucity of literature directly related to interracial communication argues for more sensitive conceptual schemes for interpersonal analysis. Although several studies of intercultural communication have already been made, few if any recent research articles have contributed to our understanding of interracial communication intra-nationally. While this may appear exceedingly strange considering the enormity of our racial problems, it is not inconsistent with the lack of pluralism which has so often characterized academic research. It is highly likely that studies in interracial communication could prove equally as rewarding to the society as intercultural studies have proved. Furthermore, inasmuch as interpersonal communication in transracial contexts, particularly in America, must often be considered intercultural, a brief look at some pertinent research in this area might help us understand what might be referred to as "transracial communication."

Since the appearance of Franz Boas's (1940) collection of articles, a variety of cultural anthropologists, speech communication scholars, and sociolinguistic experts have studied language and culture (Carroll, 1964; Hall, 1959; Hoijer, 1954; Lado, 1963; A. G. Smith, 1966; Van Nieuwenhuijze, 1963; Weinreich, 1964). Even so, the employment of research designs and methodologies similar to Boas's has not provided the theoretical framework needed to make this research applicable to transracial contexts. In *Race, Language and Culture,* Boas attempted to demonstrate the relevance of his research to everyday problems. However, the section on language is primarily classificatory, dealing with the various traits and attributes of Indian languages, and little effort is expended to draw any implications about inter-ethnic communication. It is therefore doubtful that Boas accomplished his goal.

With perhaps more currency for interpersonal communication, Edward Hall (1959) suggested the possibility of a silent language operating between people of different cultures, and even later (1966) analyzed the perception of space and time dimensions as possible factors in intercultural relationships. Although verbal language is the essential medium of interpersonal communication in that words and sentences are the means of *connecting* one person to another, nonverbal signs play extremely significant roles in communication. Perhaps, in communication across racial lines, an understanding of the nonverbal signs is even more important than an understanding of the verbal code. Nonverbal signs can often serve as double-cutting edges when we are trying to communicate in transracial contexts. In one situation, a speaker might unintentionally use an "attack" word while speaking to a member of another race and be "rescued" by his unmalicious, perhaps, friendly appearance as reflected in countenance, ease, and gestures. In another, a person might misunderstand certain intergroup signs (Black handshake, Soul fingers, Victory walk, and so on) even when such "signs" are accompanied by rather innocent words. While Edward Hall (1959) does not discuss the domestic situation, his general treatment of cultural differences is a perceptive look at communication problems between people who view time and space differently.

A variety of books (Dance, 1967, Smith, 1966, Sereno and Mortensen, 1970; and Berlo, 1960, among others) concerned with theory and process have added to our knowledge of interpersonal communication. Berlo (1960) in writing about the characteristics of the "source-encoder" identified four factors which are valuable for our discussion. According to Berlo, the factors within the source capable of increasing the fidelity of his communication are his: (1) communication skills; (2) attitudes; (3) knowledge; and (4) sociocultural position. "Communication skills," his first factor, include writing, speaking, reading, and listening, the first two being "encoding" capacities and the latter two being "decoding" capacities. A fifth communication skill crucial to both encoding and decoding is thought. To be a fuzzy thinker is to run the risk of being misunderstood.

Berlo's second factor was "attitudes." The lead article by Herbert W. Simons in Chapter 5 discussed the difficulty scholars have had in defining attitudes, but let us assume an attitude to be a predisposition, favorable or unfavorable, toward some object. Now it is possible to conceptualize what Berlo means by: (1) attitude toward self; (2) attitude toward subject matter; and (3) attitude toward receiver.

The third factor contributing to the source-encoder's credibility is his knowledge. Effective interpersonal communication requires both knowledge and understanding. The source must know what it is he wants to communicate and he must understand what communication skills can best be brought to bear on specific issues. You may possess sharp insight into inter-ethnic or interracial problems and yet not be able to communicate effectively because you do not understand how to use your communication skills. The person who enters such an interaction technically knowledgeable, but lacking understanding of communication skills, could possibly offend the receiver. Such situations can be avoided if the source-encoder concentrates on content and skill jointly; they are both indispensable to effective interpersonal communication in transracial contexts.

Perhaps more closely related to some of the concepts to be explored more thoroughly in this chapter is the factor of sociocultural position. Every person who communicates is a captive of his cultural environment. Berlo does not see this concept in relationship to interracial communication, although he gives general guidelines which he explains in terms of international differences (Berlo, 1960) and status. But it is still possible to speak of the source's sociocultural system *in re* transracial communication as well *in re* the corresponding system within the receiver. Actually, all that has been said above about the source can be applied to the "receiver-decoder." Later we shall discuss principles of communication applicable to transracial interaction, at which time specific concepts will be discussed.

From the foregoing discussion of related literature, several fundamental principles of interpersonal communication in transracial contexts can be stated. The principles derived from the body of knowledge about transracial communication behavior are placed in four categories: (1) common codification; (2) sender-receiver proximity; (3) perspective; and (4) general communication skills.

## *Principles derived from theory*

### 1. INTERRACIAL COMMUNICATION IS FACILITATED WHEN THE COMMUNICATORS SHARE A COMMON CODING SYSTEM.

Much conflict, interracial and otherwise, could be resolved and indeed prevented if people had some knowledge of each other's verbal code. When source and receiver share a codification system, their chances of achieving understanding are considerably improved. "Code" refers to the verbal and nonverbal signs of communication. It therefore serves as the primary link between source and receiver, and, if it is significantly impaired in any way, the communication process is less likely to succeed. Thus interpersonal communication depends upon a common code, and effective transracial communication requires that the communicators understand the essential elements of each other's code.

Fairly recent studies into the value of categorization (Hayek, 1952; Bruner, Goodnow, and Austin, 1956; and Triandis, 1960) have revealed that persons who categorize objects, events, and concepts in a similar manner should be able to communicate effectively. Accordingly, the work of several scholars (Homans, 1950; Runkel, 1956; and Newcomb, 1956) indicates that if persons possess cognitive similarity and have opportunity for interaction, then communication will be rewarding. These research findings may be taken as presumptive evidence that a common coding system facilitates interpersonal communication in transracial contexts.

#### Overlapping Codes

Often, in interpersonal communication between different ethnic groups, the source and receiver have overlapping codes, i.e., codes which provide an area of commonality but which also contain areas of unshared codification. A factor contributing to this situation is the relative ease with which members of minority ethnic groups learn the code of the majority society. This means that most white communicators have had limited experience in integrated communication, except for peripheral relationships with maids, gardeners, and so on, and that most white communicators do not understand Black community language. Blacks and other minority-group members have also had limited experience with integrated communication, but they have developed functional communication behavior in the native language of the majority society. Few whites have developed functional communication behavior in the language of the Black community. Usually the Black, or minority person, acquires the majority's code formally but finds great resistance to its adoption among his peers, in his home, and at play. The white communicator has usually acquired his code informally, as a matter of course. A reason for this, of course, is that the language of the majority is the language of trade, commerce, education, politics, and services, and minority groups must therefore adopt this language to some extent, even if only in their daily intercourse with the external world and not in more immediate surroundings. The figures below represent some possibilities of code overlapping.

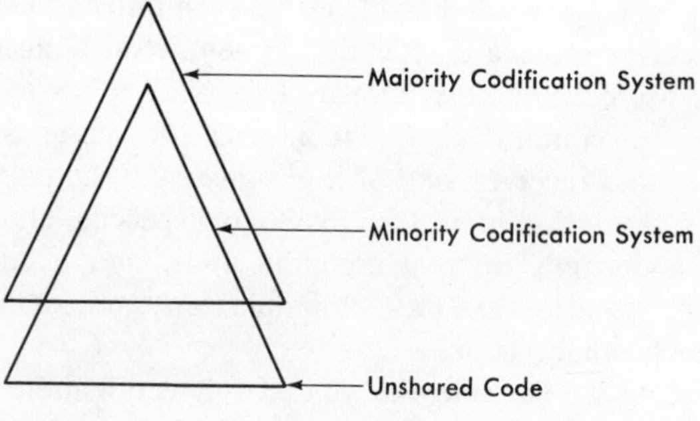


**Figure 1**

Figure 1 shows one possibility of code overlapping and an unshared area of codification. This figure might represent the Black-white codification pattern in many areas of American society. You will notice that the Minority codification system is largely enclosed by the Majority codification system. This makes it possible for interracial communication to occur when it would otherwise be impossible, as when a Black communicator reverts to the use of community language while supposedly communicating with a white receiver. Community language, consisting of Black English, slang, and communication subtleties as reflected in the nonverbal code, is represented by the area labeled "Unshared code." It is usually reserved for communication between ethnic peers and family members, and during social occasions.

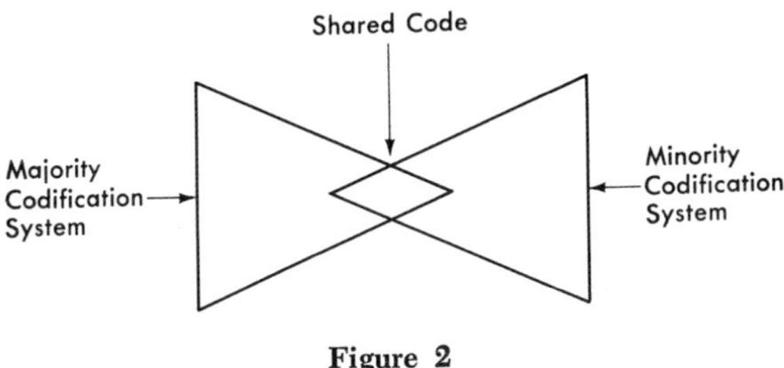


**Figure 2**

Figure 2 shows the commonality of code in the case of a minority whose cultural language is foreign to the general American codification system. This figure might represent the codification structure of many Spanish-speaking Americans, who share a small area of commonality with the larger codification system by virtue of limited participation in the society in search of employment and other necessities. Because the majority of Americans with whom they come into contact do not speak Spanish, the minority group has to learn the utilitarian words of English in order to provide for their families and get an education. Often they use Spanish in their churches, at home, and at play, much like Blacks use Black English and slang when not constrained by the formalities of the majority culture.

### Nonverbal Code

Nonverbal signs comprise a major portion of the code in effective interracial communication. Nonverbal codification, which is often used unconsciously, is indispensable to meaningful communication in transracial contexts. In order to achieve a measure of understanding, persons who communicate must possess the capacity to respond to nonverbal as well as verbal cues. It has been estimated that 65 per cent of the social meaning of communication is carried by nonverbal communication. "Action speaks louder than words," according to one adage. None of you would ever think seriously of saying "up" and simultaneously pointing a finger downward. The reason is that most Americans share a common nonverbal codification system for "up" and "down." Yet in inter-ethnic communication it is possible that a source might employ a word you think you understand, only to confuse you because the word employed and the accompanying nonverbal communication do not coincide as they should in your experience. When the word "beautiful" is used in reference to a girl you consider homely, you may have second thoughts about the exactness of the source's code especially when he says "beautiful" but recoils instead of being attracted by the girl's physical presence. Perhaps "beautiful" means something other than the receiver thinks it should, and the nonverbal communication often helps to point that out.

Ruesch and Kees (1956) identified three kinds of nonverbal communication: sign language, action language, and object language. "Sign language" is the conscious substitution of a gesture for words, numbers, or punctuation. Most Americans share a similar sign language, which means that even in interracial communication there are many areas of shared meaning. "Action language" refers to all bodily movements that are not consciously meant to communicate, but nevertheless do. Certain unintended facial expressions might lead to interracial misunderstanding. In fact, it is possible for an observer to decode the action messages of another person and arrive at an unintended conclusion. This means that close attention must be paid to the implications of action language. In a certain medical school, an experiment was conducted on the ability of minority patients to identify doctors with racial prejudice. The results showed that although each doctor performed the same tasks, the patients were consistently able to identify those who were judged to have prejudicial attitudes. Finally, "object language" refers to material and physical displays, intentional and unintentional, which communicate. Thus object language can range anywhere from sartorial outfits like the berets and leather jackets of the Black Panthers to a display of the United States Flag. Given the complexities of this phenomenon, our brief discussion has not exhausted the subject, nor was it meant to, but we hope it has provided you with some guidelines in understanding how a common code facilitates interracial communication. For additional information regarding language differences, see Frederick Williams' article on "Acquisition and Performance of Communication Behaviors" in Chapter 3 of this volume.

### 2. MEANINGFUL COMMUNICATION IN TRANSRACIAL CONTEXTS REQUIRES THE PROXIMITY OF SOURCE AND RECEIVER.

All communication events require that the participants become available to each other inasmuch as there are physical limits to the transmitting of codes, whether verbal or nonverbal. In transracial communication, where availability is more difficult, access to some of the characteristics of each other's experience determines the effectiveness of our communication. Mistakes are often made when persons of different ethnic backgrounds fail to comprehend each other's perceptions and visualizations. Minority persons often have access to white perceptions because of the necessity to function within a majority society, while whites do not often reciprocate by learning what the minority's perceptions are. Of course, there are exceptions when the majority's society is threatened by minority group protests, demonstrations or violence; during such a time the survival of the white society appears at stake and efforts to understand minority complaints are in the best interest of the majority community. In writing this essay, however, we have become more than ever convinced that transracial communication can take place in the absence of pressure for survival upon the parties involved.

### SINCERITY

Some of the mistakes of perception can be corrected if the communicators sincerely want to transcend boundaries. Nothing can happen if genuine willingness to become available to the other person is lacking. You can become available through research into the cultural background, the issues of interest, and the historical contributions of the persons you seek to understand. But more importantly, you must become geographically available. Transracial communication implies contact between the races. Reading the history of a race is not talking face to face with a member of that race. Availability is putting yourself where there can be contact. Enthusiasm about learning another's culture cannot substitute for personal availability. Proximity, of course, requires willingness. Transracial communication increases in more meaningful ways as the interaction among whites and minority groups increases as a result of open housing and open-mindedness. Willingness to send a message must be balanced by willingness to respond to a message, and the coordination of stimulus-and-response sensitivities will reduce the human distance between communicators.

### PROPINQUITY

In several studies (particularly Byrne, 1961) propinquity has been well documented as a significant variable in interpersonal attraction and repulsion. These studies, for the most part, have concentrated on intraracial groups. We can assume from our earlier discussion of ethnic groups that the subjects generally held similar well-established aspirations and sentiments, and had similar learned drives. In fact those who seem deficient in the general values of the group are often defined as "incongruents" by consensual judgment.

Persons of different ethnic groups are also often defined as "incongruents" by virtue of their heritage, skin color, or religion. Incongruence works two streets, however. It is always possible for the describer to appear deficient in the eyes of the described. And once we have defined other persons as "incongruents" we seek to avoid them or escape them when we find ourselves in their presence. Many whites and Blacks feel their incongruence so intensely that they refuse to make themselves available for communication. A few studies have verified this reaction in a converse manner, by showing that a relationship exists between similar attitudes and interpersonal attraction (A. J. Smith, 1957; Jones and Daugherty, 1959). Thus even if a "stranger" exhibited attitudes similar to those of a group, it felt more attraction to him than to someone with dissimilar attitudes (Byrne, 1961). The results strongly suggest the need for the propinquity of source and receiver if interracial communication is to be effective. Incongruence and dissimilarity of attitudes can only be overcome when we make ourselves available to each other.

3. INTERPERSONAL COMMUNICATION WITH TRANSRACIAL CONTEXTS OFTEN FAILS BECAUSE THE SENDER AND RECEIVER DO NOT SHARE NOR SEEK EACH OTHER'S POINT OF VIEW.

Human beings come together into close identification and interact sensibly with each other primarily because of the commonality of their aspirations, dreams, fears, and anxieties. Transracial communication can be constrained by the diverse points of view of the communicators, who are sometimes unable and often unwilling to view issues and arguments from another's standpoint.

The attitude that "My people must win no-matter-what" seriously endangers communication between different ethnic groups. What is required in interracial communication is the ability to predict the speech-communication behavior of the participants. The sensitivity to others will allow one communicator to empathize with another. It is only then that interpersonal communication within transracial contexts ceases to be haphazard because it is only then that foresight and expectations of another's response prove to be reasonably accurate. The matter of viewpoint can be illustrated by the varying uses of language by whites and Blacks in given situations. Some whites may think of the ghetto conflagrations between 1965 and 1968 as "riots," but Blacks speak of them as "rebellions." Furthermore, many whites may perceive the participants as "hoodlums" while their Black counterparts may speak of "freedom fighters." In such cases, the use of language becomes mostly, if not totally, a matter of standpoint. For communication to take place, Blacks and whites must be flexible enough to aggressively seek to know the other's viewpoint, which may be defined as the particular perspective, partly characterized by emotional attachments, aspirations and cultural biases, which a person has of the society. Acceptance of another's viewpoint does not commit you to agreement with that person's position; it simply opens the way for possible interracial understanding by putting you into the other's place (Mead, 1934).

Obviously, we have not exhausted the concept of perspective in the above discussion. What is significant for transracial communication is that once we grasp an appreciation for another's viewpoint, our ability to see relationships and to make judgments can be strengthened. In fact the willingness to accept the possibility of a perspective other than our own relates to the earlier section on open-mindedness.

4. THERE IS LITTLE TO SUGGEST THAT CHANGING THE GRAMMAR OF BLACKS WILL MAKE FOR SUBSTANTIALLY MORE EFFECTIVE INTER-ETHNIC COMMUNICATION.

It is argued in some circles that the major problem in interpersonal communication between Blacks and whites is the use of "bad English" or "substandard English" by Blacks. According to this theory, if all Blacks used standard American speech, we would not have interracial conflicts. While it is true that a common code contributes to interpersonal communication, it is not true that the Black users of Black English are not generally understood. Of course, there are Black English words which the average user of English might not grasp, but the same is true of English itself. There are few masters of every word in the English language, and to that extent most of us have limited vocabularies, but no one would dare suggest that we cannot communicate because we do not understand all the words that are used.

In addition, foreign speakers of English, even from Western nations, have little difficulty communicating although they possess exotic accents, often speak haltingly, sometimes have extremely basic vocabularies, and use incorrect grammar. Clearly, the principal trouble is not grammar but viewpoint.

It has been argued before that mankind is separated more by cultural difference than language (Oliver, 1962), and that thought patterns are more important than vocabulary and grammar. This is certainly the case between Blacks and whites. Grammar is an instrument used to promote clarity and understanding, but often the problems between Blacks and whites do not suffer as much for clarity as for the ability to look beyond the words to the source of the other person's ideas and to his frame of reference.

The foregoing discussion suggests that interpersonal communication between people of different races is possible, but at the same time that it does not often occur without effort. Beginning with sensitivity to the other's viewpoint and acceptance of the fact that his possibly different viewpoint grows out of peculiarly ethnic traditions and aspirations, the communicator must move beyond connection to communication. It is perfectly possible to be sensitive and yet not communicate, for this step involves committing oneself to interaction. When messages are transmitted between communicator and communicatee; they interact. And as we pointed out initially in this essay, the aim of transracial communication is understanding between persons of different races.

If sensing another individual's point of view is important, then the person who would communicate within transracial contexts should approach interaction humbly, feeling, "I do not know all I should know about this person's peculiar problems, fears, and aims." Knowing more, however, entails learning more about the person's ethnic background and point of view. As an outgrowth of sensitivity, not sentimentality, one develops a grasp of essential concepts, images, and philosophies.

Additionally, the codification system of the person with whom you want to communicate must be respected in the light of his ethnic aspirations. The importance of respecting the other's codification system is illustrated by a conversation I overheard. Two students, one white and one Black, stood in the front of the classroom discussing slavery just before class began. The white student said, "Slavery was good for the Africans because as savages they were introduced to Christianity." The Black student became exceedingly angry and retorted, "You're too stupid to talk to." At that point, the white student was dismayed and wanted to know what had he said. I explained to him that the word "savage" does not relate to the Black man's concept of himself or his ancestors. Blacks would argue that many Africans probably considered Christians to be barbarians and savages. So, in the same sense that whites do not consider their Christian ancestors savages, Blacks cannot consider their pagan ancestors savages. It is a matter of perspective. How we perceive ourselves and our roles in history and society greatly affects how we relate to others. Thus, scrutiny of one's own perceptions should always precede any extensive participation in transracial communication.

The task is challenging but rewarding, and a possible answer to intergroup conflict particularly when such conflict threatens our society. A final note—in this article, while we have sought to provide you with some fundamental principles of interpersonal communication in transracial contexts, we have not attempted to treat the subject exhaustively.

## *REFERENCES*


Allen, A., & Hernandez, D. Mexican American: Culturally deprived? Anglo: Ethnocentric? Los Angeles: (unpublished), 1969.

Berlo, D. K. *The process of communication*. New York. Holt, Rinehart & Winston, Inc., 1960.

Bettinghaus, E. *Persuasive communication*. New York. Holt, Rinehart & Winston, Inc., 1968.

Boas, F. *Language, race and culture.* New York: The Macmillan Company, 1940.

Bruner, J. S., Goodnow, J. J., & Austin, G. A. *A Study of thinking.* New York. John Wiley & Sons, Inc., 1956.

Byrne, D. Interpersonal attraction and similarity. *Journal of Abnormal Psychology*, 1961, 62, 713–715.

________ & McGraw, C. Interpersonal attraction toward Negroes. *Human Relations*, 1964, 17, 201–213.

Carroll, J. B. *Language and thought.* Englewood Cliffs, N.J.: Prentice-Hall, Inc., 1964.

Dance, F. E. X. *Human communication theory.* New York: Holt, Rinehart & Winston, Inc., 1967.

Gittler, J. *Understanding minority groups.* New York: John Wiley & Sons, Inc., 1956.

Hall, E. T. *The hidden dimension.* Garden City, N.Y.: Doubleday & Company, Inc., 1956.

________ *The silent language.* Garden City, N.Y.: Doubleday & Company, Inc., 1959.

Hayek, F. A. *The sensory order: An inquiry into the foundations of theoretical psychology.* Chicago: University of Chicago Press, 1952.

Hoijer, H. *Language in culture.* Chicago: University of Chicago Press, 1954.

Homans, G. C. *The human group.* New York: Harcourt, Brace & World, Inc., 1950.

Jones, E. E., & Daugherty, B. N. Political orientation and the perceptual effects of an anticipated interaction. *Journal of Abnormal Psychology*, LIX 1959, 59, 340–349.

Lado, R. *Linguistics across cultures.* Ann Arbor: University of Michigan Press, 1963.

Mead, G. H. *Mind, self, and society.* Chicago: University of Chicago Press, 1934.

Newcomb, T. M. The prediction of interpersonal attraction. *American Psychology*, 1956, 11, 575–586.

Oliver, R. *Culture and communication.* Springfield, Ill.: Charles C. Thomas, Publisher, 1962.

Ratcliffe, S. A. & Steil, L. K. Attitudinal differences between black and white students. *The Speech Teacher,* 1970, 19, 190–198.

Rokeach, M. *The open and closed mind.* New York: Basic Books, Inc., Publishers, 1960.

Ruesch, J., & Kees, W. *Nonverbal communication: Notes on the visual perception of human relations.* Berkeley: University of California Press, 1956.

Runkel, P. I. Cognitive similarity in facilitating communication. *Sociometry*, 1956, 19, 178–191.

Schramm, W. How communication works. In W. Schramm (Ed.), *The process and effects of mass communication*. Urbana, Illinois: University of Illinois Press, 1954. Pp. 3–26.

Sereno, K. K., & Mortenson, C. D. *Foundations of communication theory*. New York: Harper & Row, Publishers, 1970.

Smith, A. G. (Ed.) *Communication and culture*. New York: Holt, Rinehart & Winston, Inc., 1966.

Smith, A. J. Similarity of values and its relation to acceptance and the projection of similarity. *Journal of Psychology*, 1957, 43, 251–260.

Triandis, H. C. Cognitive similarity and communication in a dyad. *Human Relations*, 1960, 13, 175–183.

Van Nieuwenhuijze, C. A. O. *Cross-cultural studies*. The Hague: Mouton and Company, 1963.

Weinreich, U. *Languages in contact*. The Hague: Mouton and Company, 1964.

Westley, B. H., & MacLean, M. S., Jr. A conceptual model for communication research. *Journalism Quarterly*, 1957, 34, 31–38.

## SECTION TWO: READINGS

### *Introduction and Objectives for Reading One: "Rapping in the Ghetto"*

This selection is an extremely interesting and informative examination of the form, style, and functions of various language patterns used in Black ghettos. The student is cautioned not to allow the many illustrations to overshadow the significance of the author's comments about the nature of language and its function in various communication events in the ghetto.

After reading this selection you should be able to:

1. Identify and describe in writing four of the eight kinds of verbal behavior discussed in the reading.
2. Identify and describe two functions of "rapping."
3. Identify and describe in writing four uses of language in either a white-middle-class or non-ghetto Black community which serve essentially the same function as the kinds of language behavior described in your answer to Objective One.
4. List and describe in writing five aspects of his society which you feel explain the ghetto dweller's need for and use of the verbal behavior discussed in the reading.
5. Compare and contrast as many points as you can in Chapter 3 and this reading.

Thomas Kochman

## RAPPING IN THE GHETTO

"Rapping," "shucking," "jiving," "running it down," "gripping," "copping a plea," "signifying" and "sounding" are all part of the black ghetto idiom and describe different kinds of talking. Each has its own distinguishing features of form, style, and function; each is influenced by, and influences, the speaker, setting, and audience; and each sheds light on the black perspective and the black condition—on those orienting values and attitudes that will cause a speaker to speak or perform in his own way within the social context of the black community.

. . . . . . . . . . . . . . . . . . . . . . . . . .

While often used to mean ordinary conversation, rapping is distinctively a fluent and a lively way of talking, always characterized by a high degree of personal style. To one's own group, rapping may be descriptive of an interesting narration, a colorful rundown of some past event. An example of this kind of rap is the answer from a Chicago gang member to a youth worker who asked how his group became organized:

> Now I'm goin tell you how the jive really started. I'm goin to tell you how the club got this big. 'Bout 1956 there used to be a time when the Jackson Park show was open and the Stony show was open. Sixty-six street, Jeff, Gene, all of 'em, little bitty dudes, little bitty . . . Gene wasn't with 'em then. Gene was cribbin (living) over here. Jeff, all of 'em, little bitty dudes, you dig? All of us were little.
>
> Sixty-six (the gang on sixty-sixth street), they wouldn't allow us in the Jackson Park show. That was when the parky (?) was headin it. Everybody say, If we want to go to the show, we go! One day, who was it? Carl Robinson. He went up to the show . . . and Jeff fired on him. He came back and all this was swelled up 'bout yay big, you know. He come back over to the hood (neighborhood). He told (name unclear) and them dudes went up there. That was when mostly all the main sixty-six boys was over here like Bett Riley. All of 'em was over here. People that quit gang-bangin (fighting, especially as a group), Marvell Gates, people like that.

Excerpted from Thomas Kochman, "Rapping in the Ghetto," *TRANS-action,* VI (1969), 26–34. Copyright © February, 1969 by *TRANS-action,* Inc. New Brunswick, New Jersey. Reprinted by permission of the author and publisher.

> They went on up there, John, Roy and Skeeter went in there. And they start humbuggin (fighting) in there. That's how it all started. Sixty-six found out they couldn't beat us, at *that* time. They couldn't *whup* seven-o. Am I right Leroy? You was cribbin over here then. Am I right? We were dynamite! Used to be a time, you ain't have a passport, Man, you couldn't walk through here. And if didn't nobody know you it was worse than that. . . ."

Rapping to a woman is a colorful way of "asking for some pussy." "One needs to throw a lively rap when he is 'putting the make' on a broad." (John Horton, "Time and Cool People," *Trans*-action, April, 1967.)

According to one informant the woman is usually someone he has just seen or met, looks good, and might be willing to have sexual intercourse with him. My informant says the term would not be descriptive of talk between a couple "who have had a relationship over any length of time." Rapping then, is used at the beginning of a relationship to create a favorable impression and be persuasive at the same time. The man who has the reputation for excelling at this is the pimp, or mack man. Both terms describe a person of considerable status in the street hierarchy, who, by his lively and persuasive rapping ("macking" is also used in this context) has acquired a stable of girls to hustle for him and give him money. For most street men and many teenagers he is the model whom they try to emulate. Thus, within the community you have a pimp walk, pimp style boots and clothes, and perhaps most of all "pimp talk," is a colorful literary example of a telephone rap. One of my informants regards it as extreme, but agrees that it illustrates the language, style and technique of rapping. "Blood" is rapping to an ex-whore named Christine in an effort to trap her into his stable:

> Now try to control yourself baby. I'm the tall stud with the dreamy bedroom eyes across the hall in four-twenty. I'm the guy with the pretty towel wrapped around his sexy hips. I got the same hips on now that you X-rayed. Remember that hump of sugar your peepers feasted on?
>
> She said, "Maybe, but you shouldn't call me. I don't want an incident. What do you want? A lady doesn't accept phone calls from strangers."
>
> I said, "A million dollars and a trip to the moon with a bored, trapped, beautiful bitch, you dig? I'm no stranger. I've been popping the elastic on your panties ever since you saw me in the hall. . . ."

Rapping between men and women often is competitive and leads to a lively repartee with the women becoming as adept as the men. An example follows:

> A man coming from the bathroom forgot to zip his pants. An unescorted party of women kept watching him and laughing among themselves. The man's friends "hip" (inform) him to what's going on. He approaches one woman—"Hey baby, did you see that big black Cadillac with the full

> tires? ready to roll in action just for you." She answers—"No motherfucker, but I saw a little gray Volkswagen with two flat tires." Everybody laughs. His rap was "capped" (Excelled, topped).

When "whupping the game" on a "trick" or "lame" (trying to get goods or services from someone who looks like he can be swindled), rapping is often descriptive of the highly stylized verbal part of the maneuver. In well-established "con games" the rap is carefully prepared and used with great skill in directing the course of the transaction. An excellent illustration came from an adept hustler who was playing the "murphy" game on a white trick. The "murphy" game is designed to get the *trick* to give his money to the hustler, who in this instance poses as a "steerer" (one who directs or steers customers to a brothel), to keep the whore from stealing it. The hustler then skips with the money.

> Look Buddy, I know a fabulous house not more than two blocks away. Brother you ain't never seen more beautiful, freakier broads than are in that house. One of them, the prettiest one, can do more with a swipe than a monkey can with a banana. She's like a rubber doll; she can take a hundred positions."
>
> At this point the sucker is wild to get to this place of pure joy. He entreats the con player to take him there, not just direct him to it.
>
> The "murphy" player will prat him (pretend rejection) to enhance his desire. He will say, "Man, don't be offended, but Aunt Kate, that runs the house don't have nothing but highclass white men coming to her place. . . . You know, doctors, lawyers, big-shot politicians. You look like a clean-cut white man, but you ain't in that league are you? (Iceberg Slim, *Pimp: The Story of My Life*)

After a few more exchanges of the "murphy" dialogue, "the mark is separated from his scratch."

An analysis of rapping indicates a number of things.

■ For instance, it is revealing that one raps *to* rather than *with* a person, supporting the impression that rapping is to be regarded more as a performance than verbal exchange. As with other performances, rapping projects the personality, physical appearance and style of the performer. In each of the examples given, the intrusive "I" of the speaker was instrumental in contributing to the total impression of the rap.

■ The combination of personality and style is usually best when "asking for some pussy." It is less when "whupping the game" on someone or "running something down."

In "asking for some pussy" for example, where personality and style might be projected through non-verbal means: stance, clothing, walking, looking, one can speak of a "silent rap." The woman is won here without the use of words, or rather, with words being implied that would generally accompany the non-verbal components.

■ As a lively way of "running it down" the verbal element consists of personality and style plus information. To someone *reading* my example of the gang member's narration, the impression might be that the information would be more influential in directing the listener's response. The youth worker might be expected to say "So that's how the gang got so big," instead of "Man, that gang member is *bad* (strong, brave)" in which instance he would be responding to the personality and style of the rapper. However, if the reader would *listen* to the gang member on tape or could have been present when the gang member spoke he more likely would have reacted more to personality and style, as my informants did.

Remember that in attendance with the youth worker were members of the gang who *already knew* how the gang got started (e.g., "Am I right Leroy? You was cribbin' over here then") and for whom the information itself would have little interest. Their attention was held by the *way* the information was presented.

■ The verbal element in "whupping the game" on someone, in the preceding example, was an integral part of an overall deception in which information and personality-style were skillfully manipulated for the purpose of controlling the "trick's" response. But again, greater weight must be given to personality-style. In the "murphy game" for example, it was this element which got the trick to trust the hustler and leave his money with him for "safekeeping."

The function of rapping in each of these forms is *expressive*. By this I mean that the speaker raps to project his personality onto the scene or to evoke a generally favorable response. When rapping is used to "ask for some pussy" or to "whup the game" on someone its function is *directive*. By this I mean that rapping becomes an instrument to manipulate and control people to get them to give up or to do something. The difference between rapping to a "fox" (pretty girl) for the purpose of "getting inside her pants" and rapping to a "lame" to get something from him is operational rather than functional. The latter rap contains a concealed motivation where the former does not.

"Shucking," "shucking it," "shucking and jiving," "S-ing" and "J-ing" or just "jiving," are terms that refer to language behavior practiced by the black when confronting "the Man" (the white man, the establishment, or *any* authority figure), and to another form of language behavior practiced by blacks with each other on the peer group level.

In the South, and later in the North, the black man learned that American society had assigned to him a restrictive role and status. Among whites his behavior had to conform to this imposed station and he was constantly reminded to "keep his place." He learned that it was not acceptable in the presence of white people to show feelings of indignation, frustration, discontent, pride, ambition, or desire; that real feelings had to be concealed behind a mask of innocence, ignorance, childishness, obedience, humility and deference. The terms used by the black to describe the role he played before white folks in the South was "tomming" or "jeffing." Failure to accommodate the white Southerner in this respect was almost certain to invite psychological and often physical brutality.

. . . . . . . . . . . . . . . . . . .

In the northern cities the black encountered authority figures equivalent to Southern "crackers": policemen, judges, probation officers, truant officers, teachers and "Mr. Charlies" (bosses), and soon learned that the way to get by and avoid difficulty was to shuck. Thus, he learned to accommodate "the Man," to use the total orchestration of speech, intonation, gesture and facial expression for the purpose of producing whatever appearance would be acceptable. It was a technique and ability that was developed from fear, a respect for power, and a will to survive. This type of accommodation is exemplified by the Uncle Tom with his "Yes sir, Mr. Charlie," or "Anything you say, Mr. Charlie."

Through accommodation, many blacks became adept at concealing and controlling their emotions and at assuming a variety of postures. They became competent actors. Many developed a keen perception of what affected, motivated, appeased or satisfied the authority figures with whom they came into contact. Shucking became an effective way for many blacks to stay out of trouble, and for others a useful artifice for avoiding arrest or getting out of trouble when apprehended. Shucking it with a judge, for example, would be to feign repentance in the hope of receiving a lighter or suspended sentence.

. . . . . . . . . . . . . . . . . . .

Some field illustrations of shucking to get out of trouble came from some seventh-grade children from an inner-city school in Chicago. The children were asked to talk their way out of a troublesome situation.

> You are cursing at this old man and your mother comes walking down the stairs. She hears you.
>
> To "talk your way out of this":
>
> "I'd tell her that I was studying a scene in school for a play."
>
> What if you were in a store stealing something and the manager caught you?
>
> "I would start stuttering. Then I would say, 'Oh, Oh, I forgot. Here the money is.' "

. . . . . . . . . . . . . . . . . . .

Another example of shucking was related to me by a colleague. A black gang member was coming down the stairway from the club room with seven guns on him and encountered some policemen and detectives coming up the same stairs. If they stopped and frisked him he and others would have been arrested. A paraphrase of his shuck follows: "Man, I gotta get away from up there. There's gonna be some trouble and I don't want no part of it." This shuck worked on the minds of the policemen. It anticipated their questions as to why he was leaving the club room, and why he would be in a hurry. He also gave *them* a reason for wanting to get up to the room fast.

It ought to be mentioned at this point that there was not uniform agreement among my informants in characterizing the above examples as shucking. One informant used shucking only in the sense in which it is used among peers, e.g., bull-shitting, and characterized the above examples as jiving or whupping game. Others however, identified the above examples as shucking, and reserved jiving and whupping game for more offensive maneuvers. In fact, one of the apparent features of shucking is that the posture of the black when acting with members of the establishment be a *defensive* one.

Frederick Douglass, in telling of how he taught himself to read, would challenge a white boy with whom he was playing, by saying that he could write as well as he. Whereupon he would write down all the letters he knew. The white boy would then write down more letters than Douglass did. In this way, Douglass eventually learned all the letters of the alphabet. Some of my informants regarded the example as whupping game. Others regarded it as shucking. The former were perhaps focusing on the maneuver rather than the language used. The latter may have felt that any maneuvers designed to learn to read were justifiably defensive. One of my informants said Douglass was "shucking *in order* to whup the game." This latter response seems to be the most revealing. Just as one can rap to whup the game on someone, so one can shuck or jive for the same purpose; that is, assume a guise or posture or perform some action in a certain way that is designed to work on someone's mind to get him to give up something.

. . . . . . . . . . . . . . . . . . . . .

An eight year old boy whupped the game on me one day this way:

> My colleague and I were sitting in a room listening to a tape. The door to the room was open and outside was a soda machine. Two boys came up in the elevator, stopped at the soda machine, and then came into the room.
>
> "Do you have a dime for two nickels?" Presumably the soda machine would not accept nickels. I took out the change in my pocket, found a dime and gave it to the boy for two nickels.
>
> After accepting the dime, he looked at the change in my hand and asked, "Can I have two cents? I need carfare to get home." I gave him the two cents.

At first I assumed the verbal component of the maneuver was the rather weak, transparently false reason for wanting the two cents. Actually, as was pointed out to me later, the maneuver began with the first question which was designed to get me to show my money. He could then ask me for something that he knew I had, making my refusal more difficult. He apparently felt that the reason need not be more than plausible because the amount he wanted was small. Were the amount larger, he would no doubt have elaborated on the verbal element of the game. The form of the verbal element could be in the direction of rapping or shucking and jiving. If he were to rap the eight-year old might say, "Man, you know a cat needs to have a little bread to keep the girls in line." Were he to shuck and jive he might make the reason for needing the money more compelling, look hungry, etc.

The function of shucking and jiving as it refers to blacks and "the Man" is designed to work on the mind and emotions of the authority figure for the purpose of getting him to feel a certain way or give up something that will be to the other's advantage.

. . . . . . . . . . . . . . . . . . . .

When the maneuvers seem to be *defensive* most of my informants regarded the language behavior as shucking. When the maneuvers were *offensive* my informants tended to regard the behavior as 'whupping the game.'

. . . . . . . . . . . . . . . . . . . .

Shucking, jiving, shucking and jiving, or S-ing and J-ing, when referring to language behavior practiced by blacks, is descriptive of the talk and gestures that are appropriate to "putting someone on" by creating a false impression. The terms seem to cover a range from simply telling a lie, to bullshitting, to subtly playing with someone's mind. An important difference between this form of shucking and that described earlier is that the same talk and gestures that are deceptive to the "the Man" are often transparent to those members of one's own group who are able practitioners at shucking themselves. As Robert Conot has pointed out, "The Negro who often fools the white officer by 'shucking it' is much less likely to be successful with another Negro. . . ." Also, S-ing and J-ing within the group has play overtones in which the person being "put on" is aware of the attempts being made and goes along with it for enjoyment or in appreciation of the style.

"Running it down" is the term used by speakers in the ghetto when it is their intention to give information, either by explanation, narrative, or giving advice. In the following literary example, Sweet Mac is "running this Edith broad down" to his friends:

> Edith is the "saved" broad who can't marry out of her religion . . . or do anything else out of her religion for that matter, especially what I wanted her to do. A bogue religion, man! So dig, for the last couple weeks I been quoting the Good Book and all that stuff to her; telling her I am now saved myself, you dig. (Woodie King, Jr., "The Game," *Liberator,* August, 1965)

The following citation from Claude Brown uses the term with the additional sense of giving advice:

> If I saw him (Claude's brother) hanging out with cats I knew were weak, who might be using drugs sooner or later, I'd run it down to him.

It seems clear that running it down has simply an informative function, that of telling somebody something that he doesn't already know.

"Gripping" is of fairly recent vintage, used by black high school students in Chicago to refer to the talk and facial expression that accompanies a *partial* loss of face or self-possession, or showing of fear. Its appearance alongside "copping a plea," which refers to a total loss of face, in which one begs one's adversary for mercy, is a significant new perception. In linking it with the street code which acclaims the ability to "look tough and inviolate, fearless, secure, 'cool,' " it suggests that even the slightest weakening of this posture will be held up to ridicule and contempt. There are always contemptuous overtones attached to the use of the term when applied to the others' behavior. One is tempted to link it with the violence and toughness required to survive on the street. The intensity of both seems to be increasing. As one of my informants noted, "Today, you're *lucky* if you end up in the hospital"—that is, are not killed.

. . . . . . . . . . . . . . . . . . . .

The function of gripping and copping a plea is obviously to induce pity or to acknowledge the presence of superior strength. In so doing, one evinces noticeable feelings of fear and insecurity which also result in a loss of status among one's peers.

Signifying is the term used to describe the language behavior that, as Abrahams has defined it, attempts to "imply, goad, beg, boast by indirect verbal or gestural means." (Roger D. Abrahams, *Deep Down in the Jungle*) In Chicago it is also used as a synonym to describe language behavior more generally known as "sounding" elsewhere.

Some excellent examples of signifying as well as of other forms of language behavior come from the well known "toast" (narrative form) "The Signifying Monkey and the Lion" which was collected by Abrahams from Negro street corner bards in Philadelphia. In the above toast the monkey is trying to get the lion involved in a fight with the elephant:

Now the lion came through the jungle one peaceful day,
When the signifying monkey stopped him, and that is what he started to say:
He said, "Mr. Lion," he said, "A bad-assed mother-fucker down your way,"
He said, "Yeah! The way he talks about your folks is a certain shame.
"I even heard him curse when he mentioned your grandmother's name."
The lion's tail shot back like a forty-four
When he went down that jungle in all uproar.

Thus the monkey has goaded the lion into a fight with the elephant by "signifying," that is, indicating that the elephant has been "sounding on" (insulting) the lion. When the lion comes back, thoroughly beaten up, the monkey again "signifies" by making fun of the lion:

. . . lion came back through the jungle more dead than alive,
When the monkey started some more of that signifying jive.
He said, "Damn, Mr. Lion, you went through here yesterday, the jungle rung.
Now you come back today, damn near hung."

The monkey, of course, is delivering this taunt from a safe distance away on the limb of a tree when his foot slips and he falls to the ground, at which point,

Like a bolt of lightning, a stripe of white heat,
The lion was on the monkey with all four feet.

In desperation the monkey quickly resorts to "copping a plea":

The monkey looked up with a tear in his eyes,
He said, "Please, Mr. Lion, I apologize."

His "plea" however, fails to move the lion to show any mercy so the monkey tries another verbal ruse, "shucking":

He said, "You lemme get my head out of the sand, ass out the grass, I'll fight you like a natural man."

In this he is more successful as,

> The lion jumped back and squared for a fight.
> The motherfucking monkey jumped clear out of sight.

A safe distance away again, the monkey returns to "signifying":

> He said, "Yeah, you had me down, you had me at last,
> But you left me free, now you can still kiss my ass."

This example illustrates the methods of provocation, goading and taunting artfully practiced by a signifier.

Interestingly, when the *function* of signifying is *directive* the *tactic* employed is *indirection,* i.e., the signifier reports or repeats what someone else has said about the listener; the "report" is couched in plausible language designed to compel belief and arouse feelings of anger and hostility. There is also the implication that if the listener fails to do anything about it—what has to be "done" is usually quite clear—his status will be seriously compromised. Thus the lion is compelled to vindicate the honor of his family by fighting or else leave the impression that he is afraid, and that he is not "king" of the jungle. When used for the purpose of directing action, "signifying" is like "shucking" in also being deceptive and subtle in approach and depending for success on the naivete or gullibility of the person being "put on."

When the function of signifying is to arouse feelings of embarrassment, shame, frustration or futility, to diminish someone's status, the tactic employed is direct in the form of a taunt, as in the example where the monkey is making fun of the lion.

Sounding is the term which is today most widely known for the game of verbal insult known in the past as "Playing the Dozens," "The Dirty Dozens" or just "The Dozens." Other curent names for the game have regional distribution: Signifying or "Sigging" (Chicago), Joning (Washington, D.C.), Screaming (Harrisburg), etc. In Chicago, the term "sounding" would be descriptive of the initial remarks which are designed to sound out the other person to see whether he will play the game. The verbal insult is also subdivided, the term "signifying" applying to insults which are hurled directly at the person and the dozens applying to results hurled at your opponent's family, especially the mother.

Sounding is often catalyzed by signifying remarks referred to earlier such as "Are you going to let him say that about your mama" to spur an exchange between members of the group. It is begun on a relatively low key and built up by verbal exchanges. The game goes like this:

> One insults a member of another's family; others in the group make disapproving sounds to spur on the coming exchange. The one who has been insulted feels at this point that he must reply with a slur on the protagonist's family which is clever enough to defend his honor, (And

therefore that of his family). This, of course, leads the other (once again, more due to pressure from the crowd than actual insult) to make further jabs. This can proceed until everyone is bored with the whole affair, until one hits the other (fairly rare), or until some other subject comes up that interrupts the proceedings (the usual state of affairs). (Roger D. Abrahams, "Playing the Dozens," *Journal of American Folklore,* July–September, 1962)

. . . . . . . . . . . . . . . . . . .

An example of the "game" collected by one of my students goes:

Frank looked up and saw Leroy enter the Outpost.

Leroy walked past the room where Quinton, "Nap," "Pretty Black," "Cunny," Richard, Haywood, "Bull" and Reese sat playing cards. As Leroy neared the T.V. room, Frank shouted to him.

Frank: "Hey Leroy, your mama—calling you man."

Leroy turned and walked toward the room where the sound came from. He stood in the door and looked at Frank.

Leroy: "Look motherfuckers, I don't play that shit."

Frank (signifying): "Man, I told you cats 'bout that mama jive" (as if he were concerned about how Leroy felt)

Leroy: "That's all right Frank; you don't have to tell these funky motherfuckers nothing; I'll fuck me up somebody yet."

Frank's face lit up as if he were ready to burst his side laughing. "Cunny" became pissed at Leroy.

"Cunny": "Leroy, you stupid bastard, you let Frank make a fool of you. He said that 'bout your mama."

"Pretty Black": "Aw, fat ass head 'Cunny' shut up."

"Cunny": "Ain't that some shit. This black slick head motor flicker got nerve 'nough to call somebody 'fathead.' Boy, you so black, you sweat Permalube Oil."

This eased the tension of the group as they burst into loud laughter.

"Pretty Black": "What 'chu laughing 'bout 'Nap,' with your funky mouth smelling like dog shit."

Even Leroy laughed at this.

"Nap" "Your mama motherfucker."

"Pretty Black": "Your funky mama too."

"Nap": (strongly) "It takes twelve barrels of water to make a steamboat run; it takes an elephant's dick to make your Grandmammy come; she been elephant fucked, camel fucked and hit side the head with your Grandpappy's nuts."

Reese: "Godorr-damn; go on and rap motherfucker."

Reese began slapping each boy in his hand, giving his positive approval of "Naps" comment. "Pretty Black" in an effort not to be outdone, but directing his verbal play elsewhere stated:

"Pretty Black": "Reese, what you laughing 'bout? You so square, you shit bricked shit."

Frank: "Whoooowee!"

Reese (sounded back): "Square huh, what about your nappy ass hair before it was stewed; that shit was so bad till, when you went to bed at night, it would leave your head and go on the corner and meddle."

The boys slapped each other in the hand and cracked up.

"Pretty Black": "On the streets meddling, bet Dinky didn't offer me no pussy and I turned it down."

Frank: "Reese scared of pussy."

"Pretty Black": "Hell yeah; the greasy mother rather fuck old ugly, funky cock Sue Willie than get a piece of ass from a decent broad."

Frank: "Godorr-damn! Not Sue Willie."

"Pretty Black": "yeah ol meat-beating Reese rather screw that cross-eyed, clapsy bitch, who when she cry, tears rip down her ass."

Haywood: "Don't be so mean, Black."

Reese: "Aw shut up, you half-white bastard."

Frank: "Wait man, Haywood ain't gonna hear much more of that half-white shit; he's a brother too."

Reese: "Brother, my black ass; that white ass landlord gotta be this motherfucker's paw."

"Cunny": "Man, you better stop foolin with Haywood; he's turning red."

Haywood: "Fuck yall. (as he withdrew from the "sig" game.)

Frank: "Yeah, fuck yall; let's go to the stick hall."

The group left enroute to the billiard hall. (James Maryland, "Signifying at the Outpost," unpublished term paper for the course *Idiom of the Negro Ghettos,* January 1967)

The above example of sounding is an excellent illustration of the "game" as played by 15–17-year-old Negro boys, some of whom have already acquired the verbal skill which for them is often the basis for having a high "rep." Ability with words is apparently as highly valued as physical strength. In the sense that the status of one of the participants in the game is diminished if he has to resort to fighting to answer a verbal attack, verbal ability may be even more highly regarded than physical ability.

The relatively high value placed on verbal ability must be clear to most black boys at early age. Most boys begin their activity in sounding by compiling a repertoire of "one liners." When the game is played the one who has the greatest number of such remarks wins. Here are some examples of "one liners" collected from fifth and sixth grade black boys in Chicago:

Yo mama is so bowlegged, she looks like the bit out of a donut.

Yo mama sent her picture to the lonely hearts club, and they sent it back and said "We ain't that lonely!"

Your family is so poor the rats and roaches eat lunch out.

Your house is so small the roaches walk single file.

I walked in your house and your family was running around the table. I said, "Why you doin that?" Your mama say, "First one drops, we eat."

Real proficiency in the game comes to only a small percentage of those who play it. These players have the special skill in being able to turn around what their opponents have said and attack them with it. Thus, when someone indifferently said "fuck you" to Concho, his retort was immediate and devastating: "Man, you haven't even kissed me yet."

The "best talkers" from this group often become the successful street-corner, barber shop, and pool hall story tellers who deliver the long, rhymed, witty, narrative stories called "toasts." They are, as Roger D. Abrahams has described, the traditional "men of words" and have become on occassion entertainers as Dick Gregory and Redd Fox, who are virtuosos at repartee, and preachers, whose verbal power has been traditionally esteemed.

The function of the "dozens" or "sounding" is to borrow status from an opponent through an exercise of verbal power. The opponent feels compelled to regain his status by "sounding" back on the speaker or other group member whom he regards as more vulnerable.

The presence of a group seems to be especially important in controlling the game. First of all, one does not "play" with just anyone since the subject matter is concerned with things that in reality one is quite sensitive about. It is precisely *because* "Pretty Black" has a "Black slick head" that makes him vulnerable to "Cunny's" barb, especially now when the Afro-American "natural" hair style is in vogue. Without the control of the group "sounding" will frequently lead to a fight. This was illustrated by a tragic epilogue concerning Haywood, when Haywood was being "sounded" on in the presence of two girls by his best friend (other members of the group were absent), he refused to tolerate it. He went home, got a rifle, came back and shot and killed his friend. In the classroom from about the fourth grade on fights among black boys invariably are caused by someone "sounding" on the other person's mother.

Significantly, the subject matter of sounding is changing with the changing self-concept of the black with regard to those physical characteristics that are characteristically "Negro," and which in the past were vulnerable points in the black psyche: blackness and "nappy" hair. It ought to be said that for many blacks, blackness was always highly esteemed and it might be more accurate to regard the present sentiment of the black community toward skin color as reflecting a shifted attitude for only a *portion* of the black community. This suggests that "sounding" on someone's light skin color is not new. Nevertheless, one can regard the previously favorable attitude toward light skin color and "good hair" as the prevailing one. "Other things being equal, the more closely a woman approached her white counterpart, the more attractive she was considered to be, by both men and women alike. "Good hair" (hair that is long and soft) and light skin were the chief criteria." (Elliot Liebow, *Tally's Corner*)

The dozens has been linked to the over-all psychosocial growth of the black male. McCormick has stated that a "single round of a dozen or so exchanges frees more pent-up aggressions than will a dose of sodium pentothal." The fact that one permits a kind of abuse within the rules of the game and within the confines of the group which would otherwise not be tolerated, is filled with psychological import. It seems also important, however, to view its function from the perspective of the non-participating members of the group. Its function for them may be to incite and prod individual members of the group to combat for the purpose of energizing the elements, of simply relieving the boredom of just "hanging around" and the malaise of living in a static and restrictive environment.

A summary analysis of the different forms of language behavior which have been discussed above permit the following generalizations:

The prestige norms which influence black speech behavior are those which have been successful in manipulating and controlling people and situations. The function of all of the forms of language behavior discussed above, with the exception of "running it down," was to project personality, assert oneself, or arouse emotion, frequently with the additional purpose of getting the person to give up or do something which will be of some benefit to the speaker. Only running it down has as its primary function to communicate information and often here too, the personality and style of the speaker in the form of rapping is projected along with the information.

The purpose for which language is used suggests that the speaker views the social situations into which he moves as consisting of a series of transactions which require that he be continually ready to take advantage of a person or situation or defend himself against being victimized. He has absorbed what Horton has called "street rationality." As one of Horton's respondents put it: "The good hustler . . . conditions his mind and must never put his guard too far down, to relax, or he'll be taken."

. . . . . . . . . . . . . . . . . . . . . . . .

In conclusion, by blending style and verbal power, through rapping, sounding and running it down, the black in the ghetto establishes his personality; through shucking, gripping and copping a plea, he shows his respect for power; through jiving and signifying he stirs up excitement. With all of the above, he hopes to manipulate and control people and situations to give himself a winning edge.

## *Further reading suggested by the author*

*Deep Down in the Jungle* by Roger D. Abrahams (Hatboro, Pa.: Folklore Associates, 1964) is a collection and analysis of black narrative folklore from the streets of Philadelphia.

*Urban Blues* by Charles Keil (Chicago: University of Chicago Press, 1966) is an analysis of the contemporary blues man as an "expressive male role within urban lower-class Negro culture."

*Pimp, the Story of My Life* by Iceberg Slim (Los Angeles: Holloway House, 1967) is a revealing insight into lower class life-styles.

## *QUESTIONS FOR DISCUSSION*

1. George Herbert Mead's thoughts concerning "self-concept" seem pertinent to the effecting of transracial communication. Discuss the relationship between one's self-concept and open-mindedness in this context.
2. Provide some specific examples of the role of nonverbal language in effective and ineffective transracial communication.
3. Discuss and analyze a transracial communication event on campus or in the community in terms of the four categories discussed: (1) common codification; (2) sender-receiver proximity; (3) viewpoint; and (4) general communication skills.
4. Chapter 9 contains a discussion of the measurement of the effects of communication. Are there any particular problems or difficulties in determining the effectiveness of communication in transracial situations?
5. What are some problems that communicators may have in analyzing an audience of a different race? Does the author suggest any ways to solve these problems?
6. Do you think it is possible to teach the "masses" principles of effective transracial communication? If so, what are some methods that could be used to effect such a goal?
7. We often hear militant Black Power advocates on national television making statements about violence, Black separatism, and so on. In light of what has been discussed, how might members of different racial groups throughout the country react to these statements? In what ways might the author's suggestions concerning transracial communication change their reactions?

*chapter* **8**

# MEASURING COMMUNICATION EFFECTS

## SECTION ONE: OVERVIEW AND PERSPECTIVE

### *Objectives for Section One*

After reading this selection you should be able to:

1. State in writing a definition of communication effects and distinguish between intentional and unintentional outcomes of communication.
2. Write two definitions of measurement and state the major distinction between them.
3. Distinguish in writing between observable and nonobservable phenomena and identify the problem involved in measuring nonobservable phenomena.
4. Define in writing validity and reliability, and state why these concepts are important in measurement.
5. Define in writing correlation and explain negative, positive, and zero correlations.
6. Describe in writing one technique for using the concept of correlation in determining an instrument's reliability.
7. State in writing three reasons why measurement is important to communication.
8. Define in writing three domains of human behavior and describe how measurement is used to assess communication effects in each.
9. Name and describe in writing, for each domain of human behavior, two methods for measuring communication effects in everyday situations.

*Donald J. Cegala*

# MEASURING COMMUNICATION EFFECTS

## *Communication Effects*

In preceeding chapters it has been suggested that communication of various sorts influences the way man behaves. Communication can modify values and attitudes, impart knowledge, cause or end wars, entertain audiences, and influence countless other events in our environment. This scope of events or results influenced by communication is referred to as the *effect of communication.*

## *Intentional and Unintentional Communication*

It is important to realize that any given communication may produce several effects. We can broadly classify communication effects into two categories: (1) *intentional effects;* and (2) *unintentional effects.* (See Chapter 2 for some additional discussions of this topic.)

Donald J. Cegala *is a Ph.D. candidate in the Department of Communication at Florida State University. He received his undergraduate training in Rhetoric and Public Address at the University of Wisconsin, at Madison, and his M.A. in Communication Theory and Research at Purdue University. Mr. Cegala has conducted experimental research in the theory and measurement of attitudes, and has co-authored scholarly journal articles and convention papers on such topics as the use of behavioral objectives in speech education, the development of a measure of ego-involvement, and the use of hypnosis in communication research. He is a member of the Speech Communication Association, the International Communication Association, the American Educational Research Association, and several regional speech associations.*

As the term implies, *intentional effects* refer to those results of communication which are anticipated or expected. The protest leader speaking on campus, for example, expects certain events to result from his communication—perhaps a student strike or a change in his listeners' attitudes toward a particular issue. These anticipated outcomes of communication are generally well planned, and are directly related to the intended purpose of the communicator.

Often, however, communication affects listeners even when we do not expect any particular result. Or, the effect produced may not be the one we intended. Such outcomes of communication are said to be *unintentional effects.* They are not planned or anticipated by the communicator, and are often undetected.

Although unintentional effects can be produced by verbal communication, we often think of them as being related to nonverbal messages. One's appearance, for example, often has meaning for others. "Mod" clothes, long hair, beards, and love beads communicate rather precise meanings in our society today. To some individuals, particularly the young, these symbols communicate a sense of unity, or even brotherhood. They announce membership in a group which has been appropriately called the "now generation." The speaker addressing a young audience, perhaps more often than not, intends to be identified as a member of this group and deliberately conveys the unsaid message. But what about the variety of possible unintentional meanings these symbols communicate—such as "hippie," student protestor, trouble maker, and even communist—to other members of our society? Unintentional messages of this sort, particularly if they go undetected by the communicator, can have disastrous effects on a speaker's message. For this reason, and others which will be discussed in this chapter, we require some method for *measuring the effectiveness of communication.*

## *Measurement*

Throughout this chapter, "measurement" is discussed in two senses. The major focus is on measurement in carefully controlled experimental situations. To most people, measurement, in this sense, is *a procedure in which numerals are assigned to objects and events according to rules for the purpose of determining the amount of something.* The second way in which measurement is discussed is in relationship to its use in uncontrolled, everyday situations. We might define measurement of this type as a *systematic method for detecting and interpreting information about a particular object, event, or phenomenon.*

The basic distinction between these two types of measurement is the manner in which information is gathered and interpreted, and the degree of precision employed. Measurement in controlled experimental situations involves the employment of some type of instrument (e.g., a test) to collect data which we can subsequently analyze and interpret.[1] There are, however, many "real-life" communication situations in which there is no opportunity to collect data with a measuring instrument. Suppose, for example, you are describing the plot of a movie to your roommate. It would be very impractical, if not presumptuous, for you to administer a comprehension test to your roommate to determine how effectively you had communicated your ideas. Yet, presumably you would like to know if you had succeeded. The assessment of the effects of communication in such situations obviously requires a different type of measurement. Measurement, in this sense, involves the systematic assessment and interpretation of verbal and nonverbal "feedback." Alternative methods for measuring the effectiveness of communication will be discussed later on in the chapter; at the moment we will consider some general problems concerning measurement in speech communication.

## *Problems of Measurement*

There are inherent problems involved in the measurement of speech communication, regardless of the way "measurement" is defined. These problems are due primarily to the nature of the phenomena through which we usually attempt to measure communication—e.g., attitudes, comprehension of information. If we want to determine the length of a room, for example, we can easily do so with some standard unit of measurement such as a yardstick. The measurement of attitudes is not this easy. Although the statements "The mean audience attitude toward marijuana is 4.5" and "This room is 10 yards long" appear to be similar, they are in some respects quite different. Measuring a room with a yardstick is a straightforward procedure; the measuring of attitudes is confounded by the fact that an attitude is a nonobservable phenomenon. One can observe, and directly sense, the length of an object, but no one has ever seen or touched an attitude. Obviously, it is much more difficult to arrive at a precise unit of measurement for nonobservable phenomena than for observable phenomena.

Since we cannot measure nonobservable phenomena directly, we are forced to rely on other methods for making accurate inferences about their quantity and quality. One technique is the use of measuring instruments

[1]In Chapter 6, several electronic measuring instruments that can be used to collect data are discussed. In this chapter, "measuring instruments" refers to paper-and-pencil tests.

(paper-and-pencil tests) in controlled experimental situations. Another is the systematic detection and interpretation of verbal and nonverbal feedback in everyday situations. *Both these methods, however, depend upon the accuracy with which the key factors of a particular phenomenon are identified, assessed, and interpreted.* Suppose you are trying to measure the intelligence of a group of individuals. You could employ any one of several alternative procedures for accomplishing this goal. You might, for example, administer an intelligence test to the group. You might observe the individuals' behavior in various situations and contexts and make inferences about the amount of intelligence they possess. In order to allow you to make accurate inferences, your method of measurement has to permit you to assess those factors or qualities which are related to mental ability. A standard intelligence test, for example, is composed of several subtests, each designed to measure some factor thought to be critical in assessing mental ability (reasoning ability, vocabulary, and so on). However, since we cannot directly observe something called "intelligence," we cannot be sure that the various mental capabilities measured by an intelligence test represent all the important capabilities which *in fact* are related to mental ability. This leads us to the problem of validity.

VALIDITY. The problem of validity is somewhat analogous to the relationship between a map of a territory and the actual land it is supposed to represent. When a map accurately corresponds to the land we say that it is a valid representation of the land. By "valid," we mean that the parts of the map (lakes, mountains, roads, and so on) represent the parts of the land accurately enough so that one can use the map to discuss the land and make inferences about it. Obviously, if a map showed lakes and mountains where there were in fact no lakes and mountains, it would be a useless and inaccurate representation of the land. Similarly, in order for a measuring procedure to be useful it must allow us to identify, assess, and interpret the actual factors of the phenomenon being measured. When a measuring procedure meets this requirement, we say that it possesses *validity*. The validity of a measuring procedure, then, essentially involves the question: Does this procedure really measure what it is intended to measure?

Unless this question is answered, we cannot expect to draw any accurate inferences about the phenomenon being measured; consequently, validity is an extremely important concept in measurement, particularly when we are attempting to measure nonobservable phenomena such as information gain, IQ, attitudes, and so on.[2]

[2]A case in point is the use of intelligence tests to measure the intelligence of minority groups. Performance on these tests depends greatly on an individual's skill with middle-class, white, American English. Unsurprisingly, Black children from ghettos sometimes have lower IQ scores than middle-class, white children.

At this point in your experience with measurement it is not important that you know the methods and techniques used to establish the validity of a measuring procedure, which involve moderately sophisticated statistics and measurement theory. It is important, however, that you be aware of the *necessity* that a measuring procedure be valid. Various kinds of measuring devices that have been used in assessing communication effects will be discussed later on in the chapter, but first we shall turn our attention to another aspect of measurement very closely related to the concept of validity.

RELIABILITY. In addition to being concerned about validity, students of speech communication should also be concerned about a measuring procedure's reliability. Reliability involves the question: How *consistently* does a procedure measure what it is intended to measure? In other words, when we speak of *reliability* we are concerned with the dependability with which a phenomenon can be measured by a particular procedure. We would expect a yardstick to consistently measure the same number of yards in a given room, regardless of how many times the room was measured. One would find little use for a yardstick which measured a different number of yards each time the same room was measured. Likewise, a test of comprehension which shows an individual's comprehension to be 98 per cent on one occasion and 25 per cent the same afternoon would not be a very reliable indicator of that individual's knowledge. Surely no student would want such a test to be used to determine his final grade!

CORRELATION. The degree of consistency associated with a given measurement procedure can be represented by a statistic known as a coefficient of correlation Since a number of the articles that follow talk about correlation, it may be beneficial to discuss the concept briefly.

Correlation has to do with covariation. Coefficients of correlation indicate the degree of relationship between two sets of numbers. They range from +1, through 0, to −1. A coefficient of +1 indicates a perfect *positive (or direct)* correlation, whereas a coefficient of −1 indicates a perfect *negative (or inverse)* correlation.[3] A coefficient of correlation of 0

---

Nor is the problem of language the only one. There is reason to believe that standard intelligence tests may not test the wide variety of abilities which possibly compose the mental ability of a child who lives in a ghetto environment. It is possible that his mental ability is more accurately measured by the extent to which he survives in his adverse environment, than by his reading ability, vocabulary, or mathematical skills.

[3]We very seldom find two characteristics in the real world that are perfectly correlated. Therefore, the coefficients of correlation usually encountered are less than 1. However, the closer a correlation coefficient gets to +1 or −1, the greater the degree of relationship between the characteristics. For example,

(or near 0) represents little or no correlation. These concepts can perhaps be seen more clearly by the graphs in Figure 1.

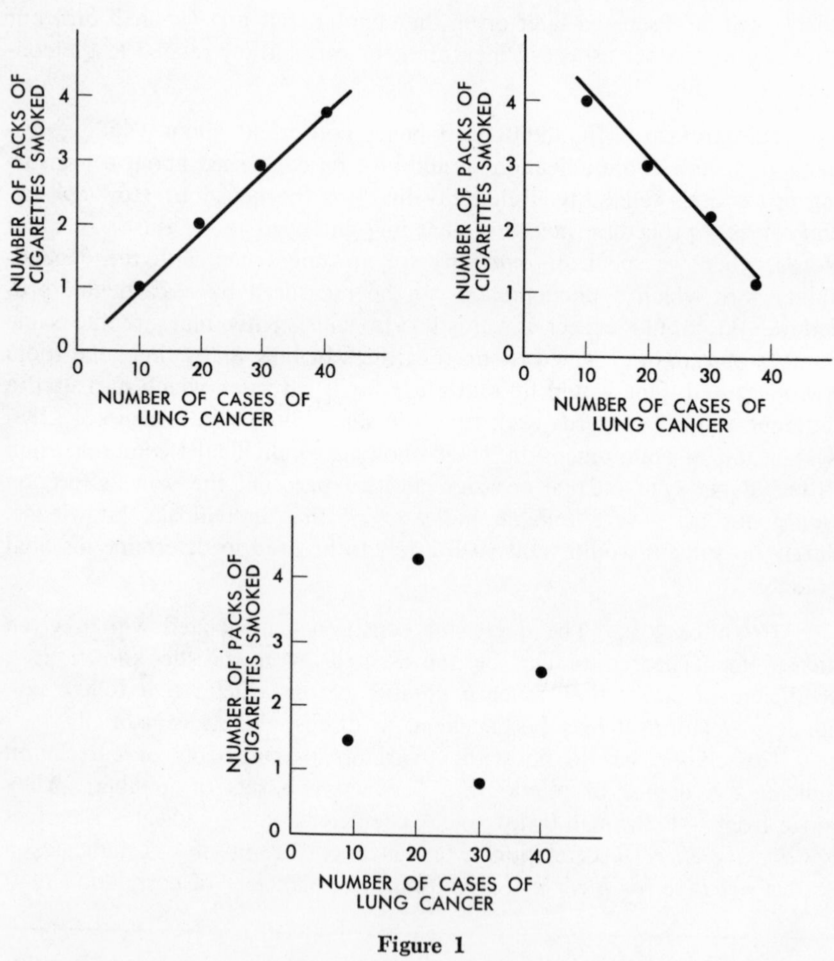


**Figure 1**

---

a correlation of −.95 indicates a higher degree of relationship than a correlation of +.80. Likewise, a correlation of +.45 indicates a higher degree of relationship than a correlation coefficient of −.15. Note that the *degree* of the relationship is indicated by the *magnitude* of the correlation coefficient and not by the sign (plus or minus) of the coefficient. The *sign* of a coefficient tells us the *direction* of the relationship, which is also very important. For example, though the correlations in graphs *a* and *b* in Figure 1 have the same magnitude, their signs imply very different things to a heavy smoker!

The graphs in Figure 1 illustrate the relationship or correlation between numbers representing two phenomena (i.e., number of packs of cigarettes smoked and number of cases of lung cancer). However, when correlation techniques are used to determine the reliability of a measuring procedure, numbers representing a *single phenomenon on different occasions* are correlated. For example, one technique that could be used to determine the reliability of a speech rating scale would be to have a number of competent raters evaluate the same speeches on two different occasions. The scores produced by the raters on the first occasion could then be correlated (using statistical procedures) with the scores produced by the same raters on the second occasion. The resulting coefficient of correlation would be an indication of the consistency, or reliability, with which raters can evaluate a speech using a particular rating scale.[4] See the study by Kibler, Barker and Enoch (1967) in the references for an example of this procedure.

It should be clear by now that both reliability and validity are important concepts in measurement. Before we can draw accurate inferences about the information obtained from a measuring procedure, we must be sure that it accurately assesses the actual factors of the phenomenon we are interested in measuring (validity) and that our measuring procedure can produce this assessment with reasonable consistency (reliability).

## *Why Measurement in Communication?*

We have so far discussed communication effects and measurement, but we have failed to consider why measurement of communication effects is important. There are at least three reasons why students of communication are interested in the measurement of communication effects.

First, measurement is important for theoretical reasons: it allows communication researchers and practitioners to determine what parts of the communication event most influence the results. For example, considerable research concerning a speaker's credibility (e.g., the speaker's competency and trustworthiness) indicates that under certain conditions highly credible speakers are more persuasive than less credible ones (Anderson and Clevenger, 1963). If we know what parts of the communication event most influence the results, we can give our attention to those parts and increase the probability of being successful communicators.

A second reason for being concerned with the measurement of communication effects is related to the concept of purpose in communication. Recall the distinction made earlier between intentional and unintentional

[4]There are other statistical methods of correlation that only require measurements to be taken on *one* occasion. The interested reader is referred to Guilford (1954).

communication effects. It was indicated that, often times, the intended effects of communication are altered by unintentional messages that are also communicated. Several agencies (e.g., the Nielson Company) serve people who are very concerned about the relationship between the purpose of their communications (e.g., influencing listeners to purchase certain products or to vote for a particular political candidate) and the actual effects produced. If we have no way of assessing the fidelity between our purpose and the actual results of our communication, we cannot determine if we have been a successful communicator.

Once communication effects have been measured, the results may suggest that a modification of communication strategies is needed. This is the third reason for the interest in measurement. The measured consequences of a given message influence plans or strategies to make future communication more effective. An advertiser may discover that his TV advertisements need more color and imagination, or a white political candidate may realize that his middle-class American image is not helping him to get votes in the ghetto.

The measurement of communication effects, then, is important for both theoretical and practical concerns. The ideal relationship between the objectives or purposes of communication and the actual results produced are diagramed in Figure 2.

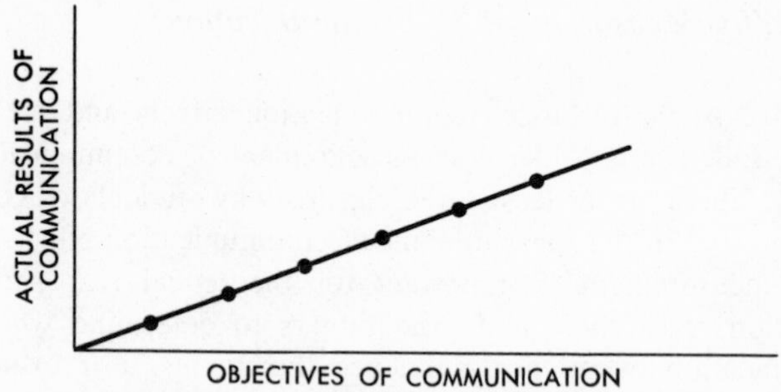


**Figure 2**

Figure 2 depicts the relationship (or correlation) between the objectives of communication and the actual results. Ideally there should be a one-to-one relationship (a perfect correlation) between the objectives of a given communication and the actual effects it produces. This is not the case in the real world. A more accurate picture of the true relationship appears in Figure 3. As Figure 3 suggests, results are sometimes in harmony with our communication objectives (points 1 and 2). But most of the time the two are somewhere between very incongruous (points 3 and 4) or very closely related (points 5 and 6).

We are concerned about measuring communication effects so we can better determine when there is harmony between objectives and results and when there is incongruity. In addition to this knowledge, the measurement of communication effects helps us to determine *why* there was an incongruity or harmony between communication results and objectives, which in turn guides us in future communication strategies.

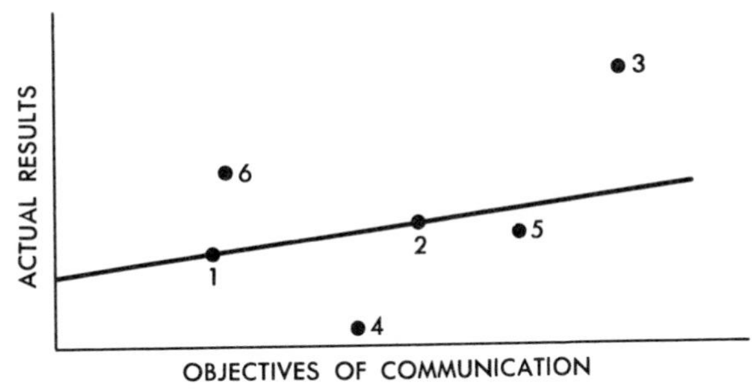


**Figure 3**

## *Uses of Measurement in Communication*

The possible results of communication include an infinite variety of human behavior. For example, we could probably never accurately determine all the effects (both intentional and unintentional) of ex-President Johnson's speech of March, 1968, in which he announced to the nation that he would not seek renomination. At best, we could only speculate about the message's impact on the audience's voting behavior, attitudes, feelings, and so on. This is perhaps the main reason why students of communication have been primarily interested in the intentional effects of messages. It is less difficult to determine if a message produced the intended effects than to determine all its possible effects.

For purposes of clarity we will discuss how measurement is used in communication with respect to three broad classes of human behavior. The first class of behavior lies in what is called the *cognitive domain.* The cognitive domain includes behavior relevant to mental processes such as thinking, reasoning, learning, and so on. The second class of behavior is that included in the *affective domain.* The affective domain also is concerned primarily with mental processes, but of a different kind. We might say that the affective domain includes mental behavior which is "emotional" in nature, e.g., values, attitudes, and aesthetic judgments. Both the cognitive and affective domains include behavior which is not directly observable, since it is mental. The third class of behavior, however, is directly observable. This is in the *psychomotor domain.* Any behavior which is directly observable—such as running, walking, writing, and so on—is classified in this domain.

### *The Cognitive Domain*

The measurement of the effects of communication in the cognitive domain is typically measurement of the effect of messages designed to inform listeners.

Considerable research in speech communication has attempted to determine the most effective means of communicating information (Petrie, 1963). Over all, these research efforts have produced a number of principles which communicators may use to maximize their efficiency. A few of these principles are listed below according to the aspect of communication to which they are related:

I. The Message
   - A. Information contained in organized informative messages is comprehended more readily than information contained in disorganized informative messages.[5]
   - B. The emphasis and repetition of major ideas increases the amount of information transmitted to listeners.
   - C. Stylistic devices, such as the use of imagery, concrete and specific words, personal pronouns, rhetorical questions, and comparison and contrast, make a message more instantly intelligible.
   - D. Well-developed major ideas are comprehended and retained more readily than details and specifics.

II. The Speaker
   - A. The use of visible action (gestures and visual aids) increases the amount of information comprehended by listeners.
   - B. Poor eye contact may affect the amount of information obtained by receivers.

III. The Listener
   - A. Males generally retain more information than females.
   - B. Intelligent listeners generally retain more information than less intelligent listeners.
   - C. Listeners of well-developed verbal ability generally retain more information than listeners with less verbal ability.
   - D. The listener's motivation is an important factor in his obtaining information.
   - E. The listener's attitudes and predispositions may affect the manner in which he receives and interprets information.

[5]Note that this principle does not apply to persuasive messages. See Chapter 5.

Students who are familiar with these and other principles of effective informative speaking can utilize them to increase the probability of successfully communicating information to others. You should realize, however, that these principles are not generalizable to all communication situations under all possible conditions. At best, they can only provide guidelines for us to follow when we are communicating information to others. A white person, for example, speaking in a Black ghetto may follow all the suggested principles of informative speaking and still not effectively communicate his ideas to listeners because of other factors which influence the speaker-audience relationship. On the other hand, Rap Brown could perhaps violate all the traditionally accepted principles and still effectively communicate to certain Black audiences.

Ideally, communicators should assess the effectiveness of their communication in every situation. If the opportunity exists, the most desirable method for determining the effectiveness of informative communication is through the use of some measuring instrument such as a paper-and-pencil test of comprehension. Data collected in this manner can be subsequently analyzed and interpreted to determine if the intended communication effects were achieved. Analysis of this kind may also help to determine if any unintentional communication has either helped or hindered anticipated outcomes. We have already discussed the fact, however, that many situations do not allow the communicator to employ measuring instruments. Unfortunately, it still may be desirable or even necessary to assess the effectiveness of communication in such situations.

The methods for assessing the effects of communication in everyday situations are usually not as precise or conclusive as paper-and-pencil tests. One of the readings following this article (Kerlinger's) is a discussion of some of the problems involved with unstructured methods of measurement. Nevertheless, the information obtained with unstructured measurement procedures is certainly better than no information at all, and can prove useful to communicators.

One might, for example, interview a sample of listeners in order to determine the effectiveness of a given informative message. Such an interview could be designed to reveal if listeners acquired the information intended to be conveyed in the message in addition to supplying data about possible unintentional communication. Although this procedure is not as precise as administering a comprehension test to all the listeners, it would provide some indication of the effectiveness of the communication.

An even simpler, but perhaps less valid, method is to interpret nonverbal feedback cues from listeners. Many people, for example, frown or become noticeably inattentive when they do not understand a message. If you have unsuccessfully tried to explain a complex idea to someone, you have probably experienced this sort of feedback. Cues of this nature, if they are detected, can provide a communicator with reasonably accurate information about the effectiveness of his communication, particularly unintentional communication. This method, however, is perhaps best used in small groups, where the communicator can easily stop talking and ask his listeners where points of his communication need clarification.

At this point you have probably thought of one or two alternative methods for assessing the effectiveness of informative communication. If not, you should take the time to do so and list as many alternative methods as you can. Keep in mind the second definition of measurement discussed earlier: *a systematic method for detecting and interpreting information about a particular object, event, or phenomenon.* The key to a successful and useful method of measurement in this sense lies in the term "systematic." A haphazard and completely untested method of measurement will lead only to invalid and unreliable data. One should not forget that even unstructured methods of measurement have to be reasonably valid and reliable, or inferences based on them will be inaccurate and useless.

### *The Affective Domain*

Although there is a wide range of behavior included in the affective domain, students of communication typically have focused their measurement on two areas: (1) attitudes; and (2) judgments of the effectiveness of speeches.

Just as there is measurement of the effectiveness of informative messages, there is measurement of the effectiveness of persuasive messages. Measurement has played a great part in aiding researchers to determine the ways in which persuasive communication is most effective. Considerable research in speech communication and related fields has focused on determining what factors effect attitudinal change in receivers of communication. Since these principles have already been enumerated and discussed in Chapter 5, space will not again be devoted to this topic. However, the reader is encouraged to reread pages 226 to 275 in light of what has been said about measurement in this chapter.

The principles derived from research on attitudes, however, can only provide guidelines for the student of communication. An accurate assessment of the effects of communication requires, in most cases, a systematic investigation by the communicator. In some situations it can be accomplished by collecting data with any one of several instruments designed to measure attitudes (Shaw and Wright, 1967).

Many times, however, the communicator must rely on other methods for assessing the effectiveness of his communication. One method, for example, might be to assess nonverbal feedback cues from listeners' facial expressions. There is evidence which suggests that facial expressions often reveal the attitudes and emotions of listeners (Davitz, 1964).

Research on kinesics has also indicated that it is possible to systematically record and interpret the bodily movements of listeners (Birdwhistell, 1956, 1964). Other studies suggest that certain speech patterns of individuals can be used to detect their internal states (Mehrabian, 1966; Mahl, 1959). Although accurate detection and interpretation of facial expressions, bodily movements, and other verbal and nonverbal cues require practice and training, the systematic employment of measuring procedures of this type can provide a communicator with valuable information about the effects of communication. Other equally valuable methods are interviewing and the observation of individual's behavior in real-life contexts. Webb et al. (1966) describe a number of fascinating methods for assessing the effectiveness of communication. Before attempting to employ such procedures, however, the student is encouraged to read the Kerlinger article following this essay, to familiarize himself with the problems of this approach to measurement.

The second major focus of measurement in the affective domain has been on speech rating scales. Speech rating scales have been used in experimental research in much the same way as measures of comprehension and attitudes. A major use of rating scales has been to determine how the parts of the communication process affect the way messages are received and interpreted by listeners. Ash (1966), for example, found that over-all ratings of speech effectiveness correlated highest with the speaker's ability to cover his subject matter, hold the audience's attention, and make his subject worthwhile to his audience. Studies like Ash's have aided speech instructors to help their students improve the effectiveness of their speaking.

Perhaps the widest use of speech rating scales, however, is evaluation in the classroom. Most speech-communication instructors use some type of rating scale to measure the effectiveness of classroom speaking. The formats of speech rating scales vary quite widely, however, particularly the criteria used to judge the effectiveness of a message. Becker (1962) reports some interesting research findings which suggest that speech raters fail to discriminate among several standard criteria included on rating scales. Raters were asked to judge speeches on the basis of 11 separate criteria. Becker then analyzed the raters' judgments and found that several criteria could be grouped together, thus reducing the *actual* criteria that the raters used from 11 to only 3: (1) content analysis; (2) delivery; and (3) language.[6] A similar study by Price (1964) found that 35 separate criteria could be reduced to 6. These results suggest that very complex

[6]This was done mathematically by a statistical method called factor analysis.

rating forms which include several criteria may not be as valid as has been assumed. The rationale for including a criterion on a rating form is that it identifies an important and separate factor of speech effectiveness. Apparently the validity of some of these assumptions, and hence the validity of multi-criteria rating scales, is somewhat questionable.

Also concerned with the validity of rating scales was a study done by Barker, Kibler, and Geter (1968). They investigated the relationship between individuals' ratings of informative speeches and their comprehension of the information contained in the messages rated. Valid ratings of informative speeches should reflect the degree to which a speaker communicates information to listeners, since this is the primary intentional effect of informative messages. Ironically, the results indicated that there was a negligible correlation between ratings of speech effectiveness and the raters' comprehension of information in the messages.

Perhaps the strongest argument in favor of speech rating scales is that they usually have fairly high coefficients of reliability (.60 to .80). A considerable amount of research concerning rating scales, however, indicates that the higher coefficients are obtained when approximately 20 or more raters are used (Thompson, 1946; Clevenger, 1962; Tracey, 1965; Marine, 1965). Other researchers have demonstrated that students' ratings of speeches correlate very positively with instructors' ratings, if the students are provided with specific criteria by which to judge the speeches. These findings have definite usefulness in the classroom, particularly in relation to peer-group evaluation (Barker and Wiseman, 1966).

The results of several experimental studies of speech rating scales suggest a number of principles that might be employed in communication situations where rating scales are used. Some of these principles are listed below:

IV. The Speakers
- A. The order in which individuals speak and the lapse of time between individual speakers may affect the rating given to a speaker.
- B. If a speaker has consistently received high ratings, judges will tend to rate him high on subsequent speeches.

V. The Raters
- A. Generally, the greater the number of raters, the higher the reliability of the ratings.
- B. Various characteristics of raters, such as sex and rigidity, may affect their judgments.
- C. Raters' biases toward the subject matter of a speech may affect their ratings.
- D. Students' ratings of speeches are generally very positively correlated with instructors' ratings.
- E. Training of raters increases the reliability of their judgments.

F. If raters know or like a speaker, their judgments tend to be more favorable.

VI. The Rating Scale

A. Rating scales with relatively few criteria (3 to 6) are just as useful and perhaps more valid than rating scales with many criteria.

B. The validity of a speech rating scale is almost always open to criticism.

Since many speech-communication instructors employ rating scales in evaluating their students' performance, it behooves students to become familiar with the findings about rating scales. Students, for example, might evaluate an instructor's rating scale in terms of the principles concerning reliability and validity. If such an evaluation should prove the rating scale to be a questionable measure of speech performance, the instructor could probably be persuaded to make the necessary adjustments in the rating scale or in classroom procedures.

## *The Psychomotor Domain*

Although psychomotor behavior related to the effects of communication is generally of the greatest interest to speech-communication researchers, it is, ironically, the least often measured in experimental situations. The reason for this is partly the difficulty of designing experiments which allow researchers to accurately observe overt behavioral change as a result of communication. Suppose, for example, that a researcher is interested in determining the effects of a message on racially prejudiced behavior. It is impossible for the researcher to observe his subjects in various situations (at home, school, work, on vacation) to see if their behavior toward Blacks, for example, has changed as a result of a message. However, these behavioral changes are precisely the results we are most often interested in assessing. Typically, we have tried to overcome the problem by measuring behavior in the cognitive and affective domains and using this information to make inferences about overt behavior. For example, we measure behavior in the cognitive domain with instruments like achievement tests, and then we use the results to make predictions about performance. Similarly, we measure attitudes in the affective domain and base inferences about behavior on those attitudes.

The difficulty in this procedure is that there is usually not a one-to-one relationship between behavior in one domain and behavior in another. The Barker, Kibler, Geter (1968) study, for example, indicated that ratings of informative speeches did not correlate with the raters' comprehension of the messages they evaluated. This phenomenon is illustrated again in the research using college grades to predict adult accomplishment. For example, several researchers have found that grades in medical school are not predictive of physicians' performance after the first few years of practice. Similar relationships have been found in using college grades to predict success in business and teaching (Hoyt, 1965).

There are comparable findings about measurement in the affective domain. Some research attempting to relate attitudinal and behavioral change has indicated that a person does not always behave in accordance with his stated attitudes (Festinger, 1964; Greenwald, 1965; Leventhal, Singer, and Jonas, 1965; Leventhal, Jonas and Trembly, 1966).

Since speech-communication students are often ultimately interested in overt behavioral responses as a result of communication, the researcher is presented with a dilemma. One answer to this dilemma appears to lie in the use of empirically validated measuring devices which can be used to predict behavior with a reasonable degree of accuracy. Although Becker (1968, 1969) and Miller (1967), among other scholars, have proposed a number of methods for increasing the accuracy of measurement in speech-communication, more research is needed to develop precise methods for predicting complex changes in human behavior.

Since little experimental research in speech communication has attempted to measure behavior in the psychomotor domain, there exist no principles to guide students in preparing messages designed to effect psychomotor behavior. However, behavior in the psychomotor domain is often more amenable to the everyday type of measurement than is behavior in either the affective or cognitive domains. Moreover, despite the problems inherent in drawing inferences about behavior in one domain from measurement of behavior in another, we may in many instances draw such inferences if our measuring procedure is valid and reliable. Since observable behavior is often the most important desired effect of communication, and in some instances is more easily measured in everyday situations, measurement of behavior in the psychomotor domain is perhaps the most useful to students in assessing the effects of communication.

We have already discussed some alternative methods for measuring observable behavior so as to make inferences about behavior in the cognitive and affective domains. However, one needn't limit measurement in the psychomotor domain to only this purpose. It is quite feasible, and in some instances most desirable, to rely *only* on observable behavior as evidence of the effectiveness of communication. For example, the president of a student organization interested in assessing the effectiveness of a campus-wide drive to gain support and membership among the students may gather his data in several ways. One might be to circulate a questionnaire designed to measure the amount of information students possessed about the organization's functions and duties. Another might be to measure students' attitudes about the organization and its importance to the university or college. A third alternative could involve a systematic observation of students' behavior—attendance at meetings, membership and degree of activity and participation in the organization, and the degree of generally active support of students in and out of the organization. Although we cannot say which procedure would best measure the effects of communication, in all probability the most important behavioral change to secure is in the psychomotor domain. This is not to say that data about students' attitudes and knowledge are unimportant, but only that measurement of actual behavior is probably a more valid and useful assessment of the effects of communication.

In the final analysis, the method measuring the effects of communication rests on the particular communication situation and the type of information desired. If very specific information is required, and if the opportunity exists, one should rely on paper-and-pencil tests or controlled observation to collect data. If, on the other hand, conditions do not permit, other methods for collecting and interpreting data must be employed. We have suggested a few of these alternative methods; however, the student is encouraged to use his imagination and creativity to devise appropriate methods for making the assessments he needs. The concepts of validity and reliability are of crucial importance, regardless of the method of measurement selected. Remember, inferences and conclusions drawn from data are only as accurate as the methods used to collect the data.

## *REFERENCES*

Anderson, K., & Clevenger, T. A summary of experimental research in ethos. *Speech Monographs*, 1963, 30, 59–78.

Ash, P. A note on the judgment of speaker effectiveness. *Journal of Applied Psychology*, 1966, 50, 204–205.

Barker, L. L., & Wiseman, G. Peer group instruction: What is it? *Speech Teacher*, 1966, 15, 220–223.

Barker, L. L., Kibler, R. J., & Geter, R. W. Two investigations of the relationship among selected ratings of speech effectiveness and comprehension. *Speech Monographs*, 1968, 35, 400–406.

Becker, S. L. The rating of speeches: Scale independence. *Speech Monographs,* 1962, 29, 38–44.

Becker, S. L., Toward an appropriate theory for contemporary speech-communication. In *What Rhetoric (Communication Theory) Is Appropriate For Contemporary Speech Communication?* D. H. Smith (Ed.), Minneapolis, Minnesota: University of Minnesota Press, 1969, Pp. 9–25.

________ New approaches to audience analysis. *In Perspectives On Communication*, C. E. Larson and F. E. X. Dance (Eds.), Milwaukee, Wis.: University of Wisconsin Press, 1968, Pp. 61–77.

Birdwhistell, R. L. *Introduction to kinesics.* Louisville: University of Kentucky Press, 1956.

———— Body behavior and communication. *International Encyclopedia of the Social Sciences.* New York: The Macmillan Company and The Free Press, 1964, pp. 379–84.

Clevenger, T. Retest reliability of judgments of general effectiveness in public speaking. *Western Speech*, 1962, 26, 216–222.

Davitz, J. R. *The communication of emotional meaning.* New York: McGraw-Hill Book Company, 1964.

Festinger, L. Behavioral support for opinion change. *Public Opinion Quarterly*, 1964, 28, 404–417.

Greenwald, A. G. Behavior change following a persuasive communication. *Journal of Personality*, 1965, 30, 370–391.

Guilford, J. *Psychometric methods.* New York: McGraw-Hill Book Company, 1954.

Hoyt, D. P. *The relationship between college grades and adult achievement.* Iowa City, Iowa: American College Testing Program, 1965.

Kibler, R. J., Barker, L. L., and Enoch, R. H. The development and preliminary assessment of a set of video-taped informative speech models. *Central States Speech Journal*, 1967, 4, 268–275.

Leventhal, H., Singer R., & Jonas, S. Effects of fear specificity of recommendations upon attitudes and behavior. *Journal of Personality and Social Psychology*, 1965, 2, 20–29.

Leventhal, H., Jonas, S., & Trembly, G. Sex differences in attitude and behavior change under conditions of fear and specific instructions. *Journal of Experimental Social Psychology*, 1966, 2, 387–399.

Mahl, G. F. Measuring the patient's anxiety during interviews from "expressive" aspects of his speech. *Transactions of the New York Academy of Science*, 1959, 21, 249–257.

Marine, D. R. An investigation of intra-speaker reliability. *Speech Teacher*, 1965, 14, 128–131.

Mehrabian, A. Immediacy: An indicator of attitudes in linguistic communication. *Journal of Personality*, 1966, 34, 26–34.

Miller, G. R. A crucial problem in attitude research. *Quarterly Journal of Speech*, 1967, 53, 235–240.

Petrie, C. Informative speaking: A summary and bibliography of related research. *Speech Monographs*, 1963, 30, 79–91.

Price, W. K. The University of Wisconsin Speech attainment test. (Doctoral dissertation, University of Wisconsin) Ann Arbor, Mich.: University MicroFilms, 1964, No. 64-13, p. 915.

Shaw, M. E., & Wright, J. M. *Scales for the measurement of attitudes.* New York: McGraw-Hill Book Company, 1967.

Thompson, W. N. A study of the characteristics of student raters in public speaking performances. *Speech Monographs*, 1946, 13, 45–53.

Tracey, W. S. Class reaction as a basis for grading. *Speech Teacher*, 1965, 14, 224–225.

Webb, E. J., Campbell, D. T., Schwartz, R. D., & Sechrest, L. *Unobtrusive measures.* Skokie, Ill.: Rand McNally & Co., 1966.

## SECTION TWO: READINGS

*Introduction and Objectives for Reading One: "Audience Analysis"*

The reader will find that this selection highlights some of the concepts and ideas discussed in the foregoing article. It should also provide some insight into the alternative methods of measuring the effects of communication.

After reading this selection you should be able to:

1. Distinguish in writing a *dominant* effect from an *idiosyncratic* one.
2. Define in writing the term *process response* and list two reasons why process effects are of interest in communication.
3. Define in writing the term *product response.*
4. List and discuss the uses of six types of instruments that measure the effects of communication.

Theodore Clevenger, Jr.

# *AUDIENCE ANALYSIS*

TYPES OF EFFECTS. Both in monitoring effects and in message pretesting, it is important to make several distinctions among types of effects. The first of these, . . . is a distinction between dominant and idiosyncratic message effects. In one sense, of course, all message effects are idiosyncratic because all message effects occur within individuals; however, some effects are much more likely to occur among individuals in a given audience than are others. An effect that we have reason to believe will occur or that we have observed to occur among a significant fraction of a given audience may be called a *dominant effect*. This terminology does not imply that dominant effects control the behavior of the individual auditor to a

From *Audience Analysis* by Theodore Clevenger, Jr., copyright © 1966 by The Bobbs-Merrill Company, Inc., reprinted by permission of the publishers.

greater extent than other effects, but simply that, when we look at the responses of all of the auditors, the dominant effects occur very frequently.

An effect that we have reason to believe will occur or that we have observed to occur among only a few auditors may be called an *idiosyncratic effect.* For many auditors the strongest effect of the speech will be the idiosyncratic effects that the message has upon them. Generally we use the dominant reactions of an audience to generalize about how the audience as a whole responded to the speech, but these dominant responses usually leave out of consideration a wealth of qualitatively different individual responses.

A second important distinction among message effects, also suggested by the TV commercial . . . is a distinction between anticipated effects and surprise effects. An *anticipated effect* is either one that the speaker deliberately set out to achieve or it is a side-effect that he recognized probably would occur and that he was prepared to accept. Of course, an anticipated effect may not occur in any sizeable fraction of an audience, but if the speaker is looking for it, then either its occurrence or its nonoccurrence will be noted. One of the purposes of audience analysis is to eliminate *surprise effects,* so if audience analysis has been effective, then most surprise effects will be idiosyncratic. When a dominant effect is unanticipated, the surprise may be a happy one or it may be disastrous.

A third and final distinction among message effects is the distinction between process and product effects. A *process effect* is one that occurs during the speech and is subject to modification by subsequent portions of the message; it is what goes on in the listener as he listens to the speech. A *product effect* is one that is left as a residue after the message has concluded. I may or may not thrill to the language of a brilliant orator (process), but whether I do or not, I may remember his words and quote them later (product).

. . . . . . . . . . . . . . . . . . . . .

PRODUCT RESPONSES. After a speech is over, the speaker may wish to know what effect it had upon the auditors. In general, he will be interested in three classes of response to the speech-as-a-whole. These three classes of "product response," as we have previously labeled them, are the auditor's internal state, his overt behavior, and his verbal behavior.

The stated principal objective of many speeches is to affect some particular internal state of the auditor: to cause him to think about a topic, to lead him to see a question in some new light, to give him information, or to change his opinion or his attitude. All of these goals have reference to internal, nonobservable states in the auditor. In general, they will be inferred from verbal behavior in much the same way as we outlined in discussing verbal behavior as an index to predisposing characteristics earlier in this chapter, and we need not discuss them further here.

Sometimes, however, the actual goal of a speech is to affect the verbal behavior of the auditor in its own right. That is, sometimes we are interested in the auditor's verbal behavior quite apart from any implications that the verbalization may have with respect to the auditor's internal states. Because we tend to confuse verbal behaviors (such as the expression "I hate war") with the internal or subjective states that they are thought to reflect (such as the actual feeling of dislike toward war), we tend to overlook the importance of influence over the auditor's verbal behavior as a desirable outcome of oral communication. We are inclined to say that we are interested in the auditor's verbalizations only as indexes to their internal states, but under some circumstances, it may actually be much more important for listeners to talk about the topic in a certain way than to harbor some particular set of feelings toward it. Very often when speakers say that they want to "inform" their audiences or "convince" them, their actual goal is to influence the auditor's verbal behavior, whether or not they are actually informed or convinced as a matter of subjective fact.

Thus, the object of brain-washing is not necessarily to effect any substantial or immediate change in the victim's way of *thinking,* but to alter his way of *talking*. He then becomes a source of favorable stimulation for others and eventually may even convince himself. If you and I disagree concerning the proper solution to a problem, and I can get you to talk about it in my terms, you will eventually capitulate to my view. If I can keep the entire community *talking* about patriotic themes regardless of how they feel about them, eventually they will whip up a wave of patriotic sentiment.

The interpretation of verbal behavior as an index to subjective states is based upon inference and hence subject to a certain unreliability. But the interpretation of verbal behavior in its own right as a legitimate product response to speaking is a matter of simple observation, and no inference is involved. When Woodrow Wilson coined the expression "Make the world safe for democracy," and when that expression was repeated by others during the succeeding years over and over again in thousands of contexts, the verbalization (quite apart from any sentiment that it might be thought to reveal) could be taken quite legitimately as a product response to Wilson's speaking. A political candidate, advertiser, religious leader, teacher, or revolutionary may well be interested in the frequency with which his verbal formulations are repeated by auditors and auditors-of-auditors when his speech is over. Such influence on their verbalization may be the most powerful and far-reaching effect of his speech.

Sometimes the speaker is interested in the auditor's overt, nonverbal behavior following the speech. The salesman is interested in getting his auditor's signature on a contract. The chemistry laboratory instructor is interested in seeing the student perform a series of manipulations with laboratory materials. The fund-drive speaker is interested in getting the auditor to make a contribution. The politician wants a vote. To be sure, these individuals may sometimes set more limited, "intermediate" goals with certain groups of auditors; the salesman may on a given occasion settle for good will, the laboratory instructor for correct answers to certain questions, the fund-drive speaker for an improved attitude, or the politician for a weakening of opposition. But on some occasions the speaker's real and immediate goal is overt, nonverbal behavior of a particular desired kind.

In this case, too, the speaker is able to observe directly the effects of his speech. No inference is involved in counting votes, sales, contributions, or properly conducted experiments. Of course, this is not to suggest that these behaviors are not accompanied by subjective events, or to imply that the speaker who is looking beyond the immediate speech should fail to note these nonobservables to whatever extent is possible; but to the extent that overt behavior is desired as an outcome of a given speech, no inference is necessary to describe the outcome of the speech; it will be observable, at least in principle.

## *Instrumentation*

Many of the types of information referred to in the preceding pages can be obtained informally, or through casual observation and inference. For example, the speaker can often obtain enough information about momentary audience interest levels during the speech simply through his unsystematic observation of auditors' overt behavior, and the salesman can keep an informal box-score on proportion of sales as a rough index of the effectiveness of his sales pitch.

However, some kinds of information (such as physiological response data) can be obtained only with the aid of special instruments. Moreover, some situations demand that more formal procedures be used to obtain data that in other situations might be obtained informally. If, for example, a speaker should wish to pretest two alternative forms of a message, and to compare process responses to the two, then it would be wise to have some more reliable basis for comparison of the process effects than his recollection of what happened in the audience during the two speeches. Here, the speaker might want to compare audience analyzer responses, or to analyze pictures of the audience during the speech, or to use some other form of data collection that would produce somewhat more reliable and permanent results. That is, he might prefer to collect his data according to more formal procedures.

We shall refer to any formal procedure for gathering data about auditors as an "instrument," and to the general problem of devising these procedures as the problem of "instrumentation." Although a virtually endless list might be compiled of instruments that are sometimes useful in audience analysis, we shall single out . . . six types of instruments as being of special significance and collectively representative. These are questionnaires, attitude tests, audience analyzers, information tests, the physiograph, and the observation inventory. . . . Some of these apply to the problem of assessing predisposing characteristics, some to process responses, some to product responses, and some to two or more of these. All but three of them are applied exclusively to verbal behavior.

QUESTIONNAIRES. Depending upon how a speaker intends to interpret the results, he may treat a questionnaire as a source of data in its own right or as a means of eliciting verbal behavior that is to be subjected to content analysis.

When used as a means of establishing predisposing characteristics of auditors, it ordinarily is designed to gather demographic information and information relating to the auditor's previous experiences. In preparing a classroom speech on Winston Churchill's eloquence, for example, a student speaker might want to know how many of his auditors were history majors, how many were majoring in English or speech, and so forth. He might also want to know how many of his auditors had even heard a Churchill speech or read one. He might want to collect some supplementary data regarding their knowledge of certain details of World War II, about which some of Churchill's most famous speeches were made. Assuming that he believes that his fellow students will give him truthful replies to his questions, he may obtain the information he requires by asking them to complete a questionnaire.

However, the questionnaire is not limited to a device for gathering demographic and background data on listeners. It may also be used to elicit verbal behavior either before or after the speech in order to estimate predisposing characteristics or product responses. For instance, if a speaker were planning to talk about wiretapping, he might want to know how his audience viewed and evaluated the practice. One approach to getting that information would be to devise a questionnaire consisting of a few leading questions such as, "What do you feel are the strongest arguments against the use of wiretapping by police?" Answers to this question could be analyzed and classified, and the speaker would have a basis for inferring dominant trends of opinion among his auditors.

ATTITUDE TESTS. Popular thinking tends to include along with questionnaires a somewhat more specialized class of instruments called opinion or attitude tests. The purpose of most of these tests is to locate the attitude of the auditor toward a given attitude object at a point on a continuum running from favorable to unfavorable. In its simplest form, the attitude test consists of a single continuous line on which the auditor is asked to place a checkmark corresponding to his feeling about the attitude object. For instance:

What is your attitude toward allowing police to make unlimited use of wiretapping in the investigation of crime?

| Strongly Approve | Approve | Undecided | Disapprove | Strongly Disapprove |
|---|---|---|---|---|
| ____ | ____ | ____ | ____ | ____ |

. . . . . . . . . . . . . . . . . . .

AUDIENCE ANALYZERS. The audience analyzer has as its central unit . . . a device for recording individual responses of auditors as they hear a speech or view a TV program or a play. Each subject has a device for registering his momentary responses. It may be a single button, an array of buttons, a three-way switch, or a dial with several possible settings. He uses the button, switch, or dial to indicate his responses according to some prearranged standard.

For example, the auditor may be asked to use his response recorder to indicate how interesting he finds the speech from moment to moment. If the response recorder is a single button, he may be asked to press the button when he finds the speech interesting, but otherwise leave it alone. Or, if the response recorder is a three-way switch, he may be asked to press the switch to the right when he thinks the speech is interesting, to the left when he thinks it is very dull, and otherwise to leave the switch in the middle.

. . . . . . . . . . . . . . . . . . .

INFORMATION TESTS. Except for teachers, a speaker seldom has an opportunity to administer information tests to his auditors as a measure of their knowledge before the speech or as a measure of their information gain afterwards. However, speaking to inform has in our technological age become a dominant form of public address, and the documentary has emerged as an important instrument of public service in broadcasting. In planning for and pretesting both informative speeches and documentaries it is helpful to know something about auditor information levels before and after the speech. The best way to get this information is through a test.

. . . . . . . . . . . . . . . . . . .

Observation Inventories. We have noted that speakers often need to observe overt, nonverbal behavior of auditors either as a means of detecting process responses or as a way of measuring the outcome of the speech. We have noted that most speakers do something of this kind on an informal basis as they talk, but it is also possible to make more systematic observations of auditor behavior by making up in advance lists of behaviors that are to be counted or otherwise observed. Such aids to observation of overt auditor response will be called observation inventories.

The simplest observation inventory is a binary judgment. Did the auditor buy (or vote for me, or contribute money) or not? A box score of such binary judgments over the entire audience is one way to measure the effectiveness of a speech, at least insofar as the speech was designed to produce immediate action.

But more sophisticated inventories are also possible. For instance we might measure attention by the proportion of time that the auditor looks at the speaker. Continuous observation of this single characteristic might be used as a basis for inferring the auditor's overall interest level and the high and low interest points of the speech for him.

Or, a number of more discrete behaviors might be noted. A list of behaviors that are presumed to reflect agreement, for example, might be compiled, and each item noted as it occurred in the auditor's behavioral pattern as he listened to the speech. A similar approach could be taken to the auditor's behavior after the speech to measure some aspects of his response to the whole speech.

## *Introduction and Objectives for Reading Two: "Observations of Behavior"*

The author of this selection considers some basic problems in using direct observation for recording and measuring behavior. He discusses problems concerning the observer, the reliability and validity of observations, and units of behavior.

After reading this article you should be able to:

1. Identify in writing two problems concerning "observer-inference" from observations of behavior.
2. Identify and describe in writing the relationship between units of observable behavior and the reliability and validity of an observer's judgment.
3. Distinguish in writing between the "molar" and "molecular" approaches to observing behavior.

Fred N. Kerlinger

# OBSERVATIONS OF BEHAVIOR

## THE OBSERVER

The major problem of behavioral observation is the observer himself. One of the difficulties with the interview . . . is the interviewer, because he is part of the measuring instrument. This problem is almost nonexistent in objective tests and scales. In behavioral observation the observer is both a crucial strength and a crucial weakness. Why? The observer must digest the information derived from his observations and then make inferences about constructs. He observes a certain behavior, say a child striking another child. Somehow he must process this observation and make an inference that the behavior is a manifestation of the construct "aggression" or "aggressive behavior," or even "hostility." The strength and the weakness of the procedure is the observer's powers of inference. If it were not for inference, a machine observer would be better than a man observer. (Sometimes it *may* be.) The strength is that the observer can relate the observed behavior to the constructs or variables of a study: he brings behavior and construct together. One of the recurring difficulties of measurement is to bridge the gap between behavior and construct. Competent observers and well-made observations help bridge this gap.

The basic weakness of the observer is that he can make quite incorrect inferences from observations, due to human fallibility. This is a formidable problem. Take two extreme cases. Suppose, on the one hand, that an observer who is strongly hostile to parochial school education observes parochial school classes. It is clear that his bias may well invalidate the observational measuring instrument.

. . . . . . . . . . . . . . . . .

On the other hand, assume that an observer could be completely objective and that he knew nothing whatever about public or parochial education. In a sense any observations he makes would not be biased, but they would be inadequate. Observation of human behavior requires com-

From Chapter 28 from *Foundations of Behavioral Research* by Fred N. Kerlinger. Copyright © 1964 by Holt, Rinehart and Winston, Inc. Reprinted by permission of Holt, Rinehart and Winston, Inc.

petent knowledge of that behavior, and even of the meaning of the behavior.

The observer-inference problem is the main difficulty. There is, however, another problem: the observer can affect the objects of observation simply by being part of the observational situation. Actually and fortunately, this is not a severe problem. Indeed, it is more of a problem to the uninitiated who seem to believe that people will act differently, even artificially, when observed. The classic educational case of this is the belief that a teacher under observation, especially by superiors, will put her best foot forward. She will act in an exemplary way not necessarily customary with her, it is thought. This may be true. A significant point is missed, however. It is not realized that a teacher cannot do what she cannot do. She cannot act in a way she has not learned to act. She cannot be "adaptable," to use one of Ryans' adjectives, if she has not learned to be adaptable.

Observers seem to have little effect on the situations they observe.[1] Individuals and groups seem to adapt rather quickly to an observer's presence and to act as they would usually act. This does not mean that the observer cannot have an effect. It means that if the observer takes care to be unobtrusive and not to give the people observed the feeling that judgments are being made, then the observer as an influential stimulus is mostly nullified.

. . . . . . . . . . . . . . . . .

## *Characteristics of Observations*

The first and most important consideration in any observation system is to know clearly what is being observed. This seems so obvious as to be trite. Let us see that it is not so obvious. Suppose we are studying the relation between *independence* and *problem-solving.* We hypothesize that the more independent a child the better he will be able to solve problems, other things equal. We wish to observe *independence,* or more accurately, *independent behavior.* Now, what *is* independent behavior? If a child persistently works by himself is this independent behavior? If a child initiates projects and games with other children, is this independent behavior? Take a much more difficult problem: What is democratic behavior in a teacher? If a teacher is nice to children, is this democratic? If she organizes children into groups, is she being democratic? Just what do we mean when we say "democratic behavior"? It should be obvious that clear knowledge of what is being observed is not so obvious.

[1] R. Heyns and R. Lippitt, "Systematic Observational Techniques," in G. Lindzey, ed., *Handbook of Social Psychology,* Vol. I. Cambridge, Mass.: Addison-Wesley, 1954, chap. 10, p. 399.

It is necessary, then, to define fairly precisely and unambiguously what is to be observed. If we are measuring *curiosity,* we must tell the observer what curious behavior is. If *cooperativeness* is being measured, we must somehow tell the observer how cooperative behavior is distinguished from any other kind of behavior. This means that we must provide the observer with some form of operational definition of the variable being measured; we must define the variable behaviorally.

. . . . . . . . . . . . . . . . . . . .

## UNITS OF BEHAVIOR

What units to use in measuring human behavior is still an unsettled problem. Here one is often faced with a clash between reliability and validity demands. Theoretically, one can attain a high degree of reliability by using small and easily observed and recorded units. One can attempt to define behavior quite operationally by listing a large number of behavioral acts, and can thus ordinarily attain a high degree of precision and reliability. Yet in so doing one may also have so reduced the behavior that it no longer bears much resemblance to the behavior one intended to observe. Thus validity has been lost.

On the other hand, one can use broad "natural" definitions and perhaps achieve a high degree of validity. One might instruct observers to observe *cooperation* and define *cooperative behavior* as "accepting other persons' approaches, suggestions, and ideas; working harmoniously with others toward goals," or some such rather broad definition. If observers have had group experience and understand group processes, then it might be expected that they could validly assess behavior as cooperative and uncooperative by using this definition. Such a broad, even vague, definition enables the observer to capture, if he can, the full flavor of cooperative behavior. But it also allows considerable ambiguity of interpretation to creep into observers' perceptions, thus lowering reliability.

Some researchers who are strongly operational in their approach insist upon highly specific definitions of the variables observed. They might list a number of specific behaviors for the observer to observe. No others would be observed and recorded. Extreme approaches like this may produce high reliability, but they may also miss part of the essential core of the variables observed. Suppose ten specific types of behavior are listed for *cooperativeness*. Suppose, too, that the universe of possible behaviors consists of 40 or 50 types. Clearly, important aspects of *cooperativeness* will be neglected. While what is measured may be reliably measured, it may be quite trivial or at least partly irrelevant to the variable *cooperativeness*.

This is the molar-molecular problem of any measurement procedure in the social sciences. The *molar approach* takes larger behavioral wholes as units of observation. Complete interaction units may be specified as observational targets. Verbal behavior may be broken down into complete interchanges between two or more individuals, or into whole paragraphs or sentences. The *molecular approach,* by contrast, takes smaller segments of behavior as units of observation. Each interchange or partial interchange may be recorded. Units of verbal behavior may be words or short phrases. The molar observer will start with a general, broadly defined variable . . . and consider and record a variety of behaviors under the one rubric. He depends on his experience and interpretation of the meaning of the actions he is observing. The molecular observer, on the other hand, seeks to push his own experience and interpretation out of the observational picture. He records what he sees—and no more.

### *Introduction and Objectives for Reading Three: "Techniques of Attitude Measurement"*

The reader should find this selection very informative. The author discusses four major types of attitude scales used in measuring communication effects. The student will find this particular article to be very closely related to Chapter 5 as well as the present chapter.

After reading this selection you should be able to:

1. List in writing two basic assumptions about test items that are common to all the four types of attitude scales discussed.
2. Compare and contrast in writing the four techniques of measuring attitudes in terms of: (1) scale construction; (2) scoring procedures; and (3) basic assumptions about the scales.

Philip Zimbardo and Ebbe B. Ebbesen

## *TECHNIQUES OF ATTITUDE MEASUREMENT*

Several different paper-and-pencil tests have been developed to measure attitudes. Of these tests, four have been fairly highly refined and have been used most extensively. These major techniques are: Thurstone's

From Philip G. Zimbardo and Ebbe B. Ebbesen, *Influencing Attitudes and Changing Behavior*, 1969, Addison-Wesley, Reading, Mass.

method of equal-appearing intervals, Likert's method of summated ratings, Guttman's scalogram, and Osgood's semantic differential. A brief review of each of these methods will hopefully provide the reader with a clearer understanding of how the social psychologist obtains the data from which he so elegantly extrapolates.

Each of the techniques to be discussed makes different assumptions about the nature of the test items that are used and the kind of information they provide about a person's attitudes. However, there are certain basic assumptions which are common to all of these methods. First of all, it is assumed that subjective attitudes can be measured by a quantitative technique, so that each person's opinion can be represented by some numerical score. Secondly, all of these methods assume that a particular test item has the same meaning for all respondents, and thus a given response will be scored identically for everyone making it. Such assumptions may not always be justified, but as yet no measurement technique has been developed which does not include them.

## *Thurstone's Method of Equal-Appearing Intervals*

The first major technique of attitude measurement was developed by Thurstone, in 1929, in his study of attitudes toward religion. The scale which he constructed introduced the metric to an area of research where it had never been used before. Thurstone assumed that one could obtain statements of opinion about a particular issue and could order them according to a dimension of expressed favorableness-unfavorableness towards the issue. Furthermore, the ordering of these statements could be such that there appeared to be an equal distance between adjacent statements on the continuum. Because of the latter assumption, one can make judgments about the degree of discrepancy between different people's attitudes. Thurstone also assumed that the statements are uncorrelated and that each statement has a position which is independent of the others. That is, acceptance of one statement does not necessarily imply the acceptance of any others.

A Thurstone scale is made up of about twenty independent statements of opinion about a particular issue. Each statement has a numerical scale value determined by its average judged position on the continuum. A person's *attitude* on the issue is measured by asking him to check those statements with which he agrees. His *score* is the mean scale value of those items which he checked. An example of a shortened version of such a scale follows:

TRAIT: ATTITUDE TOWARD OPEN HOUSING

| Scale value | | Statement |
|---|---|---|
| Least favorable | 1.5 | A. A person should refuse to rent to anyone he doesn't like. |
| | 3.0 | B. Federal laws enforcing open housing should apply only to public housing, not to private neighborhoods. |
| | 4.5 | C. Local governments should publicly urge people to engage in fair housing practices. |
| | 6.0 | D. Only in extreme cases of discrimination in housing should there be some sort of legal intervention. |
| Most favorable | 7.5 | E. A person must rent to the first eligible applicant, regardless of race, color, or creed. |

The hallmark of a Thurstone scale is that the intervals between the statements are approximately equal. This property of the scale is achieved by the method in which it is constructed. The first step is to collect a large number of opinion statements about some particular issue. Any statements which are confusing, ambiguous, double-barreled, or likely to be approved by individuals with opposed attitudes are immediately discarded. Each of the remaining statements is then sorted into one of eleven categories by a group of judges, according to the degree of favorableness or unfavorableness toward the issue expressed by the statement, *regardless* of the judges' own attitudes. These categories thus make up a scale which ranges from very favorable, through neutral, to extremely unfavorable opinions about the issue. By tabulating the ratings of all the judges, it is possible to calculate both the numerical scale position of each statement (its average scale value), as well as the extent to which the judges agreed in its placement (its spread of ratings). The statements which are selected for use on the final scale are those which have high interjudge agreement and which fall at relatively equally-spaced intervals along the continuum. A subject's attitude on the particular issue is then derived from his responses to this final set of scale items.

### *Likert's Method of Summated Ratings*

One of the practical drawbacks of the Thurstone scale is that its construction is extremely laborious and time-consuming. To cope with this problem, Likert developed a different technique which could produce an equally reliable attitude scale with relative ease. The Likert scale is made up of a series of opinion statements about some issue. However, in contrast to the Thurstone scale, a person's attitude is measured by asking him to indicate the *extent* of his agreement or disagreement with each item. This is done by having the person rate each item on a five-point scale of response (strongly agree, agree, undecided, disagree, strongly disagree). A person's attitude score is the sum of his individual ratings. An example of a single scale item is the following:

A. "People should be allowed to move into any neighborhood they choose."

| Rating value | |
|---|---|
| 1 | a) Strongly agree |
| 2 | b) Agree |
| 3 | c) Undecided |
| 4 | d) Disagree |
| 5 | e) Strongly disagree |

Likert assumes that each statement that is used in the scale is a linear function of the same attitude dimension. This assumption is the basis for the operation of adding up a person's individual scores (or summating his ratings, to put it more formally) to obtain his final score. A further implication is that the items in a scale must be highly correlated with a common attribute and thus with each other, as opposed to Thurstone's distinct and independent items. It is important to note that at no point does Likert assume equal intervals between scale values. For example, it is quite possible that the difference between "agree" and "strongly agree" is much larger than the difference between "agree" and "undecided." This means that a Likert scale can provide information on the *ordering* of people's attitudes on a continuum, but it is unable to indicate how close or how far apart different attitudes might be.

Likert's method of scale construction is similar to Thurstone's in the initial collecting and editing of a variety of opinion statements. The remaining statements are then rated by a sample group of subjects on the five-point response scale in terms of their *own* opinions about the statements. This is in contrast to the Thurstone technique, where the ratings are made by trained judges and based not on personal opinions but on some relatively objective evaluation of where the statements fall on a continuum. The final Likert scale is composed of those items which best differentiate between sample subjects with the highest and lowest total scores.

### Guttman's Scalogram

A third scaling technique is based on the assumption that a single, unidimensional trait can be measured by a set of statements which are ordered along a continuum of "difficulty of acceptance." That is, the statements range from those which are easy for most people to accept to those which few persons would endorse. Such scale items are *cumulative,* since the acceptance of one item implies that the person accepts all those of lesser magnitude (those less difficult to accept). To the extent that this is true, one can predict a person's attitude towards other statements on the basis of knowing the most difficult item he will accept. An example of such a scale might be the following:

TRAIT: ATTITUDE TOWARD OPEN HOUSING

| *Acceptability* | *Statement* |
|---|---|
| Least difficult to accept | A. Generally speaking, people should be able to live anywhere they want. |
| | B. Real estate agencies should not discriminate against minority groups. |
| | C. The city should actively support the idea of open housing. |
| | D. There should be a local review board which would pass on cases of extreme discrimination in housing. |
| Most difficult to accept | E. There should be federal laws to enforce open housing. |

In order to obtain a scale which represents a single dimension, Guttman presents sample subjects with an initial set of items and records the extent to which they respond to the items with specified answer patterns. These patterns, which are referred to as *scale types,* follow a certain step-like order. The subject may either accept none of the items in the set (score 0), accept item A only (score 1), accept items A and B only (score 2), accept items A, B, and C only (score 3), etc. If the subject gives a nonscale response pattern (e.g., accepts items C only and not those of lesser magnitude), it is assumed that he has made one or more response errors. By analyzing the number of response errors made, Guttman is able to determine the degree to which the initial set of items reflects a unidimensional attribute (that is, the extent to which they are "scalable"). The final scale is obtained by eliminating poor items and retesting sample subjects until a scalable set of items has been developed.

A person's attitude is then measured by having him check all the statements on the scale which are acceptable to him. His score is that of the appropriate scale type or (if he has given a nonscale response pattern) that of the scale type closest to his response. As the latter scoring procedure implies, it is almost impossible to develop a perfect unidimensional scale. This may be because people are actually responding not on the single dimension hypothesized, but rather on a different one, or on multiple dimensions.

## *Osgood's Semantic Differential*

The three methods just described attempt to measure attitudes by having people indicate the extent of their agreement with various opinion statements. In contrast to this approach, Osgood has studied attitudes by focusing on the *meaning* that people give to a word or concept. Underlying this technique is the basic assumption of a hypothetical semantic space of an unknown number of dimensions, in which the meaning of any word or concept can be represented as a particular point. Osgood's procedure is to have people judge a particular concept on a set of semantic scales. These scales are defined by verbal opposites with a mid-point of neutrality, and are usually composed of seven discriminable steps. For example, a particular person's meaning of the concept "integration" is measured by his ratings of it on a set of semantic scales:

| | | | | | | | | |
|---|---|---|---|---|---|---|---|---|
| good | ___ | ___ | ___ | ___ | ___ | ___ | ___ | bad |
| strong | ___ | ___ | ___ | ___ | ___ | ___ | ___ | weak |
| fast | ___ | ___ | ___ | ___ | ___ | ___ | ___ | slow |
| active | ___ | ___ | ___ | ___ | ___ | ___ | ___ | passive |

and so on.

An analysis of the ratings collected by this method may reveal the particular dimensions which people use to qualify their experience, the types of concepts that are regarded as similar or different in meaning, and the intensity of the meaning given to a particular concept. Osgood's own research has indicated that there are three dominant, independent dimensions which people use in judging concepts. He refers to these dimensions as the evaluative factor (e.g., good-bad), the potency factor (e.g., strong-weak), and the activity factor (e.g., active-passive). Although this method can provide a lot of information about a concept, it is not exactly clear how the concept's *meaning* for a person is related to opinion statements he would make about it.

## QUESTIONS FOR DISCUSSION

1. Given the two basic types of measurement discussed in the chapter, select a specific effect of communication and specify what procedures you would follow to measure the effect. Use an instrument of some kind and also measure it in everyday situations.
2. Given that the purpose and the actual result of communication are not always in harmony, discuss what factors may effect this incongruity. Try to support your observations with specific examples.
3. Consider a communication event—perhaps a Presidential address or a speech by a Black Panther—and discuss what intentional and unintentional effects might be produced by the message. How might you attempt to measure the effects?
4. A number of suggestions were made for measuring communication effects in everyday situations. How many other suggestions can you add to the list? Consider, for example, some of the methods you have for reading nonverbal cues in your own communication behavior.
5. How might one employ the various principles listed in this chapter in an effort to be a better communicator?

*epilogue:*

# A SUMMARY OF SELECTED KEY COMMUNICATION PRINCIPLES APPEARING IN THE BOOK

Throughout this book you have been introduced to a considerable number of communication principles which have been derived from theory and research. Most of them relate to rather specific elements of the communication process and some have considerably more direct application to your personal communication behavior than do others. In this Epilogue we attempt to synthesize, in one list, what appear to be the more important and relevant principles set forth in the preceding chapters. Obviously, perceptions of importance and relevance differ; some may be included which you will question and others may be omitted which you would have included. We have tried to list those principles to which the authors gave primary attention.

The purpose of the list is, in part, to summarize some of the key ideas presented in the text, but primarily to stimulate your thinking about the principles of communication which are basic to the improvement of your personal ability to communicate. One danger of listing these principles out of context is that the author's meaning might be distorted. If you have a question about what is meant by one of the principles, you should reread the pertinent chapter (given in parentheses).

Again, it must be emphasized that the principles proposed below are not "law." They are not infallible and they may even be proved incorrect in future years. They do, however, represent some contemporary thinking about communication behavior, and they are ones which, if you are a betting person, you probably would be wise to "put your money on" in your future communication behavior.

1. Experience alone does not make one a good communicator (Chapter 2).
2. Communication is a process rather than an event (Chapter 2).
3. Since all human behavior is communicative, we might say that one cannot *not* communicate (Chapter 2).
4. There is a major genetic component in the acquisition of language (Chapter 3).
5. Specific language and communication habits are culturally bound (Chapter 3).
6. Linguistic form and function vary together according to the demands of different communication situations (Chapter 3).
7. People acquire information by being repeatedly exposed to contiguous stimuli and responses (Chapter 4).
8. People tend to process information that is reinforcing and fail to process information that is nonreinforcing (Chapter 4).
9. People tend to expose themselves to information that is consistent with their attitudes and beliefs but to avoid exposure to inconsistent information (Chapter 4).
10. People tend to perceive information as consistent with their attitudes and beliefs even when it is inconsistent (Chapter 4).
11. People tend to remember information that is consistent with their attitudes and beliefs and forget information that is inconsistent (Chapter 4).
12. The mass media generally have a major impact on the diffusion of new information but have little impact on attitudes (Chapter 4).
13. The major impact of the mass media in the diffusion of information is through a multi-step flow: mass media to opinion leader to person two to person three (Chapter 4).
14. Acquisition of information most frequently occurs between a source and a receiver who are homophilous (Chapter 4).
15. Attitudes are learned and can therefore be unlearned (Chapter 5).
16. Although attitudes and behavior are positively correlated, attitudes do not predetermine behavior (Chapter 5).
17. Public attitudes are more resistant than private attitudes, especially when they have group support (Chapter 5).
18. The same individual may hold or reflect different attitudes in different social settings and in different roles (Chapter 5).
19. Perceptions of the credibility of the source, especially of exper-

tise and trustworthiness, lead to attitudinal change (Chapter 5).

20. With the passage of time, receivers sometimes tend to disassociate the source from the message, unless the source is reinstated (Chapter 5).
21. In many instances, the more a persuader asks for, the more he is likely to get (Chapter 5).
22. Organized messages do not seem to produce greater attitudinal change than disorganized messages, although they may increase the source's credibility (Chapter 5).
23. Giving equal weight to both sides of a controversial issue or stating the "facts" impartially does not persuade (Chapter 5).
24. Good evidence generally produces persuasive effects over the long run (Chapter 5).
25. There is little consistent basis for claims that logical or emotional appeals are relatively more effective (Chapter 5).
26. Strong threat appeals are generally more effective than weak ones, especially when the source is highly credible (Chapter 5).
27. Informal face-to-face communications are generally more persuasive than mass-media presentations (Chapter 5).
28. In the absence of evidence, or when issues are complex, people tend to lean on social sources of influence (Chapter 5).
29. Changes in behavior generally lead to changes in attitudes more readily than the converse (Chapter 5).
30. It is easier to reinforce existing attitudes than to convert others or reduce their hostility (Chapter 5).
31. There is probably an optimal level of activation of each individual in each communication activity in which he is engaged (Chapter 6).
32. Interracial communication is facilitated when the communicators share a common coding system (Chapter 7).
33. Meaningful communication within transracial contexts requires the proximity of source and receiver (Chapter 7).
34. Interpersonal communication within transracial contexts often fails because the sender and the receiver do not share nor seek each other's point of view (Chapter 7).
35. There is little to suggest that changing the grammar of Blacks will make for substantially more effective inter-ethnic communication (Chapter 7).
36. Emphasis and repetition of major ideas facilitates the amount of information transmitted to listeners (Chapter 8).
37. The use of visible action increases the amount of information comprehended by listeners (Chapter 8).

38. The listener's motivation is an important factor in his obtaining information (Chapter 8).
39. The listener's attitudes and predispositions may affect the manner in which information is received and interpreted (Chapter 8).
40. If a speaker has consistently received high ratings, judges will tend to give him high ratings for subsequent speeches (Chapter 8).
41. A rater's bias toward the subject matter of a speech may affect his ratings (Chapter 8).
42. If raters know or like a speaker, their ratings tend to be higher (Chapter 8).
43. The validity of a speech rating is almost always questionable (Chapter 8).

# INDEX

LIBRARY
HAMILTON
UNIVERSITY